I0053190

Dictionary of International Justice, Peace and Sustainable Development.

Key Terms and Phrases

From the Same Author:

Dictionnaire de la justice internationale, de la paix et du développement durable - Principaux termes et expressions (2ème édition revue et complétée), Editions L'Harmattan, Paris, 2011

Côte d'Ivoire – Quelques réflexions d'ordre juridique, Editions L'Harmattan, Paris, 2011

Justice internationale et liberté d'expression – Les médias face aux crimes internationaux - Préface de Loïc Hervouët, Editions L'Harmattan, Paris, 2008

La profession d'avocat dans l'espace francophone - Principaux textes et documents, Editions L'Harmattan, Paris, 2004

L'exercice occasionnel de la profession d'avocat dans l'espace francophone, Editions L'Harmattan, Paris, 2004

Devenir avocat dans l'espace francophone – Règles, textes législatifs, réglementaires, nationaux et internationaux - Préface de Ronald Montcalm, Editions L'Harmattan, Paris, 2003

Côte d'Ivoire : Procès Gbagbo : victoire d'étape pour l'ex-président ivoirien / http://www.atlantico.fr / 24 juin 2012

Côte d'Ivoire : Le procès Gbagbo devant la CPI n'aide pas à la réconciliation nationale avec le camp Ouattara / http://www.atlantico.fr / 27 janvier 2012

Sénégal : Youssou N'Dour sera-t-il le Berlusconi sénégalais ? / http://www.atlantico.fr / 4 janvier 2012

Lybie : Politique et justice internationale : je t'aime, moi non plus / http://www.atlantico.fr / 28 juin 2011

Joseph Bemba

Dictionary of International Justice, Peace and Sustainable Development.

Key Terms and Phrases

Innovations and Information, Inc. Frederick, MD

© 2012 by Joseph Bemba
All rights reserved. Published 2011
Published in the United States of America
17 16 15 14 13 12   5 4 3 2 1

All rights reserved. No part of this book may be reproduced, stored in a retrieval system, transcribed in any form or by any means, electronic, mechanical, photocopy, recording, or any other means, or translated into any language without the prior written permission of the author.

The information in this book is given in good faith. However, the publisher cannot be held responsible for any error or omission.

http://www.iandi.cc

ISBN 978-0-9853477-2-7

TABLE OF CONTENTS

FORWARD

In order to understand international justice, it is a prerequisite to first understand its language, vocabulary and terminology. Getting along well begins with knowing each other well; getting along well stems from understanding each other well. International justice, like peace and development - especially sustainable development, does not escape that obvious fact.

This dictionary gathers a list of key terms and phrases used in international justice as per the applicable international and regional legal texts: genocide, crimes against humanity, war crimes, crimes of genocide, crimes of aggression and other violations of the International Humanitarian Law. These concepts are usually strewn in scattered law texts and case law documents.

As a legal and educational tool, this book has the ambition to make accessible to all -lawyers or not, legal experts or non-experts and everyday laymen-, the sometimes "geeky" vocabulary of international justice, in order to better understand what it does and what is at stake.

Beside international justice per se, this dictionary deals with the concepts of peace, sustainable development and the related notions of democracy, human rights and fundamental freedoms, rule of Law, good governance, environmental protection that are all interrelated, indivisible and inseparable from the notion of international justice.

Definitions and segments of definitions consistent with the applicable rule of law, statements from main articles, preambles and significant extracts from fundamental texts will be covered here. Doctrinal data as well as case-law data will be progressively added to the body of work so as to ultimately develop -with the contributions of future generations-, a comprehensive tool. At the end of this document, the reader can find an alphabetical list of terms and phrases including their page numbers and source texts, and also a list of reference texts.

International justice, peace and sustainable development will be achieved when they become every-day facts of life; this entails mastering their jargon, which is an objective this dictionary seeks to contribute to.

ABBREVIATIONS

ICC: International Criminal Court
ICJ: International Court of Justice
ICTR: International Criminal Tribunal for Rwanda
ICTY: International Criminal for the former Yugoslavia
Rome Statute ICC: Rome Statute of the International Criminal Court
RPE: Rules of Procedure and Evidence
RPE – ICC: Rules of Procedure and Evidence of the International Criminal Court
RPE – ICTR: Rules of Procedure and Evidence of the International Criminal Tribunal for Rwanda
RPE – ICTY: Rules of Procedure and Evidence of the International Criminal for the former Yugoslavia
Statute ICJ: Statute of the International Court of Justice
Statute ICTR: Statute of the International Criminal Tribunal for Rwanda
Statute ICTY: Statute of the International Criminal for the former Yugoslavia
UN: United Nations
UNO: United Nations Organization

TERMS AND PHRASES

A

Admission of guilt - Guilty Plea *(Rome Statute ICC, Part 6. The trial (...), art. 64. Functions and powers of the Trial Chamber (...), paragraph 8. (a); Rome Statute ICC, art. 65. Proceedings on an admission of guilt; RPE – ICC, Rule 139. Decision on admission of guilt - RPE – ICTY, Rule 62. Initial Appearance of Accused; Rule 62bis. Guilty Pleas; Rule 62 ter. Plea Agreement Procedure - RPE – ICTR, Rule 62. Initial Appearance of Accused and Plea; Rule 62bis. Plea Agreement Procedure).*

Rome Statute ICC, Part 6. The trial (...), art. 64. Functions and powers of the Trial Chamber (...). 8. (a) At the commencement of the trial, the Trial Chamber shall have read to the accused the charges previously confirmed by the Pre-Trial Chamber. The Trial Chamber shall satisfy itself that the accused understands the nature of the charges. It shall afford him or her the opportunity to make an admission of guilt in accordance with article 65 or to plead not guilty. (…)

Rome Statute ICC, art. 65. Proceedings on an admission of guilt. 1. Where the accused makes an admission of guilt pursuant to article 64, paragraph 8 (a), the Trial Chamber shall determine whether:

(a) The accused understands the nature and consequences of the admission of guilt;

(b) The admission is voluntarily made by the accused after sufficient consultation with defence counsel; and

(c) The admission of guilt is supported by the facts of the case that are contained in:

(i) The charges brought by the Prosecutor and admitted by the accused;

(ii) Any materials presented by the Prosecutor which supplement the charges and which the accused accepts; and

(iii) Any other evidence, such as the testimony of witnesses, presented by the Prosecutor or the accused.

2. Where the Trial Chamber is satisfied that the matters referred to in paragraph 1 are established, it shall consider the admission of guilt, together with any additional evidence presented, as establishing all the essential facts that are required to prove the crime to which the admission of guilt relates, and may convict the accused of that crime.

3. Where the Trial Chamber is not satisfied that the matters referred to in paragraph 1 are established, it shall consider the admission of guilt as not having been made, in which case it shall order that the trial be continued under the ordinary trial procedures provided by this Statute and may remit the case to another Trial Chamber.

4. Where the Trial Chamber is of the opinion that a more complete presentation of the facts of the case is required in the interests of justice, in particular the interests of the victims, the Trial Chamber may:

(a) Request the Prosecutor to present additional evidence, including the testimony of witnesses; or

(b) Order that the trial be continued under the ordinary trial procedures provided by this Statute, in which case it shall consider the admission of guilt as not having been made and may remit the case to another Trial Chamber.

5. Any discussions between the Prosecutor and the defence regarding modification of the charges, the admission of guilt or the penalty to be imposed shall not be binding on the Court.

RPE – ICC, Rule 139. Decision on admission of guilt. 1. After having proceeded in accordance with article 65, paragraph 1, the Trial Chamber, in order to decide whether to proceed in accordance with article 65, paragraph 4, may invite the views of the Prosecutor and the defence.

2. The Trial Chamber shall then make its decision on the admission of guilt and shall give reasons for this decision, which shall be placed on the record.

RPE – ICTY, Rule 62. Initial Appearance of Accused. (A) Upon transfer of an accused to the seat of the Tribunal, the President shall forthwith assign the case to a Trial Chamber. The accused shall be brought before that Trial Chamber or a Judge thereof without delay, and shall be formally charged. The Trial Chamber or the Judge shall:

(i) satisfy itself, himself or herself that the right of the accused to counsel is respected;

(ii) read or have the indictment read to the accused in a language the accused understands, and satisfy itself, himself or herself that the accused understands the indictment;

(iii) inform the accused that, within thirty days of the initial appearance, he or she will be called upon to enter a plea of guilty or not guilty on each count but that, should the accused so request, he or she may immediately enter a plea of guilty or not guilty on one or more count;

(iv) if the accused fails to enter a plea at the initial or any further appearance, enter a plea of not guilty on the accused's behalf;

(v) in case of a plea of not guilty, instruct the Registrar to set a date for trial;

(vi) in case of a plea of guilty:

(a) if before the Trial Chamber, act in accordance with Rule 62*bis*, or

(b) if before a Judge, refer the plea to the Trial Chamber so that it may act in accordance with Rule 62*bis;*

(vii) instruct the Registrar to set such other dates as appropriate.

(B) Where the interests of justice so require, the Registrar may assign a duty counsel as within Rule 45 (C) to represent the accused at the initial appearance. Such assignments shall be treated in accordance with the relevant provisions of the Directive referred to in Rule 45 (A).

(C) Within 30 days of the initial appearance, if the accused has not retained permanent counsel or has not yet elected in writing to conduct his or her own defence in accordance with Rule 45 (F), permanent counsel shall be assigned by the Registrar. Should the Registrar be unable to appoint permanent counsel within the time-limit, he will seek an extension from the Trial Chamber.

Rule 62 bis. Guilty Pleas. If an accused pleads guilty in accordance with Rule 62 (vi), or requests to change his or her plea to guilty and the Trial Chamber is satisfied that:
(i) the guilty plea has been made voluntarily;
(ii) the guilty plea is informed;
(iii) the guilty plea is not equivocal; and
(iv) there is a sufficient factual basis for the crime and the accused's participation in it, either on the basis of independent indicia or on lack of any material disagreement between the parties about the facts of the case, the Trial Chamber may enter a finding of guilt and instruct the Registrar to set a date for the sentencing hearing.
Rule 62 ter. Plea Agreement Procedure. (A) The Prosecutor and the defence may agree that, upon the accused entering a plea of guilty to the indictment or to one or more counts of the indictment, the Prosecutor shall do one or more of the following before the Trial Chamber:
(i) apply to amend the indictment accordingly;
(ii) submit that a specific sentence or sentencing range is appropriate;
(iii) not oppose a request by the accused for a particular sentence or sentencing range.
(B) The Trial Chamber shall not be bound by any agreement specified in paragraph (A).
(C) If a plea agreement has been reached by the parties, the Trial Chamber shall require the disclosure of the agreement in open session or, on a showing of good cause, in closed session, at the time the accused pleads guilty in accordance with Rule 62 (vi), or requests to change his or her plea to guilty.
RPE – ICTR, Rule 62. Initial Appearance of Accused and Plea. (A) Upon his transfer to the Tribunal, the accused shall be brought before a Trial Chamber or a Judge thereof without delay, and shall be formally charged. The Trial Chamber or the Judge shall:
(i) Satisfy itself or himself that the right of the accused to counsel is respected;
(ii) Read or have the indictment read to the accused in a language he understands, and satisfy itself or himself that the accused understands the indictment;
(iii) Call upon the accused to enter a plea of guilty or not guilty on each count; should the accused fail to do so, enter a plea of not guilty on his behalf;
(iv) In case of a plea of not guilty, instruct the Registrar to set a date for trial;
(v) In case of a plea of guilty:
(a) if before a Judge, refer the plea to the Trial Chamber so that it may act in accordance with Rule 62 (B); or
(b) if before a Trial Chamber, act in accordance with Rule 62 (B).
(B) If an accused pleads guilty in accordance with Rule 62 (A)(v), or requests to change his plea to guilty, the Trial Chamber shall satisfy itself that the guilty plea:
(i) is made freely and voluntarily;
(ii) is an informed plea;
(iii) is unequivocal; and
(iv) is based on sufficient facts for the crime and accused's participation in it, either on the basis of objective indicia or of lack of any material disagreement between the parties about the facts of the case. Thereafter the Trial Chamber may enter a finding of guilt and instruct the Registrar to set a date for the sentencing hearing.

Rule 62bis. Plea Agreement Procedure. (A) The Prosecutor and the Defence may agree that, upon the accused entering a plea of guilty to the indictment or to one or more counts of the indictment, the Prosecutor shall do one or more of the following before the Trial Chamber:

(i) apply to amend the indictment accordingly;

(ii) submit that a specific sentence or sentencing range is appropriate;

(iii) not oppose a request by the accused for a particular sentence or sentencing range.

(B) The Trial Chamber shall not be bound by any agreement specified in paragraph (A).

(C) If a plea agreement has been reached by the parties, the Trial Chamber shall require the disclosure of the agreement in open session or, on a showing of good cause, in closed session, at the time the accused pleads guilty in accordance with Rule 62 (A) (v), or requests to change his or her plea to guilty.

African Charter on Human and Peoples' Rights.

Adopted June 27, 1981, Kenya, Nairobi, entered into force October 21, 1986. *Preamble.* The African States members of the Organization of African Unity, parties to the present convention entitled "*African Charter on Human and Peoples' Rights*",

Recalling Decision 115 (XVI) of the Assembly of Heads of State and Government at its Sixteenth Ordinary Session held in Monrovia, Liberia, from 17 to 20 July 1979 on the preparation of a "preliminary draft on an African Charter on Human and Peoples' Rights providing inter alia for the establishment of bodies to promote and protect human and peoples' rights";

Considering the Charter of the Organization of African Unity, which stipulates that "freedom, equality, justice and dignity are essential objectives for the achievement of the legitimate aspirations of the African peoples";

Reaffirming the pledge they solemnly made in Article 2 of the said Charter to eradicate all forms of colonialism from Africa, to coordinate and intensify their cooperation and efforts to achieve a better life for the peoples of Africa and to promote international cooperation having due regard to the Charter of the United Nations and the Universal Declaration of Human Rights;

Taking into consideration the virtues of their historical tradition and the values of African civilization which should inspire and characterize their reflection on the concept of human and peoples' rights;

Recognizing on the one hand, that fundamental human rights stem from the attributes of human beings which justifies their national and international protection and on the other hand that the reality and respect of peoples rights should necessarily guarantee human rights;

Considering that the enjoyment of rights and freedoms also implies the performance of duties on the part of everyone;

Convinced that it is henceforth essential to pay a particular attention to the right to development and that civil and political rights cannot be dissociated from economic, social and cultural rights in their conception as well as universality and that the satisfaction of economic, social and cultural rights ia a guarantee for the enjoyment of civil and political rights;

Conscious of their duty to achieve the total liberation of Africa, the peoples of which are still struggling for their dignity and genuine independence, and undertaking to eliminate colonialism, neo-colonialism, apartheid, zionism and to dismantle aggressive foreign military bases and all forms of discrimination, particularly those based on race, ethnic group, color, sex, language, religion or political opinions;

Reaffirming their adherence to the principles of human and peoples' rights and freedoms contained in the declarations, conventions and other instrument adopted by the Organization of African Unity, the Movement of Non-Aligned Countries and the United Nations;

Firmly convinced of their duty to promote and protect human and people' rights and freedoms taking into account the importance traditionally attached to these rights and freedoms in Africa;

Have agreed as follows: (...)

African Court of Justice and Human Rights *(Protocol on the Statute of the African Court of Justice and Human Rights. Adopted by the 11th Ordinary Session of the Assembly of the Union, In Sharm El-Sheikh, Egypt, 01 July 2008. Preamble; Chapter 1. Merger of the African Court on Human and Peoples'Rights and the Court of Justice of the African Union. Art. 1. Replacement of the 1998 and 2003 Protocols; Art. 2. Establishment of a single Court; Art. 3. Reference to the single Court in the Constitutive Act. (...) Annex – Statute of the African Court of Justice and Human Rights. (...) Art. 2. Functions of the Court; Art. 3. Composition; Art. 4. Qualifications of Judges (...); Art. 16. Sections of the Court; (...) Art. 25. Seat and Seal of the Court; (...) Chapter 3. Competence of the Court. Art. 28. Jurisdiction of the Court; Art. 29. Entities Eligible to Submit Cases to the Court; Art. 30. Other Entities Eligible to Submit Cases to the Court; Art. 31. Applicable Law; (...) Chapter 5. Advisory opinion. Art. 53. Request for Advisory Opinion. (...)).*

Preamble. The Member States of the African Union, Parties to this Protocol,

Recalling the objectives and principles enunciated in the Constitutive Act of the African Union, adopted on 11 July 2000 in Lomé, Togo, in particular the commitment to settle their disputes through peaceful means;

Bearing in mind their commitment to promote peace, security and stability on the Continent and to protect human and peoples' rights in accordance with the African Charter on Human and Peoples' Rights and other relevant instruments relating to human rights;

Considering that the Constitutive Act of the African Union provides for the establishment of a Court of Justice charged with hearing, among other things, all cases relating to interpretation or application of the said Act or of all other Treaties adopted within the framework of the Union;

Further considering Decisions Assembly/AU/Dec.45 (III) and Assembly/AU/Dec.83 (V) of the Assembly of the Union, adopted respectively at its Third (6-8 July 2004, Addis Ababa, Ethiopia) and Fifth (4-5 July 2005, Sirte, Libya), Ordinary Sessions, to merge the African Court on Human and Peoples' Rights and the Court of Justice of the African Union into a single Court,

Firmly convinced that the establishment of an African Court of Justice and Human Rights shall assist in the achievement of the goals pursued by the African Union and that the attainment of the objectives of the African Charter on Human and Peoples'

17

Rights requires the establishment of a judicial organ to supplement and strengthen the mission of the African Commission on Human and Peoples' Rights as well as the African Committee of Experts on the Rights and Welfare of the Child;

Taking due account of the Protocol to the African Charter on Human and Peoples' Rights on the Establishment an African Court on Human and Peoples' Rights, adopted by the Assembly of Heads of States and Governments of the Organization of African Unity on 10 June 1998 at Ouagadougou, Burkina Faso, and which entered into force on 25 January 2004;

Taking due account also of the Protocol of the Court of Justice of the African Union, adopted by the Assembly of the Union on 11 July 2003 in Maputo Mozambique;

Recalling their commitment to take all necessary measures to strengthen their common institutions and to endow them with the necessary powers and resources to carry out their missions effectively;

Cognizant of the Protocol to the African Charter on Human and Peoples' Rights on the Rights of Women in Africa, and the commitments contained in the Solemn Declaration on the gender equality in Africa (Assembly/AU/Decl.12 (III) adopted by the Assembly of the Union respectively at its Second and Third ordinary sessions held in July 2003 and 2004, in Maputo, Mozambique and in Addis Ababa, Ethiopia);

Convinced that the present Protocol shall supplement the mandate and efforts of other continental treaty bodies as well as national institutions in protecting human rights:

Have agreed as follows:

Chapter 1. Merger of the African Court on Human and Peoples' Rights and the Court of Justice of the African Union. Art. 1. Replacement of the 1998 and 2003 Protocols. The Protocol to the African Charter on Human and Peoples' Rights on the Establishment of an African Court on Human and Peoples' Rights, adopted on 10 June 1998 in Ouagadougou, Burkina Faso and which entered into force on 25 January 2004, and the Protocol of the Court of Justice of the African Union, adopted on 11 July 2003 in Maputo, Mozambique, are hereby replaced by the present Protocol and Statute annexed as its integral part hereto, subject to the provisions of Article 5, 7 and 9 of this Protocol.

Art. 2. Establishment of a single Court. The African Court on Human and Peoples' Rights established by the Protocol to the African Charter on Human and Peoples' Rights on the Establishment of an African Court on Human and Peoples' Rights and the Court of Justice of the African Union established by the Constitutive Act of the African Union, are hereby merged into a single Court and established as *"The African Court of Justice and Human Rights"*.

Art. 3. Reference to the single Court in the Constitutive Act. References made to the "Court of Justice" in the Constitutive Act of the African Union shall be read as references to the "African Court of Justice and Human Rights" established under Article 2 of this Protocol. (…)

Annex – Statute of the African Court of Justice and Human Rights. (…) Art. 2. Functions of the Court. 1. The African Court of Justice and Human Rights shall be the main judicial organ of the African Union.

2. The Court shall be constituted and function in accordance with the provisions of the present Statute.

Art. 3. Composition. 1. The Court shall consist of sixteen (16) Judges who are nationals of States Parties. Upon recommendation of the Court, the Assembly, may, review the number of Judges.

2. The Court shall not, at any one time, have more than one judge from a single Member State.

3. Each geographical region of the Continent, as determined by the Decisions of the Assembly shall, where possible, be represented by three (3) Judges except the Western Region which shall have four (4) Judges.

Art. 4. Qualifications of Judges. The Court shall be composed of impartial and independent Judges elected from among persons of high moral character, who possess the qualifications required in their respective countries for appointment to the highest judicial offices, or are jurist consults of recognized competence and experience in international law and /or, human rights law. (...)

Art. 16. Sections of the Court. The Court shall have two (2) Sections; a General Affairs Section composed of eight (8) Judges and a Human Rights Section composed of eight (8) Judges. (...)

Art. 25. Seat and Seal of the Court. 1. The Seat of the Court shall be same as the Seat of the African Court on Human and Peoples' Rights. However, the Court may sit in any other Member State, if circumstances warrant, and with the consent of the Member State concerned. The Assembly may change the seat of the Court after due consultations with the Court.

2. The Court shall have a seal bearing the inscription "The African Court of Justice and Human Rights" (...)

Chapter 3. Competence of the Court. Art. 28. Jurisdiction of the Court. The Court shall have jurisdiction over all cases and all legal disputes submitted to it in accordance with the present Statute which relate to:

a) the interpretation and application of the Constitutive Act;

b) the interpretation, application or validity of other Union Treaties and all subsidiary legal instruments adopted within the framework of the Union or the Organization of African Unity;

c) the interpretation and the application of the African Charter, the Charter on the Rights and Welfare of the Child, the Protocol to the African Charter on Human and Peoples' Rights on the Rights of Women in Africa, or any other legal instrument relating to human rights, ratified by the States Parties concerned;

d) any question of international law;

e) all acts, decisions, regulations and directives of the organs of the Union;

f) all matters specifically provided for in any other agreements that States Parties may conclude among themselves, or with the Union and which confer jurisdiction on the Court;

g) the existence of any fact which, if established, would constitute a breach of an obligation owed to a State Party or to the Union;

h) the nature or extent of the reparation to be made for the breach of an international obligation.

Art. 29. Entities Eligible to Submit Cases to the Court. 1. The following entities shall be entitled to submit cases to the Court on any issue or dispute provided for in Article 28:

a) State Parties to the present Protocol;

b) The Assembly, the Parliament and other organs of the Union authorized by the Assembly;

c) A staff member of the African Union on appeal, in a dispute and within the limits and under the terms and conditions laid down in the Staff Rules and Regulations of the Union;

2. The Court shall not be open to States, which are not members of the Union. The Court shall also have no jurisdiction to deal with a dispute involving a Member State that has not ratified the Protocol.

Art. 30. Other Entities Eligible to Submit Cases to the Court. The following entities shall also be entitled to submit cases to the Court on any violation of a right guaranteed by the African Charter, by the Charter on the Rights and Welfare of the Child, the Protocol to the African Charter on Human and Peoples' Rights on the Rights of Women in Africa, or any other legal instrument relevant to human rights ratified by the States Parties concerned:

a) State Parties to the present Protocol;

b) the African Commission on Human and Peoples' Rights;

c) the African Committee of Experts on the Rights and Welfare of the Child;

d) African Intergovernmental Organizations accredited to the Union or its organs;

e) African National Human Rights Institutions;

f) Individuals or relevant Non-Governmental Organizations accredited to the African Union or to its organs, subject to the provisions of Article 8 of the Protocol.

Art. 31. Applicable Law. 1. In carrying out its functions, the Court shall have regard to:

a) The Constitutive Act;

b) International treaties, whether general or particular, ratified by the contesting States;

c) International custom, as evidence of a general practice accepted as law;

d) The general principles of law recognized universally or by African States;

e) Subject to the provisions of paragraph 1, of Article 46 of the present Statute, judicial decisions and writings of the most highly qualified publicists of various nations as well as the regulations, directives and decisions of the Union, as subsidiary means for the determination of the rules of law;

f) Any other law relevant to the determination of the case.

2. This Article shall not prejudice the power of the Court to decide a case *ex aequo et bono,* if the parties agree thereto. (…)

Chapter 5. Advisory opinion. Art. 53. Request for Advisory Opinion. 1. The Court may give an advisory opinion on any legal question at the request of the Assembly, the Parliament, the Executive Council, the Peace and Security Council, the Economic, Social and Cultural Council (ECOSOCC), the Financial Institutions or any other organ of the Union as may be authorized by the Assembly.

2. A request for an advisory opinion shall be in writing and shall contain an exact statement of the question upon which the opinion is required and shall be accompanied by all relevant documents.

3. A request for an advisory opinion must not be related to a pending application before the African Commission or the African Committee of Experts. (…)

Seat: Arusha, Tanzania. See: Host Agreement between the Government of the United Republic of Tanzania and the African Union on the Seat of the African Court on Human and Peoples' Rights in Arusha, Tanzania.

Agenda 21 and sustainable development. United Nations. General Assembly. United Nations Conference on Environment and Development. Rio de Janeiro, 3-14 June 1992. *Chapter 1. Preamble (When the term "Governments" is used, it will be deemed to include the European Economic Community within its areas of competence. Throughout Agenda 21 the term "environmentally sound" means "environmentally safe and sound", in particular when applied to the terms "energy sources", "energy supplies", "energy systems" and "technology" or "technologies").*

1.1. Humanity stands at a defining moment in history. We are confronted with a perpetuation of disparities between and within nations, a worsening of poverty, hunger, ill health and illiteracy, and the continuing deterioration of the ecosystems on which we depend for our well-being. However, integration of environment and development concerns and greater attention to them will lead to the fulfilment of basic needs, improved living standards for all, better protected and managed ecosystems and a safer, more prosperous future. No nation can achieve this on its own; but together we can - in a global partnership for sustainable development.

1.2. This global partnership must build on the premises of General Assembly resolution 44/228 of 22 December 1989, which was adopted when the nations of the world called for the United Nations Conference on Environment and Development, and on the acceptance of the need to take a balanced and integrated approach to environment and development questions.

1.3. Agenda 21 addresses the pressing problems of today and also aims at preparing the world for the challenges of the next century. It reflects a global consensus and political commitment at the highest level on development and environment cooperation. Its successful implementation is first and foremost the responsibility of Governments. National strategies, plans, policies and processes are crucial in achieving this. International cooperation should support and supplement such national efforts. In this context, the United Nations system has a key role to play. Other international, regional and subregional organizations are also called upon to contribute to this effort. The broadest public participation and the active involvement of the non-governmental organizations and other groups should also be encouraged.

1.4. The developmental and environmental objectives of Agenda 21 will require a substantial flow of new and additional financial resources to developing countries, in order to cover the incremental costs for the actions they have to undertake to deal with global environmental problems and to accelerate sustainable development. Financial resources are also required for strengthening the capacity of international institutions for the implementation of Agenda 21. An indicative order-of-magnitude assessment of costs is included in each of the programme areas. This assessment will need to be examined and refined by the relevant implementing agencies and organizations.

1.5. In the implementation of the relevant programme areas identified in Agenda 21, special attention should be given to the particular circumstances facing the economies in transition. It must also be recognized that these countries are facing unprecedented challenges in transforming their economies, in some cases in the midst of considerable social and political tension.

1.6. The programme areas that constitute Agenda 21 are described in terms of the basis for action, objectives, activities and means of implementation. Agenda 21 is a dynamic programme. It will be carried out by the various actors according to the different situations, capacities and priorities of countries and regions in full respect of all the principles contained in the Rio Declaration on Environment and Development. It could evolve over time in the light of changing needs and circumstances. This process marks the beginning of a new global partnership for sustainable development.

(...)

Section I. Social and economic dimensions. *Chapter 2.* International cooperation to accelerate sustainable development in developing countries and related domestic policies; *Chapter 3.* Combating poverty; *Chapter 4.* Changing consumption patterns; *Chapter 5.* Demographic dynamics and sustainability; *Chapter 6.* Protecting and promoting human health conditions; *Chapter 7.* Promoting sustainable human settlement development; *Chapter 8.* Integrating environment and development in decision-making.

Section II. Conservation and management of resources for development

Chapter 9. Protection of the atmosphere; *Chapter 10.* Integrated approach to the planning and management of land resources; *Chapter 11.* Combating deforestation; *Chapter 12.* Managing fragile ecosystems: combating desertification and drought; *Chapter 13.* Managing fragile ecosystems: sustainable mountain development; *Chapter 14.* Promoting sustainable agriculture and rural development; *Chapter 15.* Conservation of biological diversity; *Chapter 16.* Environmentally sound management of biotechnology; *Chapter 17.* Protection of the oceans, all kinds of seas, including enclosed and semi-enclosed seas, and coastal areas and the protection, rational use and development of their living resources; *Chapter 18.* Protection of the quality and supply of freshwater resources: application of integrated approaches to the development, management and use of water resources; *Chapter 19.* Environmentally sound management of toxic chemicals, including prevention of illegal international traffic in toxic and dangerous products; *Chapter 20.* Environmentally Sound Management of Hazardous Wastes, Including Prevention of Illegal International Traffic in Hazardous Wastes; *Chapter 21.* Environmentally sound management of solid wastes and sewage-related issues; *Chapter 22.* Safe and environmentally sound management of radioactive wastes.

Section III. Strengthening the role of major groups

Chapter 23. Preamble; *Chapter 24.* Global action for women towards sustainable and equitable development; *Chapter 25.* Children and youth in sustainable development; *Chapter 26.* Recognizing and strengthening the role of indigenous people and their communities; *Chapter 27.* Strengthening the role of non-governmental organizations: partners for sustainable development; *Chapter 28.* Local authorities' initiatives in support of Agenda 21; *Chapter 29.* Strengthening the role of workers and their trade unions; *Chapter 30.* Strengthening the role of business and industry; *Chapter 31.* Scientific and technological community; *Chapter 32.* Strengthening the role of farmers.

Section IV. Means of implementation
Chapter 33. Financial resources and mechanisms; *Chapter 34*. Transfer of environmentally sound technology, cooperation and capacity-building; *Chapter 35*. Science for sustainable development; *Chapter 36*. Promoting education, public awareness and training; *Chapter 37*. National mechanisms and international cooperation for capacity-building in developing countries; *Chapter 38*. International institutional arrangements; *Chapter 39*. International legal instruments and mechanisms; *Chapter 40*. Information for decision-making.

American Convention on Human Rights "Pact of San Jose, Costa Rica", 22 November 1969. *Preamble.* The American states signatory to the present Convention,

Reaffirming their intention to consolidate in this hemisphere, within the framework of democratic institutions, a system of personal liberty and social justice based on respect for the essential rights of man;

Recognizing that the essential rights of man are not derived from one's being a national of a certain state, but are based upon attributes of the human personality, and that they therefore justify international protection in the form of a convention reinforcing or complementing the protection provided by the domestic law of the American states;

Considering that these principles have been set forth in the Charter of the Organization of American States, in the American Declaration of the Rights and Duties of Man, and in the Universal Declaration of Human Rights, and that they have been reaffirmed and refined in other international instruments, worldwide as well as regional in scope;

Reiterating that, in accordance with the Universal Declaration of Human Rights, the ideal of free men enjoying freedom from fear and want can be achieved only if conditions are created whereby everyone may enjoy his economic, social, and cultural rights, as well as his civil and political rights; and

Considering that the Third Special Inter-American Conference (Buenos Aires, 1967) approved the incorporation into the Charter of the Organization itself of broader standards with respect to economic, social, and educational rights and resolved that an inter-American convention on human rights should determine the structure, competence, and procedure of the organs responsible for these matters,

Have agreed upon the following: (...)

Amicus curiae *(RPE – ICC, Rule 103. Amicus curiae and other forms of submission; RPE – ICTY, Rule 74. Amicus Curiae; RPE – ICTR, Rule 74. Amicus Curiae).*
RPE – ICC, Rule 103. Amicus curiae and other forms of submission. 1. At any stage of the proceedings, a Chamber may, if it considers it desirable for the proper determination of the case, invite or grant leave to a State, organization or person to submit, in writing or orally, any observation on any issue that the Chamber deems appropriate.
2. The Prosecutor and the defence shall have the opportunity to respond to the observations submitted under sub-rule 1.

3. A written observation submitted under sub-rule 1 shall be filed with the Registrar, who shall provide copies to the Prosecutor and the defence. The Chamber shall determine what time limits shall apply to the filing of such observations.

RPE – ICTY, Rule 74. Amicus Curiae. A Chamber may, if it considers it desirable for the proper determination of the case, invite or grant leave to a State, organization or person to appear before it and make submissions on any issue specified by the Chamber.

RPE – ICTR, Rule 74. Amicus Curiae. A Chamber may, if it considers it desirable for the proper determination of the case, invite or grant leave to any State, organization or person to appear before it and make submissions on any issue specified by the Chamber.

Arab Charter on Human Rights.

Adopted by the Council of the League of Arab States, 22 May 2004, Tunis (Tunisia), entered into force March 15, 2008. *Preamble.*

Based on the faith of the Arab nation in the dignity of the human person whom God has exalted ever since the beginning of creation and in the fact that the Arab homeland is the cradle of religions and civilizations whose lofty human values affirm the human right to a decent life based on freedom, justice and equality,

In furtherance of the eternal principles of fraternity, equality and tolerance among human beings consecrated by the noble Islamic religion and the other divinely-revealed religions,

Being proud of the humanitarian values and principles that the Arab nation has established throughout its long history, which have played a major role in spreading knowledge between East and West, so making the region a point of reference for the whole world and a destination for seekers of knowledge and wisdom,

Believing in the unity of the Arab nation, which struggles for its freedom and defends the right of nations to self-determination, to the preservation of their wealth and to development; believing in the sovereignty of the law and its contribution to the protection of universal and interrelated human rights and convinced that the human person's enjoyment of freedom, justice and equality of opportunity is a fundamental measure of the value of any society,

Rejecting all forms of racism and Zionism, which constitute a violation of human rights and a threat to international peace and security, recognizing the close link that exists between human rights and international peace and security, reaffirming the principles of the Charter of the United Nations, the Universal Declaration of Human Rights and the provisions of the International Covenant on Civil and Political Rights and the International Covenant on Economic, Social and Cultural Rights, and having regard to the Cairo Declaration on Human Rights in Islam,

The States parties to the Charter have agreed as follows: (...)

Armed forces. Combatants

(Protocol Additional to the Geneva Conventions of 12 August 1949, and relating to the Protection of Victims of International Armed Conflicts (Protocol I), 8 June 1977. Part. III. Methods and Means of Warfare. Combatant and Prisoners-Of-War. Section II. Combatants and Prisoners of War.

Art. 43. Armed forces). 1. The armed forces of a Party to a conflict consist of all organized armed forces, groups and units which are under a command responsible to that Party for the conduct or its subordinates, even if that Party is represented by a government or an authority not recognized by an adverse Party. Such armed forces shall be subject to an internal disciplinary system which, inter alia, shall enforce compliance with the rules of international law applicable in armed conflict.

2. Members of the armed forces of a Party to a conflict (other than medical personnel and chaplains covered by Article 33 of the Third Convention) are combatants, that is to say, they have the right to participate directly in hostilities.

3. Whenever a Party to a conflict incorporates a paramilitary or armed law enforcement agency into its armed forces it shall so notify the other Parties to the conflict.

Assembly of States Parties *(Rome Statute ICC. Part XI. Assembly of states parties, art. 112. Assembly of States Parties).* 1. An Assembly of States Parties to this Statute is hereby established. Each State Party shall have one representative in the Assembly who may be accompanied by alternates and advisers. Other States which have signed this Statute or the Final Act may be observers in the Assembly.

2. The Assembly shall:

(a) Consider and adopt, as appropriate, recommendations of the Preparatory Commission;

(b) Provide management oversight to the Presidency, the Prosecutor and the Registrar regarding the administration of the Court;

(c) Consider the reports and activities of the Bureau established under paragraph 3 and take appropriate action in regard thereto;

(d) Consider and decide the budget for the Court;

(e) Decide whether to alter, in accordance with article 36, the number of judges;

(f) Consider pursuant to article 87, paragraphs 5 and 7, any question relating to non-cooperation;

(g) Perform any other function consistent with this Statute or the Rules of Procedure and Evidence.

3. (a) The Assembly shall have a Bureau consisting of a President, two Vice-Presidents and 18 members elected by the Assembly for three-year terms.

(b) The Bureau shall have a representative character, taking into account, in particular, equitable geographical distribution and the adequate representation of the principal legal systems of the world.

(c) The Bureau shall meet as often as necessary, but at least once a year. It shall assist the Assembly in the discharge of its responsibilities.

4. The Assembly may establish such subsidiary bodies as may be necessary, including an independent oversight mechanism for inspection, evaluation and investigation of the Court, in order to enhance its efficiency and economy.

5. The President of the Court, the Prosecutor and the Registrar or their representatives may participate, as appropriate, in meetings of the Assembly and of the Bureau.

6. The Assembly shall meet at the seat of the Court or at the Headquarters of the United Nations once a year and, when circumstances so require, hold special sessions. Except as otherwise specified in this Statute, special sessions shall be

convened by the Bureau on its own initiative or at the request of one third of the States Parties.

7. Each State Party shall have one vote. Every effort shall be made to reach decisions by consensus in the Assembly and in the Bureau. If consensus cannot be reached, except as otherwise provided in the Statute:

(a) Decisions on matters of substance must be approved by a two-thirds majority of those present and voting provided that an absolute majority of States Parties constitutes the quorum for voting;

(b) Decisions on matters of procedure shall be taken by a simple majority of States Parties present and voting.

8. A State Party which is in arrears in the payment of its financial contributions towards the costs of the Court shall have no vote in the Assembly and in the Bureau if the amount of its arrears equals or exceeds the amount of the contributions due from it for the preceding two full years. The Assembly may, nevertheless, permit such a State Party to vote in the Assembly and in the Bureau if it is satisfied that the failure to pay is due to conditions beyond the control of the State Party.

9. The Assembly shall adopt its own rules of procedure.

10. The official and working languages of the Assembly shall be those of the General Assembly of the United Nations.

Attack directed against any civilian population. See: Crimes against humanity

"Attacks" *(Protocol Additional to the Geneva Conventions of 12 August 1949, and relating to the Protection of Victims of International Armed Conflicts (Protocol I), 8 June 1977. Part. IV. Civilian Population. Section I. General Protection Against Effects of Hostilities. Chapter I. Basic rule and field of application. Art. 49. Definition of attacks and scope of application; Chapter IV. Precautionary measures. Art. 57. Precautions in attack; Art. 58. Precautions against the effects of attacks).* Art. 49. Definition of attacks and scope of application. 1. "Attacks" means acts of violence against the adversary, whether in offence or in defence.

2. The provisions of this Protocol with respect to attacks apply to all attacks in whatever territory conducted, including the national territory belonging to a Party to the conflict but under the control of an adverse Party.

3. The provisions of this section apply to any land, air or sea warfare which may affect the civilian population, individual civilians or civilian objects on land. They further apply to all attacks from the sea or from the air against objectives on land but do not otherwise affect the rules of international law applicable in armed conflict at sea or in the air.

4. The provisions of this section are additional to the rules concerning humanitarian protection contained in the Fourth Convention, particularly in part II thereof, and in other international agreements binding upon the High Contracting Parties, as well as to other rules of international law relating to the protection of civilians and civilian objects on land, at sea or in the air against the effects of hostilities.

Art. 57. Precautions in attack. 1. In the conduct of military operations, constant care shall be taken to spare the civilian population, civilians and civilian objects.

2. With respect to attacks, the following precautions shall be taken:

(a) those who plan or decide upon an attack shall:

(i) do everything feasible to verify that the objectives to be attacked are neither civilians nor civilian objects and are not subject to special protection but are military objectives within the meaning of paragraph 2 of Article 52 and that it is not prohibited by the provisions of this Protocol to attack them;

(ii) take all feasible precautions in the choice of means and methods of attack with a view to avoiding, and in any event to minimizing, incidental loss or civilian life, injury to civilians and damage to civilian objects;

(iii) refrain from deciding to launch any attack which may be expected to cause incidental loss of civilian life, injury to civilians, damage to civilian objects, or a combination thereof, which would be excessive in relation to the concrete and direct military advantage anticipated;

(b) an attack shall be cancelled or suspended if it becomes apparent that the objective is not a military one or is subject to special protection or that the attack may be expected to cause incidental loss of civilian life, injury to civilians, damage to civilian objects, or a combination thereof, which would be excessive in relation to the concrete and direct military advantage anticipated;

(c) effective advance warning shall be given of attacks which may affect the civilian population, unless circumstances do not permit.

3. When a choice is possible between several military objectives for obtaining a similar military advantage, the objective to be selected shall be that the attack on which may be expected to cause the least danger to civilian lives and to civilian objects.

4. In the conduct of military operations at sea or in the air, each Party to the conflict shall, in conformity with its rights and duties under the rules of international law applicable in armed conflict, take all reasonable precautions to avoid losses of civilian lives and damage to civilian objects.

5. No provision of this article may be construed as authorizing any attacks against the civilian population, civilians or civilian objects.

Art. 58. Precautions against the effects of attacks. The Parties to the conflict shall, to the maximum extent feasible:

(a) without prejudice to Article 49 of the Fourth Convention, endeavour to remove the civilian population, individual civilians and civilian objects under their control from the vicinity of military objectives;

(b) avoid locating military objectives within or near densely populated areas;

(c) take the other necessary precautions to protect the civilian population, individual civilians and civilian objects under their control against the dangers resulting from military operations.

C

Chambers *(Rome Statute ICC, art. 39. Chambers; See RPE – ICC, Chapter 2. Composition and administration of the Court. Section I. General provisions relating to the composition and administration of the Court. Rules 4, 5, 6, 7, 8; Statute ICTY, art. 12. Composition of the Chambers; See RPE – ICTY, Part 3. Organization of the Tribunal. Section 1. The Judges; Section 4. The Chambers; Statute ICTR, art. 11. Composition of the Chambers; See RPE – ICTR, Part. 3. Organization of the Tribunal. Section 1. The Judges; Section 4. The Chambers).*

Rome Statute ICC, art. 39. Chambers. 1. As soon as possible after the election of the judges, the Court shall organize itself into the divisions specified in article 34, paragraph (b). The Appeals Division shall be composed of the President and four other judges, the Trial Division of not less than six judges and the Pre-Trial Division of not less than six judges. The assignment of judges to divisions shall be based on the nature of the functions to be performed by each division and the qualifications and experience of the judges

elected to the Court, in such a way that each division shall contain an appropriate combination of expertise in criminal law and procedure and in international law. The Trial and Pre-Trial Divisions shall be composed predominantly of judges with criminal trial experience.

2. (a) The judicial functions of the Court shall be carried out in each division by Chambers.

(b) (i) The Appeals Chamber shall be composed of all the judges of the Appeals Division;

(ii) The functions of the Trial Chamber shall be carried out by three judges of the Trial Division;

(iii) The functions of the Pre-Trial Chamber shall be carried out either by three judges of the Pre-Trial Division or by a single judge of that division in accordance with this Statute and the Rules of Procedure and Evidence;

(c) Nothing in this paragraph shall preclude the simultaneous constitution of more than one Trial Chamber or Pre-Trial Chamber when the efficient management of the Court's workload so requires.

3. (a) Judges assigned to the Trial and Pre-Trial Divisions shall serve in those divisions for a period of three years, and thereafter until the completion of any case the hearing of which has already commenced in the division concerned.

(b) Judges assigned to the Appeals Division shall serve in that division for their entire term of office.

4. Judges assigned to the Appeals Division shall serve only in that division. Nothing in this article shall, however, preclude the temporary attachment of judges from the

Trial Division to the Pre-Trial Division or vice versa, if the Presidency considers that the efficient management of the Court's workload so requires, provided that under no circumstances shall a judge who has participated in the pre-trial phase of a case be eligible to sit on the Trial Chamber hearing that case. (...) *See: RPE – ICC, Chapter 2. Composition and administration of the Court. Section I. General provisions relating to the composition and administration of the Court. Rules 4, 5, 6, 7, 8.*

Statute ICTY, art. 12. Composition of the Chambers. 1. The Chambers shall be composed of a maximum of sixteen permanent independent judges, no two of whom may be nationals of the same State, and a maximum at any one time of twelve *ad litem* independent judges appointed in accordance with article 13 *ter*, paragraph 2, of the Statute, no two of whom may be nationals of the same State.

2. A maximum at any one time of three permanent judges and six *ad litem* judges shall be members of each Trial Chamber. Each Trial Chamber to which *ad litem* judges are assigned may be divided into sections of three judges each, composed of both permanent and *ad litem* judges, except in the circumstances specified in paragraph 5 below. A section of a Trial Chamber shall have the same powers and responsibilities as a Trial Chamber under the Statute and shall render judgement in accordance with the same rules.

3. Seven of the permanent judges shall be members of the Appeals Chamber. The Appeals Chamber shall, for each appeal, be composed of five of its members.

4. A person who for the purposes of membership of the Chambers of the International Tribunal could be regarded as a national of more than one State shall be deemed to be a national of the State in which that person ordinarily exercises civil and political rights.

5. The Secretary-General may, at the request of the President of the International Tribunal appoint, from among the *ad litem* judges elected in accordance with Article 13 *ter*, reserve judges to be present at each stage of a trial to which they have been appointed and to replace a judge if that judge is unable to continue sitting.

6. Without prejudice to paragraph 2 above, in the event that exceptional circumstances require for a permanent judge in a section of a Trial Chamber to be replaced resulting in a section solely comprised of *ad litem* judges, that section may continue to hear the case, notwithstanding that its composition no longer includes a permanent judge. (...) *See: RPE – ICTY, Part 3. Organization of the Tribunal. Section 1. The Judges; Section 4. The Chambers.*

Statute ICTR, art. 11. Composition of the Chambers. 1. The Chambers shall be composed of sixteen permanent independent judges, no two of whom may be nationals of the same State, and a maximum at any one time of nine *ad litem* independent judges appointed in accordance with article 12 *ter*, paragraph 2, of the present Statute, no two of whom may be nationals of the same State.

2. Three permanent judges and a maximum at any one time of six *ad litem* judges shall be members of each Trial Chamber. Each Trial Chamber to which ad *litem* judges are assigned may be divided into sections of three judges each, composed of both permanent and *ad litem* judges. A section of a Trial Chamber shall have the same powers and responsibilities as a Trial Chamber under the present Statute and shall render judgement in accordance with the same rules.

3. Seven of the permanent judges shall be members of the Appeals Chamber. The Appeals Chamber shall, for each appeal, be composed of five of its members.

4. A person who for the purposes of membership of the Chambers of the International Tribunal for Rwanda could be regarded as a national of more than one State shall be deemed to be a national of the State in which that person ordinarily exercises civil and political rights. (...) See: RPE – ICTR, Part. 3. Organization of the Tribunal. Section 1. The Judges; Section 4. The Chambers.

Charter of fundamental rights of the European Union. C 364/1 - Official Journal of the European Communities, 18.12.2000. *Preamble.* The peoples of Europe, in creating an ever closer union among them, are resolved to share a peaceful future based on common values.

Conscious of its spiritual and moral heritage, the Union is founded on the indivisible, *universal* values of human dignity, freedom, equality and solidarity; it is based on the principles of democracy and the rule of law. It places the individual at the heart of its activities, by establishing the citizenship of the Union and by creating an area of freedom, security and justice.

The Union contributes to the preservation and to the development of these common values while respecting the diversity of the cultures and traditions of the peoples of Europe as well as the national identities of the Member States and the organization of their public authorities at national, regional and local levels; it seeks to promote balanced and sustainable development and ensures free movement of persons, goods, services and capital, and the freedom of establishment.

To this end, it is necessary to strengthen the protection of fundamental rights in the light of changes in society, social progress and scientific and technological developments by making those rights more visible in a Charter.

This Charter reaffirms, with due regard for the powers and tasks of the Community and the Union and the principle of subsidiarity, the rights as they result, in particular, from the constitutional traditions and international obligations common to the Member States, the Treaty on European Union, the Community Treaties, the European Convention for the Protection of Human Rights and Fundamental Freedoms, the Social Charters adopted by the Community and by the Council of Europe and the case-law of the Court of Justice of the European Communities and of the European Court of Human Rights.

Enjoyment of these rights entails responsibilities and duties with regard to other persons, to the human community and to future generations.

The Union therefore recognizes the rights, freedoms and principles set out hereafter.
(...)

Charter of the United Nations, San Francisco, 26 June 1945 *(Preamble; Chapter I. Purposes and principles, Art. 1, Art. 2; Chapter II. Membership, Art. 3, Art. 4, Art. 5, Art. 6; Chapter III. Organs, Art. 7, Art. 8; Chapter XIV. The International Court of Justice, Art. 92). Preamble.* We the peoples of the United Nations,

Determined

To save succeeding generations from the scourge of war, which twice in our lifetime has brought untold sorrow to mankind, and

To reaffirm faith in fundamental human rights, in the dignity and worth of the human person, in the equal rights of men and women and of nations large and small, and

To establish conditions under which justice and respect for the obligations arising from treaties and other sources of international law can be maintained, and

To promote social progress and better standards of life in larger freedom,

And for these ends

To practice tolerance and live together in peace with one another as good neighbors, and

To unite our strength to maintain international peace and security, and

To ensure, by the acceptance of principles and the institution of methods, that armed force shall not be used, save in the common interest, and

To employ international machinery for the promotion of the economic and social advancement of all peoples,

Have resolved to combine our efforts to accomplish these aims.

Accordingly, our respective Governments, through representatives assembled in the city of San Francisco, who have exhibited their full powers found to be in good and due form, have agreed to the present Charter of the United Nations and do hereby establish an international organization to be known as the United Nations.

Chapter I. Purposes and principles. Art. 1. The Purposes of the United Nations are:

1. To maintain international peace and security, and to that end: to take effective collective measures for the prevention and removal of threats to the peace, and for the suppression of acts of aggression or other breaches of the peace, and to bring about by peaceful means, and in conformity with the principles of justice and international law, adjustment or settlement of international disputes or situations which might lead to a breach of the peace;

2. To develop friendly relations among nations based on respect for the principle of equal rights and self-determination of peoples, and to take other appropriate measures to strengthen universal peace;

3. To achieve international cooperation in solving international problems of an economic, social, cultural, or humanitarian character, and in promoting and encouraging respect for human rights and for fundamental freedoms for all without distinction as to race, sex, language, or religion; and

4. To be a center for harmonizing the actions of nations in the attainment of these common ends.

Art. 2. The Organization and its Members, in pursuit of the Purposes stated in Article 1, shall act in accordance with the following Principles.

1. The Organization is based on the principle of the sovereign equality of all its Members.

2. All Members, in order to ensure to all of them the rights and benefits resulting from membership, shall fulfil in good faith the obligations assumed by them in accordance with the present Charter.

3. All Members shall settle their international disputes by peaceful means in such a manner that international peace and security, and justice, are not endangered.

4. All Members shall refrain in their international relations from the threat or use of force against the territorial integrity or political independence of any state, or in any other manner inconsistent with the Purposes of the United Nations.

5. All Members shall give the United Nations every assistance in any action it takes in accordance with the present Charter, and shall refrain from giving assistance to any state against which the United Nations is taking preventive or enforcement action.

6. The Organization shall ensure that states which are not Members of the United Nations act in accordance with these Principles so far as may be necessary for the maintenance of international peace and security.

7. Nothing contained in the present Charter shall authorize the United Nations to intervene in matters which are essentially within the domestic jurisdiction of any state or shall require the Members to submit such matters to settlement under the present Charter; but this principle shall not prejudice the application of enforcement measures under Chapter VII.

Chapter II. Membership. Art. 3. The original Members of the United Nations shall be the states which, having participated in the United Nations Conference on International Organization at San Francisco, or having previously signed the Declaration by United Nations of January 1,1942, sign the present Charter and ratify it in accordance with Article 110.

Art. 4. 1. Membership in the United Nations is open to all other peace-loving states which accept the obligations contained in the present Charter and, in the judgment of the Organization, are able and willing to carry out these obligations.

2. The admission of any such state to membership in the United Nations will be effected by a decision of the General Assembly upon the recommendation of the Security Council.

Art. 5. A Member of the United Nations against which preventive or enforcement action has been taken by the Security Council may be suspended from the exercise of the rights and privileges of membership by the General Assembly upon the recommendation of the Security Council. The exercise of these rights and privileges may be restored by the Security Council. *Art. 6.* A Member of the United Nations which has persistently violated the Principles contained in the present Charter may be expelled from the Organization by the General Assembly upon the recommendation of the Security Council.

Chapter III. Organs. Art. 7. 1. There are established as the principal organs of the United Nations: a General Assembly, a Security Council, an Economic and Social Council, a Trusteeship Council, an International Court of Justice, and a Secretariat.

2. Such subsidiary organs as may be found necessary may be established in accordance with the present Charter.

Art. 8. The United Nations shall place no restrictions on the eligibility of men and women to participate in any capacity and under conditions of equality in its principal and subsidiary organs. (…).

Chapter XIV. The International Court of Justice. Art. 92. The International Court of Justice shall be the principal judicial organ of the United Nations. It shall function in accordance with the annexed Statute, which is based upon the Statute of the Permanent Court of International Justice and forms an integral part of the present Charter. (…).

Child *(Convention on the rights of the child. Adopted and opened for signature, ratification and accession by General Assembly resolution 44/25 of 20 November 1989. Part. I., Art.1; Art. 2; Art. 3).* Art. 1. For the purposes of the present Convention, a child means every human being below the age of eighteen years unless under the law applicable to the child, majority is attained earlier.

Art. 2. 1. States Parties shall respect and ensure the rights set forth in the present Convention to each child within their jurisdiction without discrimination of any kind, irrespective of the child's or his or her parent's or legal guardian's race, colour, sex, language, religion, political or other opinion, national, ethnic or social origin, property, disability, birth or other status.

2. States Parties shall take all appropriate measures to ensure that the child is protected against all forms of discrimination or punishment on the basis of the status, activities, expressed opinions, or beliefs of the child's parents, legal guardians, or family members.

Art. 3. 1. In all actions concerning children, whether undertaken by public or private social welfare institutions, courts of law, administrative authorities or legislative bodies, the best interests of the child shall be a primary consideration.

2. States Parties undertake to ensure the child such protection and care as is necessary for his or her well-being, taking into account the rights and duties of his or her parents, legal guardians, or other individuals legally responsible for him or her, and, to this end, shall take all appropriate legislative and administrative measures.

3. States Parties shall ensure that the institutions, services and facilities responsible for the care or protection of children shall conform with the standards established by competent authorities, particularly in the areas of safety, health, in the number and suitability of their staff, as well as competent supervision.

"Civil defence", "Civil defence organizations", "Personnel" and "Matériel" of civil defence organizations *(Protocol Additional to the Geneva Conventions of 12 August 1949, and relating to the Protection of Victims of International Armed Conflicts (Protocol I), 8 June 1977. Part. IV. Civilian Population. Section I. General Protection Against Effects of Hostilities. Chapter VI. Civil defence. Art. 61. Definitions and scope).* For the purpose of this Protocol: (1) "Civil defence" means the performance of some or all of the undermentioned humanitarian tasks intended to protect the civilian population against the dangers, and to help it to recover from the immediate effects, of hostilities or disasters and also to provide the conditions necessary for its survival. These tasks are:

(a) warning;
(b) evacuation;
(c) management of shelters;
(d) management of blackout measures;
(e) rescue;
(f) medical services, including first aid, and religious assistance;
(g) fire-fighting;
(h) detection and marking of danger areas;
(i) decontamination and similar protective measures;
(j) provision of emergency accommodation and supplies;

(k) emergency assistance in the restoration and maintenance of order in distressed areas;

(l) emergency repair of indispensable public utilities;

(m) emergency disposal of the dead;

(n) assistance in the preservation of objects essential for survival;

(o) complementary activities necessary to carry out any of the tasks mentioned above, including, but not limited to, planning and organization;

(2) "Civil defence organizations" means those establishments and other units which are organized or authorized by the competent authorities of a Party to the conflict to perform any of the tasks mentioned under (1), and which are assigned and devoted exclusively to such tasks;

(3) "Personnel" of civil defence organizations means those persons assigned by a Party to the conflict exclusively to the performance of the tasks mentioned under (1), including personnel assigned by the competent authority of that Party exclusively to the administration of these organizations;

(4) "Matériel" of civil defence organizations means equipment, supplies and transports used by these organizations for the performance of the tasks mentioned under (1).

Civil defence in occupied territories *(Protocol Additional to the Geneva Conventions of 12 August 1949, and relating to the Protection of Victims of International Armed Conflicts (Protocol I), 8 June 1977. Part. IV. Civilian Population. Section I. General Protection Against Effects of Hostilities. Chapter VI. Civil defence. Art. 63. Civil defence in occupied territories).* 1. In occupied territories, civilian civil defence organizations shall receive from the authorities the facilities necessary for the performance of their tasks. In no Circumstances shall their personnel be compelled to perform activities which would interfere with the proper performance of these tasks. The Occupying Power shall not change the structure or personnel of such organizations in any way which might jeopardize the efficient performance of their mission. These organizations shall not be required to give priority to the nationals or interests of that Power.

2. The Occupying Power shall not compel, coerce or induce civilian civil defence organizations to perform their tasks in any manner prejudicial to the interests of the civilian population.

3. The Occupying Power may disarm civil defence personnel for reasons of security.

4. The Occupying Power shall neither divert from their proper use nor requisition buildings or matériel belonging to or used by civil defence organizations if such diversion or requisition would be harmful to the civilian population.

5. Provided that the general rule in paragraph 4 continues to be observed, the Occupying Power may requisition or divert these resources, subject to the following particular conditions: (a) that the buildings or matériel are necessary for other needs of the civilian population; and

(b) that the requisition or diversion continues only while such necessity exists.

6. The Occupying Power shall neither divert nor requisition shelters provided for the use of the civilian population or needed by such population.

Civilian objects *(Protocol Additional to the Geneva Conventions of 12 August 1949, and relating to the Protection of Victims of International Armed Conflicts (Protocol I), 8 June 1977. Part. IV. Civilian Population. Section I. General Protection Against Effects of Hostilities. Chapter III. Civilian objects. Art. 52. General Protection of civilian objects).* 1. Civilian objects shall not be the object of attack or of reprisals. Civilian objects are all objects which are not military objectives as defined in paragraph 2.

2. Attacks shall be limited strictly to military objectives. In so far as objects are concerned, military objectives are limited to those objects which by their nature, location, purpose or use make an effective contribution to military action and whose total or partial destruction, capture or neutralization, in the circumstances ruling at the time, offers a definite military advantage.

3. In case of doubt whether an object which is normally dedicated to civilian purposes, such as a place of worship, a house or other dwelling or a school, is being used to make an effective contribution to military action, it shall be presumed not to be so used.

Civilians and civilian population *(Protocol Additional to the Geneva Conventions of 12 August 1949, and relating to the Protection of Victims of International Armed Conflicts (Protocol I), 8 June 1977. Part. IV. Civilian Population. Section I. General Protection Against Effects of Hostilities. Chapter II. Civilians and civilian population. Art. 50. Definition of civilians and civilian population).* 1. A civilian is any person who does not belong to one of the categories of persons referred to in Article 4 (A) (1), (2), (3) and (6) of the Third Convention and in Article 43 of this Protocol. In case of doubt whether a person is a civilian, that person shall be considered to be a civilian.

2. The civilian population comprises all persons who are civilians.

3. The presence within the civilian population of individuals who do not come within the definition of civilians does not deprive the population of its civilian character.

Convention (III) relative to the Treatment of Prisoners of War. Geneva, 12 August 1949. Art. 4. A. Prisoners of war, in the sense of the present Convention, are persons belonging to one of the following categories, who have fallen into the power of the enemy:

(1) Members of the armed forces of a Party to the conflict, as well as members of militias or volunteer corps forming part of such armed forces.

(2) Members of other militias and members of other volunteer corps, including those of organized resistance movements, belonging to a Party to the conflict and operating in or outside their own territory, even if this territory is occupied, provided that such militias or volunteer corps, including such organized resistance movements, fulfil the following conditions:

(a) that of being commanded by a person responsible for his subordinates;

(b) that of having a fixed distinctive sign recognizable at a distance;

(c) that of carrying arms openly;

(d) that of conducting their operations in accordance with the laws and customs of war.

(3) Members of regular armed forces who profess allegiance to a government or an authority not recognized by the Detaining Power.

(…) (6) Inhabitants of a non-occupied territory, who on the approach of the enemy spontaneously take up arms to resist the invading forces, without having had time to form themselves into regular armed units, provided they carry arms openly and respect the laws and customs of war.

Protocol Additional to the Geneva Conventions of 12 August 1949, and relating to the Protection of Victims of International Armed Conflicts (Protocol I), 8 June 1977. Art. 43. Armed forces. 1. The armed forces of a Party to a conflict consist of all organized armed forces, groups and units which are under a command responsible to that Party for the conduct or its subordinates, even if that Party is represented by a government or an authority not recognized by an adverse Party. Such armed forces shall be subject to an internal disciplinary system which, inter alia, shall enforce compliance with the rules of international law applicable in armed conflict.

2. Members of the armed forces of a Party to a conflict (other than medical personnel and chaplains covered by Article 33 of the Third Convention) are combatants, that is to say, they have the right to participate directly in hostilities.

3. Whenever a Party to a conflict incorporates a paramilitary or armed law enforcement agency into its armed forces it shall so notify the other Parties to the conflict.

Combatants and prisoners of war *(Protocol Additional to the Geneva Conventions of 12 August 1949, and relating to the Protection of Victims of International Armed Conflicts (Protocol I), 8 June 1977. Part. III. Methods and Means of Warfare. Combatant and Prisoners-Of-War. Section II. Combatants and Prisoners of War. Art. 44. Combatants and prisoners of war).* 1. Any combatant, as defined in Article 43, who falls into the power of an adverse Party shall be a prisoner of war.

2. While all combatants are obliged to comply with the rules of international law applicable in armed conflict, violations of these rules shall not deprive a combatant of his right to be a combatant or, if he falls into the power of an adverse Party, of his right to be a prisoner of war, except as provided in paragraphs 3 and 4.

3. In order to promote the protection of the civilian population from the effects of hostilities, combatants are obliged to distinguish themselves from the civilian population while they are engaged in an attack or in a military operation preparatory to an attack. Recognizing, however, that there are situations in armed conflicts where, owing to the nature of the hostilities an armed combatant cannot so distinguish himself, he shall retain his status as a combatant, provided that, in such situations, he carries his arms openly:

(a) during each military engagement, and

(b) during such time as he is visible to the adversary while he is engaged in a military deployment preceding the launching of an attack in which he is to participate.

Acts which comply with the requirements of this paragraph shall not be considered as perfidious within the meaning of Article 37, paragraph 1 (c).

4. A combatant who falls into the power of an adverse Party while failing to meet the requirements set forth in the second sentence of paragraph 3 shall forfeit his right to

be a prisoner of war, but he shall, nevertheless, be given protections equivalent in all respects to those accorded to prisoners of war by the Third Convention and by this Protocol. This protection includes protections equivalent to those accorded to prisoners of war by the Third Convention in the case where such a person is tried and punished for any offences he has committed.

5. Any combatant who falls into the power of an adverse Party while not engaged in an attack or in a military operation preparatory to an attack shall not forfeit his rights to be a combatant and a prisoner of war by virtue of his prior activities.

6. This Article is without prejudice to the right of any person to be a prisoner of war pursuant to Article 4 of the Third Convention.

7. This Article is not intended to change the generally accepted practice of States with respect to the wearing of the uniform by combatants assigned to the regular, uniformed armed units of a Party to the conflict.

8. In addition to the categories of persons mentioned in Article 13 of the First and Second Conventions, all members of the armed forces of a Party to the conflict, as defined in Article 43 of this Protocol, shall be entitled to protection under those Conventions if they are wounded or sick or, in the case of the Second Convention, shipwrecked at sea or in other waters.

"Contact zone". Medical aircraft in contact or similar zones

(Protocol Additional to the Geneva Conventions of 12 August 1949, and relating to the Protection of Victims of International Armed Conflicts (Protocol I), 8 June 1977. Part. II. Wounded, sick and shipwrecked. Section II. Medical transportation. Art. 26. Medical aircraft in contact or similar zones). 1. In and over those parts of the contact zone which are physically controlled by friendly forces and in and over those areas the physical control of which is not clearly established, protection for medical aircraft can be fully effective only by prior agreement between the competent military authorities of the Parties to the conflict, as provided for in Article 29. Although, in the absence of such an agreement, medical aircraft operate at their own risk, they shall nevertheless be respected after they have been recognized as such.

2. "Contact zone" means any area on land where the forward elements of opposing forces are in contact with each other, especially where they are exposed to direct fire from the ground.

Convention against torture and other cruel, inhuman or degrading treatment or punishment (Adopted and opened for signature, ratification and accession by General Assembly resolution 39/46 of 10 December 1984).

Preamble. The States Parties to this Convention,

Considering that, in accordance with the principles proclaimed in the Charter of the United Nations, recognition of the equal and inalienable rights of all members of the human family is the foundation of freedom, justice and peace in the world,

Recognizing that those rights derive from the inherent dignity of the human person,

Considering the obligation of States under the Charter, in particular Article 55, to promote universal respect for, and observance of, human rights and fundamental freedoms,

Having regard to article 5 of the Universal Declaration of Human Rights and article 7 of the International Covenant on Civil and Political Rights, both of which provide that no one shall be subjected to torture or to cruel, inhuman or degrading treatment or punishment,

Having regard also to the Declaration on the Protection of All Persons from Being Subjected to Torture and Other Cruel, Inhuman or Degrading Treatment or Punishment, adopted by the General Assembly on 9 December 1975,

Desiring to make more effective the struggle against torture and other cruel, inhuman or degrading treatment or punishment throughout the world,

Have agreed as follows: (…).

Convention for the Protection of Human Rights and Fundamental Freedoms *(as amended by Protocols Nos. 11 and 14 with Protocols Nos. 1, 4, 6, 7, 12 and 13)*. Rome, 4 November 1950. Preamble. The governments signatory hereto, being members of the Council of Europe,

Considering the Universal Declaration of Human Rights proclaimed by the General Assembly of the United Nations on 10 December 1948;

Considering that this Declaration aims at securing the universal and effective recognition and observance of the Rights therein declared;

Considering that the aim of the Council of Europe is the achievement of greater unity between its members and that one of the methods by which that aim is to be pursued is the maintenance and further realization of human rights and fundamental freedoms;

Reaffirming their profound belief in those fundamental freedoms which are the foundation of justice and peace in the world and are best maintained on the one hand by an effective political democracy and on the other by a common understanding and observance of the human rights upon which they depend;

Being resolved, as the governments of European countries which are likeminded and have a common heritage of political traditions, ideals, freedom and the rule of law, to take the first steps for the collective enforcement of certain of the rights stated in the Universal Declaration,

Have agreed as follows: (…)

Convention on Biological Diversity. *Rio de Janeiro, 5 June 1992 (Authentic text. Preamble. Art. 1. Objectives. Art. 2. Use of Terms. "Biological diversity", "Biological resources", "Biotechnology", "Country of origin of genetic resources", "Country providing genetic resources", "Domesticated or cultivated species", "Ecosystem", "Ex-situ conservation", "Genetic material", "Genetic resources", "Habitat", "In-situ conditions", "In-situ conservation", "Protected area", "Regional economic integration organization", "Sustainable use", "Technology". Art. 3. Principle. Art. 4. Jurisdictional Scope. Art. 5. Cooperation).* Preamble. The Contracting Parties,

Conscious of the intrinsic value of biological diversity and of the ecological, genetic, social, economic, scientific, educational, cultural, recreational and aesthetic values of biological diversity and its components,

Conscious also of the importance of biological diversity for evolution and for maintaining life sustaining systems of the biosphere,

Affirming that the conservation of biological diversity is a common concern of humankind,

Reaffirming that States have sovereign rights over their own biological resources,

Reaffirming also that States are responsible for conserving their biological diversity and for using their biological resources in a sustainable manner,

Concerned that biological diversity is being significantly reduced by certain human activities,

Aware of the general lack of information and knowledge regarding biological diversity and of the urgent need to develop scientific, technical and institutional capacities to provide the basic understanding upon which to plan and implement appropriate measures,

Noting that it is vital to anticipate, prevent and attack the causes of significant reduction or loss of biological diversity at source,

Noting also that where there is a threat of significant reduction or loss of biological diversity, lack of full scientific certainty should not be used as a reason for postponing measures to avoid or minimize such a threat,

Noting further that the fundamental requirement for the conservation of biological diversity is the in-situ conservation of ecosystems and natural habitats and the maintenance and recovery of viable populations of species in their natural surroundings,

Noting further that ex-situ measures, preferably in the country of origin, also have an important role to play,

Recognizing the close and traditional dependence of many indigenous and local communities embodying traditional lifestyles on biological resources, and the desirability of sharing equitably benefits arising from the use of traditional knowledge, innovations and practices relevant to the conservation of biological diversity and the sustainable use of its components,

Recognizing also the vital role that women play in the conservation and sustainable use of biological diversity and affirming the need for the full participation of women at all levels of policy-making and implementation for biological diversity conservation,

Stressing the importance of, and the need to promote, international, regional and global cooperation among States and intergovernmental organizations and the non-governmental sector for the conservation of biological diversity and the sustainable use of its components,

Acknowledging that the provision of new and additional financial resources and appropriate access to relevant technologies can be expected to make a substantial difference in the world's ability to address the loss of biological diversity,

Acknowledging further that special provision is required to meet the needs of developing countries, including the provision of new and additional financial resources and appropriate access to relevant technologies,

Noting in this regard the special conditions of the least developed countries and small island States,

Acknowledging that substantial investments are required to conserve biological diversity and that there is the expectation of a broad range of environmental, economic and social benefits from those investments,

Recognizing that economic and social development and poverty eradication are the first and overriding priorities of developing countries,

Aware that conservation and sustainable use of biological diversity is of critical importance for meeting the food, health and other needs of the growing world population, for which purpose access to and sharing of both genetic resources and technologies are essential,

Noting that, ultimately, the conservation and sustainable use of biological diversity will strengthen friendly relations among States and contribute to peace for humankind,

Desiring to enhance and complement existing international arrangements for the conservation of biological diversity and sustainable use of its components, and

Determined to conserve and sustainably use biological diversity for the benefit of present and future generations,

Have agreed as follows:

Art. 1. Objectives. The objectives of this Convention, to be pursued in accordance with its relevant provisions, are the conservation of biological diversity, the sustainable use of its components and the fair and equitable sharing of the benefits arising out of the utilization of genetic resources, including by appropriate access to genetic resources and by appropriate transfer of relevant technologies, taking into account all rights over those resources and to technologies, and by appropriate funding.

Art. 2. Use of Terms. For the purposes of this Convention:

"Biological diversity" means the variability among living organisms from all sources including, inter alia, terrestrial, marine and other aquatic ecosystems and the ecological complexes of which they are part; this includes diversity within species, between species and of ecosystems.

"Biological resources" includes genetic resources, organisms or parts thereof, populations, or any other biotic component of ecosystems with actual or potential use or value for humanity.

"Biotechnology" means any technological application that uses biological systems, living organisms, or derivatives thereof, to make or modify products or processes for specific use.

"Country of origin of genetic resources" means the country which possesses those genetic resources in in-situ conditions.

"Country providing genetic resources" means the country supplying genetic resources collected from in-situ sources, including populations of both wild and domesticated species, or taken from ex-situ sources, which may or may not have originated in that country.

"Domesticated or cultivated species" means species in which the evolutionary process has been influenced by humans to meet their needs.

"Ecosystem" means a dynamic complex of plant, animal and micro-organism communities and their non-living environment interacting as a functional unit.

"**Ex-situ conservation**" means the conservation of components of biological diversity outside their natural habitats.

"**Genetic material**" means any material of plant, animal, microbial or other origin containing functional units of heredity.

"**Genetic resources**" means genetic material of actual or potential value.

"**Habitat**" means the place or type of site where an organism or population naturally occurs.

"**In-situ conditions**" means conditions where genetic resources exist within ecosystems and natural habitats, and, in the case of domesticated or cultivated species, in the surroundings where they have developed their distinctive properties.

"**In-situ conservation**" means the conservation of ecosystems and natural habitats and the maintenance and recovery of viable populations of species in their natural surroundings and, in the case of domesticated or cultivated species, in the surroundings where they have developed their distinctive properties.

"**Protected area**" means a geographically defined area which is designated or regulated and managed to achieve specific conservation objectives.

"**Regional economic integration organization**" means an organization constituted by sovereign States of a given region, to which its member States have transferred competence in respect of matters governed by this Convention and which has been duly authorized, in accordance with its internal procedures, to sign, ratify, accept, approve or accede to it.

"**Sustainable use**" means the use of components of biological diversity in a way and at a rate that does not lead to the long-term decline of biological diversity, thereby maintaining its potential to meet the needs and aspirations of present and future generations.

"Technology" includes biotechnology.

Art. 3. Principle. States have, in accordance with the Charter of the United Nations and the principles of international law, the sovereign right to exploit their own resources pursuant to their own environmental policies, and the responsibility to ensure that activities within their jurisdiction or control do not cause damage to the environment of other States or of areas beyond the limits of national jurisdiction.

Art. 4. Jurisdictional Scope. Subject to the rights of other States, and except as otherwise expressly provided in this Convention, the provisions of this Convention apply, in relation to each Contracting Party:

(a) In the case of components of biological diversity, in areas within the limits of its national jurisdiction; and

(b) In the case of processes and activities, regardless of where their effects occur, carried out under its jurisdiction or control, within the area of its national jurisdiction or beyond the limits of national jurisdiction.

Art. 5. Cooperation. Each Contracting Party shall, as far as possible and as appropriate, cooperate with other Contracting Parties, directly or, where appropriate, through competent international organizations, in respect of areas beyond national jurisdiction and on other matters of mutual interest, for the conservation and sustainable use of biological diversity.

(...)

Convention on the elimination of all forms of discrimination against women. New York, 18 December 1979.

Preamble. The States Parties to the present Convention,

Noting that the Charter of the United Nations reaffirms faith in fundamental human rights, in the dignity and worth of the human person and in the equal rights of men and women,

Noting that the Universal Declaration of Human Rights affirms the principle of the inadmissibility of discrimination and proclaims that all human beings are born free and equal in dignity and rights and that everyone is entitled to all the rights and freedoms set forth therein, without distinction of any kind, including distinction based on sex,

Noting that the States Parties to the International Covenants on Human Rights have the obligation to ensure the equal rights of men and women to enjoy all economic, social, cultural, civil and political rights,

Considering the international conventions concluded under the auspices of the United Nations and the specialized agencies promoting equality of rights of men and women,

Noting also the resolutions, declarations and recommendations adopted by the United Nations and the specialized agencies promoting equality of rights of men and women,

Concerned, however, that despite these various instruments extensive discrimination against women continues to exist,

Recalling that discrimination against women violates the principles of equality of rights and respect for human dignity, is an obstacle to the participation of women, on equal terms with men, in the political, social, economic and cultural life of their countries, hampers the growth of the prosperity of society and the family and makes more difficult the full development of the potentialities of women in the service of their countries and of humanity,

Concerned that in situations of poverty women have the least access to food, health, education, training and opportunities for employment and other needs,

Convinced that the establishment of the new international economic order based on equity and justice will contribute significantly towards the promotion of equality between men and women,

Emphasizing that the eradication of apartheid, all forms of racism, racial discrimination, colonialism, neo-colonialism, aggression, foreign occupation and domination and interference in the internal affairs of States is essential to the full enjoyment of the rights of men and women,

Affirming that the strengthening of international peace and security, the relaxation of international tension, mutual co-operation among all States irrespective of their social and economic systems, general and complete disarmament, in particular nuclear disarmament under strict and effective international control, the affirmation of the principles of justice, equality and mutual benefit in relations among countries and the realization of the right of peoples under alien and colonial domination and foreign occupation to self-determination and independence, as well as respect for national sovereignty and territorial integrity, will promote social progress and development and as a consequence will contribute to the attainment of full equality between men and women,

Convinced that the full and complete development of a country, the welfare of the world and the cause of peace require the maximum participation of women on equal terms with men in all fields,

Bearing in mind the great contribution of women to the welfare of the family and to the development of society, so far not fully recognized, the social significance of maternity and the role of both parents in the family and in the upbringing of children, and aware that the role of women in procreation should not be a basis for discrimination but that the upbringing of children requires a sharing of responsibility between men and women and society as a whole, *Aware* that a change in the traditional role of men as well as the role of women in society and in the family is needed to achieve full equality between men and women,

Determined to implement the principles set forth in the Declaration on the Elimination of Discrimination against Women and, for that purpose, to adopt the measures required for the elimination of such discrimination in all its forms and manifestations,

Have agreed on the following: (…).

Convention on the Prevention and Punishment of the Crime of Genocide.

Approved and proposed for signature and ratification or accession by General Assembly resolution 260 A (III) of 9 December 1948.

Preamble. The Contracting Parties,

Having considered the declaration made by the General Assembly of the United Nations in its resolution 96 (I) dated 11 December 1946 that genocide is a crime under international law, contrary to the spirit and aims of the United Nations and condemned by the civilized world, Recognizing that at all periods of history genocide has inflicted great losses on humanity, and

Being convinced that, in order to liberate mankind from such an odious scourge, international co-operation is required,

Hereby agree as hereinafter provided: (…).

Convention on the rights of the child (Adopted and opened for signature, ratification and accession by General Assembly resolution 44/25 of 20 November 1989).

Preamble. The States Parties to the present Convention,

Considering that, in accordance with the principles proclaimed in the Charter of the United Nations, recognition of the inherent dignity and of the equal and inalienable rights of all members of the human family is the foundation of freedom, justice and peace in the world,

Bearing in mind that the peoples of the United Nations have, in the Charter, reaffirmed their faith in fundamental human rights and in the dignity and worth of the human person, and have determined to promote social progress and better standards of life in larger freedom, *Recognizing* that the United Nations has, in the Universal Declaration of Human Rights and in the International Covenants on

Human Rights, proclaimed and agreed that everyone is entitled to all the rights and freedoms set forth therein, without distinction of any kind, such as race, colour, sex, language, religion, political or other opinion, national or social origin, property, birth or other status,

Recalling that, in the Universal Declaration of Human Rights, the United Nations has proclaimed that childhood is entitled to special care and assistance,

Convinced that the family, as the fundamental group of society and the natural environment for the growth and well-being of all its members and particularly children, should be afforded the necessary protection and assistance so that it can fully assume its responsibilities within the community,

Recognizing that the child, for the full and harmonious development of his or her personality, should grow up in a family environment, in an atmosphere of happiness, love and understanding,

Considering that the child should be fully prepared to live an individual life in society, and brought up in the spirit of the ideals proclaimed in the Charter of the United Nations, and in particular in the spirit of peace, dignity, tolerance, freedom, equality and solidarity,

Bearing in mind that the need to extend particular care to the child has been stated in the Geneva Declaration of the Rights of the Child of 1924 and in the Declaration of the Rights of the Child adopted by the General Assembly on 20 November 1959 and recognized in the Universal Declaration of Human Rights, in the International Covenant on Civil and Political Rights (in particular in articles 23 and 24), in the International Covenant on Economic, Social and Cultural Rights (in particular in article 10) and in the statutes and relevant instruments of specialized agencies and international organizations concerned with the welfare of children, *Bearing* in mind that, as indicated in the Declaration of the Rights of the Child, "the child, by reason of his physical and mental immaturity, needs special safeguards and care, including appropriate legal protection, before as well as after birth",

Recalling the provisions of the Declaration on Social and Legal Principles relating to the Protection and Welfare of Children, with Special Reference to Foster Placement and Adoption Nationally and Internationally; the United Nations Standard Minimum Rules for the Administration of Juvenile Justice (The Beijing Rules); and the Declaration on the Protection of Women and Children in Emergency and Armed Conflict, Recognizing that, in all countries in the world, there are children living in exceptionally difficult conditions, and that such children need special consideration,

Taking due account of the importance of the traditions and cultural values of each people for the protection and harmonious development of the child,

Recognizing the importance of international co-operation for improving the living conditions of children in every country, in particular in the developing countries,

Have agreed as follows: (...).

Convention relating to the Status of Refugees. Geneva, 28 July 1951.

Preamble. The High Contracting Parties,

Considering that the Charter of the United Nations and the Universal Declaration of Human Rights approved on 10 December 1948 by the General Assembly have affirmed the principle that human beings shall enjoy fundamental rights and freedoms without discrimination,

Considering that the United Nations has, on various occasions, manifested its profound concern for refugees and endeavoured to assure refugees the widest possible exercise of these fundamental rights and freedoms,

Considering that it is desirable to revise and consolidate previous international agreements relating to the status of refugees and to extend the scope of and the protection accorded by such instruments by means of a new agreement,

Considering that the grant of asylum may place unduly heavy burdens on certain countries, and that a satisfactory solution of a problem of which the United Nations has recognized the international scope and nature cannot therefore be achieved without international co-operation,

Expressing the wish that all States, recognizing the social and humanitarian nature of the problem of refugees, will do everything within their power to prevent this problem from becoming a cause of tension between States,

Noting that the United Nations High Commissioner for Refugees is charged with the task of supervising international conventions providing for the protection of refugees, and recognizing that the effective co-ordination of measures taken to deal with this problem will depend upon the co-operation of States with the High Commissioner,

Have agreed as follows: (…).

Copenhagen Accord. 18 December 2009. United Nations. Conference of the Parties. Fifteenth session. Copenhagen, 7.18 December 2009. Agenda item 9. High-level segment. Draft decision -/CP.15. Proposal by the President. *Copenhagen Accord.*

The Heads of State, Heads of Government, Ministers, and other heads of delegation present at the United Nations Climate Change Conference 2009 in Copenhagen,

In pursuit of the ultimate objective of the Convention as stated in its Article 2,

Being guided by the principles and provisions of the Convention,

Noting the results of work done by the two Ad hoc Working Groups,

Endorsing decision x/CP.15 on the Ad hoc Working Group on Long-term Cooperative Action

and decision x/CMP.5 that requests the Ad hoc Working Group on Further Commitments of Annex I Parties under the Kyoto Protocol to continue its work,

Have agreed on this Copenhagen Accord which is operational immediately.

1. We underline that climate change is one of the greatest challenges of our time. We emphasise our strong political will to urgently combat climate change in accordance with the principle of common but differentiated responsibilities and respective capabilities. To achieve the ultimate objective of the Convention to stabilize greenhouse gas concentration in the atmosphere at a level that would prevent dangerous anthropogenic interference with the climate system, we shall, recognizing the scientific view that the increase in global temperature should be below 2 degrees Celsius, on the basis of equity and in the context of sustainable development, enhance our long-term cooperative action to combat climate change. We recognize the critical impacts of climate change and the potential impacts of response measures on countries particularly vulnerable to its adverse effects and

stress the need to establish a comprehensive adaptation programme including international support.

2. We agree that deep cuts in global emissions are required according to science, and as documented by the IPCC Fourth Assessment Report with a view to reduce global emissions so as to hold the increase in global temperature below 2 degrees Celsius, and take action to meet this objective consistent with science and on the basis of equity. We should cooperate in achieving the peaking of global and national emissions as soon as possible, recognizing that the time frame for peaking will be longer in developing countries and bearing in mind that social and economic development and poverty eradication are the first and overriding priorities of developing countries and that a low-emission development strategy is indispensable to sustainable development.

3. Adaptation to the adverse effects of climate change and the potential impacts of response measures is a challenge faced by all countries. Enhanced action and international cooperation on adaptation is urgently required to ensure the implementation of the Convention by enabling and supporting the implementation of adaptation actions aimed at reducing vulnerability and building resilience in developing countries, especially in those that are particularly vulnerable, especially least developed countries, small island developing States and Africa. We agree that developed countries shall provide adequate, predictable and sustainable financial resources, technology and capacity-building to support the implementation of adaptation action in developing countries.

4. Annex I Parties commit to implement individually or jointly the quantified economywide emissions targets for 2020, to be submitted in the format given in Appendix I by Annex I Parties to the secretariat by 31 January 2010 for compilation in an INF document. Annex I Parties that are Party to the Kyoto Protocol will thereby further strengthen the emissions reductions initiated by the Kyoto Protocol. Delivery of reductions and financing by developed countries will be measured, reported and verified in accordance with existing and any further guidelines adopted by the Conference of the Parties, and will ensure that accounting of such targets and finance is rigorous, robust and transparent.

5. Non-Annex I Parties to the Convention will implement mitigation actions, including those to be submitted to the secretariat by non-Annex I Parties in the format given in Appendix II by 31 January 2010, for compilation in an INF document, consistent with Article 4.1 and Article 4.7 and in the context of sustainable development. Least developed countries and small island developing States may undertake actions voluntarily and on the basis of support. Mitigation actions subsequently taken and envisaged by Non-Annex I Parties, including national inventory reports, shall be communicated through national communications consistent with Article 12.1(b) every two years on the basis of guidelines to be adopted by the Conference of the Parties. Those mitigation actions in national communications or otherwise communicated to the Secretariat will be added to the list in appendix II. Mitigation actions taken by Non-Annex I Parties will be subject to their domestic measurement, reporting and verification the result of which will be reported through their national communications every two years. Non-Annex I Parties will communicate information on the implementation of their actions through

National Communications, with provisions for international consultations and analysis under clearly defined guidelines that will ensure that national sovereignty is respected. Nationally appropriate mitigation actions seeking international support will be recorded in a registry along with relevant technology, finance and capacity building support. Those actions supported will be added to the list in appendix II. These supported nationally appropriate mitigation actions will be subject to international measurement, reporting and verification in accordance with guidelines adopted by the Conference of the Parties.

6.   We recognize the crucial role of reducing emission from deforestation and forest degradation and the need to enhance removals of greenhouse gas emission by forests and agree on the need to provide positive incentives to such actions through the immediate establishment of a mechanism including REDD-plus, to enable the mobilization of financial resources from developed countries.

7.   We decide to pursue various approaches, including opportunities to use markets, to enhance the cost-effectiveness of, and to promote mitigation actions. Developing countries, especially those with low emitting economies should be provided incentives to continue to develop on a low emission pathway.

8.   Scaled up, new and additional, predictable and adequate funding as well as improved access shall be provided to developing countries, in accordance with the relevant provisions of the Convention, to enable and support enhanced action on mitigation, including substantial finance to reduce emissions from deforestation and forest degradation (REDD-plus), adaptation, technology development and transfer and capacity-building, for enhanced implementation of the Convention. The collective commitment by developed countries is to provide new and additional resources, including forestry and investments through international institutions, approaching USD 30 billion for the period 2010 . 2012 with balanced allocation between adaptation and mitigation. Funding for adaptation will be prioritized for the most vulnerable developing countries, such as the least developed countries, small island developing States and Africa. In the context of meaningful mitigation actions and transparency on implementation, developed countries commit to a goal of mobilizing jointly USD 100 billion dollars a year by 2020 to address the needs of developing countries. This funding will come from a wide variety of sources, public and private, bilateral and multilateral, including alternative sources of finance. New multilateral funding for adaptation will be delivered through effective and efficient fund arrangements, with a governance structure providing for equal representation of developed and developing countries. A significant portion of such funding should flow through the Copenhagen Green Climate Fund.

9.   To this end, a High Level Panel will be established under the guidance of and accountable to the Conference of the Parties to study the contribution of the potential sources of revenue, including alternative sources of finance, towards meeting this goal.

10.   We decide that the Copenhagen Green Climate Fund shall be established as an operating entity of the financial mechanism of the Convention to support projects, programme, policies and other activities in developing countries related to mitigation including REDD-plus, adaptation, capacity-building, technology development and transfer.

11. In order to enhance action on development and transfer of technology we decide to establish a Technology Mechanism to accelerate technology development and transfer in support of action on adaptation and mitigation that will be guided by a country-driven approach and be based on national circumstances and priorities.

12. We call for an assessment of the implementation of this Accord to be completed by 2015, including in light of the Convention's ultimate objective. This would include consideration of strengthening the long-term goal referencing various matters presented by the science, including in relation to temperature rises of 1.5 degrees Celsius.

Crime against humanity of apartheid. *See: Crimes against humanity.*

Crime against humanity of deportation or forcible transfer of population. *See: Crimes against humanity.*

Crime against humanity of enforced disappearance of persons. *See: Crimes against humanity.*

Crime against humanity of enforced prostitution. See: Crimes against humanity, War crimes, Elements of Crimes.

Crime against humanity of enforced sterilization. *See: Crimes against humanity, War crimes, Elements of Crimes.*

Crime against humanity of enslavement. *See: Crimes against humanity.*

Crime against humanity of extermination. *See: Crimes against humanity.*

Crime against humanity of forced pregnancy. *See: Crimes against humanity, War crimes, Elements of Crimes.*

Crime against humanity of imprisonment or other severe deprivation of physical liberty. *See: Crimes against humanity*

Crime against humanity of murder. *See: Crimes against humanity, War crimes, Elements of Crimes.*

Crime against humanity of other inhumane acts. *See: Crimes against humanity.*

Crime against humanity of persecution. *See: Crimes against humanity.*

Crime against humanity of rape. *See: Crimes against humanity, War crimes, Elements of Crimes.*

Crime against humanity of sexual slavery. *See: Crimes against humanity, War crimes, Elements of Crimes.*

Crime against humanity of sexual violence. *See: Crimes against humanity, War crimes, Elements of Crimes.*

Crime against humanity of torture. *See: Torture, Crimes against humanity, War crimes, Elements of Crimes.*

Crime of aggression *(Rome Statute ICC. Part II. Jurisdiction, admissibility and applicable law, art. 5. Crimes within the jurisdiction of the Court).* 1. The jurisdiction of the Court shall be limited to the most serious crimes of concern to the international community as a whole. The Court has jurisdiction in accordance with this Statute with respect to the following crimes:
(a) The crime of genocide;
(b) Crimes against humanity;
(c) War crimes;
(d) The crime of aggression.
2. The Court shall exercise jurisdiction over the crime of aggression once a provision is adopted in accordance with articles 121 and 123 defining the crime and setting out the conditions under which the Court shall exercise jurisdiction with respect to this crime. Such a provision shall be consistent with the relevant provisions of the Charter of the United Nations.

Crime of apartheid. *See: Crimes against humanity*

Crime of Genocide. *See: Genocide - Crime of Genocide.*

Crimes against humanity *(London Agreement (8 August 1945), Charter of the International Military Tribunal. Art. 6. (c) - Rome Statute ICC, art. 7 (Attack directed against any civilian population, Extermination, Enslavement, Deportation or forcible transfer of population, Torture, Forced pregnancy, Persecution, The crime of apartheid, Enforced disappearance of persons) - Rome Statute ICC, Elements of Crimes, art. 7. Crimes against humanity. Introduction; Art. 7 (1) (a). Crime against humanity of murder. Elements; Art. 7 (1) (b). Crime against humanity of extermination. Elements; Art. 7 (1) (c). Crime against humanity of enslavement. Elements; Art. 7 (1) (d). Crime against humanity of deportation or forcible transfer of population. Elements; Art. 7 (1) (e). Crime against humanity of imprisonment or other severe deprivation of physical liberty. Elements; Art. 7 (1) (f). Crime against humanity of torture. Elements; Art. 7 (1) (g)-1. Crime against humanity of rape. Elements; Art. 7 (1) (g)-2. Crime against humanity of sexual slavery. Elements; Art. 7 (1) (g)-3. Crime against humanity of enforced prostitution. Elements; Art. 7 (1)* *(g)-4. Crime against humanity of forced pregnancy. Elements; Art. 7 (1) (g)-5. Crime against humanity of enforced sterilization. Elements; Art. 7 (1) (g)-6. Crime against humanity of sexual violence. Elements; Art. 7 (1) (h). Crime against humanity of persecution. Elements; Art. 7 (1) (i). Crime against humanity of enforced disappearance of persons. Elements; Art. 7 (1) (j). Crime against humanity of apartheid. Elements; Art. 7 (1) (k). Crime against humanity of other inhumane acts. Elements - Statute ICTY, art. 5. Crimes against humanity; Statute ICTR, art. 3. Crimes against Humanity).*

London Agreement (8 August 1945). Charter of the International Military Tribunal. Prosecution and punishment of major war criminals of European Axis. Agreement signed at London August 8, 1945, with charter of the International Military Tribunal. Entered into force August 8, 1945. Discrepancy in article 6 of charter rectified by protocol of October 6, 1945. Agreement by the government of the United States of America, the Provisional Government of the French Republic, the Government of the United Kingdom of Great Britain and Northern Ireland and the Government of the Union of Soviet Socialist Republics for the prosecution and punishment of the major war criminals of the European axis). Charter of the International Military Tribunal. (...) II. Jurisdiction and general principles. *Art. 6.* (c) *Crimes against humanity*: namely, murder, extermination, enslavement, deportation, and other inhumane acts committed against any civilian population, before or during the war; or persecutions on political, racial or religious grounds in execution of or in connection with any crime within the jurisdiction of the Tribunal, whether or not in violation of the domestic law of the country where perpetrated. (...)

Rome Statute ICC, art. 7. Crimes against humanity. 1. For the purpose of this Statute, 'crime against humanity' means any of the following acts when committed as part of a widespread or systematic attack directed against any civilian population, with knowledge of the attack:

(a) Murder;

(b) Extermination;

(c) Enslavement;

(d) Deportation or forcible transfer of population;

(e) Imprisonment or other severe deprivation of physical liberty in violation of fundamental rules of international law;

(f) Torture;

(g) Rape, sexual slavery, enforced prostitution, forced pregnancy, enforced sterilization, or any other form of sexual violence of comparable gravity;

(h) Persecution against any identifiable group or collectivity on political, racial, national, ethnic, cultural, religious, gender as defined in paragraph 3, or other grounds that are universally recognized as impermissible under international law, in connection with any act referred to in this paragraph or any crime within the jurisdiction of the Court;

(i) Enforced disappearance of persons;

(j) The crime of apartheid;

(k) Other inhumane acts of a similar character intentionally causing great suffering, or serious injury to body or to mental or physical health.

2. For the purpose of paragraph 1:

(a) *'Attack directed against any civilian population'* means a course of conduct involving the multiple commission of acts referred to in paragraph 1 against any civilian population, pursuant to or in furtherance of a State or organizational policy to commit such attack;

(b) *'Extermination'* includes the intentional infliction of conditions of life, *inter alia* the deprivation of access to food and medicine, calculated to bring about the destruction of part of a population;

(c) *'Enslavement'* means the exercise of any or all of the powers attaching to the right of ownership over a person and includes the exercise of such power in the course of trafficking in persons, in particular women and children;

(d) *'Deportation or forcible transfer of population'* means forced displacement of the persons concerned by expulsion or other coercive acts from the area in which they are lawfully present, without grounds permitted under international law;

(e) *'Torture'* means the intentional infliction of severe pain or suffering, whether physical or mental, upon a person in the custody or under the control of the accused; except that torture shall not include pain or suffering arising only from, inherent in or incidental to, lawful sanctions;

(f) *'Forced pregnancy'* means the unlawful confinement of a woman forcibly made pregnant, with the intent of affecting the ethnic composition of any population or carrying out other grave violations of international law. This definition shall not in any way be interpreted as affecting national laws relating to pregnancy;

(g) *'Persecution'* means the intentional and severe deprivation of fundamental rights contrary to international law by reason of the identity of the group or collectivity;

(h) *'The crime of apartheid'* means inhumane acts of a character similar to those referred to in paragraph 1, committed in the context of an institutionalized regime of systematic oppression and domination by one racial group over any other racial group or groups and committed with the intention of maintaining that regime;

(i) *'Enforced disappearance of persons'* means the arrest, detention or abduction of persons by, or with the authorization, support or acquiescence of, a State or a political organization, followed by a refusal to acknowledge that deprivation of freedom or to give information on the fate or whereabouts of those persons, with the intention of removing them from the protection of the law for a prolonged period of time.

3. For the purpose of this Statute, it is understood that the term *'gender'* refers to the two sexes, male and female, within the context of society. The term 'gender' does not indicate any meaning different from the above.

Rome Statute ICC, Elements of Crimes, art. 7. Crimes against humanity. Introduction. 1. Since article 7 pertains to international criminal law, its provisions, consistent with article 22, must be strictly construed, taking into account that crimes against humanity as defined in article 7 are among the most serious crimes of concern to the international community as a whole, warrant and entail individual criminal responsibility, and require conduct which is impermissible under generally applicable international law, as recognized by the principal legal systems of the world.

2. The last two elements for each crime against humanity describe the context in which the conduct must take place. These elements clarify the requisite participation in and knowledge of a widespread or systematic attack against a civilian population.

However, the last element should not be interpreted as requiring proof that the perpetrator had knowledge of all characteristics of the attack or the precise details of the plan or policy of the State or organization. In the case of an emerging widespread or systematic attack against a civilian population, the intent clause of the last element indicates that this mental element is satisfied if the perpetrator intended to further such an attack.

3. *'Attack directed against a civilian population'* in these context elements is understood to mean a course of conduct involving the multiple commission of acts referred to in article 7, paragraph 1, of the Statute against any civilian population, pursuant to or in furtherance of a State or organizational policy to commit such attack. The acts need not constitute a military attack. It is understood that *'policy to commit such attack'* requires that the State or organization actively promote or encourage such an attack against a civilian population *(6. A policy which has a civilian population as the object of the attack would be implemented by State or organizational action. Such a policy may, in exceptional circumstances, be implemented by a deliberate failure to take action, which is consciously aimed at encouraging such attack. The existence of such a policy cannot be inferred solely from the absence of governmental or organizational action).*

Art. 7 (1) (a). Crime against humanity of murder. *Elements.* 1. The perpetrator killed (7) one or more persons.

2. The conduct was committed as part of a widespread or systematic attack directed against a civilian population.

3. The perpetrator knew that the conduct was part of or intended the conduct to be part of a widespread or systematic attack against a civilian population.

(7. The term 'killed' is interchangeable with the term 'caused death'. This footnote applies to all elements which use either of these concepts).

Art. 7 (1) (b). Crime against humanity of extermination. *Elements.* 1. The perpetrator killed (8) one or more persons, including by inflicting conditions of life calculated to bring about the destruction of part of a population. (9).

2. The conduct constituted, or took place as part of, (10) a mass killing of members of a civilian population.

3. The conduct was committed as part of a widespread or systematic attack directed against a civilian population.

4. The perpetrator knew that the conduct was part of or intended the conduct to be part of a widespread or systematic attack directed against a civilian population.

(8. The conduct could be committed by different methods of killing, either directly or indirectly.

9. The infliction of such conditions could include the deprivation of access to food and medicine.

10. The term 'as part of' would include the initial conduct in a mass killing).

Art. 7 (1) (c). Crime against humanity of enslavement. *Elements.* 1. The perpetrator exercised any or all of the powers attaching to the right of ownership over one or more persons, such as by purchasing, selling, lending or bartering such a person or persons, or by imposing on them a similar deprivation of liberty. (11).

2. The conduct was committed as part of a widespread or systematic attack directed against a civilian population.

3. The perpetrator knew that the conduct was part of or intended the conduct to be part of a widespread or systematic attack directed against a civilian population.

(11. It is understood that such deprivation of liberty may, in some circumstances, include exacting forced labour or otherwise reducing a person to a servile status as defined in the Supplementary Convention on the Abolition of Slavery, the Slave Trade, and Institutions and Practices Similar to Slavery of 1956. It is also understood that the conduct described in this element includes trafficking in persons, in particular women and children).

Art. 7 (1) (d). Crime against humanity of deportation or forcible transfer of population. *Elements.* 1. The perpetrator deported or forcibly (12) transferred, (13) without grounds permitted under international law, one or more persons to another State or location, by expulsion or other coercive acts.

2. Such person or persons were lawfully present in the area from which they were so deported or transferred.

3. The perpetrator was aware of the factual circumstances that established the lawfulness of such presence.

4. The conduct was committed as part of a widespread or systematic attack directed against a civilian population.

5. The perpetrator knew that the conduct was part of or intended the conduct to be part of a widespread or systematic attack directed against a civilian population.

(12. The term 'forcibly' is not restricted to physical force, but may include threat of force or coercion, such as that caused by fear of violence, duress, detention, psychological oppression or abuse of power against such person or persons or another person, or by taking advantage of a coercive environment.

13. 'Deported or forcibly transferred' is interchangeable with 'forcibly displaced').

Art. 7 (1) (e). Crime against humanity of imprisonment or other severe deprivation of physical liberty. *Elements.* 1. The perpetrator imprisoned one or more persons or otherwise severely deprived one or more persons of physical liberty.

2. The gravity of the conduct was such that it was in violation of fundamental rules of international law.

3. The perpetrator was aware of the factual circumstances that established the gravity of the conduct.

4. The conduct was committed as part of a widespread or systematic attack directed against a civilian population.

5. The perpetrator knew that the conduct was part of or intended the conduct to be part of a widespread or systematic attack directed against a civilian population.

Art. 7 (1) (f). Crime against humanity of torture (14). Elements. 1. The perpetrator inflicted severe physical or mental pain or suffering upon one or more persons.

2. Such person or persons were in the custody or under the control of the perpetrator.

3. Such pain or suffering did not arise only from, and was not inherent in or incidental to, lawful sanctions.

4. The conduct was committed as part of a widespread or systematic attack directed against a civilian population.

5. The perpetrator knew that the conduct was part of or intended the conduct to be part of a widespread or systematic attack directed against a civilian population.

(14. It is understood that no specific purpose need be proved for this crime).

Art. 7 (1) (g)-1. Crime against humanity of rape. Elements. 1. The perpetrator invaded (15) the body of a person by conduct resulting in penetration, however slight, of any part of the body of the victim or of the perpetrator with a sexual organ, or of the anal or genital opening of the victim with any object or any other part of the body.

2. The invasion was committed by force, or by threat of force or coercion, such as that caused by fear of violence, duress, detention, psychological oppression or abuse of power, against such person or another person, or by taking advantage of a coercive environment, or the invasion was committed against a person incapable of giving genuine consent. (16).

3. The conduct was committed as part of a widespread or systematic attack directed against a civilian population.

4. The perpetrator knew that the conduct was part of or intended the conduct to be part of a widespread or systematic attack directed against a civilian population.

(15. The concept of 'invasion' is intended to be broad enough to be gender-neutral.

16. It is understood that a person may be incapable of giving genuine consent if affected by natural, induced or age-related incapacity. This footnote also applies to the corresponding elements of article 7 (1) (g)-3, 5 and 6).

Art. 7 (1) (g)-2. Crime against humanity of sexual slavery (17). Elements. 1. The perpetrator exercised any or all of the powers attaching to the right of ownership over one or more persons, such as by purchasing, selling, lending or bartering such a person or persons, or by imposing on them a similar deprivation of liberty. (18).

2. The perpetrator caused such person or persons to engage in one or more acts of a sexual nature.

3. The conduct was committed as part of a widespread or systematic attack directed against a civilian population.

4. The perpetrator knew that the conduct was part of or intended the conduct to be part of a widespread or systematic attack directed against a civilian population.

(17. Given the complex nature of this crime, it is recognized that its commission could involve more than one perpetrator as a part of a common criminal purpose.

18. It is understood that such deprivation of liberty may, in some circumstances, include exacting forced labour or otherwise reducing a person to a servile status as defined in the Supplementary Convention on the Abolition of Slavery, the Slave Trade, and Institutions and Practices Similar to Slavery of 1956. It is also understood that the conduct described in this element includes trafficking in persons, in particular women and children).

Art. 7 (1) (g)-3. Crime against humanity of enforced prostitution. Elements. 1. The perpetrator caused one or more persons to engage in one or more acts of a sexual nature by force, or by threat of force or coercion, such as that caused by fear of violence, duress, detention, psychological oppression or abuse of power, against such person or persons or another person, or by taking advantage of a coercive environment or such person's or persons' incapacity to give genuine consent.

2. The perpetrator or another person obtained or expected to obtain pecuniary or other advantage in exchange for or in connection with the acts of a sexual nature.

3. The conduct was committed as part of a widespread or systematic attack directed against a civilian population.

4. The perpetrator knew that the conduct was part of or intended the conduct to be part of a widespread or systematic attack directed against a civilian population.

Art. 7 (1) (g)-4. Crime against humanity of forced pregnancy. Elements. 1. The perpetrator confined one or more women forcibly made pregnant, with the intent of affecting the ethnic composition of any population or carrying out other grave violations of international law.

2. The conduct was committed as part of a widespread or systematic attack directed against a civilian population.

3. The perpetrator knew that the conduct was part of or intended the conduct to be part of a widespread or systematic attack directed against a civilian population.

Art. 7 (1) (g)-5. Crime against humanity of enforced sterilization. Elements. 1. The perpetrator deprived one or more persons of biological reproductive capacity. (19).

2. The conduct was neither justified by the medical or hospital treatment of the person or persons concerned nor carried out with their genuine consent. (20).

3. The conduct was committed as part of a widespread or systematic attack directed against a civilian population.

4. The perpetrator knew that the conduct was part of or intended the conduct to be part of a widespread or systematic attack directed against a civilian population.

(19. The deprivation is not intended to include birth-control measures which have a non permanent effect in practice.

20. It is understood that 'genuine consent' does not include consent obtained through deception).

Art. 7 (1) (g)-6. Crime against humanity of sexual violence. *Elements.* 1. The perpetrator committed an act of a sexual nature against one or more persons or caused such person or persons to engage in an act of a sexual nature by force, or by threat of force or coercion, such as that caused by fear of violence, duress, detention, psychological oppression or abuse of power, against such person or persons or another person, or by taking advantage of a coercive environment or such person's or persons' incapacity to give genuine consent.

2. Such conduct was of a gravity comparable to the other offences in article 7, paragraph 1 (g), of the Statute.

3. The perpetrator was aware of the factual circumstances that established the gravity of the conduct.

4. The conduct was committed as part of a widespread or systematic attack directed against a civilian population.

5. The perpetrator knew that the conduct was part of or intended the conduct to be part of a widespread or systematic attack directed against a civilian population.

Art. 7 (1) (h). Crime against humanity of persecution. Elements. 1. The perpetrator severely deprived, contrary to international law, (21) one or more persons of fundamental rights.

2. The perpetrator targeted such person or persons by reason of the identity of a group or collectivity or targeted the group or collectivity as such.

3. Such targeting was based on political, racial, national, ethnic, cultural, religious, gender as defined in article 7, paragraph 3, of the Statute, or other grounds that are universally recognized as impermissible under international law.

4. The conduct was committed in connection with any act referred to in article 7, paragraph 1, of the Statute or any crime within the jurisdiction of the Court. (22).

5. The conduct was committed as part of a widespread or systematic attack directed against a civilian population.

6. The perpetrator knew that the conduct was part of or intended the conduct to be part of a widespread or systematic attack directed against a civilian population.

(21. This requirement is without prejudice to paragraph 6 of the General Introduction to the Elements of Crimes.

22. It is understood that no additional mental element is necessary for this element other than that inherent in element 6).

Art. 7 (1) (i). Crime against humanity of enforced disappearance of persons *(23, 24).* **Elements.** 1. The perpetrator:

(a) Arrested, detained (25, 26) or abducted one or more persons; or

(b) Refused to acknowledge the arrest, detention or abduction, or to give information on the fate or whereabouts of such person or persons.

2. (a) Such arrest, detention or abduction was followed or accompanied by a refusal to acknowledge that deprivation of freedom or to give information on the fate or whereabouts of such person or persons; or

(b) Such refusal was preceded or accompanied by that deprivation of freedom.

3. The perpetrator was aware that: (27).

(a) Such arrest, detention or abduction would be followed in the ordinary course of events by a refusal to acknowledge that deprivation of freedom or to give information on the fate or whereabouts of such person or persons; (28) or

(b) Such refusal was preceded or accompanied by that deprivation of freedom.

4. Such arrest, detention or abduction was carried out by, or with the authorization, support or acquiescence of, a State or a political organization.

5. Such refusal to acknowledge that deprivation of freedom or to give information on the fate or whereabouts of such person or persons was carried out by, or with the authorization or support of, such State or political organization.

6. The perpetrator intended to remove such person or persons from the protection of the law for a prolonged period of time.

7. The conduct was committed as part of a widespread or systematic attack directed against a civilian population.

8. The perpetrator knew that the conduct was part of or intended the conduct to be part of a widespread or systematic attack directed against a civilian population.

(23. Given the complex nature of this crime, it is recognized that its commission will normally involve more than one perpetrator as a part of a common criminal purpose.

24. This crime falls under the jurisdiction of the Court only if the attack referred to in elements 7 and 8 occurs after the entry into force of the Statute.

25. The word 'detained' would include a perpetrator who maintained an existing detention.

26. It is understood that under certain circumstances an arrest or detention may have been lawful.

27. This element, inserted because of the complexity of this crime, is without prejudice to the General Introduction to the Elements of Crimes.

28. It is understood that, in the case of a perpetrator who maintained an existing detention, this element would be satisfied if the perpetrator was aware that such a refusal had already taken place).

Art. 7 (1) (j). Crime against humanity of apartheid. *Elements.* 1. The perpetrator committed an inhumane act against one or more persons.

2. Such act was an act referred to in article 7, paragraph 1, of the Statute, or was an act of a character similar to any of those acts. (29).

3. The perpetrator was aware of the factual circumstances that established the character of the act.

4. The conduct was committed in the context of an institutionalized regime of systematic oppression and domination by one racial group over any other racial group or groups.

5. The perpetrator intended to maintain such regime by that conduct.

6. The conduct was committed as part of a widespread or systematic attack directed against a civilian population.

7. The perpetrator knew that the conduct was part of or intended the conduct to be part of a widespread or systematic attack directed against a civilian population.

(29. It is understood that 'character' refers to the nature and gravity of the act).

Art. 7 (1) (k). Crime against humanity of other inhumane acts. *Elements.* 1. The perpetrator inflicted great suffering, or serious injury to body or to mental or physical health, by means of an inhumane act.

2. Such act was of a character similar to any other act referred to in article 7, paragraph 1, of the Statute. (30).

3. The perpetrator was aware of the factual circumstances that established the character of the act.

4. The conduct was committed as part of a widespread or systematic attack directed against a civilian population.

5. The perpetrator knew that the conduct was part of or intended the conduct to be part of a widespread or systematic attack directed against a civilian population.

(30. It is understood that 'character' refers to the nature and gravity of the act).

Statute ICTY, art. 5. Crimes against humanity. The International Tribunal shall have the power to prosecute persons responsible for the following crimes when committed in armed conflict, whether international or internal in character, and directed against any civilian population:

(a) murder;
(b) extermination;
(c) enslavement;
(d) deportation;
(e) imprisonment;
(f) torture;
(g) rape;
(h) persecutions on political, racial and religious grounds;
(i) other inhumane acts.

Statute ICTR, art. 3. Crimes against Humanity. The International Tribunal for Rwanda shall have the power to prosecute persons responsible for the following crimes when committed as part of a widespread or systematic attack against any civilian population on national, political, ethnic, racial or religious grounds:

(a) Murder;
(b) Extermination;
(c) Enslavement;
(d) Deportation;
(e) Imprisonment;
(f) Torture;
(g) Rape;
(h) Persecutions on political, racial and religious grounds;
(i) Other inhumane acts.

Crimes against peace (*London Agreement (8 August 1945). Charter of the International Military Tribunal. Prosecution and punishment of major war criminals of European Axis. Agreement signed at London August 8, 1945, with charter of the International Military Tribunal. Entered into force August 8, 1945. Discrepancy in article 6 of charter rectified by protocol of October 6, 1945. Agreement by the government of the United States of America, the Provisional Government of the French Republic, the Government of the United Kingdom of Great Britain and Northern Ireland and the Government of the Union of Soviet Socialist Republics for the prosecution and punishment of the major war criminals of the European axis). Charter of the International Military Tribunal. (...) II. Jurisdiction and general principles. Art. 6.* The Tribunal established by the Agreement referred to in Article 1 hereof for the trial and punishment of the major war criminals of the European Axis countries shall have the power to try and punish persons who, acting in the interests of the European Axis countries, whether as individuals or as members of organizations, committed any of the following crimes.

The following acts, or any of them, are crimes coming within the jurisdiction of the Tribunal for which there shall be individual responsibility:

(a) *Crimes against peace*: namely, planning, preparation, initiation or waging of a war of aggression, or a war in violation of international treaties, agreements or assurances, or participation in a common plan or conspiracy for the accomplishment of any of the foregoing (...)

D

Defence - Counsel for the defence *(RPE – ICC, Chapter 2. Composition and administration of the Court; Section 3. The Registry; Subsection 3. Counsel for the defence: Rule 20. Responsibilities of the Registrar relating to the rights of the defence: Rule 21. Assignment of legal assistance; Rule 22. Appointment and qualifications of Counsel for the defence - RPE – ICTY, Part 4. Investigations and rights of suspects; Section 2. Of Counsel. Rule 44. Appointment, Qualifications and Duties of Counsel; Rule 45. Assignment of Counsel; Rule 45bis. Detained Persons; Rule 45 ter. Assignment of Counsel in the Interests of Justice; Rule 46. Misconduct of Counsel - RPE – ICTR, Part 4. Investigations and rights of suspects; Section 2. Of Counsel. Rule 44. Appointment and Qualifications of Counsel; Rule 44 bis. Duty Counsel; Rule 45. Assignment of Counsel; Rule 45bis. Detained Persons; Rule 45 ter. Availability of Counsel; Rule 45 quarter. Assignment of Counsel in the Interests of Justice; Rule 46. Misconduct of Counsel).*

RPE – ICC, Chapter 2. Composition and administration of the Court; Section 3. The Registry; Subsection 3. Counsel for the defence.

Rule 20. Responsibilities of the Registrar relating to the rights of the defence. 1. In accordance with article 43, paragraph 1, the Registrar shall organize the staff of the Registry in a manner that promotes the rights of the defence, consistent with the principle of fair trial as defined in the Statute. For that purpose, the Registrar shall, *inter alia:*

(a) Facilitate the protection of confidentiality, as defined in article 67, paragraph 1 (b);

(b) Provide support, assistance, and information to all defence counsel appearing before the Court and, as appropriate, support for professional investigators necessary for the efficient and effective conduct of the defence;

(c) Assist arrested persons, persons to whom article 55, paragraph 2, applies and the accused in obtaining legal advice and the assistance of legal counsel;

(d) Advise the Prosecutor and the Chambers, as necessary, on relevant defence-related issues;

(e) Provide the defence with such facilities as may be necessary for the direct performance of the duty of the defence;

(f) Facilitate the dissemination of information and case law of the Court to defence counsel and, as appropriate, cooperate with national defence and bar associations or any independent representative body of counsel and legal associations referred to in sub-rule 3 to promote the specialization and training of lawyers in the law of the Statute and the Rules.

2. The Registrar shall carry out the functions stipulated in sub-rule 1, including the financial administration of the Registry, in such a manner as to ensure the professional independence of defence counsel.

3. For purposes such as the management of legal assistance in accordance with rule 21 and the development of a Code of Professional Conduct in accordance with rule 8, the Registrar shall consult, as appropriate, with any independent representative body of counsel or legal associations, including any such body the establishment of which may be facilitated by the Assembly of States Parties.

Rule 21. Assignment of legal assistance. 1. Subject to article 55, paragraph 2 (c), and article 67, paragraph 1 (d), criteria and procedures for assignment of legal assistance shall be established in the Regulations, based on a proposal by the Registrar, following consultations with any independent representative body of counsel or legal associations, as referred to in rule 20, sub-rule 3.

2. The Registrar shall create and maintain a list of counsel who meet the criteria set forth in rule 22 and the Regulations. The person shall freely choose his or her counsel from this list or other counsel who meets the required criteria and is willing to be included in the list.

3. A person may seek from the Presidency a review of a decision to refuse a request for assignment of counsel. The decision of the Presidency shall be final. If a request is refused, a further request may be made by a person to the Registrar, upon showing a change in circumstances.

4. A person choosing to represent himself or herself shall so notify the Registrar in writing at the first opportunity.

5. Where a person claims to have insufficient means to pay for legal assistance and this is subsequently found not to be so, the Chamber dealing with the case at that time may make an order of contribution to recover the cost of providing counsel.

Rule 22. Appointment and qualifications of Counsel for the defence. 1. A counsel for the defence shall have established competence in international or criminal law and procedure, as well as the necessary relevant experience, whether as judge, prosecutor, advocate or in other similar capacity, in criminal proceedings. A counsel for the defence shall have an excellent knowledge of and be fluent in at least one of the working languages of the Court. Counsel for the defence may be assisted by other persons, including professors of law, with relevant expertise.

2. Counsel for the defence engaged by a person exercising his or her right under the Statute to retain legal counsel of his or her choosing shall file a power of attorney with the Registrar at the earliest opportunity.

3. In the performance of their duties, Counsel for the defence shall be subject to the Statute, the Rules, the Regulations, the Code of Professional Conduct for Counsel adopted in accordance with rule 8 and any other document adopted by the Court that may be relevant to the performance of their duties.

RPE – ICTY, Part 4. Investigations and rights of suspects; Section 2. Of Counsel.
Rule 44. Appointment, Qualifications and Duties of Counsel.
(Adopted 11 Feb 1994, amended 25 July 1997) (A) Counsel engaged by a suspect or an accused shall file a power of attorney with the Registrar at the earliest opportunity. Subject to any determination by a Chamber pursuant to Rule 46 or 77, a

counsel shall be considered qualified to represent a suspect or accused if the counsel satisfies the Registrar that he or she:

(i) is admitted to the practice of law in a State, or is a university professor of law;

(ii) has written and oral proficiency in one of the two working languages of the Tribunal, unless the Registrar deems it in the interests of justice to waive this requirement, as provided for in paragraph (B);

(iii) is a member in good standing of an association of counsel practicing at the Tribunal recognized by the Registrar;

(iv) has not been found guilty or otherwise disciplined in relevant disciplinary proceedings against him in a national or international forum, including proceedings pursuant to the Code of Professional Conduct for Defence Counsel Appearing Before the International Tribunal, unless the Registrar deems that, in the circumstances, it would be disproportionate to exclude such counsel;

(v) has not been found guilty in relevant criminal proceedings;

(vi) has not engaged in conduct whether in pursuit of his or her profession or otherwise which is dishonest or otherwise discreditable to a counsel, prejudicial to the administration of justice, or likely to diminish public confidence in the International Tribunal or the administration of justice, or otherwise bring the International Tribunal into disrepute; and

(vii) has not provided false or misleading information in relation to his or her qualifications and fitness to practice or failed to provide relevant information.

(B) At the request of the suspect or accused and where the interests of justice so demand, the Registrar may admit a counsel who does not speak either of the two working languages of the Tribunal but who speaks the native language of the suspect or accused. The Registrar may impose such conditions as deemed appropriate, including the requirement that the counsel or accused undertake to meet all translations and interpretation costs not usually met by the Tribunal, and counsel undertakes not to request any extensions of time as a result of the fact that he does not speak one of the working languages. A suspect or accused may seek the President's review of the Registrar's decision. (Amended 14 July 2000, amended 28 July 2004)

(C) In the performance of their duties counsel shall be subject to the relevant provisions of the Statute, the Rules, the Rules of Detention and any other rules or regulations adopted by the Tribunal, the Host Country Agreement, the Code of Professional Conduct for Defence Counsel Appearing Before the International Tribunal and the codes of practice and ethics governing their profession and, if applicable, the Directive on the Assignment of Defence Counsel adopted by the Registrar and approved by the permanent Judges. (Amended 25 July 1997, amended 1 Dec 2000 and 13 Dec 2000, amended 13 Dec 2001, amended 28 July 2004)

(D) An Advisory Panel shall be established to assist the President and the Registrar in all matters relating to defence counsel. The Panel members shall be selected from representatives of professional associations and from counsel who have appeared before the Tribunal. They shall have recognized professional legal experience. The composition of the Advisory Panel shall be representative of the different legal systems. A Directive of the Registrar shall set out the structure and areas of responsibility of the Advisory Panel. (Amended 14 July 2000)

Rule 45. Assignment of Counsel. (Adopted 11 Feb 1994, revised 30 Jan 1995, revised 12 Nov 1997) (A) Whenever the interests of justice so demand, counsel shall be assigned to suspects or accused who lack the means to remunerate such counsel. Such assignments shall be treated in accordance with the procedure established in a Directive set out by the Registrar and approved by the permanent Judges. (Amended 14 July 2000, amended 12 Apr 2001)

(B) For this purpose, the Registrar shall maintain a list of counsel who:

(i) fulfil all the requirements of Rule 44, although the language requirement of Rule 44 (A)(ii) may be waived by the Registrar as provided for in the Directive;

(ii) possess established competence in criminal law and/or international criminal law/international humanitarian law/international human rights law;

(iii) possess at least seven years of relevant experience, whether as a judge, prosecutor, attorney or in some other capacity, in criminal proceedings; and

(iv) have indicated their availability and willingness to be assigned by the Tribunal to any person detained under the authority of the Tribunal lacking the means to remunerate counsel, under the terms set out in the Directive. (Amended 25 June 1996 and 5 July 1996, amended 14 July 2000, amended 28 July 2004)

(C) The Registrar shall maintain a separate list of counsel who, in addition to fulfilling the qualification requirements set out in paragraph (B), are readily available as "duty counsel" for assignment to an accused for the purposes of the initial appearance, in accordance with Rule 62. (Amended 10 July 1998, amended 14 July 2000, amended 28 July 2004)

(D) The Registrar shall, in consultation with the permanent Judges, establish the criteria for the payment of fees to assigned counsel. (Amended 12 Apr 2001, amended 12 Dec 2002)

(E) Where a person is assigned counsel and is subsequently found not to be lacking the means to remunerate counsel, the Chamber may, on application by the Registrar, make an order of contribution to recover the cost of providing counsel. (Revised 30 Jan 1995, amended 14 July 2000, amended 28 July 2004)

(F) A suspect or an accused electing to conduct his or her own defence shall so notify the Registrar in writing at the first opportunity. (Revised 30 Jan 1995, revised 12 Nov 1997)

Rule 45bis. Detained Persons. (Adopted 25 June 1996 and 5 July 1996)

Rules 44 and 45 shall apply to any person detained under the authority of the Tribunal.

Rule 45 ter. Assignment of Counsel in the Interests of Justice. (Adopted 4 November 2008) The Trial Chamber may, if it decides that it is in the interests of justice, instruct the Registrar to assign a counsel to represent the interests of the accused.

Rule 46. Misconduct of Counsel. (Adopted 11 Feb 1994, amended 13 Dec 2001) (A) If a Judge or a Chamber finds that the conduct of a counsel is offensive, abusive or otherwise obstructs the proper conduct of the proceedings, or that a counsel is negligent or otherwise fails to meet the standard of professional competence and ethics in the performance of his duties, the Chamber may, after giving counsel due warning:

(i) refuse audience to that counsel; and/or

(ii) determine, after giving counsel an opportunity to be heard, that counsel is no longer eligible to represent a suspect or an accused before the Tribunal pursuant to Rule 44 and 45. (Revised 12 Nov 1997, amended 13 Dec 2001, amended 28 July 2004)

(B) A Judge or a Chamber may also, with the approval of the President, communicate any misconduct of counsel to the professional body regulating the conduct of counsel in the counsel's State of admission or, if a university professor of law and not otherwise admitted to the profession, to the governing body of that counsel's University. (Revised 12 Nov 1997, amended 28 July 2004)

(C) Under the supervision of the President, the Registrar shall publish and oversee the implementation of a Code of Professional Conduct for defence counsel. (Amended 14 July 2000)

RPE – ICTR, Part 4. Investigations and rights of suspects; Section 2. Of Counsel.

Rule 44. Appointment and Qualifications of Counsel. (A) Counsel engaged by a suspect or an accused shall file his power of attorney with the Registrar at the earliest opportunity. Subject to verification by the Registrar, a counsel shall be considered qualified to represent a suspect or accused, provided that he is admitted to the practice of law in a State, or is a University professor of law.

(B) In the performance of their duties counsel shall be subject to the relevant provisions of the Statute, the Rules, the Rules of Detention and any other rules or regulations adopted by the Tribunal, the Host Country Agreement, the Code of Conduct and the codes of practice and ethics governing their profession and, if applicable, the Directive on the Assignment of Defence Counsel.

Rule 44bis. Duty Counsel. (A) A list of duty counsel who speak one or both working languages of the Tribunal and have indicated their willingness to be assigned pursuant to this Rule shall be kept by the Registrar.

(B) Duty counsel shall fulfill the requirements of Rule 44, and shall be situated within reasonable proximity to the Detention Facility and the Seat of the Tribunal.

(C) The Registrar shall at all times ensure that duty counsel will be available to attend the Detention Facility in the event of being summoned.

(D) If an accused, or suspect transferred under Rule 40 *bis*, is unrepresented at any time after being transferred to the Tribunal, the Registrar shall as soon as practicable summon duty counsel to represent the accused or suspect until counsel is engaged by the accused or suspect, or assigned under Rule 45.

(E) In providing initial legal advice and assistance to a suspect transferred under Rule 40 *bis*, duty counsel shall advise the suspect of his or her rights including the rights referred to in Rule 55 (A).

Rule 45. Assignment of Counsel. (A) A list of counsel who speak one or both of the working languages of the Tribunal, meet the requirements of Rule 44, have at least seven years' relevant experience, and have indicated their willingness to be assigned by the Tribunal to indigent suspects or accused, shall be kept by the Registrar.

(B) The criteria for determination of indigence shall be established by the Registrar and approved by the Judges.

(C) In assigning counsel to an indigent suspect or accused, the following procedure shall be observed:

(i) A request for assignment of counsel shall be made to the Registrar;

(ii) The Registrar shall enquire into the financial means of the suspect or accused and determine whether the criteria of indigence are met;

(iii) If he decides that the criteria are met, he shall assign counsel from the list; if he decides to the contrary, he shall inform the suspect or accused that the request is refused.

(D) If a request is refused, a further reasoned request may be made by the suspect or the accused to the Registrar upon showing a change in circumstances.

(E) The Registrar shall, in consultation with the Judges, establish the criteria for the payment of fees to assigned counsel.

(F) If a suspect or an accused elects to conduct his own defence, he shall so notify the Registrar in writing at the first opportunity.

(G) Where an alleged indigent person is subsequently found not to be indigent, the Chamber may make an order of contribution to recover the cost of providing counsel.

(H) Under exceptional circumstances, at the request of the suspect or accused or his counsel, the Chamber may instruct the Registrar to replace an assigned counsel, upon good cause being shown and after having been satisfied that the request is not designed to delay the proceedings.

(I) It is understood that Counsel will represent the accused and conduct the case to finality. Failure to do so, absent just cause approved by the Chamber, may result in forfeiture of fees in whole or in part. In such circumstances the Chamber may make an order accordingly. Counsel shall only be permitted to withdraw from the case to which he has been assigned in the most exceptional circumstances.

Rule 45bis. Detained Persons. Rules 44 and 45 shall apply to any person detained under the authority of the Tribunal.

Rule 45 ter. Availability of Counsel. (A) Counsel and Co-Counsel, whether assigned by the Registrar or appointed by the client for the purposes of proceedings before the Tribunal, shall furnish the Registrar, upon date of such assignment or appointment, a written undertaking that he will appear before the Tribunal within a reasonable time as specified by the Registrar.

(B) Failure by Counsel or Co-Counsel to appear before the Tribunal, as undertaken, shall be a ground for withdrawal by the Registrar of the assignment of such Counsel or Co-Counsel or the refusal of audience by the Tribunal or the imposition of any other sanctions by the Chamber concerned.

Rule 45 quarter. Assignment of Counsel in the Interests of Justice. The Trial Chamber may, if it decides that it is in the interests of justice, instruct the Registrar to assign a counsel to represent the interests of the accused.

Rule 46. Misconduct of Counsel. (A) A Chamber may, after a warning, impose sanctions against a counsel if, in its opinion, his conduct remains offensive or abusive, obstructs the proceedings, or is otherwise contrary to the interests of justice. This provision is applicable *mutatis mutandis* to Counsel for the prosecution.

(B) A Judge or a Chamber may also, with the approval of the President, communicate any misconduct of counsel to the professional body regulating the conduct of counsel in his State of admission or, if a professor and not otherwise admitted to the profession, to the governing body of his University.

(C) If a counsel assigned pursuant to Rule 45 is sanctioned in accordance with Sub-Rule (A) by being refused audience, the Chamber shall instruct the Registrar to replace the counsel.

(D) The Registrar may set up a Code of Professional Conduct enunciating the principles of professional ethics to be observed by counsel appearing before the Tribunal, subject to adoption by the Plenary Meeting. Amendments to the Code shall be made in consultation with representatives of the Prosecutor and Defence counsel, and subject to adoption by the Plenary Meeting. If the Registrar has strong grounds for believing that Counsel has committed a serious violation of the Code of Professional Conduct so adopted, he may report the matter to the President or the Bureau for appropriate action under this rule.

Demilitarized zones *(Protocol Additional to the Geneva Conventions of 12 August 1949, and relating to the Protection of Victims of International Armed Conflicts (Protocol I), 8 June 1977. Part. IV. Civilian Population. Section I. General Protection Against Effects of Hostilities. Chapter V. Localities and zones under special protection. Art. 60. Demilitarized zones).* 1. It is prohibited for the Parties to the conflict to extend their military operations to zones on which they have conferred by agreement the status of demilitarized zone, if such extension is contrary to the terms of this agreement.

2. The agreement shall be an express agreement, may be concluded verbally or in writing, either directly or through a Protecting Power or any impartial humanitarian organization, and may consist of reciprocal and concordant declarations. The agreement may be concluded in peacetime, as well as after the outbreak of hostilities, and should define and describe, as precisely as possible, the limits of the demilitarized zone and, if necessary, lay down the methods of supervision.

3. The subject of such an agreement shall normally be any zone which fulfils the following conditions:

(a) all combatants, as well as mobile weapons and mobile military equipment, must have been evacuated;

(b) no hostile use shall be made of fixed military installations or establishments;

(c) no acts of hostility shall be committed by the authorities or by the population; and

(d) any activity linked to the military effort must have ceased.

The Parties to the conflict shall agree upon the interpretation to be given to the condition laid down in subparagraph (d) and upon persons to be admitted to the demilitarized zone other than those mentioned in paragraph 4.

4. The presence, in this zone, of persons specially protected under the Conventions and this Protocol, and of police forces retained for the sole purpose of maintaining law and order, is not contrary to the conditions laid down in paragraph 3.

5. The Party which is in control of such a zone shall mark it, so far as possible, by such signs as may be agreed upon with the other Party, which shall be displayed where they are clearly visible, especially on its perimeter and limits and on highways.

6. If the fighting draws near to a demilitarized zone, and if the Parties to the conflict have so agreed, none of them may use the zone for purposes related to the conduct of military operations or unilaterally revoke its status.

7. If one of the Parties to the conflict commits a material breach of the provisions of paragraphs 3 or 6, the other Party shall be released from its obligations under the agreement conferring upon the zone the status of demilitarized zone. In such an eventuality, the zone loses its status but shall continue to enjoy the protection provided by the other provisions of this Protocol and the other rules of international law applicable in armed conflict.

Deportation or forcible transfer of population. *See: Crimes against humanity.*

Development. Right to Development. Declaration on the Right to Development *(Adopted by General Assembly resolution 41/128 of 4 December 1986).*

The General Assembly,

Bearing in mind the purposes and principles of the Charter of the United Nations relating to the achievement of international co-operation in solving international problems of an economic, social, cultural or humanitarian nature, and in promoting and encouraging respect for human rights and fundamental freedoms for all without distinction as to race, sex, language or religion,

Recognizing that development is a comprehensive economic, social, cultural and political process, which aims at the constant improvement of the well-being of the entire population and of all individuals on the basis of their active, free and meaningful participation in development and in the fair distribution of benefits resulting therefrom,

Considering that under the provisions of the Universal Declaration of Human Rights everyone is entitled to a social and international order in which the rights and freedoms set forth in that Declaration can be fully realized,

Recalling the provisions of the International Covenant on Economic, Social and Cultural Rights and of the International Covenant on Civil and Political Rights,

Recalling further the relevant agreements, conventions, resolutions, recommendations and other instruments of the United Nations and its specialized agencies concerning the integral development of the human being, economic and social progress and development of all peoples, including those instruments concerning decolonization, the prevention of discrimination, respect for and observance of, human rights and fundamental freedoms, the maintenance of international peace and security and the further promotion of friendly relations and co-operation among States in accordance with the Charter,

Recalling the right of peoples to self-determination, by virtue of which they have the right freely to determine their political status and to pursue their economic, social and cultural development,

Recalling also the right of peoples to exercise, subject to the relevant provisions of both International Covenants on Human Rights, full and complete sovereignty over all their natural wealth and resources,

Mindful of the obligation of States under the Charter to promote universal respect for and observance of human rights and fundamental freedoms for all without distinction of any kind such as race, colour, sex, language, religion, political or other opinion, national or social origin, property, birth or other status,

Considering that the elimination of the massive and flagrant violations of the human rights of the peoples and individuals affected by situations such as those resulting from colonialism, neo-colonialism, apartheid, all forms of racism and racial discrimination, foreign domination and occupation, aggression and threats against national sovereignty, national unity and territorial integrity and threats of war would contribute to the establishment of circumstances propitious to the development of a great part of mankind,

Concerned at the existence of serious obstacles to development, as well as to the complete fulfilment of human beings and of peoples, constituted, inter alia, by the denial of civil, political, economic, social and cultural rights, and considering that all human rights and fundamental freedoms are indivisible and interdependent and that, in order to promote development, equal attention and urgent consideration should be given to the implementation, promotion and protection of civil, political, economic, social and cultural rights and that, accordingly, the promotion of, respect for and enjoyment of certain human rights and fundamental freedoms cannot justify the denial of other human rights and fundamental freedoms,

Considering that international peace and security are essential elements for the realization of the right to development,

Reaffirming that there is a close relationship between disarmament and development and that progress in the field of disarmament would considerably promote progress in the field of development and that resources released through disarmament measures should be devoted to the economic and social development and well-being of all peoples and, in particular, those of the developing countries,

Recognizing that the human person is the central subject of the development process and that development policy should therefore make the human being the main participant and beneficiary of development,

Recognizing that the creation of conditions favourable to the development of peoples and individuals is the primary responsibility of their States,

Aware that efforts at the international level to promote and protect human rights should be accompanied by efforts to establish a new international economic order,

Confirming that the right to development is an inalienable human right and that equality of opportunity for development is a prerogative both of nations and of individuals who make up nations,

Proclaims the following Declaration on the Right to Development:

Art. 1. 1. The right to development is an inalienable human right by virtue of which every human person and all peoples are entitled to participate in, contribute to, and enjoy economic, social, cultural and political development, in which all human rights and fundamental freedoms can be fully realized.

2. The human right to development also implies the full realization of the right of peoples to self-determination, which includes, subject to the relevant provisions of both International Covenants on Human Rights, the exercise of their inalienable right to full sovereignty over all their natural wealth and resources.

Art. 2. 1. The human person is the central subject of development and should be the active participant and beneficiary of the right to development.

2. All human beings have a responsibility for development, individually and collectively, taking into account the need for full respect for their human rights and fundamental freedoms as well as their duties to the community, which alone can ensure the free and complete fulfilment of the human being, and they should therefore promote and protect an appropriate political, social and economic order for development.

3. States have the right and the duty to formulate appropriate national development policies that aim at the constant improvement of the well-being of the entire population and of all individuals, on the basis of their active, free and meaningful participation in development and in the fair distribution of the benefits resulting therefrom.

Art. 3. 1. States have the primary responsibility for the creation of national and international conditions favourable to the realization of the right to development.

2. The realization of the right to development requires full respect for the principles of international law concerning friendly relations and co-operation among States in accordance with the Charter of the United Nations.

3. States have the duty to co-operate with each other in ensuring development and eliminating obstacles to development. States should realize their rights and fulfil their duties in such a manner as to promote a new international economic order based on sovereign equality, interdependence, mutual interest and co-operation among all States, as well as to encourage the observance and realization of human rights.

Art. 4. 1. States have the duty to take steps, individually and collectively, to formulate international development policies with a view to facilitating the full realization of the right to development.

2. Sustained action is required to promote more rapid development of developing countries. As a complement to the efforts of developing countries, effective international co-operation is essential in providing these countries with appropriate means and facilities to foster their comprehensive development.

Art. 5. States shall take resolute steps to eliminate the massive and flagrant violations of the human rights of peoples and human beings affected by situations such as those resulting from apartheid, all forms of racism and racial discrimination, colonialism, foreign domination and occupation, aggression, foreign interference and threats against national sovereignty, national unity and territorial integrity, threats of war and refusal to recognize the fundamental right of peoples to self-determination.

Art. 6. 1. All States should co-operate with a view to promoting, encouraging and strengthening universal respect for and observance of all human rights and fundamental freedoms for all without any distinction as to race, sex, language or religion.

2. All human rights and fundamental freedoms are indivisible and interdependent; equal attention and urgent consideration should be given to the implementation, promotion and protection of civil, political, economic, social and cultural rights.

3. States should take steps to eliminate obstacles to development resulting from failure to observe civil and political rights, as well as economic social and cultural rights.

Art. 7. All States should promote the establishment, maintenance and strengthening of international peace and security and, to that end, should do their utmost to achieve general and complete disarmament under effective international control, as well as to ensure that the resources released by effective disarmament measures are used for comprehensive development, in particular that of the developing countries.

Art. 8. 1. States should undertake, at the national level, all necessary measures for the realization of the right to development and shall ensure, inter alia, equality of opportunity for all in their access to basic resources, education, health services, food, housing, employment and the fair distribution of income. Effective measures should be undertaken to ensure that women have an active role in the development process. Appropriate economic and social reforms should be carried out with a view to eradicating all social injustices.

2. States should encourage popular participation in all spheres as an important factor in development and in the full realization of all human rights.

Art. 9. 1. All the aspects of the right to development set forth in the present Declaration are indivisible and interdependent and each of them should be considered in the context of the whole.

2. Nothing in the present Declaration shall be construed as being contrary to the purposes and principles of the United Nations, or as implying that any State, group or person has a right to engage in any activity or to perform any act aimed at the violation of the rights set forth in the Universal Declaration of Human Rights and in the International Covenants on Human Rights.

Art. 10. Steps should be taken to ensure the full exercise and progressive enhancement of the right to development, including the formulation, adoption and implementation of policy, legislative and other measures at the national and international levels.

"Discrimination against women" *(Convention on the elimination of all forms of discrimination against women, New York, 18 December 1979. Part. I., Art. 2).* For the purposes of the present Convention, the term "discrimination against women" shall mean any distinction, exclusion or restriction made on the basis of sex which has the effect or purpose of impairing or nullifying the recognition, enjoyment or exercise by women, irrespective of their marital status, on a basis of equality of men and women, of human rights and fundamental freedoms in the political, economic, social, cultural, civil or any other field.

"Distinctive emblem" *(Protocol Additional to the Geneva Conventions of 12 August 1949, and relating to the Protection of Victims of International Armed Conflicts (Protocol I), 8 June 1977. Part. II. Wounded, sick and shipwrecked, Section I: General Protection. Art. 8. Terminology).* For the purposes of this Protocol: (…) l) "Distinctive emblem" means the distinctive emblem of the red cross, red crescent or red lion and sun on a white ground when used for the protection of medical units and transports, or medical and religious personnel, equipment or supplies.

"Distinctive signal" *(Protocol Additional to the Geneva Conventions of 12 August 1949, and relating to the Protection of Victims of International Armed Conflicts (Protocol I), 8 June 1977. Part. II. Wounded, sick and shipwrecked,*

Section I: General Protection. Art. 8. Terminology). For the purposes of this Protocol: (…) m) "Distinctive signal" means any signal or message specified for the identification exclusively of medical units or transports in Chapter III of Annex I to this Protocol.

E

Elements of Crimes *(Rome Statute ICC, art. 9. Elements of Crimes; Elements of Crimes. General introduction). Rome Statute ICC, art. 9. Elements of Crimes.* 1. Elements of Crimes shall assist the Court in the interpretation and application of articles 6, 7 and 8. They shall be adopted by a two-thirds majority of the members of the Assembly of States Parties.

2. Amendments to the Elements of Crimes may be proposed by:

(a) Any State Party;

(b) The judges acting by an absolute majority;

(c) The Prosecutor.

Such amendments shall be adopted by a two-thirds majority of the members of the Assembly of States Parties.

3. The Elements of Crimes and amendments thereto shall be consistent with this Statute.

Elements of Crimes. General introduction. 1. Pursuant to article 9, the following Elements of Crimes shall assist the Court in the interpretation and application of articles 6, 7 and 8, consistent with the Statute. The provisions of the Statute, including article 21 and the general principles set out in Part 3, are applicable to the Elements of Crimes.

2. As stated in article 30, unless otherwise provided, a person shall be criminally responsible and liable for punishment for a crime within the jurisdiction of the Court only if the material elements are committed with intent and knowledge. Where no reference is made in the Elements of Crimes to a mental element for any particular conduct, consequence or circumstance listed, it is understood that the relevant mental element, i.e., intent, knowledge or both, set out in article 30 applies. Exceptions to the article 30 standard, based on the Statute, including applicable law under its relevant provisions, are indicated below.

3. Existence of intent and knowledge can be inferred from relevant facts and circumstances.

4. With respect to mental elements associated with elements involving value judgement, such as those using the terms 'inhumane' or 'severe', it is not necessary that the perpetrator personally completed a particular value judgement, unless otherwise indicated.

5. Grounds for excluding criminal responsibility or the absence thereof are generally not specified in the elements of crimes listed under each crime *(This paragraph is without prejudice to the obligation of the Prosecutor under article 54, paragraph 1, of the Statute).*

6. The requirement of 'unlawfulness' found in the Statute or in other parts of international law, in particular international humanitarian law, is generally not specified in the elements of crimes.

7. The elements of crimes are generally structured in accordance with the following principles:

– As the elements of crimes focus on the conduct, consequences and circumstances associated with each crime, they are generally listed in that order;

– When required, a particular mental element is listed after the affected conduct, consequence or circumstance;

– Contextual circumstances are listed last.

8. As used in the Elements of Crimes, the term 'perpetrator' is neutral as to guilt or innocence. The elements, including the appropriate mental elements, apply, *mutatis mutandis*, to all those whose criminal responsibility may fall under articles 25 and 28 of the Statute.

9. A particular conduct may constitute one or more crimes.

10. The use of short titles for the crimes has no legal effect. (…)

"Enforced disappearance" *(International Convention for the Protection of All Persons from Enforced Disappearance. 20 December 2006. Part. I., Art. 2).* For the purposes of this Convention, "enforced disappearance" is considered to be the arrest, detention, abduction or any other form of deprivation of liberty by agents of the State or by persons or groups of persons acting with the authorization, support or acquiescence of the State, followed by a refusal to acknowledge the deprivation of liberty or by concealment of the fate or whereabouts of the disappeared person, which place such a person outside the protection of the law.

Enforced disappearance of persons. *See: Crimes against humanity.*

Enslavement. *See: Crimes against humanity.*

Environment and Development. Rio Declaration on Environment and Development.
United Nations, General Assembly. The United Nations Conference on Environment and Development,

Having met at Rio de Janeiro from 3 to 14 June 1992,

Reaffirming the Declaration of the United Nations Conference on the Human Environment, adopted at Stockholm on 16 June 1972, and seeking to build upon it,

With the goal of establishing a new and equitable global partnership through the creation of new levels of cooperation among States, key sectors of societies and people,

Working towards international agreements which respect the interests of all and protect the integrity of the global environmental and developmental system,

Recognizing the integral and interdependent nature of the Earth, our home,

Proclaims that:

Principle 1. Human beings are at the centre of concerns for sustainable development. They are entitled to a healthy and productive life in harmony with nature.

Principle 2. States have, in accordance with the Charter of the United Nations and the principles of international law, the sovereign right to exploit their own resources pursuant to their own environmental and developmental policies, and the responsibility to ensure that activities within their jurisdiction or control do not cause damage to the environment of other States or of areas beyond the limits of national jurisdiction.

Principle 3. The right to development must be fulfilled so as to equitably meet developmental and environmental needs of present and future generations.

Principle 4. In order to achieve sustainable development, environmental protection shall constitute an integral part of the development process and cannot be considered in isolation from it.

Principle 5. All States and all people shall cooperate in the essential task of eradicating poverty as an indispensable requirement for sustainable development, in order to decrease the disparities in standards of living and better meet the needs of the majority of the people of the world.

Principle 6. The special situation and needs of developing countries, particularly the least developed and those most environmentally vulnerable, shall be given special priority. International actions in the field of environment and development should also address the interests and needs of all countries.

Principle 7. States shall cooperate in a spirit of global partnership to conserve, protect and restore the health and integrity of the Earth's ecosystem. In view of the different contributions to global environmental degradation, States have common but differentiated responsibilities. The developed countries acknowledge the responsibility that they bear in the international pursuit to sustainable development in view of the pressures their societies place on the global environment and of the technologies and financial resources they command.

Principle 8. To achieve sustainable development and a higher quality of life for all people, States should reduce and eliminate unsustainable patterns of production and consumption and promote appropriate demographic policies.

Principle 9. States should cooperate to strengthen endogenous capacity-building for sustainable development by improving scientific understanding through exchanges of scientific and technological knowledge, and by enhancing the development, adaptation, diffusion and transfer of technologies, including new and innovative technologies.

Principle 10. Environmental issues are best handled with participation of all concerned citizens, at the relevant level. At the national level, each individual shall have appropriate access to information concerning the environment that is held by public authorities, including information on hazardous materials and activities in their communities, and the opportunity to participate in decision-making processes. States shall facilitate and encourage public awareness and participation by making information widely available. Effective access to judicial and administrative proceedings, including redress and remedy, shall be provided.

Principle 11. States shall enact effective environmental legislation. Environmental standards, management objectives and priorities should reflect the environmental and development context to which they apply. Standards applied by some countries may be inappropriate and of unwarranted economic and social cost to other countries, in particular developing countries.

Principle 12. States should cooperate to promote a supportive and open international economic system that would lead to economic growth and sustainable development in all countries, to better address the problems of environmental degradation. Trade policy measures for environmental purposes should not constitute a means of arbitrary or unjustifiable discrimination or a disguised restriction on international trade. Unilateral actions to deal with environmental challenges outside the jurisdiction of the importing country should be avoided. Environmental measures addressing transboundary or global environmental problems should, as far as possible, be based on an international consensus.

Principle 13. States shall develop national law regarding liability and compensation for the victims of pollution and other environmental damage. States shall also cooperate in an expeditious and more determined manner to develop further international law regarding liability and compensation for adverse effects of environmental damage caused by activities within their jurisdiction or control to areas beyond their jurisdiction.

Principle 14. States should effectively cooperate to discourage or prevent the relocation and transfer to other States of any activities and substances that cause severe environmental degradation or are found to be harmful to human health.

Principle 15. In order to protect the environment, the precautionary approach shall be widely applied by States according to their capabilities. Where there are threats of serious or irreversible damage, lack of full scientific certainty shall not be used as a reason for postponing cost-effective measures to prevent environmental degradation.

Principle 16. National authorities should endeavour to promote the internalization of environmental costs and the use of economic instruments, taking into account the approach that the polluter should, in principle, bear the cost of pollution, with due regard to the public interest and without distorting international trade and investment.

Principle 17. Environmental impact assessment, as a national instrument, shall be undertaken for proposed activities that are likely to have a significant adverse impact on the environment and are subject to a decision of a competent national authority.

Principle 18. States shall immediately notify other States of any natural disasters or other emergencies that are likely to produce sudden harmful effects on the environment of those States. Every effort shall be made by the international community to help States so afflicted.

Principle 19. States shall provide prior and timely notification and relevant information to potentially affected States on activities that may have a significant adverse transboundary environmental effect and shall consult with those States at an early stage and in good faith.

Principle 20. Women have a vital role in environmental management and development. Their full participation is therefore essential to achieve sustainable development.

Principle 21. The creativity, ideals and courage of the youth of the world should be mobilized to forge a global partnership in order to achieve sustainable development and ensure a better future for all.

Principle 22. Indigenous people and their communities and other local communities have a vital role in environmental management and development because of their knowledge and traditional practices. States should recognize and duly support their identity, culture and interests and enable their effective participation in the achievement of sustainable development.

Principle 23. The environment and natural resources of people under oppression, domination and occupation shall be protected.

Principle 24. Warfare is inherently destructive of sustainable development. States shall therefore respect international law providing protection for the environment in times of armed conflict and cooperate in its further development, as necessary.

Principle 25. Peace, development and environmental protection are interdependent and indivisible.

Principle 26. States shall resolve all their environmental disputes peacefully and by appropriate means in accordance with the Charter of the United Nations.

Principle 27. States and people shall cooperate in good faith and in a spirit of partnership in the fulfilment of the principles embodied in this Declaration and in the further development of international law in the field of sustainable development.

Escape *(Rome Statute ICC, Part X. Enforcement, art. 111. Escape; RPE – ICC, Section VI. Escape, Rule 225. Measures under article 111 in the event of escape).*
Rome Statute ICC, Part X. Enforcement, art. 111. Escape. If a convicted person escapes from custody and flees the State of enforcement, that State may, after consultation with the Court, request the person's surrender from the State in which the person is located pursuant to existing bilateral or multilateral arrangements, or may request that the Court seek the person's surrender, in accordance with Part 9. It may direct that the person be delivered to the State in which he or she was serving the sentence or to another State designated by the Court.
RPE – ICC, Section VI. Escape, Rule 225. Measures under article 111 in the event of escape. 1. If the sentenced person has escaped, the State of enforcement shall, as soon as possible, advise the Registrar by any medium capable of delivering a written record. The Presidency shall then proceed in accordance with Part 9.
2. However, if the State in which the sentenced person is located agrees to surrender him or her to the State of enforcement, pursuant to either international agreements or its national legislation, the State of enforcement shall so advise the Registrar in writing. The person shall be surrendered to the State of enforcement as soon as possible, if necessary in consultation with the Registrar, who shall provide all necessary assistance, including, if necessary, the presentation of requests for transit to the States concerned, in accordance with rule 207. The costs associated with the surrender of the sentenced person shall be borne by the Court if no State assumes responsibility for them.
3. If the sentenced person is surrendered to the Court pursuant to Part 9, the Court shall transfer him or her to the State of enforcement. Nevertheless, the Presidency may, acting on its own motion or at the request of the Prosecutor or of the initial State of enforcement and in accordance with article 103 and rules 203 to 206,

designate another State, including the State to the territory of which the sentenced person has fled.

4. In all cases, the entire period of detention in the territory of the State in which the sentenced person was in custody after his or her escape and, where sub-rule 3 is applicable, the period of detention at the seat of the Court following the surrender of the sentenced person from the State in which he or she was located shall be deducted from the sentence remaining to be served.

European Court of Human Rights *(Convention for the Protection of Human Rights and Fundamental Freedoms. Rome, 4.XI.1950. Section 2. European Court of Human Rights. Art. 19. Establishment of the Court; Art. 20. Number of judges; Art. 21. Criteria for office; (...) Art. 32. Jurisdiction of the Court; Art. 33. Inter-State cases; Art. 34. Individual applications; Art. 35. Admissibility criteria; Art. 36. Third party intervention - Rules of Court. Rule 19. Seat of the Court).*

Convention for the Protection of Human Rights and Fundamental Freedoms. *Rome, 4.XI.1950. Section 2. European Court of Human Rights.*

Art. 19. Establishment of the Court. To ensure the observance of the engagements undertaken by the High Contracting Parties in the Convention and the Protocols thereto, there shall be set up a European Court of Human Rights, hereinafter referred to as "the Court". It shall function on a permanent basis.

Art. 20. Number of judges. The Court shall consist of a number of judges equal to that of the High Contracting Parties.

Art. 21. Criteria for office. 1. The judges shall be of high moral character and must either possess the qualifications required for appointment to high judicial office or be jurisconsults of recognized competence.

2. The judges shall sit on the Court in their individual capacity.

3. During their term of office the judges shall not engage in any activity which is incompatible with their independence, impartiality or with the demands of a full-time office; all questions arising from the application of this paragraph shall be decided by the Court. (...)

Art. 32. Jurisdiction of the Court. 1. The jurisdiction of the Court shall extend to all matters concerning the interpretation and application of the Convention and the Protocols thereto which are referred to it as provided in Articles 33, 34, 46 and 47.

2. In the event of dispute as to whether the Court has jurisdiction, the Court shall decide.

Art. 33. Inter-State cases. Any High Contracting Party may refer to the Court any alleged breach of the provisions of the Convention and the Protocols thereto by another High Contracting Party.

Art. 34. Individual applications. The Court may receive applications from any person, non-governmental organization or group of individuals claiming to be the victim of a violation by one of the High Contracting Parties of the rights set forth in the Convention or the Protocols thereto. The High Contracting Parties undertake not to hinder in any way the effective exercise of this right.

Art. 35. Admissibility criteria. 1. The Court may only deal with the matter after all domestic remedies have been exhausted, according to the generally recognized rules of international law, and within a period of six months from the date on which the final decision was taken.

2. The Court shall not deal with any application submitted under Article 34 that

(a) is anonymous; or

(b) is substantially the same as a matter that has already been examined by the Court or has already been submitted to another procedure of international investigation or settlement and contains no relevant new information.

3. The Court shall declare inadmissible any individual application submitted under Article 34 if it considers that:

(a) the application is incompatible with the provisions of the Convention or the Protocols thereto, manifestly ill-founded, or an abuse of the right of individual application; or

(b) the applicant has not suffered a significant disadvantage, unless respect for human rights as defined in the Convention and the Protocols thereto requires an examination of the application on the merits and provided that no case may be rejected on this ground which has not been duly considered by a domestic tribunal.

4. The Court shall reject any application which it considers inadmissible under this Article. It may do so at any stage of the proceedings.

Art. 36. Third party intervention. 1. In all cases before a Chamber or the Grand Chamber, a High Contracting Party one of whose nationals is an applicant shall have the right to submit written comments and to take part in hearings.

2. The President of the Court may, in the interest of the proper administration of justice, invite any High Contracting Party which is not a party to the proceedings or any person concerned who is not the applicant to submit written comments or take part in hearing.

3. In all cases before a Chamber or the Grand Chamber, the Council of Europe Commissioner for Human Rights may submit written comments and take part in hearings. (...)

Rules of Court. Rule 19. Seat of the Court. 1. The seat of the Court shall be at the seat of the Council of Europe at Strasbourg. The Court may, however, if it considers it expedient, perform its functions elsewhere in the territories of the member States of the Council of Europe.

2. The Court may decide, at any stage of the examination of an application, that it is necessary that an investigation or any other function be carried out elsewhere by it or one or more of its members.

Extermination. *See: Crimes against humanity.*

Extradition *(Rome Statute ICC, art. 102. Use of terms).* For the purposes of this Statute:

(...) (b) "extradition" means the delivering up of a person by one State to another as provided by treaty, convention or national legislation.

F

Forced pregnancy. *See: Crimes against humanity, War crimes, Elements of Crimes.*

"Frontier worker" *(International Convention on the protection of the rights of all migrant workers and members of their families. Adopted by General Assembly resolution 45/158 of 18 December 1990. Part. I., Scope and Definitions, Art. 2).* For the purposes of the present Convention: 2.(a) The term "frontier worker" refers to a migrant worker who retains his or her habitual residence in a neighbouring State to which he or she normally returns every day or at least once a week.

G

General protection *(Protocol Additional to the Geneva Conventions of 12 August 1949, and relating to the Protection of Victims of International Armed Conflicts (Protocol I), 8 June 1977. Part. IV. Civilian Population. Section I. General Protection Against Effects of Hostilities. Chapter VI. Civil defence. Art. 62. General protection; Art. 52. General Protection of civilian objects). Art. 62. General protection.* 1. Civilian civil defence organizations and their personnel shall be respected and protected, subject to the provisions of this Protocol, particularly the provisions of this section. They shall be entitled to perform their civil defence tasks except in case of imperative military necessity.

2. The provisions of paragraph 1 shall also apply to civilians who, although not members of civilian civil defence organizations, respond to an appeal from the competent authorities and perform civil defence tasks under their control.

3. Buildings and materiel used for civil defence purposes and shelters provided for the civilian population are covered by Article 52. Objects used for civil defence purposes may not be destroyed or diverted from their proper use except by the Party to which they belong.

Art. 52. General Protection of civilian objects). 1. Civilian objects shall not be the object of attack or of reprisals. Civilian objects are all objects which are not military objectives as defined in paragraph 2.

2. Attacks shall be limited strictly to military objectives. In so far as objects are concerned, military objectives are limited to those objects which by their nature, location, purpose or use make an effective contribution to military action and whose total or partial destruction, capture or neutralization, in the circumstances ruling at the time, offers a definite military advantage.

3. In case of doubt whether an object which is normally dedicated to civilian purposes, such as a place of worship, a house or other dwelling or a school, is being used to make an effective contribution to military action, it shall be presumed not to be so used.

General Protection of civilian objects *(Protocol Additional to the Geneva Conventions of 12 August 1949, and relating to the Protection of Victims of International Armed Conflicts (Protocol I), 8 June 1977. Part. IV. Civilian Population. Section I. General Protection Against Effects of Hostilities. Chapter III. Civilian objects. Art. 52. General Protection of civilian objects).* 1. Civilian objects shall not be the object of attack or of reprisals. Civilian objects are all objects which are not military objectives as defined in paragraph 2.

2. Attacks shall be limited strictly to military objectives. In so far as objects are concerned, military objectives are limited to those objects which by their nature,

location, purpose or use make an effective contribution to military action and whose total or partial destruction, capture or neutralization, in the circumstances ruling at the time, offers a definite military advantage.

3. In case of doubt whether an object which is normally dedicated to civilian purposes, such as a place of worship, a house or other dwelling or a school, is being used to make an effective contribution to military action, it shall be presumed not to be so used.

General protection of medical duties *(Protocol Additional to the Geneva Conventions of 12 August 1949, and relating to the Protection of Victims of International Armed Conflicts (Protocol I), 8 June 1977. Part. II. Wounded, sick and shipwrecked. Section I. General Protection. Art. 16. General protection of medical duties).* 1. Under no circumstances shall any person be punished for carrying out medical activities compatible with medical ethics, regardless of the person benefiting therefrom.

2. Persons engaged in medical activities shall not be compelled to perform acts or to carry out work contrary to the rules of medical ethics or to other medical rules designed for the benefit of the wounded and sick or to the provisions of the Conventions or of this Protocol, or to refrain from performing acts or from carrying out work required by those rules and provisions.

3. No person engaged in medical activities shall be compelled to give to anyone belonging either to an adverse Party, or to his own Party except as required by the law of the latter Party, any information concerning the wounded and sick who are, or who have been, under his care, if such information would, in his opinion, prove harmful to the patients concerned or to their families. Regulations for the compulsory notification of communicable diseases shall, however, be respected.

Geneva Conventions of 12 August 1949: "First Convention", "Second Convention", "Third Convention" and "Fourth Convention" *(Protocol Additional to the Geneva Conventions of 12 August 1949, and relating to the Protection of Victims of International Armed Conflicts (Protocol I), 8 June 1977. Part I. General provisions. Art 2. Definitions).* For the purposes of this Protocol (a) "First Convention", "Second Convention", "Third Convention" and "Fourth Convention" mean, respectively, the Geneva Convention for the Amelioration of the Condition of the Wounded and Sick in Armed Forces in the Field of 12 August 1949; the Geneva Convention for the Amelioration of the Condition of Wounded, Sick and Ship-wrecked Members of Armed Forces at Sea of 12 August 1949; the Geneva Convention relative to the Treatment of Prisoners of War of 12 August 1949; the Geneva Convention relative to the Protection of Civilian Persons in Time of War of 12 August 1949; "the Conventions" means the four Geneva Conventions of 12 August 1949 for the protection of war victims.

(See: Protocol Additional to the Geneva Conventions of 12 August 1949, and relating to the Protection of Victims of International Armed Conflicts (Protocol I), 8 June 1977; Protocol Additional to the Geneva Conventions of 12 August 1949, and relating to the Protection of Victims of Non-International Armed Conflicts (Protocol

II), 8 June 1977; Protocol additional to the Geneva Conventions of 12 August 1949, and relating to the adoption of an additional distinctive emblem (Protocol III), 8 December 2005).

Genocide by causing serious bodily or mental harm. *See: Genocide - Crime of Genocide.*

Genocide - Crime of Genocide (Convention on the Prevention and Punishment of the Crime of Genocide, New York, 9 December 1948. Preamble. Art. 1; Art. 2; Art. 3: Art. 4; Art. 5; Art. 6; Art. 7; (…); Genocide (Rome Statute ICC, art. 6); Elements of Crimes. Art. 6. Genocide. Introduction; Art. 6 (a). Genocide by killing. Elements; Art. 6 (b). Genocide by causing serious bodily or mental harm. Elements; Art. 6 (c). Genocide by deliberately inflicting conditions of life calculated to bring about physical destruction. Elements; Art. 6 (d). Genocide by imposing measures intended to prevent births. Elements; Art. 6 (e). Genocide by forcibly transferring children. Elements; Genocide (Statute ICTY, art. 4); Genocide (Statute ICTR, art. 2)).

Convention on the Prevention and Punishment of the Crime of Genocide. Adopted by Resolution 260 (III) A of the U.N. General Assembly on 9 December 1948, New York. *Preamble.* The Contracting Parties,

Having considered the declaration made by the General Assembly of the United Nations in its resolution 96 (I) dated 11 December 1946 that genocide is a crime under international law, contrary to the spirit and aims of the United Nations and condemned by the civilized world,

Recognizing that at all periods of history genocide has inflicted great losses on humanity, and *Being* convinced that, in order to liberate mankind from such an odious scourge, international co-operation is required,

Hereby agree as hereinafter provided:

Art. 1. The Contracting Parties confirm that genocide, whether committed in time of peace or in time of war, is a crime under international law which they undertake to prevent and to punish.

Art. 2. In the present Convention, genocide means any of the following acts committed with intent to destroy, in whole or in part, a national, ethnical, racial or religious group, as such:

(a) Killing members of the group;

(b) Causing serious bodily or mental harm to members of the group;

(c) Deliberately inflicting on the group conditions of life calculated to bring about its physical destruction in whole or in part;

(d) Imposing measures intended to prevent births within the group;

(e) Forcibly transferring children of the group to another group.

Art. 3. The following acts shall be punishable:

(a) Genocide;

(b) Conspiracy to commit genocide;

(c) Direct and public incitement to commit genocide;

(d) Attempt to commit genocide;

(e) Complicity in genocide.

Art. 4. Persons committing genocide or any of the other acts enumerated in article 3 shall be punished, whether they are constitutionally responsible rulers, public officials or private individuals.

Art. 5. The Contracting Parties undertake to enact, in accordance with their respective Constitutions, the necessary legislation to give effect to the provisions of the present Convention, and, in particular, to provide effective penalties for persons guilty of genocide or any of the other acts enumerated in article 3.

Art. 6. Persons charged with genocide or any of the other acts enumerated in article 3 shall be tried by a competent tribunal of the State in the territory of which the act was committed, or by such international penal tribunal as may have jurisdiction with respect to those Contracting Parties which shall have accepted its jurisdiction.

Art. 7. Genocide and the other acts enumerated in article 3 shall not be considered as political crimes for the purpose of extradition. The Contracting Parties pledge themselves in such cases to grant extradition in accordance with their laws and treaties in force. (…)

Genocide *(Rome Statute ICC, art. 6).* For the purpose of this Statute, 'genocide' means any of the following acts committed with intent to destroy, in whole or in part, a national, ethnical, racial or religious group, as such:

(a) Killing members of the group;

(b) Causing serious bodily or mental harm to members of the group;

(c) Deliberately inflicting on the group conditions of life calculated to bring about its physical destruction in whole or in part;

(d) Imposing measures intended to prevent births within the group;

(e) Forcibly transferring children of the group to another group.

Elements of Crimes. Art. 6. **Genocide. Introduction.** With respect to the last element listed for each crime:

– The term 'in the context of' would include the initial acts in an emerging pattern;

– The term 'manifest' is an objective qualification;

– Notwithstanding the normal requirement for a mental element provided for in article 30, and recognizing that knowledge of the circumstances will usually be addressed in proving genocidal intent, the appropriate requirement, if any, for a mental element regarding this circumstance will need to be decided by the Court on a case-by-case basis.

Art. 6 (a). **Genocide by killing. Elements.** 1. The perpetrator killed one or more persons *(The term 'killed' is interchangeable with the term 'caused death').*

2. Such person or persons belonged to a particular national, ethnical, racial or religious group.

3. The perpetrator intended to destroy, in whole or in part, that national, ethnical, racial or religious group, as such.

4. The conduct took place in the context of a manifest pattern of similar conduct directed against that group or was conduct that could itself effect such destruction.

Art. 6 (b). **Genocide by causing serious bodily or mental harm. Elements.** 1. The perpetrator caused serious bodily or mental harm to one or more persons *(This conduct may include, but is not necessarily restricted to, acts of torture, rape, sexual violence or inhuman or degrading treatment).*

2. Such person or persons belonged to a particular national, ethnical, racial or religious group.

3. The perpetrator intended to destroy, in whole or in part, that national, ethnical, racial or religious group, as such.

4. The conduct took place in the context of a manifest pattern of similar conduct directed against that group or was conduct that could itself effect such destruction.

Art. 6 (c). **Genocide by deliberately inflicting conditions of life calculated to bring about physical destruction. Elements.** 1. The perpetrator inflicted certain conditions of life upon one or more persons.

2. Such person or persons belonged to a particular national, ethnical, racial or religious group.

3. The perpetrator intended to destroy, in whole or in part, that national, ethnical, racial or religious group, as such.

4. The conditions of life were calculated to bring about the physical destruction of that group, in whole or in part *(The term 'conditions of life' may include, but is not necessarily restricted to, deliberate deprivation of resources indispensable for survival, such as food or medical services, or systematic expulsion from homes).*

5. The conduct took place in the context of a manifest pattern of similar conduct directed against that group or was conduct that could itself effect such destruction.

Art. 6 (d). **Genocide by imposing measures intended to prevent births. Elements.** 1. The perpetrator imposed certain measures upon one or more persons.

2. Such person or persons belonged to a particular national, ethnical, racial or religious group.

3. The perpetrator intended to destroy, in whole or in part, that national, ethnical, racial or religious group, as such.

4. The measures imposed were intended to prevent births within that group.

5. The conduct took place in the context of a manifest pattern of similar conduct directed against that group or was conduct that could itself effect such destruction.

Art. 6 (e). **Genocide by forcibly transferring children. Elements.** 1. The perpetrator forcibly transferred one or more persons *(The term 'forcibly' is not restricted to physical force, but may include threat of force or coercion, such as that caused by fear of violence, duress, detention, psychological oppression or abuse of power, against such person or persons or another person, or by taking advantage of a coercive environment).*

2. Such person or persons belonged to a particular national, ethnical, racial or religious group.

3. The perpetrator intended to destroy, in whole or in part, that national, ethnical, racial or religious group, as such.

4. The transfer was from that group to another group.

5. The person or persons were under the age of 18 years.

6. The perpetrator knew, or should have known, that the person or persons were under the age of 18 years.

7. The conduct took place in the context of a manifest pattern of similar conduct directed against that group or was conduct that could itself effect such destruction.

Genocide (*Statute ICTY, art. 4*). 1. The International Tribunal shall have the power to prosecute persons committing genocide as defined in paragraph 2 of this article or of committing any of the other acts enumerated in paragraph 3 of this article.

2. Genocide means any of the following acts committed with intent to destroy, in whole or in part, a national, ethnical, racial or religious group, as such:
a) killing members of the group;
b) causing serious bodily or mental harm to members of the group;
c) deliberately inflicting on the group conditions of life calculated to bring about its physical destruction in whole or in part;
d) imposing measures intended to prevent births within the group;
e) forcibly transferring children of the group to another group;
3. The following acts shall be punishable:
(a) genocide;
(b) conspiracy to commit genocide;
(c) direct and public incitement to commit genocide;
(d) attempt to commit genocide;
(e) complicity in genocide.

Genocide (*Statute ICTR, art. 2*). 1. The International Tribunal for Rwanda shall have the power to prosecute persons committing genocide as defined in paragraph 2 of this Article or of committing any of the other acts enumerated in paragraph 3 of this Article.
2. Genocide means any of the following acts committed with intent to destroy, in whole or in part, a national, ethnical, racial or religious group, as such:
(a) Killing members of the group;
(b) Causing serious bodily or mental harm to members of the group;
(c) Deliberately inflicting on the group conditions of life calculated to bring about its physical destruction in whole or in part;
(d) Imposing measures intended to prevent births within the group;
(e) Forcibly transferring children of the group to another group.
3. The following acts shall be punishable:
(a) Genocide;
(b) Conspiracy to commit genocide;
(c) Direct and public incitement to commit genocide;
(d) Attempt to commit genocide;
(e) Complicity in genocide.

Genocide by deliberately inflicting conditions of life calculated to bring about physical destruction. *See: Genocide - Crime of Genocide.*

Genocide by forcibly transferring children. *See: Genocide - Crime of Genocide.*

Genocide by imposing measures intended to prevent births. *See: Genocide - Crime of Genocide.*

Genocide by killing. *See: Genocide - Crime of Genocide.*

Grave breaches of the Geneva Conventions of 12 August 1949 and of the Additional Protocols *(Convention (I) for the Amelioration of the Condition of the Wounded and Sick in Armed Forces in the Field. Geneva, 12 August 1949. Chapter IX. Repression of Abuses and Infractions. Art. 49; Art. 50. Convention (II) for the Amelioration of the Condition of Wounded, Sick and Shipwrecked Members of Armed Forces at Sea. Geneva, 12 August 1949. Chapter VIII. Repression of Abuses and Infractions. Art. 50; Art. 51. Convention (III) relative to the Treatment of Prisoners of War. Geneva, 12 August 1949. Part. VI. Execution of the Convention. Section I. General Provisions. Art. 129; Art. 130. Convention (IV) relative to the Protection of Civilian Persons in Time of War. Geneva, 12 August 1949. Part. IV. Execution of the Convention. Section I. General Provisions. Art. 146; Art. 147. Protocol Additional to the Geneva Conventions of 12 August 1949, and relating to the Protection of Victims of International Armed Conflicts (Protocol I), 8 June 1977. Part. II. Wounded, sick and shipwrecked. Section I. General Protection. Art. 11. Protection of persons. Part. V. Execution of the Conventions and of its Protocols. Section II. Repression of Breaches of the Conventions and of this Protocol. Art. 85. Repression of breaches of this Protocol).* **Convention (I) for the Amelioration of the Condition of the Wounded and Sick in Armed Forces in the Field.** *Geneva, 12 August 1949. Chapter IX. Repression of Abuses and Infractions. Art. 49.* The High Contracting Parties undertake to enact any legislation necessary to provide effective penal sanctions for persons committing, or ordering to be committed, any of the grave breaches of the present Convention defined in the following Article.*

Each High Contracting Party shall be under the obligation to search for persons alleged to have committed, or to have ordered to be committed, such grave breaches, and shall bring such persons, regardless of their nationality, before its own courts. It may also, if it prefers, and in accordance with the provisions of its own legislation, hand such persons over for trial to another High Contracting Party concerned, provided such High Contracting Party has made out a prima facie case.

Each High Contracting Party shall take measures necessary for the suppression of all acts contrary to the provisions of the present Convention other than the grave breaches defined in the following Article.

In all circumstances, the accused persons shall benefit by safeguards of proper trial and defence, which shall not be less favourable than those provided by Article 105 and those following, of the Geneva Convention relative to the Treatment of Prisoners of War of 12 August 1949.

Art. 50. Grave breaches to which the preceding Article relates shall be those involving any of the following acts, if committed against persons or property protected by the Convention: wilful killing, torture or inhuman treatment, including biological experiments, wilfully causing great suffering or serious injury to body or health, and extensive destruction and appropriation of property, not justified by military necessity and carried out unlawfully and wantonly.

Convention (II) for the Amelioration of the Condition of Wounded, Sick and Shipwrecked Members of Armed Forces at Sea. *Geneva, 12 August 1949. Chapter VIII. Repression of Abuses and Infractions. Art. 50.* The High Contracting Parties undertake to enact any legislation necessary to provide effective penal sanctions for persons committing, or ordering to be committed, any of the grave breaches of the present Convention defined in the following Article.

Each High Contracting Party shall be under the obligation to search for persons alleged to have committed, or to have ordered to be committed, such grave breaches, and shall bring such persons, regardless of their nationality, before its own courts. It may also, if it prefers, and in accordance with the provisions of its own legislation, hand such persons over for trial to another High Contracting Party concerned, provided such High Contracting Party has made out a prima facie case.

Each High Contracting Party shall take measures necessary for the suppression of all acts contrary to the provisions of the present Convention other than the grave breaches defined in the following Article.

In all circumstances, the accused persons shall benefit by safeguards of proper trial and defence, which shall not be less favourable than those provided by Article 105 and those following of the Geneva Convention relative to the Treatment of Prisoners of War of August 12, 1949.

Art. 51. Grave breaches to which the preceding Article relates shall be those involving any of the following acts, if committed against persons or property protected by the Convention: wilful killing, torture or inhuman treatment, including biological experiments, wilfully causing great suffering or serious injury to body or health, and extensive destruction and appropriation of property, not justified by military necessity and carried out unlawfully and wantonly.

Convention (III) relative to the Treatment of Prisoners of War. Geneva, 12 August 1949. *Part. VI. Execution of the Convention. Section I. General Provisions. Art. 129.*
The High Contracting Parties undertake to enact any legislation necessary to provide effective penal sanctions for persons committing, or ordering to be committed, any of the grave breaches of the present Convention defined in the following Article.

Each High Contracting Party shall be under the obligation to search for persons alleged to have committed, or to have ordered to be committed, such grave breaches, and shall bring such persons, regardless of their nationality, before its own courts. It may also, if it prefers, and in accordance with the provisions of its own legislation, hand such persons over for trial to another High Contracting Party concerned, provided such High Contracting Party has made out a prima facie case.

Each High Contracting Party shall take measures necessary for the suppression of all acts contrary to the provisions of the present Convention other than the grave breaches defined in the following Article.

In all circumstances, the accused persons shall benefit by safeguards of proper trial and defence, which shall not be less favourable than those provided by Article 105 and those following of the present Convention.

Art. 130. Grave breaches to which the preceding Article relates shall be those involving any of the following acts, if committed against persons or property protected by the Convention: wilful killing, torture or inhuman treatment, including biological experiments, wilfully causing great suffering or serious injury to body or health, compelling a prisoner of war to serve in the forces of the hostile Power, or wilfully depriving a prisoner of war of the rights of fair and regular trial prescribed in this Convention.

Convention (IV) relative to the Protection of Civilian Persons in Time of War. *Geneva, 12 August 1949. Part. IV. Execution of the Convention. Section I. General Provisions. Art. 146.* The High Contracting Parties undertake to enact any legislation necessary to provide effective penal sanctions for persons committing, or ordering to be committed, any of the grave breaches of the present Convention defined in the following Article.

Each High Contracting Party shall be under the obligation to search for persons alleged to have committed, or to have ordered to be committed, such grave breaches, and shall bring such persons, regardless of their nationality, before its own courts. It may also, if it prefers, and in accordance with the provisions of its own legislation, hand such persons over for trial to another High Contracting Party concerned, provided such High Contracting Party has made out a prima facie case.

Each High Contracting Party shall take measures necessary for the suppression of all acts contrary to the provisions of the present Convention other than the grave breaches defined in the following Article.

In all circumstances, the accused persons shall benefit by safeguards of proper trial and defence, which shall not be less favourable than those provided by Article 105 and those following of the Geneva Convention relative to the Treatment of Prisoners of War of 12 August 1949.

Art. 147. Grave breaches to which the preceding Article relates shall be those involving any of the following acts, if committed against persons or property protected by the present Convention: wilful killing, torture or inhuman treatment, including biological experiments, wilfully causing great suffering or serious injury to body or health, unlawful deportation or transfer or unlawful confinement of a protected person, compelling a protected person to serve in the forces of a hostile Power, or wilfully depriving a protected person of the rights of fair and regular trial prescribed in the present Convention, taking of hostages and extensive destruction and appropriation of property, not justified by military necessity and carried out unlawfully and wantonly.

Protocol Additional to the Geneva Conventions of 12 August 1949, and relating to the Protection of Victims of International Armed Conflicts (Protocol I), *8 June 1977. Part. II. Wounded, sick and shipwrecked. Section I. General Protection. Art. 11. Protection of persons.* 1. The physical or mental health and integrity of persons who are in the power of the adverse Party or who are interned, detained or otherwise deprived of liberty as a result of a situation referred to in Article 1 shall not be endangered by any unjustified act or omission. Accordingly, it is prohibited to subject the persons described in this Article to any medical procedure which is not indicated by the state of health of the person concerned and which is not consistent with generally accepted medical standards which would be applied under similar medical circumstances to persons who are nationals of the Party conducting the procedure and who are in no way deprived of liberty.

2. It is, in particular, prohibited to carry out on such persons, even with their consent:

(a) physical mutilations;

(b) medical or scientific experiments;

(c) removal of tissue or organs for transplantation, except where these acts are justified in conformity with the conditions provided for in paragraph 1.

3. Exceptions to the prohibition in paragraph 2 (c) may be made only in the case of donations of blood for transfusion or of skin for grafting, provided that they are given voluntarily and without any coercion or inducement, and then only for therapeutic purposes, under conditions consistent with generally accepted medical standards and controls designed for the benefit of both the donor and the recipient.

4. Any wilful act or omission which seriously endangers the physical or mental health or integrity of any person who is in the power of a Party other than the one on which he depends and which either violates any of the prohibitions in paragraphs 1 and 2 or fails to comply with the requirements of paragraph 3 shall be a grave breach of this Protocol.

5. The persons described in paragraph 1 have the right to refuse any surgical operation. In case of refusal, medical personnel shall endeavour to obtain a written statement to that effect, signed or acknowledged by the patient.

6. Each Party to the conflict shall keep a medical record for every donation of blood for transfusion or skin for grafting by persons referred to in paragraph 1, if that donation is made under the responsibility of that Party. In addition, each Party to the conflict shall endeavour to keep a record of all medical procedures undertaken with respect to any person who is interned, detained or otherwise deprived of liberty as a result of a situation referred to in Article 1. These records shall be available at all times for inspection by the Protecting Power. *Part. V. Execution of the Conventions and of its Protocols. Section II. Repression of Breaches of the Conventions and of this Protocol. Art. 85. Repression of breaches of this Protocol.* 1. The provisions of the Conventions relating to the repression of breaches and grave breaches, supplemented by this Section, shall apply to the repression of breaches and grave breaches of this Protocol.

2. Acts described as grave breaches in the Conventions are grave breaches of this Protocol if committed against persons in the power of an adverse Party protected by Articles 44, 45 and 73 of this Protocol, or against the wounded, sick and shipwrecked of the adverse Party who are protected by this Protocol, or against those medical or religious personnel, medical units or medical transports which are under the control of the adverse Party and are protected by this Protocol.

3. In addition to the grave breaches defined in Article 11, the following acts shall be regarded as grave breaches of this Protocol, when committed wilfully, in violation of the relevant provisions of this Protocol, and causing death or serious injury to body or health:

(a) making the civilian population or individual civilians the object of attack;

(b) launching an indiscriminate attack affecting the civilian population or civilian objects in the knowledge that such attack will cause excessive loss of life, injury to civilians or damage to civilian objects, as defined in Article 57, paragraph 2 (a)(iii);

(c) launching an attack against works or installations containing dangerous forces in the knowledge that such attack will cause excessive loss of life, injury to civilians or damage to civilian objects, as defined in Article 57, paragraph 2 (a)(iii);

(d) making non-defended localities and demilitarized zones the object of attack;

(e) making a person the object of attack in the knowledge that he is hors de combat;

(f) the perfidious use, in violation of Article 37, of the distinctive emblem of the red cross, red crescent or red lion and sun or of other protective signs recognized by the Conventions or this Protocol.

4. In addition to the grave breaches defined in the preceding paragraphs and in the Conventions, the following shall be regarded as grave breaches of this Protocol, when committed wilfully and in violation of the Conventions or the Protocol:

(a) the transfer by the occupying Power of parts of its own civilian population into the territory it occupies, or the deportation or transfer of all or parts of the population of the occupied territory within or outside this territory, in violation of Article 49 of the Fourth Convention;

(b) unjustifiable delay in the repatriation of prisoners of war or civilians;

(c) practices of apartheid and other inhuman and degrading practices involving outrages upon personal dignity, based on racial discrimination;

(d) making the clearly-recognized historic monuments, works of art or places of worship which constitute the cultural or spiritual heritage of peoples and to which special protection has been given by special arrangement, for example, within the framework of a competent international organization, the object of attack, causing as a result extensive destruction thereof, where there is no evidence of the violation by the adverse Party of Article 53, subparagraph (b), and when such historic monuments, works of art and places of worship are not located in the immediate proximity of military objectives;

(e) depriving a person protected by the Conventions or referred to in paragraph 2 of this Article of the rights of fair and regular trial.

5. Without prejudice to the application of the Conventions and of this Protocol, grave breaches of these instruments shall be regarded as war crimes.

See: International Criminal Tribunal for the Former Yugoslavia – ICTY. Updated Statute Of the ICTY, adopted 25 may 1993 by Resolution 827, as amended 13 May 1998 by Resolution 1166; 30 November 2000 by Resolution 1329; 17 May 2002 by Resolution 1411; 14 August 2002 by Resolution 1431; 19 May 2003 by Resolution 1481; 20 April 2005 by Resolution 1597; 28 February 2006 by Resolution 1660; 29 September 2008 by Resolution 1837; 7 July 2009 by Resolution 1877: *Art. 1. Competence of the International Tribunal.* The International Tribunal shall have the power to prosecute persons responsible for serious violations of international humanitarian law committed in the territory of the former Yugoslavia since 1991 in accordance with the provisions of the present Statute.

Art. 2. Grave breaches of the Geneva Conventions of 1949. The International Tribunal shall have the power to prosecute persons committing or ordering to be committed grave breaches of the Geneva Conventions of 12 August 1949, namely the following acts against persons or property protected under the provisions of the relevant Geneva Convention:

(a) wilful killing;

(b) torture or inhuman treatment, including biological experiments;

(c) wilfully causing great suffering or serious injury to body or health;

(d) extensive destruction and appropriation of property, not justified by military necessity and carried out unlawfully and wantonly;

(e) compelling a prisoner of war or a civilian to serve in the forces of a hostile power;

(f) wilfully depriving a prisoner of war or a civilian of the rights of fair and regular trial;

(g) unlawful deportation or transfer or unlawful confinement of a civilian;

(h) taking civilians as hostages.

H

Human Environment. Stockholm Declaration on the Human Environment. 16 June 1972. Declaration of the United Nations Conference on the Human Environment. Stockholm, 5-16 June 1972.

The United Nations Conference on the Human Environment,

Having met at Stockholm from 5 to 16 June 1972,

Having considered the need for a common outlook and for common principles to inspire and guide the peoples of the world in the preservation and enhancement of the human environment,

Proclaims that:

Preamble

1. Man is both creature and moulder of his environment, which gives him physical sustenance and affords him the opportunity for intellectual, moral, social and spiritual growth. In the long and tortuous evolution of the human race on this planet a stage has been reached when, through the rapid acceleration of science and technology, man has acquired the power to transform his environment in countless ways and on an unprecedented scale. Both aspects of man's environment, the natural and the man-made, are essential to his well-being and to the enjoyment of basic human rights the right to life itself.

2. The protection and improvement of the human environment is a major issue which affects the wellbeing of peoples and economic development throughout the world; it is the urgent desire of the peoples of the whole world and the duty of all Governments.

3. Man has constantly to sum up experience and go on discovering, inventing, creating and advancing. In our time, man's capability to transform his surroundings, if used wisely, can bring to all peoples the benefits of development and the opportunity to enhance the quality of life. Wrongly or heedlessly applied, the same power can do incalculable harm to human beings and the human environment. We see around us growing evidence of man-made harm in many regions of the earth: dangerous levels of pollution in water, air, earth and living beings; major and undesirable disturbances to the ecological balance of the biosphere; destruction and depletion of irreplaceable resources; and gross deficiencies, harmful to the physical, mental and social health of man, in the man-made environment, particularly in the living and working environment.

4. In the developing countries most of the environmental problems are caused by under-development. Millions continue to live far below the minimum levels required for a decent human existence, deprived of adequate food and clothing, shelter and education, health and sanitation. Therefore, the developing countries must direct their efforts to development, bearing in mind their priorities and the need to

safeguard and improve the environment. For the same purpose, the industrialized countries should make efforts to reduce the gap themselves and the developing countries. In the industrialized countries, environmental problems are generally related to industrialization and technological development.

5. The natural growth of population continuously presents problems for the preservation of the environment, and adequate policies and measures should be adopted, as appropriate, to face these problems. Of all things in the world, people are the most precious. It is the people that propel social progress, create social wealth, develop science and technology and, through their hard work, continuously transform the human environment. Along with social progress and the advance of production, science and technology, the capability of man to improve the environment increases with each passing day.

6. A point has been reached in history when we must shape our actions throughout the world with a more prudent care for their environmental consequences. Through ignorance or indifference we can do massive and irreversible harm to the earthly environment on which our life and well being depend. Conversely, through fuller knowledge and wiser action, we can achieve for ourselves and our posterity a better life in an environment more in keeping with human needs and hopes. There are broad vistas for the enhancement of environmental quality and the creation of a good life. What is needed is an enthusiastic but calm state of mind and intense but orderly work. For the purpose of attaining freedom in the world of nature, man must use knowledge to build, in collaboration with nature, a better environment. To defend and improve the human environment for present and future generations has become an imperative goal for mankind, a goal to be pursued together with, and in harmony with, the established and fundamental goals of peace and of worldwide economic and social development.

7. To achieve this environmental goal will demand the acceptance of responsibility by citizens and communities and by enterprises and institutions at every level, all sharing equitably in common efforts. Individuals in all walks of life as well as organizations in many fields, by their values and the sum of their actions, will shape the world environment of the future. Local and national governments will bear the greatest burden for large-scale environmental policy and action within their jurisdictions. International cooperation is also needed in order to raise resources to support the developing countries in carrying out their responsibilities in this field. A growing class of environmental problems, because they are regional or global in extent or because they affect the common international realm, will require extensive cooperation among nations and action by international organizations in the common interest. The Conference calls upon Governments and peoples to exert common efforts for the preservation and improvement of the human environment, for the benefit of all the people and for their posterity.

Principles

States the common conviction that:

Principle 1. Man has the fundamental right to freedom, equality and adequate conditions of life, in an environment of a quality that permits a life of dignity and well-being, and he bears a solemn responsibility to protect and improve the environment for present and future generations. In this respect, policies promoting or perpetuating apartheid, racial segregation, discrimination, colonial and other forms of oppression and foreign domination stand condemned and must be eliminated.

Principle 2. The natural resources of the earth, including the air, water, land, flora and fauna and especially representative samples of natural ecosystems, must be safeguarded for the benefit of present and future generations through careful planning or management, as appropriate.

Principle 3. The capacity of the earth to produce vital renewable resources must be maintained and, wherever practicable, restored or improved.

Principle 4. Man has a special responsibility to safeguard and wisely manage the heritage of wildlife and its habitat, which are now gravely imperilled by a combination of adverse factors. Nature conservation, including wildlife, must therefore receive importance in planning for economic development.

Principle 5. The non-renewable resources of the earth must be employed in such a way as to guard against the danger of their future exhaustion and to ensure that benefits from such employment are shared by all mankind.

Principle 6. The discharge of toxic substances or of other substances and the release of heat, in such quantities or concentrations as to exceed the capacity of the environment to render them harmless, must be halted in order to ensure that serious or irreversible damage is not inflicted upon ecosystems. The just struggle of the peoples of ill countries against pollution should be supported.

Principle 7. States shall take all possible steps to prevent pollution of the seas by substances that are liable to create hazards to human health, to harm living resources and marine life, to damage amenities or to interfere with other legitimate uses of the sea.

Principle 8. Economic and social development is essential for ensuring a favorable living and working environment for man and for creating conditions on earth that are necessary for the improvement of the quality of life.

Principle 9. Environmental deficiencies generated by the conditions of under-development and natural disasters pose grave problems and can best be remedied by accelerated development through the transfer of substantial quantities of financial and technological assistance as a supplement to the domestic effort of the developing countries and such timely assistance as may be required.

Principle 10. For the developing countries, stability of prices and adequate earnings for primary commodities and raw materials are essential to environmental management, since economic factors as well as ecological processes must be taken into account.

Principle 11. The environmental policies of all States should enhance and not adversely affect the present or future development potential of developing countries, nor should they hamper the attainment of better living conditions for all, and appropriate steps should be taken by States and international organizations with a view to reaching agreement on meeting the possible national and international economic consequences resulting from the application of environmental measures.

Principle 12. Resources should be made available to preserve and improve the environment, taking into account the circumstances and particular requirements of developing countries and any costs which may emanate from their incorporating environmental safeguards into their development planning and the need for making available to them, upon their request, additional international technical and financial assistance for this purpose.

Principle 13. In order to achieve a more rational management of resources and thus to improve the environment, States should adopt an integrated and coordinated approach to their development planning so as to ensure that development is compatible with the need to protect and improve environment for the benefit of their population.

Principle 14. Rational planning constitutes an essential tool for reconciling any conflict between the needs of development and the need to protect and improve the environment.

Principle 15. Planning must be applied to human settlements and urbanization with a view to avoiding adverse effects on the environment and obtaining maximum social, economic and environmental benefits for all. In this respect projects which arc designed for colonialist and racist domination must be abandoned.

Principle 16. Demographic policies which are without prejudice to basic human rights and which are deemed appropriate by Governments concerned should be applied in those regions where the rate of population growth or excessive population concentrations are likely to have adverse effects on the environment of the human environment and impede development.

Principle 17. Appropriate national institutions must be entrusted with the task of planning, managing or controlling the environmental resources of States with a view to enhancing environmental quality.

Principle 18. Science and technology, as part of their contribution to economic and social development, must be applied to the identification, avoidance and control of environmental risks and the solution of environmental problems and for the common good of mankind.

Principle 19. Education in environmental matters, for the younger generation as well as adults, giving due consideration to the underprivileged, is essential in order to broaden the basis for an enlightened opinion and responsible conduct by individuals, enterprises and communities in protecting and improving the environment in its full human dimension. It is also essential that mass media of communications avoid contributing to the deterioration of the environment, but, on the contrary, disseminates information of an educational nature on the need to project and improve the environment in order to enable mal to develop in every respect.

Principle 20. Scientific research and development in the context of environmental problems, both national and multinational, must be promoted in all countries, especially the developing countries. In this connection, the free flow of up-to-date scientific information and transfer of experience must be supported and assisted, to facilitate the solution of environmental problems; environmental technologies should be made available to developing countries on terms which would encourage their wide dissemination without constituting an economic burden on the developing countries.

Principle 21. States have, in accordance with the Charter of the United Nations and the principles of international law, the sovereign right to exploit their own resources pursuant to their own environmental policies, and the responsibility to ensure that activities within their jurisdiction or control do not cause damage to the environment of other States or of areas beyond the limits of national jurisdiction.

Principle 22. States shall cooperate to develop further the international law regarding liability and compensation for the victims of pollution and other environmental damage caused by activities within the jurisdiction or control of such States to areas beyond their jurisdiction.

Principle 23. Without prejudice to such criteria as may be agreed upon by the international community, or to standards which will have to be determined nationally, it will be essential in all cases to consider the systems of values prevailing in each country, and the extent of the applicability of standards which are valid for the most advanced countries but which may be inappropriate and of unwarranted social cost for the developing countries.

Principle 24. International matters concerning the protection and improvement of the environment should be handled in a cooperative spirit by all countries, big and small, on an equal footing. Cooperation through multilateral or bilateral arrangements or other appropriate means is essential to effectively control, prevent, reduce and eliminate adverse environmental effects resulting from activities conducted in all spheres, in such a way that due account is taken of the sovereignty and interests of all States.

Principle 25. States shall ensure that international organizations play a coordinated, efficient and dynamic role for the protection and improvement of the environment.

Principle 26. Man and his environment must be spared the effects of nuclear weapons and all other means of mass destruction. States must strive to reach prompt agreement, in the relevant international organs, on the elimination and complete destruction of such weapons.

Human Rights. Vienna Declaration and Programme of Action

(World Conference on Human Rights, 14-15 June 1993, Vienna, Austria. Vienna Declaration and Programme of Action, 15 June 1993. Preamble). The World Conference on Human Rights,

Considering that the promotion and protection of human rights is a matter of priority for the international community, and that the Conference affords a unique opportunity to carry out a comprehensive analysis of the international human rights system and of the machinery for the protection of human rights, in order to enhance and thus promote a fuller observance of those rights, in a just and balanced manner,

Recognizing and affirming that all human rights derive from the dignity and worth inherent in the human person, and that the human person is the central subject of human rights and fundamental freedoms, and consequently should be the principal beneficiary and should participate actively in the realization of these rights and freedoms,

Reaffirming their commitment to the purposes and principles contained in the Charter of the United Nations and the Universal Declaration of Human Rights,

Reaffirming the commitment contained in Article 56 of the Charter of the United Nations to take joint and separate action, placing proper emphasis on developing effective international cooperation for the realization of the purposes set out in Article 55, including universal respect for, and observance of, human rights and fundamental freedoms for all,

Emphasizing the responsibilities of all States, in conformity with the Charter of the United Nations, to develop and encourage respect for human rights and fundamental freedoms for all, without distinction as to race, sex, language or religion,

Recalling the Preamble to the Charter of the United Nations, in particular the determination to reaffirm faith in fundamental human rights, in the dignity and worth of the human person, and in the equal rights of men and women and of nations large and small,

Recalling also the determination expressed in the Preamble of the Charter of the United Nations to save succeeding generations from the scourge of war, to establish conditions under which justice and respect for obligations arising from treaties and other sources of international law can be maintained, to promote social progress and better standards of life in larger freedom, to practice tolerance and good neighbourliness, and to employ international machinery for the promotion of the economic and social advancement of all peoples,

Emphasizing that the Universal Declaration of Human Rights, which constitutes a common standard of achievement for all peoples and all nations, is the source of inspiration and has been the basis for the United Nations in making advances in standard setting as contained in the existing international human rights instruments, in particular the International Covenant on Civil and Political Rights and the International Covenant on Economic, Social and Cultural Rights,

Considering the major changes taking place on the international scene and the aspirations of all the peoples for an international order based on the principles enshrined in the Charter of the United Nations, including promoting and encouraging respect for human rights and fundamental freedoms for all and respect for the principle of equal rights and self-determination of peoples, peace, democracy, justice, equality, rule of law, pluralism, development, better standards of living and solidarity,

Deeply concerned by various forms of discrimination and violence, to which women continue to be exposed all over the world,

Recognizing that the activities of the United Nations in the field of human rights should be rationalized and enhanced in order to strengthen the United Nations machinery in this field and to further the objectives of universal respect for observance of international human rights standards,

Having taken into account the Declarations adopted by the three regional meetings at Tunis, San José and Bangkok and the contributions made by Governments, and bearing in mind the suggestions made by intergovernmental and non-governmental organizations, as well as the studies prepared by independent experts during the preparatory process leading to the World Conference on Human Rights,

Welcoming the International Year of the World's Indigenous People 1993 as a reaffirmation of the commitment of the international community to ensure their enjoyment of all human rights and fundamental freedoms and to respect the value and diversity of their cultures and identities,

Recognizing also that the international community should devise ways and means to remove the current obstacles and meet challenges to the full realization of all human rights and to prevent the continuation of human rights violations resulting therefrom throughout the world,

Invoking the spirit of our age and the realities of our time which call upon the peoples of the world and all States Members of the United Nations to rededicate themselves to the global task of promoting and protecting all human rights and fundamental freedoms so as to secure full and universal enjoyment of these rights,
Determined to take new steps forward in the commitment of the international community with a view to achieving substantial progress in human rights endeavours by an increased and sustained effort of international cooperation and solidarity,
Solemnly adopts the Vienna Declaration and Programme of Action. (...)

Human Settlements (*United Nations Conference on Human Settlements (Habitat II), Istanbul, Turkey, 3-14 June 1996. Istanbul Declaration on Human Settlements).*
1. We, the Heads of State or Government and the official delegations of countries assembled at the United Nations Conference on Human Settlements (Habitat II) in Istanbul, Turkey from 3 to 14 June 1996, take this opportunity to endorse the universal goals of ensuring adequate shelter for all and making human settlements safer, healthier and more liveable, equitable, sustainable and productive. Our deliberations on the two major themes of the Conference - adequate shelter for all and sustainable human settlements development in an urbanizing world - have been inspired by the Charter of the United Nations and are aimed at reaffirming existing and forging new partnerships for action at the international, national and local levels to improve our living environment. We commit ourselves to the objectives, principles and recommendations contained in the Habitat Agenda and pledge our mutual support for its implementation.
2. We have considered, with a sense of urgency, the continuing deterioration of conditions of shelter and human settlements. At the same time, we recognize cities and towns as centres of civilization, generating economic development and social, cultural, spiritual and scientific advancement. We must take advantage of the opportunities presented by our settlements and preserve their diversity to promote solidarity among all our peoples.
3. We reaffirm our commitment to better standards of living in larger freedom for all humankind. We recall the first United Nations Conference on Human Settlements, held at Vancouver, Canada, the celebration of the International Year of Shelter for the Homeless and the Global Strategy for Shelter to the Year 2000, all of which have contributed to increased global awareness of the problems of human settlements and called for action to achieve adequate shelter for all. Recent United Nations world conferences, including, in particular, the United Nations Conference on Environment and Development, have given us a comprehensive agenda for the equitable attainment of peace, justice and democracy built on economic development, social development and environmental protection as interdependent and mutually reinforcing components of sustainable development. We have sought to integrate the outcomes of these conferences into the Habitat Agenda.
4. To improve the quality of life within human settlements, we must combat the deterioration of conditions that in most cases, particularly in developing countries, have reached crisis proportions. To this end, we must address comprehensively, inter alia, unsustainable consumption and production patterns, particularly in industrialized countries; unsustainable population changes, including changes in

structure and distribution, giving priority consideration to the tendency towards excessive population concentration; homelessness; increasing poverty; unemployment; social exclusion; family instability; inadequate resources; lack of basic infrastructure and services; lack of adequate planning; growing insecurity and violence; environmental degradation; and increased vulnerability to disasters.

5. The challenges of human settlements are global, but countries and regions also face specific problems which need specific solutions. We recognize the need to intensify our efforts and cooperation to improve living conditions in the cities, towns and villages throughout the world, particularly in developing countries, where the situation is especially grave, and in countries with economies in transition. In this connection, we acknowledge that globalization of the world economy presents opportunities and challenges for the development process, as well as risks and uncertainties, and that achievement of the goals of the Habitat Agenda would be facilitated by, inter alia, positive actions on the issues of financing of development, external debt, international trade and transfer of technology. Our cities must be places where human beings lead fulfilling lives in dignity, good health, safety, happiness and hope.

6. Rural and urban development are interdependent. In addition to improving the urban habitat, we must also work to extend adequate infrastructure, public services and employment opportunities to rural areas in order to enhance their attractiveness, develop an integrated network of settlements and minimize rural-to-urban migration. Small- and medium-sized towns need special focus.

7. As human beings are at the centre of our concern for sustainable development, they are the basis for our actions as in implementing the Habitat Agenda. We recognize the particular needs of women, children and youth for safe, healthy and secure living conditions. We shall intensify our efforts to eradicate poverty and discrimination, to promote and protect all human rights and fundamental freedoms for all, and to provide for basic needs, such as education, nutrition and life-span health care services, and, especially, adequate shelter for all. To this end, we commit ourselves to improving the living conditions in human settlements in ways that are consonant with local needs and realities, and we acknowledge the need to address the global, economic, social and environmental trends to ensure the creation of better living environments for all people. We shall also ensure the full and equal participation of all women and men, and the effective participation of youth, in political, economic and social life. We shall promote full accessibility for people with disabilities, as well as gender equality in policies, programmes and projects for shelter and sustainable human settlements development. We make these commitments with particular reference to the more than one billion people living in absolute poverty and to the members of vulnerable and disadvantaged groups identified in the Habitat Agenda.

8. We reaffirm our commitment to the full and progressive realization of the right to adequate housing as provided for in international instruments. To that end, we shall seek the active participation of our public, private and non-governmental partners at all levels to ensure legal security of tenure, protection from discrimination and equal access to affordable, adequate housing for all persons and their families.

9. We shall work to expand the supply of affordable housing by enabling markets to perform efficiently and in a socially and environmentally responsible manner, enhancing access to land and credit and assisting those who are unable to participate in housing markets.

10. In order to sustain our global environment and improve the quality of living in our human
settlements, we commit ourselves to sustainable patterns of production, consumption, transportation and settlements development; pollution prevention; respect for the carrying capacity of ecosystems; and the preservation of opportunities for future generations. In this connection, we shall cooperate in a spirit of global partnership to conserve, protect and restore the health and integrity of the Earth's ecosystem. In view of different contributions to global environmental degradation, we reaffirm the principle that countries have common but differentiated responsibilities. We also recognize that we must take these actions in a manner consistent with the precautionary principle approach, which shall be widely applied according to the capabilities of countries. We shall also promote healthy living environments, especially through the provision of adequate quantities of safe water and effective management of waste.

11. We shall promote the conservation, rehabilitation and maintenance of buildings, monuments, open spaces, landscapes and settlement patterns of historical, cultural, architectural, natural, religious and spiritual value.

12. We adopt the enabling strategy and the principles of partnership and participation as the most democratic and effective approach for the realization of our commitments. Recognizing local authorities as our closest partners, and as essential, in the implementation of the Habitat Agenda, we must, within the legal framework of each country, promote decentralization through democratic local authorities and work to strengthen their financial and institutional capacities in accordance with the conditions of countries, while ensuring their transparency, accountability and responsiveness to the needs of people, which are key requirements for Governments at all levels. We shall also increase our cooperation with parliamentarians, the private sector, labour unions and non-governmental and other civil society organizations with due respect for their autonomy. We shall also enhance the role of women and encourage socially and environmentally responsible corporate investment by the private sector. Local action should be guided and stimulated through local programmes based on Agenda 21, the Habitat Agenda, or any other equivalent programme, as well as drawing upon the experience of worldwide cooperation initiated in Istanbul by the World Assembly of Cities and Local Authorities, without prejudice to national policies, objectives, priorities and programmes. The enabling strategy includes a responsibility for Governments to implement special measures for members of disadvantaged and vulnerable groups when appropriate.

13. As the implementation of the Habitat Agenda will require adequate funding, we must mobilize financial resources at the national and international levels, including new and additional resources from all sources - multilateral and bilateral, public and private. In this connection, we must facilitate capacitybuilding and promote the transfer of appropriate technology and know-how. Furthermore, we reiterate the

commitments set out in recent United Nations conferences, especially those in Agenda 21 on funding and technology transfer.

14. We believe that the full and effective implementation of the Habitat Agenda will require the strengthening of the role and functions of the United Nations Centre for Human Settlements (Habitat), taking into account the need for the Centre to focus on well-defined and thoroughly developed objectives and strategic issues. To this end, we pledge our support for the successful implementation of the Habitat Agenda and its global plan of action. Regarding the implementation of the Habitat Agenda, we fully recognize the contribution of the regional and national action plans prepared for this Conference.

15. This Conference in Istanbul marks a new era of cooperation, an era of a culture of solidarity. As we move into the twenty-first century, we offer a positive vision of sustainable human settlements, a sense of hope for our common future and an exhortation to join a truly worthwhile and engaging challenge, that of building together a world where everyone can live in a safe home with the promise of a decent life of dignity, good health, safety, happiness and hope.

I

Indictment *(Statute ICTY, art. 18. Investigation and preparation of indictment;
art. 19. Review of the indictment; art. 20. Commencement and conduct of trial
proceedings (See: RPE – ICTY, Part. 5. Pre-Trial proceedings, Section 1.
Indictments: Rule 47 Submission of Indictment by the Prosecutor; Rule 48 Joinder of
Accused; Rule 49 Joinder of Crimes; Rule 50 Amendment of Indictment; Rule 51
Withdrawal of Indictment; Rule 52 Public Character of Indictment; Rule 53 Non-
disclosure; Rule 53 bis Service of Indictment) – Statute ICTR, art. 17. Investigation
and Preparation of Indictment; art. 18. Review of the Indictment; art. 19.
Commencement and conduct of trial proceedings (See: RPE – ICTR, Part 5. Pre-
Trial Proceedings, Section 1. Indictments; Rule 47. Submission of Indictment by the
Prosecutor ; Rule 48. Joinder of Accused; Rule 48 bis. Joinder of Trials; Rule 49.
Joinder of Crimes; Rule 50. Amendment of Indictment; Rule 51. Withdrawal of
Indictment; Rule 52. Public Character of Indictment; Rule 53. Non-Disclosure; Rule
53 bis: Service of Indictment).*

Statute ICTY, art. 18. Investigation and preparation of indictment. 1. The Prosecutor
shall initiate investigations *ex-officio* or on the basis of information obtained from
any source, particularly from Governments, United Nations organs,
intergovernmental and non-governmental organizations. The Prosecutor shall assess
the information received or obtained and decide whether there is sufficient basis to
proceed.

2. The Prosecutor shall have the power to question suspects, victims and witnesses,
to collect evidence and to conduct on-site investigations. In carrying out these tasks,
the Prosecutor may, as appropriate, seek the assistance of the State authorities
concerned.

3. If questioned, the suspect shall be entitled to be assisted by counsel of his own
choice, including the right to have legal assistance assigned to him without payment
by him in any such case if he does not have sufficient means to pay for it, as well as
to necessary translation into and from a language he speaks and understands.

4. Upon a determination that a *prima facie* case exists, the Prosecutor shall prepare
an indictment containing a concise statement of the facts and the crime or crimes
with which the accused is charged under the Statute. The indictment shall be
transmitted to a judge of the Trial Chamber.

Art. 19. Review of the indictment. 1. The judge of the Trial Chamber to whom the
indictment has been transmitted shall review it. If satisfied that a *prima facie* case
has been established by the Prosecutor, he shall confirm the indictment. If not so
satisfied, the indictment shall be dismissed.

2. Upon confirmation of an indictment, the judge may, at the request of the
Prosecutor, issue such orders and warrants for the arrest, detention, surrender or

transfer of persons, and any other orders as may be required for the conduct of the trial.

Art. 20. Commencement and conduct of trial proceedings. 1. The Trial Chambers shall ensure that a trial is fair and expeditious and that proceedings are conducted in accordance with the rules of procedure and evidence, with full respect for the rights of the accused and due regard for the protection of victims and witnesses.

2. A person against whom an indictment has been confirmed shall, pursuant to an order or an arrest warrant of the International Tribunal, be taken into custody, immediately informed of the charges against him and transferred to the International Tribunal.

3. The Trial Chamber shall read the indictment, satisfy itself that the rights of the accused are respected, confirm that the accused understands the indictment, and instruct the accused to enter a plea. The Trial Chamber shall then set the date for trial.

4. The hearings shall be public unless the Trial Chamber decides to close the proceedings in accordance with its rules of procedure and evidence.

See: RPE – ICTY, Part. 5. Pre-Trial proceedings, Section 1. Indictments: Rule 47 Submission of Indictment by the Prosecutor; Rule 48 Joinder of Accused; Rule 49 Joinder of Crimes; Rule 50 Amendment of Indictment; Rule 51 Withdrawal of Indictment; Rule 52 Public Character of Indictment; Rule 53 Non-disclosure; Rule 53bis Service of Indictment.

Statute ICTR, art. 17. Investigation and preparation of indictment. 1. The Prosecutor shall initiate investigations ex-officio or on the basis of information obtained from any source, particularly from Governments, United Nations organs, intergovernmental and non-governmental organizations. The Prosecutor shall assess the information received or obtained and decide whether there is sufficient basis to proceed.

2. The Prosecutor shall have the power to question suspects, victims and witnesses, to collect evidence and to conduct on-site investigations. In carrying out these tasks, the Prosecutor may, as appropriate, seek the assistance of the State authorities concerned.

3. If questioned, the suspect shall be entitled to be assisted by counsel of his or her own choice, including the right to have legal assistance assigned to the suspect without payment by him or her in any such case if he or she does not have sufficient means to pay for it, as well as necessary translation into and from a language he or she speaks and understands.

4. Upon a determination that a prima facie case exists, the Prosecutor shall prepare an indictment containing a concise statement of the facts and the crime or crimes with which the accused is charged under the Statute. The indictment shall be transmitted to a judge of the Trial Chamber.

Art. 18. Review of the Indictment. 1. The judge of the Trial Chamber to whom the indictment has been transmitted shall review it. If satisfied that a prima facie case has been established by the Prosecutor, he or she shall confirm the indictment. If not so satisfied, the indictment shall be dismissed.

2. Upon confirmation of an indictment, the judge may, at the request of the Prosecutor, issue such orders and warrants for the arrest, detention, surrender or

transfer of persons, and any other orders as may be required for the conduct of the trial.

Art. 19. Commencement and conduct of trial proceedings. 1. The Trial Chambers shall ensure that a trial is fair and expeditious and that proceedings are conducted in accordance with the rules of procedure and evidence, with full respect for the rights of the accused with due regard for the protection of victims and witnesses.

2. A person against whom an indictment has been confirmed shall, pursuant to an order or an arrest warrant of the International Tribunal for Rwanda, be taken into custody, immediately informed of the charges against him or her and transferred to the International Tribunal for Rwanda.

3.The Trial Chamber shall read the indictment, satisfy itself that the rights of the accused are respected, confirm that the accused understands the indictment, and instruct the accused to enter a plea. The Trial Chamber shall then set the date for trial.

4. The hearings shall be public unless the Trial Chamber decides to close the proceedings in accordance with its rules of procedure and evidence.

See: RPE – ICTR, Part 5. Pre-Trial Proceedings, Section 1. Indictments; Rule 47. Submission of Indictment by the Prosecutor ; Rule 48. Joinder of Accused; Rule 48bis. Joinder of Trials; Rule 49. Joinder of Crimes; Rule 50. Amendment of Indictment; Rule 51. Withdrawal of Indictment; Rule 52. Public Character of Indictment; Rule 53. Non-Disclosure; Rule 53bis. Service of Indictment.

*See: Rome Statute ICC, **Part V. Investigation and prosecution:** Art. 53 Initiation of an investigation; Art. 54 Duties and powers of the Prosecutor with respect to investigations; Art. 55 Rights of persons during an investigation; Art. 56 Role of the Pre-Trial Chamber in relation to a unique investigative Opportunity; Art. 57 Functions and powers of the Pre-Trial Chamber; Art. 58 Issuance by the Pre-Trial Chamber of a warrant of arrest or a summons to appear; Art. 59 Arrest proceedings in the custodial State; Art. 60 Initial proceedings before the Court; Art. 61 Confirmation of the charges before trial; **RPE – ICC, Chapter 5. Investigation and prosecution.***

Indiscriminate attacks *(Protocol Additional to the Geneva Conventions of 12 August 1949, and relating to the Protection of Victims of International Armed Conflicts (Protocol I), 8 June 1977. Part. IV. Civilian Population. Section I. General Protection Against Effects of Hostilities. Chapter II. Civilians and civilian population. Art. 51. Protection of the civilian population).* (...) 4. Indiscriminate attacks are prohibited. Indiscriminate attacks are:

(a) those which are not directed at a specific military objective;

(b) those which employ a method or means of combat which cannot be directed at a specific military objective; or

(c) those which employ a method or means of combat the effects of which cannot be limited as required by this Protocol; and consequently, in each such case, are of a nature to strike military objectives and civilians or civilian objects without distinction.

5. Among others, the following types of attacks are to be considered as indiscriminate:

(a) an attack by bombardment by any methods or means which treats as a single military objective a number of clearly separated and distinct military objectives located in a city, town, village or other area containing a similar concentration of civilians or civilian objects; and

(b) an attack which may be expected to cause incidental loss of civilian life, injury to civilians, damage to civilian objects, or a combination thereof, which would be excessive in relation to the concrete and direct military advantage anticipated.

6. Attacks against the civilian population or civilians by way of reprisals are prohibited.

7. The presence or movements of the civilian population or individual civilians shall not be used to render certain points or areas immune from military operations, in particular in attempts to shield military objectives from attacks or to shield, favour or impede military operations. The Parties to the conflict shall not direct the movement of the civilian population or individual civilians in order to attempt to shield military objectives from attacks or to shield military operations.

8. Any violation of these prohibitions shall not release the Parties to the conflict from their legal obligations with respect to the civilian population and civilians, including the obligation to take the precautionary measures provided for in Article 57.

Inter-American Convention against terrorism *(AG/RES XXXII-0/02-Adopted at the second plenary session held on June 3, 2002). Preamble; Art. 1. Object and purposes (...)). Preamble. The States Parties to this Convention,*

Bearing in mind the purposes and principles of the Charter of the Organization of American States and the Charter of the United Nations;

Considering that terrorism represents a serious threat to democratic values and to international peace and security and is a cause of profound concern to all member states;

Reaffirming the need to adopt effective steps in the inter-American system to prevent, punish, and eliminate terrorism through the broadest cooperation;

Recognizing that the serious economic harm to states which may result from terrorist acts is one of the factors that underscore the need for cooperation and the urgency of efforts to eradicate terrorism;

Reaffirming the commitment of the states to prevent, combat, punish, and eliminate terrorism; and

Bearing in mind resolution RC.23/RES. 1/01 rev. 1 corr. 1, "Strengthening Hemispheric Cooperation to Prevent, Combat, and Eliminate Terrorism," adopted at the Twenty-third Meeting of Consultation of Ministers of Foreign Affairs,

Have agreed to the following:

Art. 1. Object and purposes. The purposes of this Convention are to prevent, punish, and eliminate terrorism. To that end, the states parties agree to adopt the necessary measures and to strengthen cooperation among them, in accordance with the terms of this Convention. (...)

Inter-American Court on Human Rights (Statute of the Inter-American Court on Human Rights. O.A.S. Res. 448, October 1979, La Paz, Bolivia. Chapter 1.

General provisions. Art. 1. Nature and Legal Organization; Art. 2. Jurisdiction; Art. 3. Seat; Chapter 2. Composition of the Court. Art. 4. Composition; Art. 5. Judicial Terms (…)).

Chapter 1. General provisions. Art. 1. Nature and Legal Organization. The Inter-American Court of Human Rights is an autonomous judicial institution whose purpose is the application and interpretation of the American Convention on Human Rights. The Court exercises its functions in accordance with the provisions of the aforementioned Convention and the present Statute.

Art. 2. Jurisdiction. The Court shall exercise adjudicatory and advisory jurisdiction:

1. Its adjudicatory jurisdiction shall be governed by the provisions of Articles 61, 62 and 63 of the Convention, and

2. Its advisory jurisdiction shall be governed by the provisions of Article 64 of the Convention.

Art. 3. Seat. 1. The seat of the Court shall be San Jose, Costa Rica; however, the Court may convene in any member state of the Organization of American States (OAS) when a majority of the Court considers it desirable, and with the prior consent of the State concerned.

2. The seat of the Court may be changed by a vote of two-thirds of the States Parties to the Convention, in the OAS General Assembly.

Chapter 2. Composition of the Court. Art. 4. Composition. 1. The Court shall consist of seven judges, nationals of the member states of the OAS, elected in an individual capacity from among jurists of the highest moral authority and of recognized competence in the field of human rights, who possess the qualifications required for the exercise of the highest judicial functions under the law of the State of which they are nationals or of the State that proposes them as candidates.

2. No two judges may be nationals of the same State.

Art. 5. Judicial Terms. 1. The judges of the Court shall be elected for a term of six years and may be reelected only once. A judge elected to replace a judge whose term has not expired shall complete that term.

2. The terms of office of the judges shall run from January 1 of the year following that of their election to December 31 of the year in which their terms expire.

3. The judges shall serve until the end of their terms. Nevertheless, they shall continue to hear the cases they have begun to hear and that are still pending, and shall not be replaced by the newly elected judges in the handling of those cases. (…)

International Convention for the Protection of All Persons from Enforced Disappearance. 20 December 2006.

Preamble. The States Parties to this Convention,

Considering the obligation of States under the Charter of the United Nations to promote universal respect for, and observance of, human rights and fundamental freedoms,

Having regard to the Universal Declaration of Human Rights,

Recalling the International Covenant on Economic, Social and Cultural Rights, the International Covenant on Civil and Political Rights and the other relevant international instruments in the fields of human rights, humanitarian law and international criminal law,

Also recalling the Declaration on the Protection of All Persons from Enforced Disappearance adopted by the General Assembly of the United Nations in its resolution 47/133 of 18 December 1992,

Aware of the extreme seriousness of enforced disappearance, which constitutes a crime and, in certain circumstances defined in international law, a crime against humanity,

Determined to prevent enforced disappearances and to combat impunity for the crime of enforced disappearance,

Considering the right of any person not to be subjected to enforced disappearance, the right of victims to justice and to reparation,

Affirming the right of any victim to know the truth about the circumstances of an enforced disappearance and the fate of the disappeared person, and the right to freedom to seek, receive and impart information to this end,

Have agreed on the following articles: (…).

International Convention on the Elimination of All Forms of Racial Discrimination *(Adopted and opened for signature and ratification by General Assembly resolution 2106 (XX) of 21 December 1965). Preamble.* The States Parties to this Convention,

Considering that the Charter of the United Nations is based on the principles of the dignity and equality inherent in all human beings, and that all Member States have pledged themselves to take joint and separate action, in co-operation with the Organization, for the achievement of one of the purposes of the United Nations which is to promote and encourage universal respect for and observance of human rights and fundamental freedoms for all, without distinction as to race, sex, language or religion,

Considering that the Universal Declaration of Human Rights proclaims that all human beings are born free and equal in dignity and rights and that everyone is entitled to all the rights and freedoms set out therein, without distinction of any kind, in particular as to race, colour or national origin,

Considering that all human beings are equal before the law and are entitled to equal protection of the law against any discrimination and against any incitement to discrimination,

Considering that the United Nations has condemned colonialism and all practices of segregation and discrimination associated therewith, in whatever form and wherever they exist, and that the Declaration on the Granting of Independence to Colonial Countries and Peoples of 14 December 1960 (General Assembly resolution 1514 (XV)) has affirmed and solemnly proclaimed the necessity of bringing them to a speedy and unconditional end,

Considering that the United Nations Declaration on the Elimination of All Forms of Racial Discrimination of 20 November 1963 (General Assembly resolution 1904 (XVIII)) solemnly affirms the necessity of speedily eliminating racial discrimination throughout the world in all its forms and manifestations and of securing understanding of and respect for the dignity of the human person,

Convinced that any doctrine of superiority based on racial differentiation is scientifically false, morally condemnable, socially unjust and dangerous, and that there is no justification for racial discrimination, in theory or in practice, anywhere,

Reaffirming that discrimination between human beings on the grounds of race, colour or ethnic origin is an obstacle to friendly and peaceful relations among nations and is capable of disturbing peace and security among peoples and the harmony of persons living side by side even within one and the same State,

Convinced that the existence of racial barriers is repugnant to the ideals of any human society,

Alarmed by manifestations of racial discrimination still in evidence in some areas of the world and by governmental policies based on racial superiority or hatred, such as policies of apartheid, segregation or separation,

Resolved to adopt all necessary measures for speedily eliminating racial discrimination in all its forms and manifestations, and to prevent and combat racist doctrines and practices in order to promote understanding between races and to build an international community free from all forms of racial segregation and racial discrimination,

Bearing in mind the Convention concerning Discrimination in respect of Employment and Occupation adopted by the International Labour Organisation in 1958, and the Convention against Discrimination in Education adopted by the United Nations Educational, Scientific and Cultural Organization in 1960,

Desiring to implement the principles embodied in the United Nations Declaration on the Elimination of All Forms of Racial Discrimination and to secure the earliest adoption of practical measures to that end,

Have agreed as follows: (…).

International Convention on the Protection of the Rights of All Migrant Workers and Members of their Families. Adopted by General Assembly resolution 45/158 of 18 December 1990.

Preamble. The States Parties to the present Convention,

Taking into account the principles embodied in the basic instruments of the United Nations concerning human rights, in particular the Universal Declaration of Human Rights, the International Covenant on Economic, Social and Cultural Rights, the International Covenant on Civil and Political Rights, the International Convention on the Elimination of All Forms of Racial Discrimination, the Convention on the Elimination of All Forms of Discrimination against Women and the Convention on the Rights of the Child,

Taking into account also the principles and standards set forth in the relevant instruments elaborated within the framework of the International Labour Organisation, especially the Convention concerning Migration for Employment (No. 97), the Convention concerning Migrations in Abusive Conditions and the Promotion of Equality of Opportunity and Treatment of Migrant Workers (No.143), the Recommendation concerning Migration for Employment (No. 86), the Recommendation concerning Migrant Workers (No.151), the Convention concerning Forced or Compulsory Labour (No. 29) and the Convention concerning Abolition of Forced Labour (No. 105),

Reaffirming the importance of the principles contained in the Convention against Discrimination in Education of the United Nations Educational, Scientific and Cultural Organization,

Recalling the Convention against Torture and Other Cruel, Inhuman or Degrading Treatment or Punishment, the Declaration of the Fourth United Nations Congress on the Prevention of Crime and the Treatment of Offenders, the Code of Conduct for Law Enforcement Officials, and the Slavery Conventions,

Recalling that one of the objectives of the International Labour Organisation, as stated in its Constitution, is the protection of the interests of workers when employed in countries other than their own, and bearing in mind the expertise and experience of that organization in matters related to migrant workers and members of their families,

Recognizing the importance of the work done in connection with migrant workers and members of their families in various organs of the United Nations, in particular in the Commission on Human Rights and the Commission for Social Development, and in the Food and Agriculture Organization of the United Nations, the United Nations Educational, Scientific and Cultural Organization and the World Health Organization, as well as in other international organizations,

Recognizing also the progress made by certain States on a regional or bilateral basis towards the protection of the rights of migrant workers and members of their families, as well as the importance and usefulness of bilateral and multilateral agreements in this field,

Realizing the importance and extent of the migration phenomenon, which involves millions of people and affects a large number of States in the international community,

Aware of the impact of the flows of migrant workers on States and people concerned, and desiring to establish norms which may contribute to the harmonization of the attitudes of States through the acceptance of basic principles concerning the treatment of migrant workers and members of their families,

Considering the situation of vulnerability in which migrant workers and members of their families frequently find themselves owing, among other things, to their absence from their State of origin and to the difficulties they may encounter arising from their presence in the State of employment,

Convinced that the rights of migrant workers and members of their families have not been sufficiently recognized everywhere and therefore require appropriate international protection,

Taking into account the fact that migration is often the cause of serious problems for the members of the families of migrant workers as well as for the workers themselves, in particular because of the scattering of the family,

Bearing in mind that the human problems involved in migration are even more serious in the case of irregular migration and convinced therefore that appropriate action should be encouraged in order to prevent and eliminate clandestine movements and trafficking in migrant workers, while at the same time assuring the protection of their fundamental human rights,

Considering that workers who are non-documented or in an irregular situation are frequently employed under less favourable conditions of work than other workers and that certain employers find this an inducement to seek such labour in order to reap the benefits of unfair competition,

Considering also that recourse to the employment of migrant workers who are in an irregular situation will be discouraged if the fundamental human rights of all migrant workers are more widely recognized and, moreover, that granting certain additional rights to migrant workers and members of their families in a regular situation will encourage all migrants and employers to respect and comply with the laws and procedures established by the States concerned,

Convinced, therefore, of the need to bring about the international protection of the rights of all migrant workers and members of their families, reaffirming and establishing basic norms in a comprehensive convention which could be applied universally,

Have agreed as follows: (…).

International Court of Justice – ICJ *(Charter of the United Nations, San Francisco, 26 June 1945, Chapter XIV. The International Court of Justice, Art. 92; Art. 93; Art. 94; Art. 95; Art. 96 – Statute ICJ, Art. 1; Chapter 1. Organization of the Court. Art. 2 (...); Chapter 2. Competence of the Court. Art. 34; Art. 35; Art. 36; Art. 37; Art. 38).*

Charter of the United Nations, San Francisco, 26 June 1945, Chapter XIV. The International Court of Justice, Art. 92. The International Court of Justice shall be the principal judicial organ of the United Nations. It shall function in accordance with the annexed Statute, which is based upon the Statute of the Permanent Court of International Justice and forms an integral part of the present Charter.

Art. 93. 1. All Members of the United Nations are *ipso facto* parties to the Statute of the International Court of Justice.

2. A state which is not a Member of the United Nations may become a party to the Statute of
the International Court of Justice on conditions to be determined in each case by the General Assembly upon the recommendation of the Security Council.

Art. 94. 1. Each Member of the United Nations undertakes to comply with the decision of the International Court of Justice in any case to which it is a party.

2. If any party to a case fails to perform the obligations incumbent upon it under a judgment rendered by the Court, the other party may have recourse to the Security Council, which may, if it deems necessary, make recommendations or decide upon measures to be taken to give effect to the judgment.

Art. 95. Nothing in the present Charter shall prevent Members of the United Nations from entrusting the solution of their differences to other tribunals by virtue of agreements already in existence or which may be concluded in the future.

Art. 96. 1. The General Assembly or the Security Council may request the International Court of Justice to give an advisory opinion on any legal question.

2. Other organs of the United Nations and specialized agencies, which may at any time be so authorized by the General Assembly, may also request advisory opinions of the Court on legal
questions arising within the scope of their activities.

Statute ICJ, Art. 1. The International Court of Justice established by the Charter of the United Nations as the principal judicial organ of the United Nations shall be constituted and shall function in accordance with the provisions of the present Statute.

Chapter 1. Organization of the Court. Art. 2. The Court shall be composed of a body of independent judges, elected regardless of their nationality from among persons of high moral character, who possess the qualifications required in their respective countries for appointment to the highest judicial offices, or are jurisconsults of recognized competence in international law. (...)

Chapter 2. Competence of the Court. Art. 34. 1. Only states may be parties in cases before the Court.

2. The Court, subject to and in conformity with its Rules, may request of public international organizations information relevant to cases before it, and shall receive such information presented by such organizations on their own initiative.

3. Whenever the construction of the constituent instrument of a public international organization or of an international convention adopted thereunder is in question in a case before the Court, the Registrar shall so notify the public international organization concerned and shall communicate to it copies of all the written proceedings.

Art. 35. 1. The Court shall be open to the states parties to the present Statute.

2. The conditions under which the Court shall be open to other states shall, subject to the special provisions contained in treaties in force, be laid down by the Security Council, but in no case shall such conditions place the parties in a position of inequality before the Court.

3. When a state which is not a Member of the United Nations is a party to a case, the Court shall fix the amount which that party is to contribute towards the expenses of the Court. This provision shall not apply if such state is bearing a share of the expenses of the Court.

Art. 36. 1. The jurisdiction of the Court comprises all cases which the parties refer to it and all matters specially provided for in the Charter of the United Nations or in treaties and conventions in force.

2. The states parties to the present Statute may at any time declare that they recognize as compulsory ipso facto and without special agreement, in relation to any other state accepting the same obligation, the jurisdiction of the Court in all legal disputes concerning:

a. the interpretation of a treaty;

b. any question of international law;

c. the existence of any fact which, if established, would constitute a breach of an international obligation;

d. the nature or extent of the reparation to be made for the breach of an international obligation.

3. The declarations referred to above may be made unconditionally or on condition of reciprocity on the part of several or certain states, or for a certain time.

4. Such declarations shall be deposited with the Secretary-General of the United Nations, who shall transmit copies thereof to the parties to the Statute and to the Registrar of the Court.

5. Declarations made under Article 36 of the Statute of the Permanent Court of International Justice and which are still in force shall be deemed, as between the

parties to the present Statute, to be acceptances of the compulsory jurisdiction of the International Court of Justice for the period which they still have to run and in accordance with their terms.

6. In the event of a dispute as to whether the Court has jurisdiction, the matter shall be settled by the decision of the Court.

Art. 37. Whenever a treaty or convention in force provides for reference of a matter to a tribunal to have been instituted by the League of Nations, or to the Permanent Court of International Justice, the matter shall, as between the parties to the present Statute, be referred to the International Court of Justice.

Art. 38. 1. The Court, whose function is to decide in accordance with international law such disputes as are submitted to it, shall apply:

a. international conventions, whether general or particular, establishing rules expressly recognized by the contesting states;

b. international custom, as evidence of a general practice accepted as law;

c. the general principles of law recognized by civilized nations;

d. subject to the provisions of Article 59, judicial decisions and the teachings of the most highly qualified publicists of the various nations, as subsidiary means for the determination of rules of law.

2. This provision shall not prejudice the power of the Court to decide a case *ex aequo et bono*, if the parties agree thereto.

See: Charter of the United Nations.

International Covenant on Civil and Political Rights. Adopted and opened for signature, ratification and accession by General Assembly resolution 2200A (XXI) of 16 December 1966 *(Preamble. Part. I., Art. 1. Part. II., Art. 2; Art. 3; Art. 4. Part. III., Art. 6; Art. 7; Art. 8). Preamble.* The States Parties to the present Covenant,

Considering that, in accordance with the principles proclaimed in the Charter of the United Nations, recognition of the inherent dignity and of the equal and inalienable rights of all members of the human family is the foundation of freedom, justice and peace in the world,

Recognizing that these rights derive from the inherent dignity of the human person,

Recognizing that, in accordance with the Universal Declaration of Human Rights, the ideal of free human beings enjoying civil and political freedom and freedom from fear and want can only be achieved if conditions are created whereby everyone may enjoy his civil and political rights, as well as his economic, social and cultural rights,

Considering the obligation of States under the Charter of the United Nations to promote universal respect for, and observance of, human rights and freedoms,

Realizing that the individual, having duties to other individuals and to the community to which he belongs, is under a responsibility to strive for the promotion and observance of the rights recognized in the present Covenant,

Agree upon the following articles:

Part. I., Art. 1. 1. All peoples have the right of self-determination. By virtue of that right they freely determine their political status and freely pursue their economic, social and cultural development.

2. All peoples may, for their own ends, freely dispose of their natural wealth and resources without prejudice to any obligations arising out of international economic

co-operation, based upon the principle of mutual benefit, and international law. In no case may a people be deprived of its own means of subsistence.

3. The States Parties to the present Covenant, including those having responsibility for the administration of Non-Self-Governing and Trust Territories, shall promote the realization of the right of self-determination, and shall respect that right, in conformity with the provisions of the Charter of the United Nations.

Part. II, Art. 2. 1. Each State Party to the present Covenant undertakes to respect and to ensure to all individuals within its territory and subject to its jurisdiction the rights recognized in the present Covenant, without distinction of any kind, such as race, colour, sex, language, religion, political or other opinion, national or social origin, property, birth or other status.

2. Where not already provided for by existing legislative or other measures, each State Party to the present Covenant undertakes to take the necessary steps, in accordance with its constitutional processes and with the provisions of the present Covenant, to adopt such laws or other measures as may be necessary to give effect to the rights recognized in the present Covenant.

3. Each State Party to the present Covenant undertakes:

(a) To ensure that any person whose rights or freedoms as herein recognized are violated shall have an effective remedy, notwithstanding that the violation has been committed by persons acting in an official capacity;

(b) To ensure that any person claiming such a remedy shall have his right thereto determined by competent judicial, administrative or legislative authorities, or by any other competent authority provided for by the legal system of the State, and to develop the possibilities of judicial remedy;

(c) To ensure that the competent authorities shall enforce such remedies when granted.

Art. 3. The States Parties to the present Covenant undertake to ensure the equal right of men and women to the enjoyment of all civil and political rights set forth in the present Covenant.

Art. 4. 1. In time of public emergency which threatens the life of the nation and the existence of which is officially proclaimed, the States Parties to the present Covenant may take measures derogating from their obligations under the present Covenant to the extent strictly required by the exigencies of the situation, provided that such measures are not inconsistent with their other obligations under international law and do not involve discrimination solely on the ground of race, colour, sex, language, religion or social origin.

2. No derogation from articles 6, 7, 8 (paragraphs I and 2), 11, 15, 16 and 18 may be made under this provision.

3. Any State Party to the present Covenant availing itself of the right of derogation shall immediately inform the other States Parties to the present Covenant, through the intermediary of the Secretary-General of the United Nations, of the provisions from which it has derogated and of the reasons by which it was actuated. A further communication shall be made, through the same intermediary, on the date on which it terminates such derogation. (…).

Part. III., Art. 6. 1. Every human being has the inherent right to life. This right shall be protected by law. No one shall be arbitrarily deprived of his life.

2. In countries which have not abolished the death penalty, sentence of death may be imposed only for the most serious crimes in accordance with the law in force at the time of the commission of the crime and not contrary to the provisions of the present Covenant and to the Convention on the Prevention and Punishment of the Crime of Genocide. This penalty can only be carried out pursuant to a final judgement rendered by a competent court.

3. When deprivation of life constitutes the crime of genocide, it is understood that nothing in this article shall authorize any State Party to the present Covenant to derogate in any way from any obligation assumed under the provisions of the Convention on the Prevention and Punishment of the Crime of Genocide.

4. Anyone sentenced to death shall have the right to seek pardon or commutation of the sentence. Amnesty, pardon or commutation of the sentence of death may be granted in all cases.

5. Sentence of death shall not be imposed for crimes committed by persons below eighteen years of age and shall not be carried out on pregnant women.

6. Nothing in this article shall be invoked to delay or to prevent the abolition of capital punishment by any State Party to the present Covenant.

Art. 7. No one shall be subjected to torture or to cruel, inhuman or degrading treatment or punishment. In particular, no one shall be subjected without his free consent to medical or scientific experimentation.

Art. 8. 1. No one shall be held in slavery; slavery and the slave-trade in all their forms shall be prohibited.

2. No one shall be held in servitude.

3. (a) No one shall be required to perform forced or compulsory labour;

(b) Paragraph 3 (a) shall not be held to preclude, in countries where imprisonment with hard labour may be imposed as a punishment for a crime, the performance of hard labour in pursuance of a sentence to such punishment by a competent court;

(c) For the purpose of this paragraph the term "forced or compulsory labour" shall not include:

(i) Any work or service, not referred to in subparagraph (b), normally required of a person who is under detention in consequence of a lawful order of a court, or of a person during conditional release from such detention;

(ii) Any service of a military character and, in countries where conscientious objection is recognized, any national service required by law of conscientious objectors;

(iii) Any service exacted in cases of emergency or calamity threatening the life or well-being of the community;

(iv) Any work or service which forms part of normal civil obligations. (...).

International Covenant on Economic, Social and Cultural Rights.

New York, **16 December 1966** (Preamble. Part. I. Art. 1. Part. II. Art. 2; Art. 3; Art. 4; Art. 5. Part. III. Art. 6; Art. 7; Art. 8; Art. 9; Art. 10; Art. 11; Art. 12; Art. 13; Art. 14; Art. 15. Part. IV. Art. 16 (...); Art. 23; Art. 24; Art. 25 (...)).

Preamble. The States Parties to the present Covenant,

Considering that, in accordance with the principles proclaimed in the Charter of the United Nations, recognition of the inherent dignity and of the equal and inalienable rights of all members of the human family is the foundation of freedom, justice and peace in the world,

Recognizing that these rights derive from the inherent dignity of the human person,

Recognizing that, in accordance with the Universal Declaration of Human Rights, the ideal of free human beings enjoying freedom from fear and want can only be achieved if conditions are created whereby everyone may enjoy his economic, social and cultural rights, as well as his civil and political rights,

Considering the obligation of States under the Charter of the United Nations to promote universal respect for, and observance of, human rights and freedoms,

Realizing that the individual, having duties to other individuals and to the community to which he belongs, is under a responsibility to strive for the promotion and observance of the rights recognized in the present Covenant,

Agree upon the following articles:

Part. I. Art. 1. 1. All peoples have the right of self-determination. By virtue of that right they freely determine their political status and freely pursue their economic, social and cultural development.

2. All peoples may, for their own ends, freely dispose of their natural wealth and resources without prejudice to any obligations arising out of international economic co-operation, based upon the principle of mutual benefit, and international law. In no case may a people be deprived of its own means of subsistence.

3. The States Parties to the present Covenant, including those having responsibility for the administration of Non-Self-Governing and Trust Territories, shall promote the realization of the right of self-determination, and shall respect that right, in conformity with the provisions of the Charter of the United Nations.

Part. II. Art. 2. 1. Each State Party to the present Covenant undertakes to take steps, individually and through international assistance and co-operation, especially economic and technical, to the maximum of its available resources, with a view to achieving progressively the full realization of the rights recognized in the present Covenant by all appropriate means, including particularly the adoption of legislative measures.

2. The States Parties to the present Covenant undertake to guarantee that the rights enunciated in the present Covenant will be exercised without discrimination of any kind as to race, colour, sex, language, religion, political or other opinion, national or social origin, property, birth or other status.

3. Developing countries, with due regard to human rights and their national economy, may determine to what extent they would guarantee the economic rights recognized in the present Covenant to non-nationals.

Art. 3. The States Parties to the present Covenant undertake to ensure the equal right of men and women to the enjoyment of all economic, social and cultural rights set forth in the present Covenant.

Art. 4. The States Parties to the present Covenant recognize that, in the enjoyment of those rights provided by the State in conformity with the present Covenant, the State may subject such rights only to such limitations as are determined by law only in so far as this may be compatible with the nature of these rights and solely for the purpose of promoting the general welfare in a democratic society.

Art. 5. 1. Nothing in the present Covenant may be interpreted as implying for any State, group or person any right to engage in any activity or to perform any act aimed at the destruction of any of the rights or freedoms recognized herein, or at their limitation to a greater extent than is provided for in the present Covenant.

2. No restriction upon or derogation from any of the fundamental human rights recognized or existing in any country in virtue of law, conventions, regulations or custom shall be admitted on the pretext that the present Covenant does not recognize such rights or that it recognizes them to a lesser extent.

Part. III. Art. 6. 1. The States Parties to the present Covenant recognize the right to work, which includes the right of everyone to the opportunity to gain his living by work which he freely chooses or accepts, and will take appropriate steps to safeguard this right.

2. The steps to be taken by a State Party to the present Covenant to achieve the full realization of this right shall include technical and vocational guidance and training programmes, policies and techniques to achieve steady economic, social and cultural development and full and productive employment under conditions safeguarding fundamental political and economic freedoms to the individual.

Art. 7. The States Parties to the present Covenant recognize the right of everyone to the enjoyment of just and favourable conditions of work which ensure, in particular:

(a) Remuneration which provides all workers, as a minimum, with:

(i) Fair wages and equal remuneration for work of equal value without distinction of any kind, in particular women being guaranteed conditions of work not inferior to those enjoyed by men, with equal pay for equal work;

(ii) A decent living for themselves and their families in accordance with the provisions of the present Covenant;

(b) Safe and healthy working conditions;

(c) Equal opportunity for everyone to be promoted in his employment to an appropriate higher level, subject to no considerations other than those of seniority and competence;

(d) Rest, leisure and reasonable limitation of working hours and periodic holidays with pay, as well as remuneration for public holidays.

Art. 8. 1. The States Parties to the present Covenant undertake to ensure:

(a) The right of everyone to form trade unions and join the trade union of his choice, subject only to the rules of the organization concerned, for the promotion and protection of his economic and social interests. No restrictions may be placed on the exercise of this right other than those prescribed by law and which are necessary in a democratic society in the interests of national security or public order or for the protection of the rights and freedoms of others; (b) The right of trade unions to establish national federations or confederations and the right of the latter to form or join international trade-union organizations;

(c) The right of trade unions to function freely subject to no limitations other than those prescribed by law and which are necessary in a democratic society in the interests of national security or public order or for the protection of the rights and freedoms of others;

(d) The right to strike, provided that it is exercised in conformity with the laws of the particular country.

2. This article shall not prevent the imposition of lawful restrictions on the exercise of these rights by members of the armed forces or of the police or of the administration of the State.

3. Nothing in this article shall authorize States Parties to the International Labour Organisation Convention of 1948 concerning Freedom of Association and Protection of the Right to Organize to take legislative measures which would prejudice, or apply the law in such a manner as would prejudice, the guarantees provided for in that Convention.

Art. 9. The States Parties to the present Covenant recognize the right of everyone to social security, including social insurance.

Art. 10. The States Parties to the present Covenant recognize that:

1. The widest possible protection and assistance should be accorded to the family, which is the natural and fundamental group unit of society, particularly for its establishment and while it is responsible for the care and education of dependent children. Marriage must be entered into with the free consent of the intending spouses.

2. Special protection should be accorded to mothers during a reasonable period before and after childbirth. During such period working mothers should be accorded paid leave or leave with adequate social security benefits.

3. Special measures of protection and assistance should be taken on behalf of all children and young persons without any discrimination for reasons of parentage or other conditions. Children and young persons should be protected from economic and social exploitation. Their employment in work harmful to their morals or health or dangerous to life or likely to hamper their normal development should be punishable by law. States should also set age limits below which the paid employment of child labour should be prohibited and punishable by law.

Art. 11. 1. The States Parties to the present Covenant recognize the right of everyone to an adequate standard of living for himself and his family, including adequate food, clothing and housing, and to the continuous improvement of living conditions. The States Parties will take appropriate steps to ensure the realization of this right, recognizing to this effect the essential importance of international co-operation based on free consent.

2. The States Parties to the present Covenant, recognizing the fundamental right of everyone to be free from hunger, shall take, individually and through international co-operation, the measures, including specific programmes, which are needed:

(a) To improve methods of production, conservation and distribution of food by making full use of technical and scientific knowledge, by disseminating knowledge of the principles of nutrition and by developing or reforming agrarian systems in such a way as to achieve the most efficient development and utilization of natural resources;

(b) Taking into account the problems of both food-importing and food-exporting countries, to ensure an equitable distribution of world food supplies in relation to need.

Art. 12. 1. The States Parties to the present Covenant recognize the right of everyone to the enjoyment of the highest attainable standard of physical and mental health.

2. The steps to be taken by the States Parties to the present Covenant to achieve the full realization of this right shall include those necessary for:

(a) The provision for the reduction of the stillbirth-rate and of infant mortality and for the healthy development of the child;

(b) The improvement of all aspects of environmental and industrial hygiene;

(c) The prevention, treatment and control of epidemic, endemic, occupational and other diseases;

(d) The creation of conditions which would assure to all medical service and medical attention in the event of sickness.

Art. 13. 1. The States Parties to the present Covenant recognize the right of everyone to education. They agree that education shall be directed to the full development of the human personality and the sense of its dignity, and shall strengthen the respect for human rights and fundamental freedoms. They further agree that education shall enable all persons to participate effectively in a free society, promote understanding, tolerance and friendship among all nations and all racial, ethnic or religious groups, and further the activities of the United Nations for the maintenance of peace.

2. The States Parties to the present Covenant recognize that, with a view to achieving the full realization of this right:

(a) Primary education shall be compulsory and available free to all;

(b) Secondary education in its different forms, including technical and vocational secondary education, shall be made generally available and accessible to all by every appropriate means, and in particular by the progressive introduction of free education;

(c) Higher education shall be made equally accessible to all, on the basis of capacity, by every appropriate means, and in particular by the progressive introduction of free education;

(d) Fundamental education shall be encouraged or intensified as far as possible for those persons who have not received or completed the whole period of their primary education;

(e) The development of a system of schools at all levels shall be actively pursued, an adequate fellowship system shall be established, and the material conditions of teaching staff shall be continuously improved.

3. The States Parties to the present Covenant undertake to have respect for the liberty of parents and, when applicable, legal guardians to choose for their children schools, other than those established by the public authorities, which conform to such minimum educational standards as may be laid down or approved by the State and to ensure the religious and moral education of their children in conformity with their own convictions.

4. No part of this article shall be construed so as to interfere with the liberty of individuals and bodies to establish and direct educational institutions, subject always to the observance of the principles set forth in paragraph I of this article and to the requirement that the education given in such institutions shall conform to such minimum standards as may be laid down by the State.

Art. 14. Each State Party to the present Covenant which, at the time of becoming a Party, has not been able to secure in its metropolitan territory or other territories under its jurisdiction compulsory primary education, free of charge, undertakes, within two years, to work out and adopt a detailed plan of action for the progressive implementation, within a reasonable number of years, to be fixed in the plan, of the principle of compulsory education free of charge for all.

Art. 15. 1. The States Parties to the present Covenant recognize the right of everyone:
(a) To take part in cultural life;
(b) To enjoy the benefits of scientific progress and its applications;
(c) To benefit from the protection of the moral and material interests resulting from any scientific, literary or artistic production of which he is the author.
2. The steps to be taken by the States Parties to the present Covenant to achieve the full realization of this right shall include those necessary for the conservation, the development and the diffusion of science and culture.
3. The States Parties to the present Covenant undertake to respect the freedom indispensable for scientific research and creative activity.
4. The States Parties to the present Covenant recognize the benefits to be derived from the encouragement and development of international contacts and co-operation in the scientific and cultural fields.

Part. IV. Art. 16. 1. The States Parties to the present Covenant undertake to submit in conformity with this part of the Covenant reports on the measures which they have adopted and the progress made in achieving the observance of the rights recognized herein.
2. (a) All reports shall be submitted to the Secretary-General of the United Nations, who shall transmit copies to the Economic and Social Council for consideration in accordance with the provisions of the present Covenant;
(b) The Secretary-General of the United Nations shall also transmit to the specialized agencies copies of the reports, or any relevant parts therefrom, from States Parties to the present Covenant which are also members of these specialized agencies in so far as these reports, or parts therefrom, relate to any matters which fall within the responsibilities of the said agencies in accordance with their constitutional instruments. (...).

Art. 23. The States Parties to the present Covenant agree that international action for the achievement of the rights recognized in the present Covenant includes such methods as the conclusion of conventions, the adoption of recommendations, the furnishing of technical assistance and the holding of regional meetings and technical meetings for the purpose of consultation and study organized in conjunction with the Governments concerned.

Art. 24. Nothing in the present Covenant shall be interpreted as impairing the provisions of the Charter of the United Nations and of the constitutions of the specialized agencies which define the respective responsibilities of the various organs of the United Nations and of the specialized agencies in regard to the matters dealt with in the present Covenant.

Art. 25. Nothing in the present Covenant shall be interpreted as impairing the inherent right of all peoples to enjoy and utilize fully and freely their natural wealth and resources. (...).

International Criminal Court – ICC. Text of the Rome Statute circulated as document A/CONF.183/9 of 17 July 1998 and corrected by process-verbaux of 10 November 1998, 12 July 1999, 30 November 1999, 8 May 2000, 17 January 2001 and 16 January 2002. The Statute entered into force on 1 July 2002 *(Preamble; Part I. Establishment of the Court. Art. 1. The Court; Art. 2. Relationship of the Court with the United Nations; Art. 3. Seat of the Court; Art. 4. Legal status and powers of the Court. Part II. Jurisdiction, admissibility and applicable law. Art. 5. Crimes within the jurisdiction of the Court; (...) Art. 11. Jurisdiction ratione temporis. (...) Art. 21. Applicable law. Part. III. General principles of Criminal Law. Art. 22. Nullum crimen sine lege; Art. 23. Nulla poena sine lege; Art. 24. Non-retroactivity ratione personae; Art. 25. Individual criminal responsibility; Art. 26. Exclusion of jurisdiction over persons under eighteen; Art. 27. Irrelevance of official capacity; Art. 28. Responsibility of commanders and other superiors; Art. 29. Non-applicability of statute of limitations. (...) Part. VII. Penalties. Art. 77. Applicable penalties). Preamble.* The States Parties to this Statute,

Conscious that all peoples are united by common bonds, their cultures pieced together in a shared heritage, and concerned that this delicate mosaic may be shattered at any time,

Mindful that during this century millions of children, women and men have been victims of unimaginable atrocities that deeply shock the conscience of humanity,

Recognizing that such grave crimes threaten the peace, security and well-being of the world,

Affirming that the most serious crimes of concern to the international community as a whole must not go unpunished and that their effective prosecution must be ensured by taking measures at the national level and by enhancing international cooperation,

Determined to put an end to impunity for the perpetrators of these crimes and thus to contribute to the prevention of such crimes,

Recalling that it is the duty of every State to exercise its criminal jurisdiction over those responsible for international crimes,

Reaffirming the Purposes and Principles of the Charter of the United Nations, and in particular that all States shall refrain from the threat or use of force against the territorial integrity or political independence of any State, or in any other manner inconsistent with the Purposes of the United Nations,

Emphasizing in this connection that nothing in this Statute shall be taken as authorizing any State Party to intervene in an armed conflict or in the internal affairs of any State,

Determined to these ends and for the sake of present and future generations, to establish an independent permanent International Criminal Court in relationship with the United Nations system, with jurisdiction over the most serious crimes of concern to the international community as a whole,

Emphasizing that the International Criminal Court established under this Statute shall be complementary to national criminal jurisdictions,

Resolved to guarantee lasting respect for and the enforcement of international justice,

Have agreed as follows:

Part I. Establishment of the Court. Art. 1. The Court. An International Criminal Court ('the Court') is hereby established. It shall be a permanent institution and shall have the power to exercise its jurisdiction over persons for the most serious crimes of international concern, as referred to in this Statute, and shall be complementary to national criminal jurisdictions. The jurisdiction and functioning of the Court shall be governed by the provisions of this Statute.

Art. 2. Relationship of the Court with the United Nations. The Court shall be brought into relationship with the United Nations through an agreement to be approved by the Assembly of States Parties to this Statute and thereafter concluded by the President of the Court on its behalf.

Art. 3. Seat of the Court. 1. The seat of the Court shall be established at The Hague in the Netherlands ('the host State').

2. The Court shall enter into a headquarters agreement with the host State, to be approved by the Assembly of States Parties and thereafter concluded by the President of the Court on its behalf.

3. The Court may sit elsewhere, whenever it considers it desirable, as provided in this Statute.

Art. 4. Legal status and powers of the Court. 1. The Court shall have international legal personality. It shall also have such legal capacity as may be necessary for the exercise of its functions and the fulfilment of its purposes.

2. The Court may exercise its functions and powers, as provided in this Statute, on the territory of any State Party and, by special agreement, on the territory of any other State.

Part II. Jurisdiction, admissibility and applicable law. Art. 5. Crimes within the jurisdiction of the Court. 1. The jurisdiction of the Court shall be limited to the most serious crimes of concern to the international community as a whole. The Court has jurisdiction in accordance with this Statute with respect to the following crimes:

(a) The crime of genocide;

(b) Crimes against humanity;

(c) War crimes;

(d) The crime of aggression.

2. The Court shall exercise jurisdiction over the crime of aggression once a provision is adopted in accordance with articles 121 and 123 defining the crime and setting out the conditions under which the Court shall exercise jurisdiction with respect to this crime. Such a provision shall be consistent with the relevant provisions of the Charter of the United Nations. (...)

Art. 11. Jurisdiction ratione temporis. 1. The Court has jurisdiction only with respect to crimes committed after the entry into force of this Statute.

2. If a State becomes a Party to this Statute after its entry into force, the Court may exercise its jurisdiction only with respect to crimes committed after the entry into force of this Statute for that State, unless that State has made a declaration under article 12, paragraph 3. (...)

Art. 21. Applicable law. 1. The Court shall apply:

(a) In the first place, this Statute, Elements of Crimes and its Rules of Procedure and Evidence;

(b) In the second place, where appropriate, applicable treaties and the principles and rules of international law, including the established principles of the international law of armed conflict;

(c) Failing that, general principles of law derived by the Court from national laws of legal systems of the world including, as appropriate, the national laws of States that would normally exercise jurisdiction over the crime, provided that those principles are not inconsistent with this Statute and with international law and internationally recognized norms and standards.

2. The Court may apply principles and rules of law as interpreted in its previous decisions.

3. The application and interpretation of law pursuant to this article must be consistent with internationally recognized human rights, and be without any adverse distinction founded on grounds such as gender as defined in article 7, paragraph 3, age, race, colour, language, religion or belief, political or other opinion, national, ethnic or social origin, wealth, birth or other status.

Part. III. General principles of Criminal Law

Art. 22. Nullum crimen sine lege. 1. A person shall not be criminally responsible under this Statute unless the conduct in question constitutes, at the time it takes place, a crime within the jurisdiction of the Court.

2. The definition of a crime shall be strictly construed and shall not be extended by analogy. In case of ambiguity, the definition shall be interpreted in favour of the person being investigated, prosecuted or convicted.

3. This article shall not affect the characterization of any conduct as criminal under international law independently of this Statute.

Art. 23. Nulla poena sine lege. A person convicted by the Court may be punished only in accordance with this Statute.

Art. 24. Non-retroactivity ratione personae. 1. No person shall be criminally responsible under this Statute for conduct prior to the entry into force of the Statute.

2. In the event of a change in the law applicable to a given case prior to a final judgement, the law more favourable to the person being investigated, prosecuted or convicted shall apply.

Art. 25. Individual criminal responsibility. 1. The Court shall have jurisdiction over natural persons pursuant to this Statute.

2. A person who commits a crime within the jurisdiction of the Court shall be individually responsible and liable for punishment in accordance with this Statute.

3. In accordance with this Statute, a person shall be criminally responsible and liable for punishment for a crime within the jurisdiction of the Court if that person:

(a) Commits such a crime, whether as an individual, jointly with another or through another person, regardless of whether that other person is criminally responsible;

(b) Orders, solicits or induces the commission of such a crime which in fact occurs or is attempted;

(c) For the purpose of facilitating the commission of such a crime, aids, abets or otherwise assists in its commission or its attempted commission, including providing the means for its commission;

(d) In any other way contributes to the commission or attempted commission of such a crime by a group of persons acting with a common purpose. Such contribution shall be intentional and shall either:

(i) Be made with the aim of furthering the criminal activity or criminal purpose of the group, where such activity or purpose involves the commission of a crime within the jurisdiction of the Court; or

(ii) Be made in the knowledge of the intention of the group to commit the crime;

(e) In respect of the crime of genocide, directly and publicly incites others to commit genocide;

(f) Attempts to commit such a crime by taking action that commences its execution by means of a substantial step, but the crime does not occur because of circumstances independent of the person's intentions. However, a person who abandons the effort to commit the crime or otherwise prevents the completion of the crime shall not be liable for punishment under this Statute for the attempt to commit that crime if that person completely and voluntarily gave up the criminal purpose.

4. No provision in this Statute relating to individual criminal responsibility shall affect the responsibility of States under international law.

Art. 26. Exclusion of jurisdiction over persons under eighteen. The Court shall have no jurisdiction over any person who was under the age of 18 at the time of the alleged commission of a crime.

Art. 27. Irrelevance of official capacity. 1. This Statute shall apply equally to all persons without any distinction based on official capacity. In particular, official capacity as a Head of State or Government, a member of a Government or parliament, an elected representative or a

government official shall in no case exempt a person from criminal responsibility under this Statute, nor shall it, in and of itself, constitute a ground for reduction of sentence.

2. Immunities or special procedural rules which may attach to the official capacity of a person, whether under national or international law, shall not bar the Court from exercising its jurisdiction over such a person.

Art. 28. Responsibility of commanders and other superiors. In addition to other grounds of criminal responsibility under this Statute for crimes within the jurisdiction of the Court:

(a) A military commander or person effectively acting as a military commander shall be criminally responsible for crimes within the jurisdiction of the Court committed by forces under his or her effective command and control, or effective authority and control as the case may be, as a result of his or her failure to exercise control properly over such forces, where:

(i) That military commander or person either knew or, owing to the circumstances at the time, should have known that the forces were committing or about to commit such crimes; and

(ii) That military commander or person failed to take all necessary and reasonable measures within his or her power to prevent or repress their commission or to submit the matter to the competent authorities for investigation and prosecution.

(b) With respect to superior and subordinate relationships not described in paragraph (a), a superior shall be criminally responsible for crimes within the jurisdiction of the Court committed by subordinates under his or her effective authority and control, as a result of his or her failure to exercise control properly over such subordinates, where:

(i) The superior either knew, or consciously disregarded information which clearly indicated, that the subordinates were committing or about to commit such crimes;

(ii) The crimes concerned activities that were within the effective responsibility and control of the superior; and

(iii) The superior failed to take all necessary and reasonable measures within his or her power to prevent or repress their commission or to submit the matter to the competent authorities for investigation and prosecution.

Art. 29. Non-applicability of statute of limitations.

The crimes within the jurisdiction of the Court shall not be subject to any statute of limitations. (...)

Part. VII. Penalties. Art. 77. Applicable penalties. 1. Subject to article 110, the Court may impose one of the following penalties on a person convicted of a crime referred to in article 5 of this Statute:

(a) Imprisonment for a specified number of years, which may not exceed a maximum of 30 years; or

(b) A term of life imprisonment when justified by the extreme gravity of the crime and the individual circumstances of the convicted person.

2. In addition to imprisonment, the Court may order:

(a) A fine under the criteria provided for in the Rules of Procedure and Evidence;

(b) A forfeiture of proceeds, property and assets derived directly or indirectly from that crime, without prejudice to the rights of bona fide third parties. (...)

International Military Tribunal. London Agreement (8 August 1945). Charter of the International Military Tribunal. *Prosecution and punishment of major war criminals of European Axis. Agreement signed at London August 8, 1945, with charter of the International Military Tribunal. Entered into force August 8, 1945. Discrepancy in article 6 of charter rectified by protocol of October 6, 1945. Agreement by the government of the United States of America, the Provisional Government of the French Republic, the Government of the United Kingdom of Great Britain and Northern Ireland and the Government of the Union of Soviet Socialist Republics for the prosecution and punishment of the major war criminals of the European axis.*

Whereas the United Nations have from time to time made declarations of their intention that War Criminals shall be brought to justice;

And whereas the Moscow Declaration of the 30th October 1943 on German atrocities in Occupied Europe stated that those German Officers and men and members of the Nazi Party who have been responsible for or have taken a consenting part in atrocities and crimes will be sent back to the countries in which their abominable deeds were done in order that they may be judged and punished according to the laws of these liberated countries and of the free Governments that will be created therein;

And whereas this Declaration was stated to be without prejudice to the case of major criminals whose offenses have no particular geographical location and who will be punished by the joint decision of the Governments of the Allies;

Now therefore the Government of the United States of America, the Provisional Government of the French Republic, the Government of the United Kingdom of Great Britain and Northern Ireland and the Government of the Union of Soviet Socialist Republics (hereinafter called "the Signatories") acting in the interests of all the United Nations and by their representatives duly authorized thereto have concluded this Agreement.

Art. 1. There shall be established after consultation with the Control Council for Germany an International Military Tribunal for the trial of war criminals whose offenses have no particular geographical location whether they be accused individually or in their capacity as members of organizations or groups or in both capacities.

Art. 2. The constitution, jurisdiction and functions of the International Military Tribunal shall be those set out in the Charter annexed to this Agreement, which Charter shall form an integral part of this Agreement. (...)

Charter of the International Military Tribunal. (...) II. Jurisdiction and general principles.

Art. 6. The Tribunal established by the Agreement referred to in Article 1 hereof for the trial and punishment of the major war criminals of the European Axis countries shall have the power to try and punish persons who, acting in the interests of the European Axis countries, whether as individuals or as members of organizations, committed any of the following crimes.

The following acts, or any of them, are crimes coming within the jurisdiction of the Tribunal for which there shall be individual responsibility:

(a) *Crimes against peace*: namely, planning, preparation, initiation or waging of a war of aggression, or a war in violation of international treaties, agreements or assurances, or participation in a common plan or conspiracy for the accomplishment of any of the foregoing;

(b) *War Crimes*: namely, violations of the laws or customs of war. Such violations shall include, but not be limited to, murder, ill-treatment or deportation to slave labor or for any other purpose of civilian population of or in occupied territory, murder or ill-treatment of prisoners of war or persons on the seas, killing of hostages, plunder of public or private property, wanton destruction of cities, towns or villages, or devastation not justified by military necessity;

(c) *Crimes against humanity*: namely, murder, extermination, enslavement, deportation, and other inhumane acts committed against any civilian population, before or during the war; or persecutions on political, racial or religious grounds in execution of or in connection with any crime within the jurisdiction of the Tribunal, whether or not in violation of the domestic law of the country where perpetrated.

Leaders, organizers, instigators and accomplices participating in the formulation or execution of a common plan or conspiracy to commit any of the foregoing crimes are responsible for all acts performed by any persons in execution of such plan.

Art. 7. The official position of defendants, whether as Heads of State or responsible officials in Government Departments, shall not be considered as freeing them from responsibility or mitigating punishment.

Art. 8. The fact that the Defendant acted pursuant to order of his Government or of a superior shall not free him from responsibility, but may be considered in mitigation of punishment if the Tribunal determines that justice so requires.

Art. 9. At the trial of any individual member of any group or organization the Tribunal may declare (in connection with any act of which the individual may be convicted) that the group or organization of which the individual was a member was a criminal organization.

After receipt of the Indictment the Tribunal shall give such notice as it thinks fit that the prosecution intends to ask the Tribunal to make such declaration and any member of the organization will be entitled to apply to the Tribunal for leave to be heard by the Tribunal upon the question of the criminal character of the organization. The Tribunal shall have power to allow or reject the application. If the application is allowed, the Tribunal may direct in what manner the applicants shall be represented and heard. (...)

"Itinerant worker" *(International Convention on the protection of the rights of all migrant workers and members of their families. Adopted by General Assembly resolution 45/158 of 18 December 1990. Part. I., Scope and Definitions, Art. 2).* For the purposes of the present Convention: 2.(e) The term "itinerant worker" refers to a migrant worker who, having his or her habitual residence in one State, has to travel to another State or States for short periods, owing to the nature of his or her occupation.

K

Kyoto Protocol to the United Nations Framework Convention on Climate Change. Kyoto, 11 December 1997 *(Preamble; Art. 1; Art. 3)*.

Preamble. The Parties to this Protocol,
Being Parties to the United Nations Framework Convention on Climate Change, hereinafter referred to as "the Convention",
In pursuit of the ultimate objective of the Convention as stated in its Article 2,
Recalling the provisions of the Convention,
Being guided by Article 3 of the Convention,
Pursuant to the Berlin Mandate adopted by decision 1/CP.1 of the Conference of the Parties to the Convention at its first session,
Have agreed as follows:
Art. 1. For the purposes of this Protocol, the definitions contained in Article 1 of the Convention shall apply. In addition:
1. "Conference of the Parties" means the Conference of the Parties to the Convention.
2. "Convention" means the United Nations Framework Convention on Climate Change, adopted in New York on 9 May 1992.
3. "Intergovernmental Panel on Climate Change" means the Intergovernmental Panel on Climate Change established in 1988 jointly by the World Meteorological Organization and the United Nations Environment Programme.
4. "Montreal Protocol" means the Montreal Protocol on Substances that Deplete the Ozone Layer, adopted in Montreal on 16 September 1987 and as subsequently adjusted and amended.
5. "Parties present and voting" means Parties present and casting an affirmative or negative vote.
6. "Party" means, unless the context otherwise indicates, a Party to this Protocol.
7. "Party included in Annex I" means a Party included in Annex I to the Convention, as may be amended, or a Party which has made a notification under Article 4, paragraph 2 (g), of the Convention.
(...)
Art. 3. 1. The Parties included in Annex I shall, individually or jointly, ensure that their aggregate anthropogenic carbon dioxide equivalent emissions of the greenhouse gases listed in Annex A do not exceed their assigned amounts, calculated pursuant to their quantified emission limitation and reduction commitments inscribed in Annex B and in accordance with the provisions of this Article, with a view to reducing their overall emissions of such gases by at least 5 per cent below 1990 levels in the commitment period 2008 to 2012.

2. Each Party included in Annex I shall, by 2005, have made demonstrable progress in achieving its commitments under this Protocol.

3. The net changes in greenhouse gas emissions by sources and removals by sinks resulting from direct human-induced land-use change and forestry activities, limited to afforestation, reforestation and deforestation since 1990, measured as verifiable changes in carbon stocks in each commitment period, shall be used to meet the commitments under this Article of each Party included in Annex I. The greenhouse gas emissions by sources and removals by sinks associated with those activities shall be reported in a transparent and verifiable manner and reviewed in accordance with Articles 7 and 8.

4. Prior to the first session of the Conference of the Parties serving as the meeting of the Parties to this Protocol, each Party included in Annex I shall provide, for consideration by the Subsidiary Body for Scientific and Technological Advice, data to establish its level of carbon stocks in 1990 and to enable an estimate to be made of its changes in carbon stocks in subsequent years. The Conference of the Parties serving as the meeting of the Parties to this Protocol shall, at its first session or as soon as practicable thereafter, decide upon modalities, rules and guidelines as to how, and which, additional human-induced activities related to changes in greenhouse gas emissions by sources and removals by sinks in the agricultural soils and the land-use change and forestry categories shall be added to, or subtracted from, the
assigned amounts for Parties included in Annex I, taking into account uncertainties, transparency in reporting, verifiability, the methodological work of the Intergovernmental Panel on Climate Change, the advice provided by the Subsidiary Body for Scientific and Technological Advice in accordance with Article 5 and the decisions of the Conference of the Parties. Such a decision shall apply in the second and subsequent commitment periods. A Party may choose to apply such a decision on these additional human-induced activities for its first commitment period, provided that these activities have taken place since 1990.

5. The Parties included in Annex I undergoing the process of transition to a market economy whose base year or period was established pursuant to decision 9/CP.2 of the Conference of the Parties at its second session shall use that base year or period for the implementation of their commitments under this Article. Any other Party included in Annex I undergoing the process of transition to a market economy which has not yet submitted its first national communication under Article 12 of the Convention may also notify the Conference of the Parties serving as the meeting of the Parties to this Protocol that it intends to use an historical base year or period other than 1990 for the implementation of its commitments under this Article. The Conference of the Parties serving as the meeting of the Parties to this Protocol shall decide on the acceptance of such notification.

6. Taking into account Article 4, paragraph 6, of the Convention, in the implementation of their commitments under this Protocol other than those under this Article, a certain degree of flexibility shall be allowed by the Conference of the Parties serving as the meeting of the Parties to this Protocol to the Parties included in Annex I undergoing the process of transition to a market economy.

7. In the first quantified emission limitation and reduction commitment period, from 2008 to 2012, the assigned amount for each Party included in Annex I shall be equal to the percentage

inscribed for it in Annex B of its aggregate anthropogenic carbon dioxide equivalent emissions of the greenhouse gases listed in Annex A in 1990, or the base year or period determined in accordance with paragraph 5 above, multiplied by five. Those Parties included in Annex I for whom land-use change and forestry constituted a net source of greenhouse gas emissions in 1990 shall include in their 1990 emissions base year or period the aggregate anthropogenic carbon dioxide equivalent emissions by sources minus removals by sinks in 1990 from land-use change for the purposes of calculating their assigned amount.

8. Any Party included in Annex I may use 1995 as its base year for hydrofluorocarbons, perfluorocarbons and sulphur hexafluoride, for the purposes of the calculation referred to in paragraph 7 above.

9. Commitments for subsequent periods for Parties included in Annex I shall be established in amendments to Annex B to this Protocol, which shall be adopted in accordance with the provisions of Article 21, paragraph 7. The Conference of the Parties serving as the meeting of

the Parties to this Protocol shall initiate the consideration of such commitments at least seven years before the end of the first commitment period referred to in paragraph 1 above.

10. Any emission reduction units, or any part of an assigned amount, which a Party acquires from another Party in accordance with the provisions of Article 6 or of Article 17 shall be added to the assigned amount for the acquiring Party.

11. Any emission reduction units, or any part of an assigned amount, which a Party transfers to another Party in accordance with the provisions of Article 6 or of Article 17 shall be subtracted from the assigned amount for the transferring Party.

12. Any certified emission reductions which a Party acquires from another Party in accordance with the provisions of Article 12 shall be added to the assigned amount for the acquiring Party.

13. If the emissions of a Party included in Annex I in a commitment period are less than its assigned amount under this Article, this difference shall, on request of that Party, be added to the assigned amount for that Party for subsequent commitment periods.

14. Each Party included in Annex I shall strive to implement the commitments mentioned in paragraph 1 above in such a way as to minimize adverse social, environmental and economic impacts on developing country Parties, particularly those identified in Article 4, paragraphs 8 and 9, of the Convention. In line with relevant decisions of the Conference of the Parties on the implementation of those paragraphs, the Conference of the Parties serving as the meeting of the Parties to this Protocol shall, at its first session, consider what actions are necessary to minimize the adverse effects of climate change and/or the impacts of response measures on Parties referred to in those paragraphs. Among the issues to be considered shall be the establishment of funding, insurance and transfer of technology.

(...)

M

"Medical aircraft" *(Protocol Additional to the Geneva Conventions of 12 August 1949, and relating to the Protection of Victims of International Armed Conflicts (Protocol I), 8 June 1977. Part. II. Wounded, sick and shipwrecked, Section I: General Protection. Art. 8. Terminology).* For the purposes of this Protocol: (…) j) "Medical aircraft" means any medical transports by air.

"Medical personnel" *(Protocol Additional to the Geneva Conventions of 12 August 1949, and relating to the Protection of Victims of International Armed Conflicts (Protocol I), 8 June 1977. Part. II. Wounded, sick and shipwrecked, Section I: General Protection. Art. 8. Terminology).* For the purposes of this Protocol: (…) c) "Medical personnel" means those persons assigned, by a Party to the conflict, exclusively to the medical purposes enumerated under e) or to the administration of medical units or to the operation or administration of medical transports. Such assignments may be either permanent or temporary. The term includes:
i) medical personnel of a Party to the conflict, whether military or civilian, including those described in the First and Second Conventions, and those assigned to civil defence organizations;
ii) medical personnel of national Red Cross (Red Crescent, Red Lion and Sun) Societies and other national voluntary aid societies duly recognized and authorized by a Party to the conflict;
iii) medical personnel or medical units or medical transports described in Article 9, paragraph 2.
Art. 9. Field of application (...). 2. The relevant provisions of Articles 27 and 32 of the First Convention shall apply to permanent medical units and transports (other than hospital ships, to which Article 25 of the Second Convention applies) and their personnel made available to a Party to the conflict for humanitarian purposes:
(a) by a neutral or other State which is not a Party to that conflict;
(b) by a recognized and authorized aid society of such a State;
(c) by an impartial international humanitarian organization.
"Permanent medical personnel", "permanent medical units" and "permanent medical transports"; "Temporary medical personnel" "temporary medical-units" and "temporary medical transports" *(Protocol Additional to the Geneva Conventions of 12 August 1949, and relating to the Protection of Victims of International Armed Conflicts (Protocol I), 8 June 1977. Part. II. Wounded, sick and shipwrecked, Section I: General Protection. Art. 8. Terminology).* For the purposes of this Protocol: (…) k) "Permanent medical personnel", "permanent medical units" and "permanent medical transports" mean those assigned exclusively to medical

129

purposes for an indeterminate period. "Temporary medical personnel" "temporary medical-units" and "temporary medical transports" mean those devoted exclusively to medical purposes for limited periods during the whole of such periods. Unless otherwise specified, the terms "medical personnel", "medical units" and "medical transports" cover both permanent and temporary categories.

"Medical ships and craft" *(Protocol Additional to the Geneva Conventions of 12 August 1949, and relating to the Protection of Victims of International Armed Conflicts (Protocol I), 8 June 1977. Part. II. Wounded, sick and shipwrecked, Section I: General Protection. Art. 8. Terminology).* For the purposes of this Protocol: (…) i) "Medical ships and craft" means any medical transports by water.

"Medical transportation" *(Protocol Additional to the Geneva Conventions of 12 August 1949, and relating to the Protection of Victims of International Armed Conflicts (Protocol I), 8 June 1977. Part. II. Wounded, sick and shipwrecked, Section I: General Protection. Art. 8. Terminology).* For the purposes of this Protocol: (…) f) "Medical transportation" means the conveyance by land, water or air of the wounded, sick, shipwrecked, medical personnel, religious personnel, medical equipment or medical supplies protected by the Conventions and by this Protocol.

"Medical transports" *(Protocol Additional to the Geneva Conventions of 12 August 1949, and relating to the Protection of Victims of International Armed Conflicts (Protocol I), 8 June 1977. Part. II. Wounded, sick and shipwrecked, Section I: General Protection. Art. 8. Terminology).* For the purposes of this Protocol: (…) g) "Medical transports" means any means of transportation, whether military or civilian, permanent or temporary, assigned exclusively to medical transportation and under the control of a competent authority of a Party to the conflict.

"Medical units" *(Protocol Additional to the Geneva Conventions of 12 August 1949, and relating to the Protection of Victims of International Armed Conflicts (Protocol I), 8 June 1977. Part. II. Wounded, sick and shipwrecked, Section I: General Protection. Art. 8. Terminology).* For the purposes of this Protocol: (…) e) "Medical units" means establishments and other units, whether military or civilian, organized for medical purposes, namely the search for, collection, transportation, diagnosis or treatment - including first-aid treatment - of the wounded, sick and shipwrecked, or for the prevention of disease. The term includes for example, hospitals and other similar units, blood transfusion centres, preventive medicine centres and institutes, medical depots and the medical and pharmaceutical stores of such units. Medical units may be fixed or mobile, permanent or temporary.

"Medical vehicles" *(Protocol Additional to the Geneva Conventions of 12 August 1949, and relating to the Protection of Victims of International Armed Conflicts (Protocol I), 8 June 1977. Part. II. Wounded, sick and shipwrecked,*

Section I: General Protection. Art. 8. Terminology). For the purposes of this Protocol: (…) h) "Medical vehicles" means any medical transports by land.

"Members of the family" (International Convention on the protection of the rights of all migrant workers and members of their families. Adopted by General Assembly resolution 45/158 of 18 December 1990. Part. I., Scope and Definitions, Art. 4). For the purposes of the present Convention the term "members of the family" refers to persons married to migrant workers or having with them a relationship that, according to applicable law, produces effects equivalent to marriage, as well as their dependent children and other dependent persons who are recognized as members of the family by applicable legislation or applicable bilateral or multilateral agreements between the States concerned.

Mercenaries (Protocol Additional to the Geneva Conventions of 12 August 1949, and relating to the Protection of Victims of International Armed Conflicts (Protocol I), 8 June 1977. Part. III. Methods and Means of Warfare. Combatant and Prisoners-Of-War. Section II. Combatants and Prisoners of War. Art. 47. Mercenaries). 1. A mercenary shall not have the right to be a combatant or a prisoner of war.
2. A mercenary is any person who:
(a) is specially recruited locally or abroad in order to fight in an armed conflict;
(b) does, in fact, take a direct part in the hostilities;
(c) is motivated to take part in the hostilities essentially by the desire for private gain and, in fact, is promised, by or on behalf of a Party to the conflict, material compensation substantially in excess of that promised or paid to combatants of similar ranks and functions in the armed forces of that Party;
(d) is neither a national of a Party to the conflict nor a resident of territory controlled by a Party to the conflict;
(e) is not a member of the armed forces of a Party to the conflict; and
(f) has not been sent by a State which is not a Party to the conflict on official duty as a member of its armed forces.

"Migrant worker" (International Convention on the protection of the rights of all migrant workers and members of their families. Adopted by General Assembly resolution 45/158 of 18 December 1990. Part. I., Scope and Definitions, Art. 2). For the purposes of the present Convention: 1. The term "migrant worker" refers to a person who is to be engaged, is engaged or has been engaged in a remunerated activity in a State of which he or she is not a national.

Misconduct of a less serious nature *(Rome Statute ICC, Part 4. Composition and organization of the Court, art. 47. Disciplinary measures - RPE – ICC, Chapter 2. Composition and administration of the Court, Section 4. Situations that may affect the functioning of the Court, Subsection 1. Removal from office and disciplinary measures, Rule 23. General principle, Rule 25. Definition of misconduct of a less serious nature).*
Rome Statute ICC, Part 4. Composition and organization of the Court, art. 47. Disciplinary measures. A judge, Prosecutor, Deputy Prosecutor, Registrar or Deputy

Registrar who has committed misconduct of a less serious nature than that set out in article 46, paragraph 1, shall be subject to disciplinary measures, in accordance with the Rules of Procedure and Evidence.

RPE – ICC, Chapter 2. Composition and administration of the Court, Section 4. Situations that may affect the functioning of the Court, Subsection 1. Removal from office and disciplinary measures, Rule 23. General principle. A judge, the Prosecutor, a Deputy Prosecutor, the Registrar and a Deputy Registrar shall be removed from office or shall be subject to disciplinary measures in such cases and with such guarantees as are established in the Statute and the Rules.

Rule 25. Definition of misconduct of a less serious nature. 1. For the purposes of article 47, 'misconduct of a less serious nature' shall be constituted by conduct that:

(a) If it occurs in the course of official duties, causes or is likely to cause harm to the proper administration of justice before the Court or the proper internal functioning of the Court, such as:

(i) Interfering in the exercise of the functions of a person referred to in article 47;

(ii) Repeatedly failing to comply with or ignoring requests made by the Presiding Judge or by the Presidency in the exercise of their lawful authority;

(iii) Failing to enforce the disciplinary measures to which the Registrar or a Deputy Registrar and other officers of the Court are subject when a judge knows or should know of a serious breach of duty on their part; or

(b) If it occurs outside the course of official duties, causes or is likely to cause harm to the standing of the Court.

2. Nothing in this rule precludes the possibility of the conduct set out in sub-rule 1 (a) constituting 'serious misconduct' or "serious breach of duty' for the purposes of article 46, paragraph 1 (a).

N

NEPAD – New partnership for Africa's Development. Abuja, Nigeria, October 2001. Original document. (…) *I. Introduction.* 1. This *New Partnership for Africa's Development* is a pledge by African leaders, based on a common vision and a firm and shared conviction, that they have a pressing duty to eradicate poverty and to place their countries, both individually and collectively, on a path of sustainable growth and development and, at the same time, to participate actively in the world economy and body politic. The Programme is anchored on the determination of Africans to extricate themselves and the continent from the malaise of underdevelopment and exclusion in a globalising world.

2. The poverty and backwardness of Africa stand in stark contrast to the prosperity of the developed world. The continued marginalisation of Africa from the globalization process and the social exclusion of the vast majority of its peoples constitute a serious threat to global stability.

3. Historically accession to the institutions of the international community, the credit and aid binomial has underlined the logic of African development. Credit has led to the debt deadlock which, from instalments to rescheduling, still exists and hinders the growth of African countries. The limits of this option have been reached. Concerning the other element of the binomial, aid, we can also note the reduction of private aid and the upper limit of public aid, which is below the target set in the 1970s.

4. In Africa, 340 million people, or half the population, live on less than US $1 per day. The mortality rate of children under 5 years of age is 140 per 1000, and life expectancy at birth is only 54 years. Only 58 per cent of the population have access to safe water. The rate of illiteracy for people over 15 is 41 per cent. There are only 18 mainline telephones per 1000 people in Africa, compared with 146 for the world as a whole and 567 for high-income countries.

5. The *New Partnership for Africa's Development* calls for the reversal of this abnormal situation by changing the relationship that underpins it. Africans are appealing neither for the further entrenchment of dependency through aid, nor for marginal concessions.

6. We are convinced that an historic opportunity presents itself to end the scourge of underdevelopment that afflicts Africa. The resources, including capital, technology and human skills, that are required to launch a global war on poverty and underdevelopment exist in abundance and are within our reach. What is required to mobilise these resources and to use them properly, is bold and imaginative leadership that is genuinely committed to a sustained human development effort and the eradication of poverty, as well as a new global partnership based on shared responsibility and mutual interest.

7. Across the continent, Africans declare that we will no longer allow ourselves to be conditioned by circumstance. We will determine our own destiny and call on the rest of the world to complement our efforts. There are already signs of progress and hope. Democratic regimes that are committed to the protection of human rights, peoplecentred development and market-oriented economies are on the increase. African peoples have begun to demonstrate their refusal to accept poor economic and political leadership. These developments are, however, uneven and inadequate and need to be further expedited.

8. The *New Partnership for Africa's Development* is about consolidating and accelerating these gains. It is a call for a new relationship of partnership between Africa and the international community, especially the highly industrialised countries, to overcome the development chasm that has widened over centuries of unequal relations. (...)

Non-defended localities *(Protocol Additional to the Geneva Conventions of 12 August 1949, and relating to the Protection of Victims of International Armed Conflicts (Protocol I), 8 June 1977. Part. IV. Civilian Population. Section I. General Protection Against Effects of Hostilities. Chapter V. Localities and zones under special protection. Art. 59. Non-defended localities).* 1. It is prohibited for the Parties to the conflict to attack, by any means whatsoever, non-defended localities.

2. The appropriate authorities of a Party to the conflict may declare as a non-defended locality any inhabited place near or in a zone where armed forces are in contact which is open for occupation by an adverse Party. Such a locality shall fulfil the following conditions:

(a) all combatants, as well as mobile weapons and mobile military equipment must have been evacuated;

(b) no hostile use shall be made of fixed military installations or establishments;

(c) no acts of hostility shall be committed by the authorities or by the population; and

(d) no activities in support of military operations shall be undertaken.

3. The presence, in this locality, of persons specially protected under the Conventions and this Protocol, and of police forces retained for the sole purpose of maintaining law and order, is not contrary to the conditions laid down in paragraph 2.

4. The declaration made under paragraph 2 shall be addressed to the adverse Party and shall define and describe, as precisely as possible, the limits of the non-defended locality. The Party to the conflict to which the declaration is addressed shall acknowledge its receipt and shall treat the locality as a non-defended locality unless the conditions laid down in paragraph 2 are not in fact fulfilled, in which event it shall immediately so inform the Party making the declaration. Even if the conditions laid down in paragraph 2 are not fulfilled, the locality shall continue to enjoy the protection provided by the other provisions of this Protocol and the other rules of international law applicable in armed conflict.

5. The Parties to the conflict may agree on the establishment of non-defended localities even if such localities do not fulfil the conditions laid down in paragraph 2. The agreement should define and describe, as precisely as possible, the limits of the non-defended locality; if necessary, it may lay down the methods of supervision.

6. The Party which is in control of a locality governed by such an agreement shall mark it, so far as possible, by such signs as may be agreed upon with the other Party, which shall be displayed where they are clearly visible, especially on its perimeter and limits and on highways.

7. A locality loses its status as a non-defended locality when its ceases to fulfil the conditions laid down in paragraph 2 or in the agreement referred to in paragraph 5. In such an eventuality, the locality shall continue to enjoy the protection provided by the other provisions of this Protocol and the other rules of international law applicable in armed conflict.

O

Objects indispensable to the survival of the civilian population

(Protocol Additional to the Geneva Conventions of 12 August 1949, and relating to the Protection of Victims of International Armed Conflicts (Protocol I), 8 June 1977. Part. IV. Civilian Population. Section I. General Protection Against Effects of Hostilities. Chapter III. Civilian objects. Art. 54. Protection of objects indispensable to the survival of the civilian population). 1. Starvation of civilians as a method of warfare is prohibited.

2. It is prohibited to attack, destroy, remove or render useless objects indispensable to the survival of the civilian population, such as food-stuffs, agricultural areas for the production of food-stuffs, crops, livestock, drinking water installations and supplies and irrigation works, for the specific purpose of denying them for their sustenance value to the civilian population or to the adverse Party, whatever the motive, whether in order to starve out civilians, to cause them to move away, or for any other motive.

3. The prohibitions in paragraph 2 shall not apply to such of the objects covered by it as are used by an adverse Party:

(a) as sustenance solely for the members of its armed forces; or

(b) if not as sustenance, then in direct support of military action, provided, however, that in no event shall actions against these objects be taken which may be expected to leave the civilian population with such inadequate food or water as to cause its starvation or force its movement.

4. These objects shall not be made the object of reprisals.

5. In recognition of the vital requirements of any Party to the conflict in the defence of its national territory against invasion, derogation from the prohibitions contained in paragraph 2 may be made by a Party to the conflict within such territory under its own control where required by imperative military necessity.

P

Pacific settlement of disputes *(Charter of the United Nations, San Francisco, 26 June 1945, Chapter VI, Art. 33, Art. 34, Art. 35, Art. 36, Art. 37, Art. 38).*

Art. 33. 1. The parties to any dispute, the continuance of which is likely to endanger the maintenance of international peace and security, shall, first of all, seek a solution by negotiation, enquiry, mediation, conciliation, arbitration, judicial settlement, resort to regional agencies or arrangements, or other peaceful means of their own choice.

2. The Security Council shall, when it deems necessary, call upon the parties to settle their dispute by such means.

Art. 34. The Security Council may investigate any dispute, or any situation which might lead to international friction or give rise to a dispute, in order to determine whether the continuance of the dispute or situation is likely to endanger the maintenance of international peace and security.

Art. 35. 1. Any Member of the United Nations may bring any dispute, or any situation of the nature referred to in Article 34, to the attention of the Security Council or of the General Assembly.

2. A state which is not a Member of the United Nations may bring to the attention of the Security Council or of the General Assembly any dispute to which it is a party if it accepts in advance, for the purposes of the dispute, the obligations of pacific settlement provided in the present Charter.

3. The proceedings of the General Assembly in respect of matters brought to its attention under this Article will be subject to the provisions of Articles 11 and 12.

Art. 36. 1. The Security Council may, at any stage of a dispute of the nature referred to in Article 33 or of a situation of like nature, recommend appropriate procedures or methods of adjustment.

2. The Security Council should take into consideration any procedures for the settlement of the dispute which have already been adopted by the parties.

3. In making recommendations under this Article the Security Council should also take into consideration that legal disputes should as a general rule be referred by the parties to the International Court of Justice in accordance with the provisions of the Statute of the Court. *Art. 37.* 1. Should the parties to a dispute of the nature referred to in Article 33 fail to settle it by the means indicated in that Article, they shall refer it to the Security Council.

2. If the Security Council deems that the continuance of the dispute is in fact likely to endanger the maintenance of international peace and security, it shall decide whether to take action under Article 36 or to recommend such terms of settlement as it may consider appropriate.

Art. 38. Without prejudice to the provisions of Articles 33 to 37, the Security Council may, if all the parties to any dispute so request, make recommendations to the parties with a view to a pacific settlement of the dispute.

Peace. An Agenda for Peace *(United Nations. General Assembly. Security Council. An Agenda for Peace. Preventive diplomacy, peacemaking and peace-keeping, post-conflict peace-building. Report of the Secretary-General pursuant to the statement adopted by the Summit Meeting of the Security Council on 31 January 1992. A/47/277 - S/24111, 17 June 1992. II. Definitions. III. Preventive diplomacy (...) Demilitarized zones; IV. Peacemaking (...) Use of military force).* II. Definitions. 20. The terms preventive diplomacy, peacemaking and peace-keeping are integrally related and as used in this report are defined as follows:

Preventive diplomacy is action to prevent disputes from arising between parties, to prevent existing disputes from escalating into conflicts and to limit the spread of the latter when they occur.

Peacemaking is action to bring hostile parties to agreement, essentially through such peaceful means as those foreseen in Chapter VI of the Charter of the United Nations.

Peace-keeping is the deployment of a United Nations presence in the field, hitherto with the consent of all the parties concerned, normally involving United Nations military and/or police personnel and frequently civilians as well. Peace-keeping is a technique that expands the possibilities for both the prevention of conflict and the making of peace.

21. The present report in addition will address the critically related concept of **post-conflict peace-building** - action to identify and support structures which will tend to strengthen and solidify peace in order to avoid a relapse into conflict. Preventive diplomacy seeks to resolve disputes before violence breaks out; peacemaking and peace-keeping are required to halt conflicts and preserve peace once it is attained. If successful, they strengthen the opportunity for post-conflict peace-building, which can prevent the recurrence of violence among nations and peoples.

22. These four areas for action, taken together, and carried out with the backing of all Members, offer a coherent contribution towards securing peace in the spirit of the Charter.

(...) *III. Preventive diplomacy (...)* **Demilitarized zones.**

33. In the past, demilitarized zones have been established by agreement of the parties at the conclusion of a conflict. In addition to the deployment of United Nations personnel in such zones as part of peace-keeping operations, consideration should now be given to the usefulness of such zones as a form of preventive deployment, on both sides of a border, with the agreement of the two parties, as a means of separating potential belligerents, or on one side of the line, at the request of one party, for the purpose of removing any pretext for attack. Demilitarized zones would serve as symbols of the international community's concern that conflict be prevented.

(...) *VI. Post-conflict peace-building (...)* 58. (...) Just as demilitarized zones may serve the cause of preventive diplomacy and preventive deployment to avoid conflict, so may demilitarization assist in keeping the peace or in post-conflict peace-building, as a measure for heightening the sense of security and encouraging the parties to turn their energies to the work of peaceful restoration of their societies. (...)

IV. Peacemaking (...) **Use of military force**

42. It is the essence of the concept of collective security as contained in the Charter that if peaceful means fail, the measures provided in Chapter VII should be used, on the decision of the Security Council, to maintain or restore international peace and security in the face of a "threat to the peace, breach of the peace, or act of aggression". The Security Council has not so far made use of the most coercive of these measures - the action by military force foreseen in Article 42. In the situation between Iraq and Kuwait, the Council chose to authorize Member States to take measures on its behalf. The Charter, however, provides a detailed approach which now merits the attention of all Member States.

43. Under Article 42 of the Charter, the Security Council has the authority to take military action to maintain or restore international peace and security. While such action should only be taken when all peaceful means have failed, the option of taking it is essential to the credibility of the United Nations as a guarantor of international security. This will require bringing into being, through negotiations, the special agreements foreseen in Article 43 of the Charter, whereby Member States undertake to make armed forces, assistance and facilities available to the Security Council for the purposes stated in Article 42, not only on an ad hoc basis but on a permanent basis. Under the political circumstances that now exist for the first time since the Charter was adopted, the long-standing obstacles to the conclusion of such special agreements should no longer prevail. The ready availability of armed forces on call could serve, in itself, as a means of deterring breaches of the peace since a potential aggressor would know that the Council had at its disposal a means of response. Forces under Article 43 may perhaps never be sufficiently large or well enough equipped to deal with a threat from a major army equipped with sophisticated weapons. They would be useful, however, in meeting any threat posed by a military force of a lesser order. I recommend that the Security Council initiate negotiations in accordance with Article 43, supported by the Military Staff Committee, which may be augmented if necessary by others in accordance with Article 47, paragraph 2, of the Charter. It is my view that the role of the Military Staff Committee should be seen in the context of Chapter VII, and not that of the planning or conduct of peace-keeping operations. (...)

VI. Post-conflict peace-building.

55. Peacemaking and peace-keeping operations, to be truly successful, must come to include comprehensive efforts to identify and support structures which will tend to consolidate peace and advance a sense of confidence and well-being among people. Through agreements ending civil strife, these may include disarming the previously warring parties and the restoration of order, the custody and possible destruction of weapons, repatriating refugees, advisory and training support for security personnel, monitoring elections, advancing efforts to protect human rights, reforming or strengthening governmental institutions and promoting formal and informal processes of political participation.

56. In the aftermath of international war, post-conflict peace-building may take the form of concrete cooperative projects which link two or more countries in a mutually beneficial undertaking that can not only contribute to economic and social

development but also enhance the confidence that is so fundamental to peace. I have in mind, for example, projects that bring States together to develop agriculture, improve transportation or utilize resources such as water or electricity that they need to share, or joint programmes through which barriers between nations are brought down by means of freer travel, cultural exchanges and mutually beneficial youth and educational projects. Reducing hostile perceptions through educational exchanges and curriculum reform may be essential to forestall a re-emergence of cultural and national tensions which could spark renewed hostilities.

57. In surveying the range of efforts for peace, the concept of peace-building as the construction of a new environment should be viewed as the counterpart of preventive diplomacy, which seeks to avoid the breakdown of peaceful conditions. When conflict breaks out, mutually reinforcing efforts at peacemaking and peace-keeping come into play. Once these have achieved their objectives, only sustained, cooperative work to deal with underlying economic, social, cultural and humanitarian problems can place an achieved peace on a durable foundation. Preventive diplomacy is to avoid a crisis; post-conflict peace-building is to prevent a recurrence. (...)

Perfidy and Ruses of war. Prohibition of Perfidy *(Protocol Additional to the Geneva Conventions of 12 August 1949, and relating to the Protection of Victims of International Armed Conflicts (Protocol I), 8 June 1977. Part III. Methods and Means of Warfare Combatant and Prisoners-Of-War. Section I. Methods and Means of Warfare. Art. 37. Prohibition of Perfidy).* 1. It is prohibited to kill, injure or capture an adversary by resort to perfidy. Acts inviting the confidence of an adversary to lead him to believe that he is entitled to, or is obliged to accord, protection under the rules of international law applicable in armed conflict, with intent to betray that confidence, shall constitute perfidy. The following acts are examples of perfidy:

(a) the feigning of an intent to negotiate under a flag of truce or of a surrender;

(b) the feigning of an incapacitation by wounds or sickness;

(c) the feigning of civilian, non-combatant status; and

(d) the feigning of protected status by the use of signs, emblems or uniforms of the United Nations or of neutral or other States not Parties to the conflict.

2. Ruses of war are not prohibited. Such ruses are acts which are intended to mislead an adversary or to induce him to act recklessly but which infringe no rule of international law applicable in armed conflict and which are not perfidious because they do not invite the confidence of an adversary with respect to protection under that law. The following are examples of such ruses: the use of camouflage, decoys, mock operations and misinformation.

Persecution. *See: Crimes against humanity.*

Population and development. International Conference on Population and development, Cairo, 5-13 September 1994 *(Programme of Action. Chapter 1. Preamble; Chapter 2. Principles). Chapter 1. Preamble.* 1.1. The

1994 International Conference on Population and Development occurs at a defining moment in the history of international cooperation. With the growing recognition of global population, development and environmental interdependence, the opportunity to adopt suitable macro- and socio-economic policies to promote sustained economic growth in the context of sustainable development in all countries and to mobilize human and financial resources for global problem- solving has never been greater. Never before has the world community had so many resources, so much knowledge and such powerful technologies at its disposal which, if suitably redirected, could foster sustained economic growth and sustainable development. None the less, the effective use of resources, knowledge and technologies is conditioned by political and economic obstacles at the national and international levels. Therefore, although ample resources have been available for some time, their use for socially equitable and environmentally sound development has been seriously limited.

1.2.   The world has undergone far-reaching changes in the past two decades. Significant progress in many fields important for human welfare has been made through national and international efforts. However, the developing countries are still facing serious economic difficulties and an unfavourable international economic environment, and the number of people living in absolute poverty has increased in many countries. Around the world many of the basic resources on which future generations will depend for their survival and well-being are being depleted and environmental degradation is intensifying, driven by unsustainable patterns of production and consumption, unprecedented growth in population, widespread and persistent poverty, and social and economic inequality. Ecological problems, such as global climate change, largely driven by unsustainable patterns of production and consumption, are adding to the threats to the well-being of future generations. There is an emerging global consensus on the need for increased international cooperation in regard to population in the context of sustainable development, for which Agenda 21 provides a framework. Much has been achieved in this respect, but more needs to be done.

1.3.   The world population is currently estimated at 5.6 billion. While the rate of growth is on the decline, absolute increments have been increasing, currently exceeding 86 million persons per annum. Annual population increments are likely to remain above 86 million until the year 2015.

1.4.   During the remaining six years of this critical decade, the world's nations by their actions or inactions will choose from among a range of alternative demographic futures. The low, medium and high variants of the United Nations population projections for the coming 20 years range from a low of 7.1 billion people to the medium variant of 7.5 billion and a high of 7.8 billion. The difference of 720 million people in the short span of 20 years exceeds the current population of the African continent. Further into the future, the projections diverge even more significantly. By the year 2050, the United Nations projections range from 7.9 billion to the medium variant of 9.8 billion and a high of 11.9 billion. Implementation of the goals and objectives contained in the present 20-year Programme of Action, which address many of the fundamental population, health, education and development challenges facing the entire human community, would result in world population growth during this period and beyond at levels below the United Nations medium projection.

1.5. The International Conference on Population and Development is not an isolated event. Its Programme of Action builds on the considerable international consensus that has developed since the World Population Conference at Bucharest in 1974 and the International Conference on Population at Mexico City in 1984, to consider the broad issues of and interrelationships between population, sustained economic growth and sustainable development, and advances in the education, economic status and empowerment of women. The 1994 Conference was explicitly given a broader mandate on development issues than previous population conferences, reflecting the growing awareness that population, poverty, patterns of production and consumption and the environment are so closely interconnected that none of them can be considered in isolation.

1.6. The International Conference on Population and Development follows and builds on other important recent international activities, and its recommendations should be supportive of, consistent with and based on the agreements reached at the following:

(a) The World Conference to Review and Appraise the Achievements of the United Nations Decade for Women: Equality, Development and Peace, held in Nairobi in 1985;

(b) The World Summit for Children, held in New York in 1990;

(c) The United Nations Conference on Environment and Development, held in Rio de Janeiro in 1992;

(d) The International Conference on Nutrition, held in Rome in 1992;

(e) The World Conference on Human Rights, held in Vienna in 1993;

(f) The International Year of the World's Indigenous People, 1993, which would lead to the International Decade of the World's Indigenous People;

(g) The Global Conference on the Sustainable Development of Small Island Developing States, held in Barbados in 1994;

(h) The International Year of the Family, 1994.

1.7. The Conference outcomes are closely related to and will make significant contributions to other major conferences in 1995 and 1996, such as the World Summit for Social Development, the Fourth World Conference on Women: Action for Equality, Development and Peace, the Second United Nations Conference on Human Settlements (Habitat II), the elaboration of the Agenda for Development, as well as the celebration of the fiftieth anniversary of the United Nations. These events are expected to highlight further the call of the 1994 Conference for greater investment in people, and for a new action agenda for the empowerment of women to ensure their full participation at all levels in the social, economic and political lives of their communities.

1.8. Over the past 20 years, many parts of the world have undergone remarkable demographic, social, economic, environmental and political change. Many countries have made substantial progress in expanding access to reproductive health care and lowering birth rates, as well as in lowering death rates and raising education and income levels, including the educational and economic status of women. While the advances of the past two decades in areas such as increased use of contraception, decreased maternal mortality, implemented sustainable development plans and projects and enhanced educational programmes provide a basis for optimism about successful implementation of the present Programme of Action, much remains to be accomplished. The world as a whole has changed in ways that create important new opportunities for addressing population and development issues. Among the most significant are the major shifts in attitude among the world's people and their leaders in regard to reproductive health, family planning and population growth, resulting, inter alia, in the new comprehensive concept of reproductive health, including family planning and sexual health, as defined in the present Programme of Action. A particularly encouraging trend has been the strengthening of political commitment to population-related policies and family-planning programmes by many Governments. In this regard, sustained economic growth in the context of sustainable development will enhance the ability of countries to meet the pressures of expected population growth; will facilitate the demographic transition in countries where there is an imbalance between demographic rates and social, economic and environmental goals; and will permit the balance and integration of the population dimension into other development- related policies.

1.9.   The population and development objectives and actions of the present Programme of Action will collectively address the critical challenges and interrelationships between population and sustained economic growth in the context of sustainable development. In order to do so, adequate mobilization of resources at the national and international levels will be required as well as new and additional resources to the developing countries from all available funding mechanisms, including multilateral, bilateral and private sources. Financial resources are also required to strengthen the capacity of national, regional, subregional and international institutions to implement this Programme of Action.

1.10. The two decades ahead are likely to produce a further shift of rural populations to urban areas as well as continued high levels of migration between countries. These migrations are an important part of the economic transformations occurring around the world, and they present serious new challenges. Therefore, these issues must be addressed with more emphasis within population and development policies. By the year 2015, nearly 56 per cent of the global population is expected to live in urban areas, compared to under 45 per cent in 1994. The most rapid rates of urbanization will occur in the developing countries. The urban population of the developing regions was just 26 per cent in 1975, but is projected to rise to 50 per cent by 2015. This change will place enormous strain on existing social services and infrastructure, much of which will not be able to expand at the same rate as that of urbanization.

1.11. Intensified efforts are needed in the coming 5, 10 and 20 years, in a range of population and development activities, bearing in mind the crucial contribution that early stabilization of the world population would make towards the achievement of sustainable development. The present Programme of Action addresses all those issues, and more, in a comprehensive and integrated framework designed to improve the quality of life of the current world population and its future generations. The recommendations for action are made in a spirit of consensus and international cooperation, recognizing that the formulation and implementation of population-related policies is the responsibility of each country and should take into account the economic, social and environmental diversity of conditions in each country, with full respect for the various religious and ethical values, cultural backgrounds and philosophical convictions of its people, as well as the shared but differentiated responsibilities of all the world's people for a common future.

1.12. The present Programme of Action recommends to the international community a set of important population and development objectives, as well as qualitative and quantitative goals that are mutually supportive and of critical importance to these objectives. Among these objectives and goals are: sustained economic growth in the context of sustainable development; education, especially for girls; gender equity and equality; infant, child and maternal mortality reduction; and the provision of universal access to reproductive health services, including family planning and sexual health.

1.13. Many of the quantitative and qualitative goals of the present Programme of Action clearly require additional resources, some of which could become available from a reordering of priorities at the individual, national and international levels. However, none of the actions required - nor all of them combined - is expensive in the context of either current global development or military expenditures. A few would require little or no additional financial resources, in that they involve changes in lifestyles, social norms or government policies that can be largely brought about and sustained through greater citizen action and political leadership. But to meet the resource needs of those actions that do require increased expenditures over the next two decades, additional commitments will be required on the part of both developing and developed countries. This will be particularly difficult in the case of some developing countries and some countries with economies in transition that are experiencing extreme resource constraints.

1.14. The present Programme of Action recognizes that over the next 20 years Governments are not expected to meet the goals and objectives of the International Conference on Population and Development single-handedly. All members of and groups in society have the right, and indeed the responsibility, to play an active part in efforts to reach those goals. The increased level of interest manifested by non-governmental organizations, first in the context of the United Nations Conference on Environment and Development and the World Conference on Human Rights, and now in these deliberations, reflects an important and in many places rapid change in the relationship between Governments and a variety of non-governmental institutions. In nearly all countries new partnerships are emerging between government, business, non-governmental organizations and community groups, which will have a direct and positive bearing on the implementation of the present Programme of Action.

1.15. While the International Conference on Population and Development does not create any new international human rights, it affirms the application of universally recognized human rights standards to all aspects of population programmes. It also represents the last opportunity in the twentieth century for the international community to collectively address the critical challenges and interrelationships between population and development. The Programme of Action will require the establishment of common ground, with full respect for the various religious and ethical values and cultural backgrounds. The impact of this Conference will be measured by the strength of the specific commitments made here and the consequent actions to fulfil them, as part of a new global partnership among all the world's countries and peoples, based on a sense of shared but differentiated responsibility for each other and for our planetary home.

Chapter 2. Principles.

The implementation of the recommendations contained in the Programme of Action is the sovereign right of each country, consistent with national laws and development priorities, with full respect for the various religious and ethical values and cultural backgrounds of its people, and in conformity with universally recognized international human rights. International cooperation and universal solidarity, guided by the principles of the Charter of the United Nations, and in a spirit of partnership, are crucial in order to improve the quality of life of the peoples of the world. In addressing the mandate of the International Conference on Population and Development and its overall theme, the interrelationships between population, sustained economic growth and sustainable development, and in their deliberations, the participants were and will continue to be guided by the following set of principles:

Principle 1. All human beings are born free and equal in dignity and rights. Everyone is entitled to all the rights and freedoms set forth in the Universal Declaration of Human Rights, without distinction of any kind, such as race, colour, sex, language, religion, political or other opinion, national or social origin, property, birth or other status. Everyone has the right to life, liberty and security of person.

Principle 2. Human beings are at the centre of concerns for sustainable development. They are entitled to a healthy and productive life in harmony with nature. People are the most important and valuable resource of any nation. Countries should ensure that all individuals are given the opportunity to make the most of their potential. They have the right to an adequate standard of living for themselves and their families, including adequate food, clothing, housing, water and sanitation.

Principle 3. The right to development is a universal and inalienable right and an integral part of fundamental human rights, and the human person is the central subject of development. While development facilitates the enjoyment of all human rights, the lack of development may not be invoked to justify the abridgement of internationally recognized human rights. The right to development must be fulfilled so as to equitably meet the population, development and environment needs of present and future generations.

Principle 4. Advancing gender equality and equity and the empowerment of women, and the elimination of all kinds of violence against women, and ensuring women's ability to control their own fertility, are cornerstones of population and development-related programmes. The human rights of women and the girl child are an inalienable, integral and indivisible part of universal human rights. The full and equal participation of women in civil, cultural, economic, political and social life, at the national, regional and international levels, and the eradication of all forms of discrimination on grounds of sex, are priority objectives of the international community.

Principle 5. Population-related goals and policies are integral parts of cultural, economic and social development, the principal aim of which is to improve the quality of life of all people.

Principle 6. Sustainable development as a means to ensure human well-being, equitably shared by all people today and in the future, requires that the

145

interrelationships between population, resources, the environment and development should be fully recognized, properly managed and brought into harmonious, dynamic balance. To achieve sustainable development and a higher quality of life for all people, States should reduce and eliminate unsustainable patterns of production and consumption and promote appropriate policies, including population-related policies, in order to meet the needs of current generations without compromising the ability of future generations to meet their own needs.

Principle 7. All States and all people shall cooperate in the essential task of eradicating poverty as an indispensable requirement for sustainable development, in order to decrease the disparities in standards of living and better meet the needs of the majority of the people of the world. The special situation and needs of developing countries, particularly the least developed, shall be given special priority. Countries with economies in transition, as well as all other countries, need to be fully integrated into the world economy.

Principle 8. Everyone has the right to the enjoyment of the highest attainable standard of physical and mental health. States should take all appropriate measures to ensure, on a basis of equality of men and women, universal access to health-care services, including those related to reproductive health care, which includes family planning and sexual health. Reproductive health-care programmes should provide the widest range of services without any form of coercion. All couples and individuals have the basic right to decide freely and responsibly the number and spacing of their children and to have the information, education and means to do so.

Principle 9. The family is the basic unit of society and as such should be strengthened. It is entitled to receive comprehensive protection and support. In different cultural, political and social systems, various forms of the family exist. Marriage must be entered into with the free consent of the intending spouses, and husband and wife should be equal partners.

Principle 10. Everyone has the right to education, which shall be directed to the full development of human resources, and human dignity and potential, with particular attention to women and the girl child. Education should be designed to strengthen respect for human rights and fundamental freedoms, including those relating to population and development. The best interests of the child shall be the guiding principle of those responsible for his or her education and guidance; that responsibility lies in the first place with the parents.

Principle 11. All States and families should give the highest possible priority to children. The child has the right to standards of living adequate for its well-being and the right to the highest attainable standards of health, and the right to education. The child has the right to be cared for, guided and supported by parents, families and society and to be protected by appropriate legislative, administrative, social and educational measures from all forms of physical or mental violence, injury or abuse, neglect or negligent treatment, maltreatment or exploitation, including sale, trafficking, sexual abuse, and trafficking in its organs.

Principle 12. Countries receiving documented migrants should provide proper treatment and adequate social welfare services for them and their families, and should ensure their physical safety and security, bearing in mind the special circumstances and needs of countries, in particular developing countries, attempting to meet these objectives or requirements with regard to undocumented migrants, in conformity with the provisions of relevant conventions and international instruments and documents. Countries should guarantee to all migrants all basic human rights as included in the Universal Declaration of Human Rights.

Principle 13. Everyone has the right to seek and to enjoy in other countries asylum from persecution. States have responsibilities with respect to refugees as set forth in the Geneva Convention on the Status of Refugees and its 1967 Protocol.

Principle 14. In considering the population and development needs of indigenous people, States should recognize and support their identity, culture and interests, and enable them to participate fully in the economic, political and social life of the country, particularly where their health, education and well-being are affected.

Principle 15. Sustained economic growth, in the context of sustainable development, and social progress require that growth be broadly based, offering equal opportunities to all people. All countries should recognize their common but differentiated responsibilities. The developed countries acknowledge the responsibility that they bear in the international pursuit of sustainable development, and should continue to improve their efforts to promote sustained economic growth and to narrow imbalances in a manner that can benefit all countries, particularly the developing countries. (…)

Presumption of innocence *(Universal Declaration of Human Rights, Paris, 10 December 1948. Art. 11. (1); International Covenant on Civil and Political Rights. Adopted and opened for signature, ratification and accession by General Assembly resolution 2200A (XXI) of 16 December 1966. Art. 14. (2); Convention for the Protection of Human Rights and Fundamental Freedoms. Rome, 4.XI.1950 (as amended by Protocols Nos. 11 and 14 with Protocols Nos. 1, 4, 6, 7, 12 and 13). Art. 6. Right to a fair trial. (2); Rome Statute ICC. Part VI. The trial, art. 66. Presumption of innocence; ICTY - Rules Covering the Detention of Persons Awaiting Trial or Appeal Before the Tribunal or Otherwise Detained on the Authority of the Tribunal ("Rules of detention"). Basic principles, Rule 5; ICTR - Rules Covering the Detention of Persons Awaiting Trial or Appeal Before the Tribunal or Otherwise Detained on the Authority of the Tribunal ("Rules of detention"). Basic provisions, Rule 5).*

Universal Declaration of Human Rights, Paris, 10 December 1948. Art. 11. (1). Everyone charged with a penal offence has the right to be presumed innocent until proved guilty according to law in a public trial at which he has had all the guarantees necessary for his defence.

International Covenant on Civil and Political Rights. Adopted and opened for signature, ratification and accession by General Assembly resolution 2200A (XXI) of 16 December 1966. Art. 14. (2). Everyone charged with a criminal offence shall have the right to be presumed innocent until proved guilty according to law.

Convention for the Protection of Human Rights and Fundamental Freedoms. Rome, 4.XI.1950 (as amended by Protocols Nos. 11 and 14 with Protocols Nos. 1, 4, 6, 7, 12 and 13). Art. 6. Right to a fair trial. (2). Everyone charged with a criminal offence shall be presumed innocent until proved guilty according to law.

Rome Statute ICC. Part VI. The trial, art. 66. Presumption of innocence. 1. Everyone shall be presumed innocent until proved guilty before the Court in accordance with the applicable law.

2. The onus is on the Prosecutor to prove the guilt of the accused.

3. In order to convict the accused, the Court must be convinced of the guilt of the accused beyond reasonable doubt.

ICTY - Rules Covering the Detention of Persons Awaiting Trial or Appeal Before the Tribunal or Otherwise Detained on the Authority of the Tribunal ("Rules of detention"). Basic principles, Rule 5. All detainees, other than those who have been convicted by the Tribunal, are presumed to be innocent until found guilty and are to be treated as such at all times.

ICTR - Rules Covering the Detention of Persons Awaiting Trial or Appeal Before the Tribunal or Otherwise Detained on the Authority of the Tribunal ("Rules of detention"). Basic provisions, Rule 5. All detainees, other than those who have been convicted by the Tribunal, are presumed to be innocent until found guilty and are to be treated as such at all times.

Prisoners of War *(Convention (III) relative to the Treatment of Prisoners of War. Geneva, 12 August 1949. Part. I. General Provisions. Art. 4 A) B) C); Art. 5. Part. II. General Protection of Prisoners of War. Art. 12; Art. 13; Art. 14; Art. 15; Art. 16. Part. III. Captivity. Section VI. Relations Between Prisoners of War and the Authorities. Chapter I. Complaints of Prisoners of War Respecting the Conditions of Captivity. Art. 78. Chapter II. Prisoner of War Representatives. Art. 79; Art. 80; Art. 81). Part. I. General Provisions. Art. 4.* A. Prisoners of war, in the sense of the present Convention, are persons belonging to one of the following categories, who have fallen into the power of the enemy:

(1) Members of the armed forces of a Party to the conflict, as well as members of militias or volunteer corps forming part of such armed forces.

(2) Members of other militias and members of other volunteer corps, including those of organized resistance movements, belonging to a Party to the conflict and operating in or outside their own territory, even if this territory is occupied, provided that such militias or volunteer corps, including such organized resistance movements, fulfil the following conditions:

(a) that of being commanded by a person responsible for his subordinates;

(b) that of having a fixed distinctive sign recognizable at a distance;

(c) that of carrying arms openly;

(d) that of conducting their operations in accordance with the laws and customs of war.

(3) Members of regular armed forces who profess allegiance to a government or an authority not recognized by the Detaining Power.

(4) Persons who accompany the armed forces without actually being members thereof, such as civilian members of military aircraft crews, war correspondents, supply contractors, members of labour units or of services responsible for the welfare of the armed forces, provided that they have received authorization, from the armed forces which they accompany, who shall provide them for that purpose with an identity card similar to the annexed model. (5) Members of crews, including masters,

pilots and apprentices, of the merchant marine and the crews of civil aircraft of the Parties to the conflict, who do not benefit by more favourable treatment under any other provisions of international law.

(6) Inhabitants of a non-occupied territory, who on the approach of the enemy spontaneously take up arms to resist the invading forces, without having had time to form themselves into regular armed units, provided they carry arms openly and respect the laws and customs of war.

B. The following shall likewise be treated as prisoners of war under the present Convention: (1) Persons belonging, or having belonged, to the armed forces of the occupied country, if the occupying Power considers it necessary by reason of such allegiance to intern them, even though it has originally liberated them while hostilities were going on outside the territory it occupies, in particular where such persons have made an unsuccessful attempt to rejoin the armed forces to which they belong and which are engaged in combat, or where they fail to comply with a summons made to them with a view to internment.

(2) The persons belonging to one of the categories enumerated in the present Article, who have been received by neutral or non-belligerent Powers on their territory and whom these Powers are required to intern under international law, without prejudice to any more favourable treatment which these Powers may choose to give and with the exception of Articles 8, 10, 15, 30, fifth paragraph, 58-67, 92, 126 and, where diplomatic relations exist between the Parties to the conflict and the neutral or non-belligerent Power concerned, those Articles concerning the Protecting Power. Where such diplomatic relations exist, the Parties to a conflict on whom these persons depend shall be allowed to perform towards them the functions of a Protecting Power as provided in the present Convention, without prejudice to the functions which these Parties normally exercise in conformity with diplomatic and consular usage and treaties.

C. This Article shall in no way affect the status of medical personnel and chaplains as provided for in Article 33 of the present Convention.

Art. 5. The present Convention shall apply to the persons referred to in Article 4 from the time they fall into the power of the enemy and until their final release and repatriation.

Should any doubt arise as to whether persons, having committed a belligerent act and having fallen into the hands of the enemy, belong to any of the categories enumerated in Article 4, such persons shall enjoy the protection of the present Convention until such time as their status has been determined by a competent tribunal.

Part. II. General Protection of Prisoners of War. Art. 12. Prisoners of war are in the hands of the enemy Power, but not of the individuals or military units who have captured them. Irrespective of the individual responsibilities that may exist, the Detaining Power is responsible for the treatment given them.

Prisoners of war may only be transferred by the Detaining Power to a Power which is a party to the Convention and after the Detaining Power has satisfied itself of the willingness and ability of such transferee Power to apply the Convention. When prisoners of war are transferred under such circumstances, responsibility for the application of the Convention rests on the Power accepting them while they are in its custody.

Nevertheless, if that Power fails to carry out the provisions of the Convention in any important respect, the Power by whom the prisoners of war were transferred shall, upon being notified by the Protecting Power, take effective measures to correct the situation or shall request the return of the prisoners of war. Such requests must be complied with.

Art. 13. Prisoners of war must at all times be humanely treated. Any unlawful act or omission by the Detaining Power causing death or seriously endangering the health of a prisoner of war in its custody is prohibited, and will be regarded as a serious breach of the present Convention. In particular, no prisoner of war may be subjected to physical mutilation or to medical or scientific experiments of any kind which are not justified by the medical, dental or hospital treatment of the prisoner concerned and carried out in his interest.

Likewise, prisoners of war must at all times be protected, particularly against acts of violence or intimidation and against insults and public curiosity.

Measures of reprisal against prisoners of war are prohibited.

Art. 14. Prisoners of war are entitled in all circumstances to respect for their persons and their honour. Women shall be treated with all the regard due to their sex and shall in all cases benefit by treatment as favourable as that granted to men.

Prisoners of war shall retain the full civil capacity which they enjoyed at the time of their capture. The Detaining Power may not restrict the exercise, either within or without its own territory, of the rights such capacity confers except in so far as the captivity requires.

Art. 15. The Power detaining prisoners of war shall be bound to provide free of charge for their maintenance and for the medical attention required by their state of health.

Art. 16. Taking into consideration the provisions of the present Convention relating to rank and sex, and subject to any privileged treatment which may be accorded to them by reason of their state of health, age or professional qualifications, all prisoners of war shall be treated alike by the Detaining Power, without any adverse distinction based on race, nationality, religious belief or political opinions, or any other distinction founded on similar criteria.

Part. III. Captivity. Section VI. Relations Between Prisoners of War and the Authorities. Chapter I. Complaints of Prisoners of War Respecting the Conditions of Captivity. Art. 78. Prisoners of war shall have the right to make known to the military authorities in whose power they are, their requests regarding the conditions of captivity to which they are subjected.

They shall also have the unrestricted right to apply to the representatives of the Protecting Powers either through their prisoners' representative or, if they consider it necessary, direct, in order to draw their attention to any points on which they may have complaints to make regarding their conditions of captivity.

These requests and complaints shall not be limited nor considered to be a part of the correspondence quota referred to in Article 71. They must be transmitted immediately. Even if they are recognized to be unfounded, they may not give rise to any punishment.

Prisoners' representatives may send periodic reports on the situation in the camps and the needs of the prisoners of war to the representatives of the Protecting Powers.

Chapter II. Prisoner of War Representatives. Art. 79. In all places where there are prisoners of war, except in those where there are officers, the prisoners shall freely elect by secret ballot, every six months, and also in case of vacancies, prisoners' representatives entrusted with representing them before the military authorities, the Protecting Powers, the International Committee of the Red Cross and any other organization which may assist them. These prisoners' representatives shall be eligible for re-election.

In camps for officers and persons of equivalent status or in mixed camps, the senior officer among the prisoners of war shall be recognized as the camp prisoners' representative. In camps for officers, he shall be assisted by one or more advisers chosen by the officers; in mixed camps, his assistants shall be chosen from among the prisoners of war who are not officers and shall be elected by them.

Officer prisoners of war of the same nationality shall be stationed in labour camps for prisoners of war, for the purpose of carrying out the camp administration duties for which the prisoners of war are responsible. These officers may be elected as prisoners' representatives under the first paragraph of this Article. In such a case the assistants to the prisoners' representatives shall be chosen from among those prisoners of war who are not officers.

Every representative elected must be approved by the Detaining Power before he has the right to commence his duties. Where the Detaining Power refuses to approve a prisoner of war elected by his fellow prisoners of war, it must inform the Protecting Power of the reason for such refusal.

In all cases the prisoners' representative must have the same nationality, language and customs as the prisoners of war whom he represents. Thus, prisoners of war distributed in different sections of a camp, according to their nationality, language or customs, shall have for each section their own prisoners' representative, in accordance with the foregoing paragraphs.

Art. 80. Prisoners' representatives shall further the physical, spiritual and intellectual well-being of prisoners of war.

In particular, where the prisoners decide to organize amongst themselves a system of mutual assistance, this organization will be within the province of the prisoners' representative, in addition to the special duties entrusted to him by other provisions of the present Convention.

Prisoners' representatives shall not be held responsible, simply by reason of their duties, for any offences committed by prisoners of war.

Art 81. Prisoners' representatives shall not be required to perform any other work, if the accomplishment of their duties is thereby made more difficult.

Prisoners' representatives may appoint from amongst the prisoners such assistants as they may require. All material facilities shall be granted them, particularly a certain freedom of movement necessary for the accomplishment of their duties (inspection of labour detachments, receipt of supplies, etc.).

Prisoners' representatives shall be permitted to visit premises where prisoners of war are detained, and every prisoner of war shall have the right to consult freely his prisoners' representative.

All facilities shall likewise be accorded to the prisoners' representatives for communication by post and telegraph with the detaining authorities, the Protecting Powers, the International Committee of the Red Cross and their delegates, the Mixed

Medical Commissions and the bodies which give assistance to prisoners of war. Prisoners' representatives of labour detachments shall enjoy the same facilities for communication with the prisoners' representatives of the principal camp. Such communications shall not be restricted, nor considered as forming a part of the quota mentioned in Article 71.

Prisoners' representatives who are transferred shall be allowed a reasonable time to acquaint their successors with current affairs.

In case of dismissal, the reasons therefore shall be communicated to the Protecting Power.

Prisoners' representatives *(Convention (III) relative to the Treatment of Prisoners of War. Geneva, 12 August 1949. Part. III. Captivity. Section VI. Relations Between Prisoners of War and the Authorities. Chapter I. Complaints of Prisoners of War Respecting the Conditions of Captivity. Art. 78. Chapter II. Prisoner of War Representatives. Art. 79; Art. 80; Art. 81). Art. 78.* Prisoners of war shall have the right to make known to the military authorities in whose power they are, their requests regarding the conditions of captivity to which they are subjected.

They shall also have the unrestricted right to apply to the representatives of the Protecting Powers either through their prisoners' representative or, if they consider it necessary, direct, in order to draw their attention to any points on which they may have complaints to make regarding their conditions of captivity.

These requests and complaints shall not be limited nor considered to be a part of the correspondence quota referred to in Article 71. They must be transmitted immediately. Even if they are recognized to be unfounded, they may not give rise to any punishment.

Prisoners' representatives may send periodic reports on the situation in the camps and the needs of the prisoners of war to the representatives of the Protecting Powers.

Art. 79. In all places where there are prisoners of war, except in those where there are officers, the prisoners shall freely elect by secret ballot, every six months, and also in case of vacancies, prisoners' representatives entrusted with representing them before the military authorities, the Protecting Powers, the International Committee of the Red Cross and any other organization which may assist them. These prisoners' representatives shall be eligible for re-election.

In camps for officers and persons of equivalent status or in mixed camps, the senior officer among the prisoners of war shall be recognized as the camp prisoners' representative. In camps for officers, he shall be assisted by one or more advisers chosen by the officers; in mixed camps, his assistants shall be chosen from among the prisoners of war who are not officers and shall be elected by them.

Officer prisoners of war of the same nationality shall be stationed in labour camps for prisoners of war, for the purpose of carrying out the camp administration duties for which the prisoners of war are responsible. These officers may be elected as prisoners' representatives under the first paragraph of this Article. In such a case the assistants to the prisoners' representatives shall be chosen from among those prisoners of war who are not officers.

Every representative elected must be approved by the Detaining Power before he has the right to commence his duties. Where the Detaining Power refuses to approve a prisoner of war elected by his fellow prisoners of war, it must inform the Protecting Power of the reason for such refusal.

In all cases the prisoners' representative must have the same nationality, language and customs as the prisoners of war whom he represents. Thus, prisoners of war distributed in different sections of a camp, according to their nationality, language or customs, shall have for each section their own prisoners' representative, in accordance with the foregoing paragraphs.

Art. 80. Prisoners' representatives shall further the physical, spiritual and intellectual well-being of prisoners of war.

In particular, where the prisoners decide to organize amongst themselves a system of mutual assistance, this organization will be within the province of the prisoners' representative, in addition to the special duties entrusted to him by other provisions of the present Convention.

Prisoners' representatives shall not be held responsible, simply by reason of their duties, for any offences committed by prisoners of war.

Art 81. Prisoners' representatives shall not be required to perform any other work, if the accomplishment of their duties is thereby made more difficult.

Prisoners' representatives may appoint from amongst the prisoners such assistants as they may require. All material facilities shall be granted them, particularly a certain freedom of movement necessary for the accomplishment of their duties (inspection of labour detachments, receipt of supplies, etc.).

Prisoners' representatives shall be permitted to visit premises where prisoners of war are detained, and every prisoner of war shall have the right to consult freely his prisoners' representative.

All facilities shall likewise be accorded to the prisoners' representatives for communication by post and telegraph with the detaining authorities, the Protecting Powers, the International Committee of the Red Cross and their delegates, the Mixed Medical Commissions and the bodies which give assistance to prisoners of war. Prisoners' representatives of labour detachments shall enjoy the same facilities for communication with the prisoners' representatives of the principal camp. Such communications shall not be restricted, nor considered as forming a part of the quota mentioned in Article 71.

Prisoners' representatives who are transferred shall be allowed a reasonable time to acquaint their successors with current affairs.

In case of dismissal, the reasons therefore shall be communicated to the Protecting Power.

"Project-tied worker" *(International Convention on the protection of the rights of all migrant workers and members of their families. Adopted by General Assembly resolution 45/158 of 18 December 1990. Part. 1., Scope and Definitions, Art. 2).* For the purposes of the present Convention: 2.(f) The term "project-tied worker" refers to a migrant worker admitted to a State of employment for a defined period to work solely on a specific project being carried out in that State by his or her employer.

Prosecutor - The Office of the Prosecutor *(Rome Statute ICC, art. 42. The Office of the Prosecutor; See RPE – ICC, Chapter 2. Composition and administration of the Court. Section 2. The Office of the Prosecutor. Rules 9, 10, 11; Statute ICTY, art. 16. The Prosecutor; See RPE – ICTY, Part 3. Organization of the Tribunal. Section 6. The Prosecutor; Statute ICTR, art. 15. The Prosecutor; See RPE – ICTR, Part 3. Organization of the Tribunal. Section 6. The Prosecutor).*

Rome Statute ICC, art. 42. The Office of the Prosecutor. 1. The Office of the Prosecutor shall act independently as a separate organ of the Court. It shall be responsible for receiving referrals and any substantiated information on crimes within the jurisdiction of the Court, for examining them and for conducting investigations and prosecutions before the Court. A member of the Office shall not seek or act on instructions from any external source.

2. The Office shall be headed by the Prosecutor. The Prosecutor shall have full authority over the management and administration of the Office, including the staff, facilities and other resources thereof. The Prosecutor shall be assisted by one or more Deputy Prosecutors, who shall be entitled to carry out any of the acts required of the Prosecutor under this Statute. The Prosecutor and the Deputy Prosecutors shall be of different nationalities. They shall serve on a full-time basis.

3. The Prosecutor and the Deputy Prosecutors shall be persons of high moral character, be highly competent in and have extensive practical experience in the prosecution or trial of criminal cases. They shall have an excellent knowledge of and be fluent in at least one of the working languages of the Court.

4. The Prosecutor shall be elected by secret ballot by an absolute majority of the members of the Assembly of States Parties. The Deputy Prosecutors shall be elected in the same way from a list of candidates provided by the Prosecutor. The Prosecutor shall nominate three candidates for each position of Deputy Prosecutor to be filled. Unless a shorter term is decided upon at the time of their election, the Prosecutor and the Deputy Prosecutors shall hold office for a term of nine years and shall not be eligible for re-election. (...) *See: RPE – ICC, Chapter 2. Composition and administration of the Court. Section 2. The Office of the Prosecutor. Rules 9, 10, 11.*

Statute ICTY, art. 16. The Prosecutor. 1. The Prosecutor shall be responsible for the investigation and prosecution of persons responsible for serious violations of international humanitarian law committed in the territory of the former Yugoslavia since 1 January 1991.

2. The Prosecutor shall act independently as a separate organ of the International Tribunal. He or she shall not seek or receive instructions from any Government or from any other source.

3. The Office of the Prosecutor shall be composed of a Prosecutor and such other qualified staff as may be required.

4. The Prosecutor shall be appointed by the Security Council on nomination by the Secretary-General. He or she shall be of high moral character and possess the highest level of competence and experience in the conduct of investigations and prosecutions of criminal cases. The Prosecutor shall serve for a four-year term and be eligible for reappointment. The terms and conditions of service of the Prosecutor shall be those of an Under-Secretary-General of the United Nations.

5. The staff of the Office of the Prosecutor shall be appointed by the Secretary-General on the recommendation of the Prosecutor. *See: RPE – ICTY, Part 3. Organization of the Tribunal. Section 6. The Prosecutor.*

Statute ICTR, art. 15. *The Prosecutor.* 1. The Prosecutor shall be responsible for the investigation and prosecution of persons responsible for serious violations of international humanitarian law committed in the territory of Rwanda and Rwandan citizens responsible for such violations committed in the territory of neighbouring States, between 1 January 1994 and 31 December 1994.

2. The Prosecutor shall act independently as a separate organ of the International Tribunal for Rwanda. He or she shall not seek or receive instructions from any government or from any other source.

3. The Office of the Prosecutor shall be composed of a Prosecutor and such other qualified staff as may be required.

4. The Prosecutor shall be appointed by the Security Council on nomination by the Secretary- General. He or she shall be of high moral character and possess the highest level of competence and experience in the conduct of investigations and prosecutions of criminal cases. The Prosecutor shall serve for a four-year term and be eligible for reappointment. The terms and conditions of service of the Prosecutor shall be those of an Under-Secretary-General of the United Nations.

5. The staff of the Office of the Prosecutor shall be appointed by the Secretary-General on the
recommendation of the Prosecutor. **See:** *RPE – ICTR, Part 3. Organization of the Tribunal. Section 6. The Prosecutor.*

Protection and care *(Protocol Additional to the Geneva Conventions of 12 August 1949, and relating to the Protection of Victims of International Armed Conflicts (Protocol I), 8 June 1977. Part. II. Wounded, sick and shipwrecked. Section I. General Protection. Art. 10. Protection and care).* 1. All the wounded, sick and shipwrecked, to whichever Party they belong, shall be respected and protected.

2. In all circumstances they shall be treated humanely and shall receive, to the fullest extent practicable and with the least possible delay, the medical care and attention required by their condition. There shall be no distinction among them founded on any grounds other than medical ones.

Protection of children *(Protocol Additional to the Geneva Conventions of 12 August 1949, and relating to the Protection of Victims of International Armed Conflicts (Protocol I), 8 June 1977. Part. IV. Civilian Population. Section III. Treatment of Persons in the Power of a Party to the Conflict. Chapter II. Measures in favour of women and children. Art. 77. Protection of children; Art. 78. Evacuation of children). Art. 77. Protection of children.* 1. Children shall be the object of special respect and shall be protected against any form of indecent assault. The Parties to the conflict shall provide them with the care and aid they require, whether because of their age or for any other reason.

2. The Parties to the conflict shall take all feasible measures in order that children who have not attained the age of fifteen years do not take a direct part in hostilities and, in particular, they shall refrain from recruiting them into their armed forces. In

recruiting among those persons who have attained the age of fifteen years but who have not attained the age of eighteen years the Parties to the conflict shall endeavour to give priority to those who are oldest.

3. If, in exceptional cases, despite the provisions of paragraph 2, children who have not attained the age of fifteen years take a direct part in hostilities and fall into the power of an adverse Party, they shall continue to benefit from the special protection accorded by this Article, whether or not they are prisoners of war.

4. If arrested, detained or interned for reasons related to the armed conflict, children shall be held in quarters separate from the quarters of adults, except where families are accommodated as family units as provided in Article 75, paragraph 5.

5 . The death penalty for an offence related to the armed conflict shall not be executed on persons who had not attained the age of eighteen years at the time the offence was committed. *Art. 75. Fundamental guarantees, paragraph 5.* Women whose liberty has been restricted for reasons related to the armed conflict shall be held in quarters separated from men's quarters. They shall be under the immediate supervision of women. Nevertheless, in cases where families are detained or interned, they shall, whenever possible, be held in the same place and accommodated as family units.

Art. 78. Evacuation of children. 1. No Party to the conflict shall arrange for the evacuation of children, other than its own nationals, to a foreign country except for a temporary evacuation where compelling reasons of the health or medical treatment of the children or, except in occupied territory, their safety, so require. Where the parents or legal guardians can be found, their written consent to such evacuation is required. If these persons cannot be found, the written consent to such evacuation of the persons who by law or custom are primarily responsible for the care of the children is required. Any such evacuation shall be supervised by the Protecting Power in agreement with the Parties concerned, namely, the Party arranging for the evacuation, the Party receiving the children and any Parties whose nationals are being evacuated. In each case, all Parties to the conflict shall take all feasible precautions to avoid endangering the evacuation.

2. Whenever an evacuation occurs pursuant to paragraph 1, each child's education, including his religious and moral education as his parents desire, shall be provided while he is away with the greatest possible continuity.

3. With a view to facilitating the return to their families and country of children evacuated pursuant to this Article, the authorities of the Party arranging for the evacuation and, as appropriate, the authorities of the receiving country shall establish for each child a card with photographs, which they shall send to the Central Tracing Agency of the International Committee of the Red Cross. Each card shall bear, whenever possible, and whenever it involves no risk of harm to the child, the following information:

(a) surname(s) of the child;
(b) the child's first name(s);
(c) the child's sex;
(d) the place and date of birth (or, if that date is not known, the approximate age);
(e) the father's full name;
(f) the mother's full name and her maiden name;

(g) the child's next-of-kin;

(h) the child's nationality;

(i) the child's native language, and any other languages he speaks;

(j) the address of the child's family;

(k) any identification number for the child;

(l) the child's state of health;

(m) the child's blood group;

(n) any distinguishing features;

(o) the date on which and the place where the child was found;

(p) the date on which and the place from which the child left the country;

(q) the child's religion, if any;

(r) the child's present address in the receiving country;

(s) should the child die before his return, the date, place and circumstances of death and place of interment.

Protection of civilian medical and religious personnel *(Protocol Additional to the Geneva Conventions of 12 August 1949, and relating to the Protection of Victims of International Armed Conflicts (Protocol I), 8 June 1977. Part. II. Wounded, sick and shipwrecked. Section I. General Protection. Art. 15. Protection of civilian medical and religious personnel).* 1. Civilian medical personnel shall be respected and protected.

2. If needed, all available help shall be afforded to civilian medical personnel in an area where civilian medical services are disrupted by reason of combat activity.

3. The Occupying Power shall afford civilian medical personnel in occupied territories every assistance to enable them to perform, to the best of their ability, their humanitarian functions. The Occupying Power may not require that, in the performance of those functions, such personnel shall give priority to the treatment of any person except on medical grounds. They shall not be compelled to carry out tasks which are not compatible with their humanitarian mission.

4. Civilian medical personnel shall have access to any place where their services are essential, subject to such supervisory and safety measures as the relevant Party to the conflict may deem necessary.

5. Civilian religious personnel shall be respected and protected. The provisions of the Conventions and of this Protocol concerning the protection and identification of medical personnel shall apply equally to such persons.

Protection of cultural objects and of places of worship *(Protocol Additional to the Geneva Conventions of 12 August 1949, and relating to the Protection of Victims of International Armed Conflicts (Protocol I), 8 June 1977. Part. IV. Civilian Population. Section I. General Protection Against Effects of Hostilities. Chapter III. Civilian objects. Art. 53. Protection of cultural objects and of places of worship).* Without prejudice to the provisions of the Hague Convention for the Protection of Cultural Property in the Event of Armed Conflict of 14 May 1954, and of other relevant international instruments, it is prohibited:

(a) to commit any acts of hostility directed against the historic monuments, works of art or places of worship which constitute the cultural or spiritual heritage of peoples;

(b) to use such objects in support of the military effort;

(c) to make such objects the object of reprisals.

Protection of journalists. Measures or protection for journalists

(Protocol Additional to the Geneva Conventions of 12 August 1949, and relating to the Protection of Victims of International Armed Conflicts (Protocol I), 8 June 1977. Part. IV. Civilian Population. Section III. Treatment of Persons in the Power of a Party to the Conflict. Chapter III. Journalists. Art. 79. Measures or protection for journalists). 1. Journalists engaged in dangerous professional missions in areas of armed conflict shall be considered as civilians within the meaning of Article 50, paragraph 1.

2. They shall be protected as such under the Conventions and this Protocol, provided that they take no action adversely affecting their status as civilians, and without prejudice to the right of war correspondents accredited to the armed forces to the status provided for in Article 4 (A) (4) of the Third Convention.

3. They may obtain an identity card similar to the model in Annex II of this Protocol. This card, which shall be issued by the government of the State of which the Journalist is a national or in whose territory he resides or in which the news medium employing him is located, shall attest to his status as a journalist.

Protection of medical units *(Protocol Additional to the Geneva Conventions of 12 August 1949, and relating to the Protection of Victims of International Armed Conflicts (Protocol I), 8 June 1977. Part. II. Wounded, sick and shipwrecked. Section I. General Protection. Art. 12. Protection of medical units).* 1. Medical units shall be respected and protected at all times and shall not be the object of attack.

2. Paragraph 1 shall apply to civilian medical units, provided that they:

(a) belong to one of the Parties to the conflict;

(b) are recognized and authorized by the competent authority of one of the Parties to the conflict; or

(c) are authorized in conformity with Article 9, paragraph 2, of this Protocol or Article 27 of the First Convention.

3. The Parties to the conflict are invited to notify each other of the location of their fixed medical units. The absence of such notification shall not exempt any of the Parties from the obligation to comply with the provisions of paragraph 1.

4. Under no circumstances shall medical units be used in an attempt to shield military objectives from attack. Whenever possible, the Parties to the conflict shall ensure that medical units are so sited that attacks against military objectives do not imperil their safety.

Protection of objects indispensable to the survival of the civilian population *(Protocol Additional to the Geneva Conventions of 12 August 1949, and relating to the Protection of Victims of International Armed Conflicts (Protocol I), 8 June 1977. Part. IV. Civilian Population. Section I. General Protection Against Effects of Hostilities. Chapter III. Civilian objects. Art. 54. Protection of objects*

indispensable to the survival of the civilian population). 1. Starvation of civilians as a method of warfare is prohibited.

2. It is prohibited to attack, destroy, remove or render useless objects indispensable to the survival of the civilian population, such as food-stuffs, agricultural areas for the production of food-stuffs, crops, livestock, drinking water installations and supplies and irrigation works, for the specific purpose of denying them for their sustenance value to the civilian population or to the adverse Party, whatever the motive, whether in order to starve out civilians, to cause them to move away, or for any other motive.

3. The prohibitions in paragraph 2 shall not apply to such of the objects covered by it as are used by an adverse Party:

(a) as sustenance solely for the members of its armed forces; or

(b) if not as sustenance, then in direct support of military action, provided, however, that in no event shall actions against these objects be taken which may be expected to leave the civilian population with such inadequate food or water as to cause its starvation or force its movement.

4. These objects shall not be made the object of reprisals.

5. In recognition of the vital requirements of any Party to the conflict in the defence of its national territory against invasion, derogation from the prohibitions contained in paragraph 2 may be made by a Party to the conflict within such territory under its own control where required by imperative military necessity.

Protection of persons *(Protocol Additional to the Geneva Conventions of 12 August 1949, and relating to the Protection of Victims of International Armed Conflicts (Protocol I), 8 June 1977. Part. II. Wounded, sick and shipwrecked. Section I. General Protection. Art. 11.* Protection of persons). 1. The physical or mental health and integrity of persons who are in the power of the adverse Party or who are interned, detained or otherwise deprived of liberty as a result of a situation referred to in Article 1 shall not be endangered by any unjustified act or omission. Accordingly, it is prohibited to subject the persons described in this Article to any medical procedure which is not indicated by the state of health of the person concerned and which is not consistent with generally accepted medical standards which would be applied under similar medical circumstances to persons who are nationals of the Party conducting the procedure and who are in no way deprived of liberty.

2. It is, in particular, prohibited to carry out on such persons, even with their consent:

(a) physical mutilations;

(b) medical or scientific experiments;

(c) removal of tissue or organs for transplantation, except where these acts are justified in conformity with the conditions provided for in paragraph 1.

3. Exceptions to the prohibition in paragraph 2 (c) may be made only in the case of donations of blood for transfusion or of skin for grafting, provided that they are given voluntarily and without any coercion or inducement, and then only for therapeutic purposes, under conditions consistent with generally accepted medical standards and controls designed for the benefit of both the donor and the recipient.

4. Any wilful act or omission which seriously endangers the physical or mental health or integrity of any person who is in the power of a Party other than the one on

which he depends and which either violates any of the prohibitions in paragraphs 1 and 2 or fails to comply with the requirements of paragraph 3 shall be a grave breach of this Protocol.

5. The persons described in paragraph 1 have the right to refuse any surgical operation. In case of refusal, medical personnel shall endeavour to obtain a written statement to that effect, signed or acknowledged by the patient.

6. Each Party to the conflict shall keep a medical record for every donation of blood for transfusion or skin for grafting by persons referred to in paragraph 1, if that donation is made under the responsibility of that Party. In addition, each Party to the conflict shall endeavour to keep a record of all medical procedures undertaken with respect to any person who is interned, detained or otherwise deprived of liberty as a result of a situation referred to in Article 1. These records shall be available at all times for inspection by the Protecting Power.

Protection of persons who have taken part in hostilities *(Protocol Additional to the Geneva Conventions of 12 August 1949, and relating to the Protection of Victims of International Armed Conflicts (Protocol I), 8 June 1977. Part. III. Methods and Means of Warfare. Combatant and Prisoners-Of-War. Section II. Combatants and Prisoners of War. Art. 45. Protection of persons who have taken part in hostilities; Section III. Treatment of Persons in the Power of a Party to the Conflict. Chapter I. Field of application and protection of persons and objects. Art. 75. Fundamental guarantees). Art. 45. Protection of persons who have taken part in hostilities.* 1. A person who takes part in hostilities and falls into the power of an adverse Party shall be presumed to be a prisoner of war, and therefore shall be protected by the Third Convention, if he claims the status of prisoner of war, or if he appears to be entitled to such status, or if the Party on which he depends claims such status on his behalf by notification to the detaining Power or to the Protecting Power. Should any doubt arise as to whether any such person is entitled to the status of prisoner of war, he shall continue to have such status and, therefore, to be protected by the Third Convention and this Protocol until such time as his status has been determined by a competent tribunal.

2. If a person who has fallen into the power of an adverse Party is not held as a prisoner of war and is to be tried by that Party for an offence arising out of the hostilities, he shall have the right to assert his entitlement to prisoner-of-war status before a judicial tribunal and to have that question adjudicated. Whenever possible under the applicable procedure, this adjudication shall occur before the trial for the offence. The representatives of the Protecting Power shall be entitled to attend the proceedings in which that question is adjudicated, unless, exceptionally, the proceedings are held in camera in the interest of State security. In such a case the detaining Power shall advise the Protecting Power accordingly.

3. Any person who has taken part in hostilities, who is not entitled to prisoner-of-war status and who does not benefit from more favourable treatment in accordance with the Fourth Convention shall have the right at all times to the protection of Article 75 of this Protocol. In occupied territory, any such person, unless he is held as a spy, shall also be entitled, notwithstanding Article 5 of the Fourth Convention, to his rights of communication under that Convention.

Section III. Treatment of Persons in the Power of a Party to the Conflict. Chapter I. Field of application and protection of persons and objects. Art. 75. Fundamental guarantees. 1. In so far as they are affected by a situation referred to in Article 1 of this Protocol, persons who are in the power of a Party to the conflict and who do not benefit from more favourable treatment under the Conventions or under this Protocol shall be treated humanely in all circumstances and shall enjoy, as a minimum, the protection provided by this Article without any adverse distinction based upon race, colour, sex, language, religion or belief, political or other opinion, national or social origin, wealth, birth or other status, or on any other similar criteria. Each Party shall respect the person, honour, convictions and religious practices of all such persons.
2. The following acts are and shall remain prohibited at any time and in any place whatsoever, whether committed by civilian or by military agents:
(a) violence to the life, health, or physical or mental well-being of persons, in particular:
(i) murder;
(ii) torture of all kinds, whether physical or mental;
(iii) corporal punishment; and
(iv) mutilation;
(b) outrages upon personal dignity, in particular humiliating and degrading treatment, enforced prostitution and any form of indecent assault;
(c) the taking of hostages;
(d) collective punishments; and
(e) threats to commit any of the foregoing acts.
3. Any person arrested, detained or interned for actions related to the armed conflict shall be informed promptly, in a language he understands, of the reasons why these measures have been taken. Except in cases of arrest or detention for penal offences, such persons shall be released with the minimum delay possible and in any event as soon as the circumstances justifying the arrest, detention or internment have ceased to exist.
4. No sentence may be passed and no penalty may be executed on a person found guilty of a penal offence related to the armed conflict except pursuant to a conviction pronounced by an impartial and regularly constituted court respecting the generally recognized principles of regular judicial procedure, which include the following:
(a) the procedure shall provide for an accused to be informed without delay of the particulars of the offence alleged against him and shall afford the accused before and during his trial all necessary rights and means of defence;
(b) no one shall be convicted of an offence except on the basis of individual penal responsibility;
(c) no one shall be accused or convicted of a criminal offence on account or any act or omission which did not constitute a criminal offence under the national or international law to which he was subject at the time when it was committed; nor shall a heavier penalty be imposed than that which was applicable at the time when the criminal offence was committed; if, after the commission of the offence, provision is made by law for the imposition of a lighter penalty, the offender shall benefit thereby;
(d) anyone charged with an offence is presumed innocent until proved guilty according to law;

(e) anyone charged with an offence shall have the right to be tried in his presence;

(f) no one shall be compelled to testify against himself or to confess guilt;

(g) anyone charged with an offence shall have the right to examine, or have examined, the witnesses against him and to obtain the attendance and examination of witnesses on his behalf under the same conditions as witnesses against him;

(h) no one shall be prosecuted or punished by the same Party for an offence in respect of which a final judgement acquitting or convicting that person has been previously pronounced under the same law and judicial procedure;

(i) anyone prosecuted for an offence shall have the right to have the judgement pronounced publicly; and

(j) a convicted person shall be advised on conviction or his judicial and other remedies and of the time-limits within which they may be exercised.

5. Women whose liberty has been restricted for reasons related to the armed conflict shall be held in quarters separated from men's quarters. They shall be under the immediate supervision of women. Nevertheless, in cases where families are detained or interned, they shall, whenever possible, be held in the same place and accommodated as family units.

6. Persons who are arrested, detained or interned for reasons related to the armed conflict shall enjoy the protection provided by this Article until their final release, repatriation or re-establishment, even after the end of the armed conflict.

7. In order to avoid any doubt concerning the prosecution and trial of persons accused of war crimes or crimes against humanity, the following principles shall apply:

(a) persons who are accused of such crimes should be submitted for the purpose of prosecution and trial in accordance with the applicable rules of international law; and

(b) any such persons who do not benefit from more favourable treatment under the Conventions or this Protocol shall be accorded the treatment provided by this Article, whether or not the crimes of which they are accused constitute grave breaches of the Conventions or of this Protocol.

8. No provision of this Article may be construed as limiting or infringing any other more favourable provision granting greater protection, under any applicable rules of international law, to persons covered by paragraph 1.

Protection of the civilian population *(Protocol Additional to the Geneva Conventions of 12 August 1949, and relating to the Protection of Victims of International Armed Conflicts (Protocol I), 8 June 1977. Part. IV. Civilian Population. Section I. General Protection Against Effects of Hostilities. Chapter II. Civilians and civilian population. Art. 51. Protection of the civilian population; Chapter IV. Precautionary measures. Art. 57. Precautions in attack; Art. 58. Precautions against the effects of attacks). Art. 51. Protection of the civilian population.* 1. The civilian population and individual civilians shall enjoy general protection against dangers arising from military operations. To give effect to this protection, the following rules, which are additional to other applicable rules of international law, shall be observed in all circumstances.

2. The civilian population as such, as well as individual civilians, shall not be the object of attack. Acts or threats of violence the primary purpose of which is to spread terror among the civilian population are prohibited.

3. Civilians shall enjoy the protection afforded by this section, unless and for such time as they take a direct part in hostilities.

4. Indiscriminate attacks are prohibited. Indiscriminate attacks are:

(a) those which are not directed at a specific military objective;

(b) those which employ a method or means of combat which cannot be directed at a specific military objective; or

(c) those which employ a method or means of combat the effects of which cannot be limited as required by this Protocol; and consequently, in each such case, are of a nature to strike military objectives and civilians or civilian objects without distinction.

5. Among others, the following types of attacks are to be considered as indiscriminate:

(a) an attack by bombardment by any methods or means which treats as a single military objective a number of clearly separated and distinct military objectives located in a city, town, village or other area containing a similar concentration of civilians or civilian objects; and

(b) an attack which may be expected to cause incidental loss of civilian life, injury to civilians, damage to civilian objects, or a combination thereof, which would be excessive in relation to the concrete and direct military advantage anticipated.

6. Attacks against the civilian population or civilians by way of reprisals are prohibited.

7. The presence or movements of the civilian population or individual civilians shall not be used to render certain points or areas immune from military operations, in particular in attempts to shield military objectives from attacks or to shield, favour or impede military operations. The Parties to the conflict shall not direct the movement of the civilian population or individual civilians in order to attempt to shield military objectives from attacks or to shield military operations.

8. Any violation of these prohibitions shall not release the Parties to the conflict from their legal obligations with respect to the civilian population and civilians, including the obligation to take the precautionary measures provided for in Article 57.

Art. 57. Precautions in attack. 1. In the conduct of military operations, constant care shall be taken to spare the civilian population, civilians and civilian objects.

2. With respect to attacks, the following precautions shall be taken:

(a) those who plan or decide upon an attack shall:

(i) do everything feasible to verify that the objectives to be attacked are neither civilians nor civilian objects and are not subject to special protection but are military objectives within the meaning of paragraph 2 of Article 52 and that it is not prohibited by the provisions of this Protocol to attack them;

(ii) take all feasible precautions in the choice of means and methods of attack with a view to avoiding, and in any event to minimizing, incidental loss or civilian life, injury to civilians and damage to civilian objects;

(iii) refrain from deciding to launch any attack which may be expected to cause incidental loss of civilian life, injury to civilians, damage to civilian objects, or a combination thereof, which would be excessive in relation to the concrete and direct military advantage anticipated;

(b) an attack shall be cancelled or suspended if it becomes apparent that the objective is not a military one or is subject to special protection or that the attack may be expected to cause incidental loss of civilian life, injury to civilians, damage to civilian objects, or a combination thereof, which would be excessive in relation to the concrete and direct military advantage anticipated;

(c) effective advance warning shall be given of attacks which may affect the civilian population, unless circumstances do not permit.

3. When a choice is possible between several military objectives for obtaining a similar military advantage, the objective to be selected shall be that the attack on which may be expected to cause the least danger to civilian lives and to civilian objects.

4. In the conduct of military operations at sea or in the air, each Party to the conflict shall, in conformity with its rights and duties under the rules of international law applicable in armed conflict, take all reasonable precautions to avoid losses of civilian lives and damage to civilian objects.

5. No provision of this article may be construed as authorizing any attacks against the civilian population, civilians or civilian objects.

Art. 58. Precautions against the effects of attacks. The Parties to the conflict shall, to the maximum extent feasible:

(a) without prejudice to Article 49 of the Fourth Convention, endeavour to remove the civilian population, individual civilians and civilian objects under their control from the vicinity of military objectives;

(b) avoid locating military objectives within or near densely populated areas;

(c) take the other necessary precautions to protect the civilian population, individual civilians and civilian objects under their control against the dangers resulting from military operations.

Protection of the natural environment *(Protocol Additional to the Geneva Conventions of 12 August 1949, and relating to the Protection of Victims of International Armed Conflicts (Protocol I), 8 June 1977. Part. IV. Civilian Population. Section I. General Protection Against Effects of Hostilities. Chapter III. Civilian objects. Art. 55. Protection of the natural environment).* 1. Care shall be taken in warfare to protect the natural environment against widespread, long-term and severe damage. This protection includes a prohibition of the use of methods or means of warfare which are intended or may be expected to cause such damage to the natural environment and thereby to prejudice the health or survival of the population.

2. Attacks against the natural environment by way of reprisals are prohibited.

Protection of the victims and witnesses *(Rome Statute ICC, art. 68. Protection of the victims and witnesses and their participation in the proceedings; RPE – ICC, Section 3. Victims and witnesses, Subsection 2. Protection of victims and witnesses - Statute ICTY, art. 22. Protection of victims and witnesses; RPE – ICTY,*

Rule 69. Protection of Victims and Witnesses - Statute ICTR, art. 21. Protection of Victims and Witnesses; RPE – ICTR, Rule 69. Protection of Victims and Witnesses).
Rome Statute ICC, art. 68. **Protection of the victims and witnesses and their participation in the proceedings.** 1. The Court shall take appropriate measures to protect the safety, physical and psychological well-being, dignity and privacy of victims and witnesses. In so doing, the Court shall have regard to all relevant factors, including age, gender as defined in article 7, paragraph 3, and health, and the nature of the crime, in particular, but not limited to, where the crime involves sexual or gender violence or violence against children. The Prosecutor shall take such measures particularly during the investigation and prosecution of such crimes. These measures shall not be prejudicial to or inconsistent with the rights of the accused and a fair and impartial trial.
2. As an exception to the principle of public hearings provided for in article 67, the Chambers of the Court may, to protect victims and witnesses or an accused, conduct any part of the proceedings *in camera* or allow the presentation of evidence by electronic or other special means. In particular, such measures shall be implemented in the case of a victim of sexual violence or a child who is a victim or a witness, unless otherwise ordered by the Court, having regard to all the circumstances, particularly the views of the victim or witness.
3. Where the personal interests of the victims are affected, the Court shall permit their views and concerns to be presented and considered at stages of the proceedings determined to be appropriate by the Court and in a manner which is not prejudicial to or inconsistent with the rights of the accused and a fair and impartial trial. Such views and concerns may be presented by the legal representatives of the victims where the Court considers it appropriate, in accordance with the Rules of Procedure and Evidence.
4. The Victims and Witnesses Unit may advise the Prosecutor and the Court on appropriate protective measures, security arrangements, counselling and assistance as referred to in article 43, paragraph 6.
5. Where the disclosure of evidence or information pursuant to this Statute may lead to the grave endangerment of the security of a witness or his or her family, the Prosecutor may, for the purposes of any proceedings conducted prior to the commencement of the trial, withhold such evidence or information and instead submit a summary thereof. Such measures shall be exercised in a manner which is not prejudicial to or inconsistent with the rights of the accused and a fair and impartial trial.
6. A State may make an application for necessary measures to be taken in respect of the protection of its servants or agents and the protection of confidential or sensitive information.
See: RPE – ICC, Section 3. Victims and witnesses, Subsection 2. Protection of victims and witnesses. Rule 87. Protective measures; Rule 88. Special measures; Subsection 3. Participation of victims in the proceedings; Rule 89. Application for participation of victims in the proceedings; Rule 90. Legal representatives of victims; Rule 91. Participation of legal representatives in the proceedings; Rule 92. Notification to victims and their legal representatives; Rule 93. Views of victims or their legal representatives; Subsection 4. Reparations to victims; Rule 94. Procedure upon request; Rule 95. Procedure on the motion of the Court; Rule 96. Publication

of reparation proceedings; Rule 97. Assessment of reparations; Rule 98. Trust Fund; Rule 99. Cooperation and protective measures for the purpose of forfeiture under articles 57, paragraph 3 (e), and 75, paragraph 4.

Statute ICTY, art. 22. Protection of victims and witnesses. The International Tribunal shall provide in its rules of procedure and evidence for the protection of victims and witnesses. Such protection measures shall include, but shall not be limited to, the conduct of in camera proceedings and the protection of the victim's identity.

See: RPE – ICTY, Rule 69. Protection of Victims and Witnesses.

(A) In exceptional circumstances, the Prosecutor may apply to a Judge or Trial Chamber to order the non-disclosure of the identity of a victim or witness who may be in danger or at risk until such person is brought under the protection of the Tribunal.

(B) In the determination of protective measures for victims and witnesses, the Judge or Trial Chamber may consult the Victims and Witnesses Section.

(C) Subject to Rule 75, the identity of the victim or witness shall be disclosed in sufficient time prior to the trial to allow adequate time for preparation of the defence.

Statute ICTR, art. 21. **Protection of Victims and Witnesses.** The International Tribunal for Rwanda shall provide in its Rules of Procedure and Evidence for the protection of victims and witnesses. Such protection measures shall include, but shall not be limited to, the conduct of in camera proceedings and the protection of the victim's identity.

See: RPE – ICTR, Rule 69. Protection of Victims and Witnesses.

(A) In exceptional circumstances, either of the parties may apply to a Trial Chamber to order the non-disclosure of the identity of a victim or witness who may be in danger or at risk, until the Chamber decides otherwise.

(B) In the determination of protective measures for victims and witnesses, the Trial Chamber may consult the Victims and Witness Support Unit.

(C) Subject to Rule 75, the identity of the victim or witness shall be disclosed within such time as determined by Trial Chamber to allow adequate time for preparation of the Prosecution and the Defence.

Protection of women *(Protocol Additional to the Geneva Conventions of 12 August 1949, and relating to the Protection of Victims of International Armed Conflicts (Protocol I), 8 June 1977. Part. IV. Civilian Population. Section III. Treatment of Persons in the Power of a Party to the Conflict. Chapter II. Measures in favour of women and children. Art. 76. Protection of women).* 1. Women shall be the object of special respect and shall be protected in particular against rape, forced prostitution and any other form of indecent assault.

2. Pregnant women and mothers having dependent infants who are arrested, detained or interned for reasons related to the armed conflict, shall have their cases considered with the utmost priority.

3. To the maximum extent feasible, the Parties to the conflict shall endeavour to avoid the pronouncement of the death penalty on pregnant women or mothers having dependent infants, for an offence related to the armed conflict. The death penalty for such offences shall not be executed on such women.

Protection of works and installations containing dangerous forces

(Protocol Additional to the Geneva Conventions of 12 August 1949, and relating to the Protection of Victims of International Armed Conflicts (Protocol I), 8 June 1977. Part. IV. Civilian Population. Section I. General Protection Against Effects of Hostilities. Chapter III. Civilian objects. Art. 56. Protection of works and installations containing dangerous forces). 1. Works or installations containing dangerous forces, namely dams, dykes and nuclear electrical generating stations, shall not be made the object of attack, even where these objects are military objectives, if such attack may cause the release of dangerous forces and consequent severe losses among the civilian population. Other military objectives located at or in the vicinity of these works or installations shall not be made the object of attack if such attack may cause the release of dangerous forces from the works or installations and consequent severe losses among the civilian population.

2. The special protection against attack provided by paragraph 1 shall cease:

(a) for a dam or a dyke only if it is used for other than its normal function and in regular, significant and direct support of military operations and if such attack is the only feasible way to terminate such support;

(b) for a nuclear electrical generating station only if it provides electric power in regular, significant and direct support of military operations and if such attack is the only feasible way to terminate such support;

(c) for other military objectives located at or in the vicinity of these works or installations only if they are used in regular, significant and direct support of military operations and if such attack is the only feasible way to terminate such support.

3. In all cases, the civilian population and individual civilians shall remain entitled to all the protection accorded them by international law, including the protection of the precautionary measures provided for in Article 57. If the protection Ceases and any of the works, installations or military objectives mentioned in paragraph 1 is attacked, all practical precautions shall be taken to avoid the release of the dangerous forces.

4. It is prohibited to make any of the works, installations or military objectives mentioned in paragraph 1 the object of reprisals.

5. The Parties to the conflict shall endeavour to avoid locating any military objectives in the vicinity of the works or installations mentioned in paragraph 1. Nevertheless, installations erected for the sole purpose of defending the protected works or installations from attack are permissible and shall not themselves be made the object of attack, provided that they are not used in hostilities except for defensive actions necessary to respond to attacks against the protected works or installations and that their armament is limited to weapons capable only of repelling hostile action against the protected works or installations.

6. The High Contracting Parties and the Parties to the conflict are urged to conclude further agreements among themselves to provide additional protection for objects containing dangerous forces.

7. In order to facilitate the identification of the objects protected by this article, the Parties to the conflict may mark them with a special sign consisting of a group of three bright orange circles placed on the same axis, as specified in Article 16 of Annex I to this Protocol [Article 17 of Amended Annex]. The absence of such

marking in no way relieves any Party to the conflict of its obligations under this Article.

"Protecting Power" (Protocol Additional to the Geneva Conventions of 12 August 1949, and relating to the Protection of Victims of International Armed Conflicts (Protocol I), 8 June 1977. Part I. General provisions. Art 2. Definitions). For the purposes of this Protocol (…) (c) "Protecting Power" means a neutral or other State not a Party to the conflict which has been designated by a Party to the conflict and accepted by the adverse Party and has agreed to carry out the functions assigned to a Protecting Power under the Conventions and this Protocol.

Protocol to Prevent, Suppress and Punish Trafficking in Persons Especially Women and Children, supplementing the United Nations Convention against Transnational Organized Crime.
Adopted and opened for signature, ratification and accession by General Assembly resolution 55/25 of 15 November 2000. *Preamble*. The States Parties to this Protocol,

Declaring that effective action to prevent and combat trafficking in persons, especially women and children, requires a comprehensive international approach in the countries of origin, transit and destination that includes measures to prevent such trafficking, to punish the traffickers and to protect the victims of such trafficking, including by protecting their internationally recognized human rights,

Taking into account the fact that, despite the existence of a variety of international instruments containing rules and practical measures to combat the exploitation of persons, especially women and children, there is no universal instrument that addresses all aspects of trafficking in persons,

Concerned that, in the absence of such an instrument, persons who are vulnerable to trafficking will not be sufficiently protected,

Recalling General Assembly resolution 53/111 of 9 December 1998, in which the Assembly decided to establish an open-ended intergovernmental ad hoc committee for the purpose of elaborating a comprehensive international convention against transnational organized crime and of discussing the elaboration of, inter alia, an international instrument addressing trafficking in women and children,

Convinced that supplementing the United Nations Convention against Transnational Organized Crime with an international instrument for the prevention, suppression and punishment of trafficking in persons, especially women and children, will be useful in preventing and combating that crime,

Have agreed as follows: (…).

Q

Qualified persons *(Protocol Additional to the Geneva Conventions of 12 August 1949, and relating to the Protection of Victims of International Armed Conflicts (Protocol I), 8 June 1977. Part I. General provisions. Art 6. Qualified persons).* 1. The High Contracting Parties shall, also in peacetime, endeavour, with the assistance of the national Red Cross (Red Crescent, Red Lion and Sun) Societies, to train qualified personnel to facilitate the application of the Conventions and of this Protocol, and in particular the activities of the Protecting Powers.

2. The recruitment and training of such personnel are within domestic jurisdiction.

3. The International Committee of the Red Cross shall hold at the disposal of the High Contracting Parties the lists of persons so trained which the High Contracting Parties may have established and may have transmitted to it for that purpose.

4. The conditions governing the employment of such personnel outside the national territory shall, in each case, be the subject of special agreements between the Parties concerned.

R

"Racial discrimination" (International Convention on the Elimination of All Forms of Racial Discrimination (Adopted and opened for signature and ratification by General Assembly resolution 2106 (XX) of 21 December 1965. Part. I., Art. 1). 1. In this Convention, the term "racial discrimination" shall mean any distinction, exclusion, restriction or preference based on race, colour, descent, or national or ethnic origin which has the purpose or effect of nullifying or impairing the recognition, enjoyment or exercise, on an equal footing, of human rights and fundamental freedoms in the political, economic, social, cultural or any other field of public life.

2. This Convention shall not apply to distinctions, exclusions, restrictions or preferences made by a State Party to this Convention between citizens and non-citizens.

3. Nothing in this Convention may be interpreted as affecting in any way the legal provisions of States Parties concerning nationality, citizenship or naturalization, provided that such provisions do not discriminate against any particular nationality.

4. Special measures taken for the sole purpose of securing adequate advancement of certain racial or ethnic groups or individuals requiring such protection as may be necessary in order to ensure such groups or individuals equal enjoyment or exercise of human rights and fundamental freedoms shall not be deemed racial discrimination, provided, however, that such measures do not, as a consequence, lead to the maintenance of separate rights for different racial groups and that they shall not be continued after the objectives for which they were taken have been achieved.

"Refugee" *(Convention relating to the Status of Refugees. Geneva, 28 July 1951.Chapter I. General provisions, Art. 1. Definition of the term "refugee").*

A. For the purposes of the present Convention, the term "refugee, shall apply to any person who:

(1) Has been considered a refugee under the Arrangements of 12 May 1926 and 30 June 1928 or under the Conventions of 28 October 1933 and 10 February 1938, the Protocol of 14 September 1939 or the Constitution of the International Refugee Organization;

Decisions of non-eligibility taken by the International Refugee Organization during the period of its activities shall not prevent the status of refugee being accorded to persons who fulfil the conditions of paragraph 2 of this section;

(2) As a result of events occurring before I January 1951 and owing to well-founded fear of being persecuted for reasons of race, religion, nationality, membership of a particular social group or political opinion, is outside the country of his nationality

and is unable, or owing to such fear, is unwilling to avail himself of the protection of that country; or who, not having a nationality and being outside the country of his former habitual residence as a result of such events, is unable or, owing to such fear, is unwilling to return to it.

In the case of a person who has more than one nationality, the term "the country of his nationality" shall mean each of the countries of which he is a national, and a person shall not be deemed to be lacking the protection of the country of his nationality if, without any valid reason based on well-founded fear, he has not availed himself of the protection of one of the countries of which he is a national.

B. (1) For the purposes of this Convention, the words "events occurring before I January 1951" in article 1, section A, shall be understood to mean either (a) "events occurring in Europe before I January 1951"; or (b) "events occurring in Europe or elsewhere before I January 1951"; and each Contracting State shall make a declaration at the time of signature, ratification or accession, specifying which of these meanings it applies for the purpose of its obligations under this Convention.

(2) Any Contracting State which has adopted alternative (a) may at any time extend its obligations by adopting alternative (b) by means of a notification addressed to the Secretary-General of the United Nations.

C. This Convention shall cease to apply to any person falling under the terms of section A if:

(1) He has voluntarily re-availed himself of the protection of the country of his nationality; or

(2) Having lost his nationality, he has voluntarily reacquired it; or

(3) He has acquired a new nationality, and enjoys the protection of the country of his new nationality; or

(4) He has voluntarily re-established himself in the country which he left or outside which he remained owing to fear of persecution; or

(5) He can no longer, because the circumstances in connection with which he has been recognized as a refugee have ceased to exist, continue to refuse to avail himself of the protection of the country of his nationality;

Provided that this paragraph shall not apply to a refugee falling under section A (I) of this article who is able to invoke compelling reasons arising out of previous persecution for refusing to avail himself of the protection of the country of nationality;

(6) Being a person who has no nationality he is, because the circumstances in connection with which he has been recognized as a refugee have ceased to exist, able to return to the country of his former habitual residence;

Provided that this paragraph shall not apply to a refugee falling under section A (I) of this article who is able to invoke compelling reasons arising out of previous persecution for refusing to return to the country of his former habitual residence.

D. This Convention shall not apply to persons who are at present receiving from organs or agencies of the United Nations other than the United Nations High Commissioner for Refugees protection or assistance.

When such protection or assistance has ceased for any reason, without the position of such persons being definitively settled in accordance with the relevant resolutions adopted by the General Assembly of the United Nations, these persons shall ipso facto be entitled to the benefits of this Convention.

E. This Convention shall not apply to a person who is recognized by the competent authorities of the country in which he has taken residence as having the rights and obligations which are attached to the possession of the nationality of that country.

F. The provisions of this Convention shall not apply to any person with respect to whom there are serious reasons for considering that:

(a) He has committed a crime against peace, a war crime, or a crime against humanity, as defined in the international instruments drawn up to make provision in respect of such crimes;

(b) He has committed a serious non-political crime outside the country of refuge prior to his admission to that country as a refugee;

(c) He has been guilty of acts contrary to the purposes and principles of the United Nations.

Registry *(Rome Statute ICC, art. 43. The Registry; See RPE – ICC, Chapter 2. Composition and administration of the Court. Section 3. The Registry. Subsection 1. General provisions relating to the Registry. Rules 12, 13, 14, 15; Subsection 3. Counsel for the defence. Rules 20, 21, 22; Statute ICTY, art. 17. The Registry; See RPE – ICTY, Part 3. Organization of the Tribunal. Section 5. The Registry; Statute ICTR, art. 16. The Registry; See RPE – ICTR, Part 3. Organization of the Tribunal. Section 5. The Registrar).*

Rome Statute ICC, *art. 43. The Registry.* 1. The Registry shall be responsible for the non-judicial aspects of the administration and servicing of the Court, without prejudice to the functions and powers of the Prosecutor in accordance with article 42.

2. The Registry shall be headed by the Registrar, who shall be the principal administrative officer of the Court. The Registrar shall exercise his or her functions under the authority of the President of the Court.

3. The Registrar and the Deputy Registrar shall be persons of high moral character, be highly competent and have an excellent knowledge of and be fluent in at least one of the working languages of the Court.

4. The judges shall elect the Registrar by an absolute majority by secret ballot, taking into account any recommendation by the Assembly of States Parties. If the need arises and upon the recommendation of the Registrar, the judges shall elect, in the same manner, a Deputy Registrar.

5. The Registrar shall hold office for a term of five years, shall be eligible for reelection once and shall serve on a full-time basis. The Deputy Registrar shall hold office for a term of five years or such shorter term as may be decided upon by an absolute majority of the judges, and may be elected on the basis that the Deputy Registrar shall be called upon to serve as required.

6. The Registrar shall set up a Victims and Witnesses Unit within the Registry. This Unit shall provide, in consultation with the Office of the Prosecutor, protective measures and security arrangements, counselling and other appropriate assistance for witnesses, victims who appear before the Court, and others who are at risk on account of testimony given by such witnesses. The Unit shall include staff with expertise in trauma, including trauma related to crimes of sexual violence. *See: RPE – ICC, Chapter 2. Composition and administration of the Court. Section 3. The*

Registry. Subsection 1. General provisions relating to the Registry. Rules 12, 13, 14, 15; Subsection 3. Counsel for the defence. Rules 20, 21, 22.
Statute ICTY, art. 17. The Registry. 1. The Registry shall be responsible for the administration and servicing of the International Tribunal.
2. The Registry shall consist of a Registrar and such other staff as may be required.
3. The Registrar shall be appointed by the Secretary-General after consultation with the President of the International Tribunal. He or she shall serve for a four-year term and be eligible for reappointment. The terms and conditions of service of the Registrar shall be those of an Assistant Secretary-General of the United Nations.
4. The staff of the Registry shall be appointed by the Secretary-General on the recommendation of the Registrar. *See: RPE – ICTY, Part 3. Organization of the Tribunal. Section 5. The Registry.*
Statute ICTR, art. 16. The Registry. 1. The Registry shall be responsible for the administration and servicing of the International Tribunal for Rwanda.
2. The Registry shall consist of a Registrar and such other staff as may be required.
3. The Registrar shall be appointed by the Secretary-General after consultation with the President of the International Tribunal for Rwanda. He or she shall serve for a four-year term and be eligible for re-appointment. The terms and conditions of service of the Registrar shall be those of an Assistant Secretary-General of the United Nations.
4. The Staff of the Registry shall be appointed by the Secretary-General on the recommendation of the Registrar. *See: RPE – ICTR, Part 3. Organization of the Tribunal. Section 5. The Registrar.*

"Religious personnel" *(Protocol Additional to the Geneva Conventions of 12 August 1949, and relating to the Protection of Victims of International Armed Conflicts (Protocol I), 8 June 1977. Part. II. Wounded, sick and shipwrecked, Section I: General Protection. Art. 8. Terminology).* For the purposes of this Protocol: (…) d) "Religious personnel" means military or civilian persons, such as chaplains, who are exclusively engaged in the work of their ministry and attached:
i) to the armed forces of a Party to the conflict;
ii) to medical units or medical transports of a Party to the conflict;
iii) to medical units or medical transports described in Article 9, Paragraph 2; or
iv) to civil defence organizations of a Party to the conflict.
The attachment of religious personnel may be either permanent or temporary, and the relevant provisions mentioned under k) apply to them.
Art. 9. Field of application (…). 2. The relevant provisions of Articles 27 and 32 of the First Convention shall apply to permanent medical units and transports (other than hospital ships, to which Article 25 of the Second Convention applies) and their personnel made available to a Party to the conflict for humanitarian purposes:
(a) by a neutral or other State which is not a Party to that conflict;
(b) by a recognized and authorized aid society of such a State;
(c) by an impartial international humanitarian organization.
(…) k) "Permanent medical personnel", "permanent medical units" and "permanent medical transports" mean those assigned exclusively to medical purposes for an indeterminate period. "Temporary medical personnel" "temporary medical-units" and "temporary medical transports" mean those devoted exclusively

173

to medical purposes for limited periods during the whole of such periods. Unless otherwise specified, the terms "medical personnel", "medical units" and "medical transports" cover both permanent and temporary categories.

Right to a fair trial *(International Covenant on Civil and Political Rights. Adopted and opened for signature, ratification and accession by General Assembly resolution 2200A (XXI) of 16 December 1966. Art. 14; Convention for the Protection of Human Rights and Fundamental Freedoms. Rome, 4.XI.1950 (as amended by Protocols Nos. 11 and 14 with Protocols Nos. 1, 4, 6, 7, 12 and 13). Art. 6. Right to a fair trial; Rome Statute ICC, art. 67. Rights of the accused; Statute ICTY, art. 21. Rights of the accused; Statute ICTR, art. 20. Rights of the Accused).*

International Covenant on Civil and Political Rights. Adopted and opened for signature, ratification and accession by General Assembly resolution 2200A (XXI) of 16 December 1966. Art. 14. 1. All persons shall be equal before the courts and tribunals. In the determination of any criminal charge against him, or of his rights and obligations in a suit at law, everyone shall be entitled to a fair and public hearing by a competent, independent and impartial tribunal established by law. The press and the public may be excluded from all or part of a trial for reasons of morals, public order (ordre public) or national security in a democratic society, or when the interest of the private lives of the parties so requires, or to the extent strictly necessary in the opinion of the court in special circumstances where publicity would prejudice the interests of justice; but any judgement rendered in a criminal case or in a suit at law shall be made public except where the interest of juvenile persons otherwise requires or the proceedings concern matrimonial disputes or the guardianship of children.

2. Everyone charged with a criminal offence shall have the right to be presumed innocent until proved guilty according to law.

3. In the determination of any criminal charge against him, everyone shall be entitled to the following minimum guarantees, in full equality:

(a) To be informed promptly and in detail in a language which he understands of the nature and cause of the charge against him;

(b) To have adequate time and facilities for the preparation of his defence and to communicate with counsel of his own choosing;

(c) To be tried without undue delay;

(d) To be tried in his presence, and to defend himself in person or through legal assistance of his own choosing; to be informed, if he does not have legal assistance, of this right; and to have legal assistance assigned to him, in any case where the interests of justice so require, and without payment by him in any such case if he does not have sufficient means to pay for it; (e) To examine, or have examined, the witnesses against him and to obtain the attendance and examination of witnesses on his behalf under the same conditions as witnesses against him; (f) To have the free assistance of an interpreter if he cannot understand or speak the language used in court;

(g) Not to be compelled to testify against himself or to confess guilt.

4. In the case of juvenile persons, the procedure shall be such as will take account of their age and the desirability of promoting their rehabilitation.

5. Everyone convicted of a crime shall have the right to his conviction and sentence being reviewed by a higher tribunal according to law.

6. When a person has by a final decision been convicted of a criminal offence and when subsequently his conviction has been reversed or he has been pardoned on the ground that a new or newly discovered fact shows conclusively that there has been a miscarriage of justice, the person who has suffered punishment as a result of such conviction shall be compensated according to law, unless it is proved that the non-disclosure of the unknown fact in time is wholly or partly attributable to him.

7. No one shall be liable to be tried or punished again for an offence for which he has already been finally convicted or acquitted in accordance with the law and penal procedure of each country.

Convention for the Protection of Human Rights and Fundamental Freedoms. Rome, 4.XI.1950 (as amended by Protocols Nos. 11 and 14 with Protocols Nos. 1, 4, 6, 7, 12 and 13). Art. 6. Right to a fair trial. 1. In the determination of his civil rights and obligations or of any criminal charge against him, everyone is entitled to a fair and public hearing within a reasonable time by an independent and impartial tribunal established by law. Judgment shall be pronounced publicly but the press and public may be excluded from all or part of the trial in the interests of morals, public order or national security in a democratic society, where the interests of juveniles or the protection of the private life of the parties so require, or to the extent strictly necessary in the opinion of the court in special circumstances where publicity would prejudice the interests of justice.

2. Everyone charged with a criminal offence shall be presumed innocent until proved guilty according to law.

3. Everyone charged with a criminal offence has the following minimum rights:

a. to be informed promptly, in a language which he understands and in detail, of the nature and cause of the accusation against him;

b. to have adequate time and facilities for the preparation of his defence;

c. to defend himself in person or through legal assistance of his own choosing or, if he has not sufficient means to pay for legal assistance, to be given it free when the interests of justice so require;

d. to examine or have examined witnesses against him and to obtain the attendance and examination of witnesses on his behalf under the same conditions as witnesses against him;

e. to have the free assistance of an interpreter if he cannot understand or speak the language used in court.

Rome Statute ICC, art. 67. Rights of the accused. 1. In the determination of any charge, the accused shall be entitled to a public hearing, having regard to the provisions of this Statute, to a fair hearing conducted impartially, and to the following minimum guarantees, in full equality:

(a) To be informed promptly and in detail of the nature, cause and content of the charge, in a language which the accused fully understands and speaks;

(b) To have adequate time and facilities for the preparation of the defence and to communicate freely with counsel of the accused's choosing in confidence;

(c) To be tried without undue delay;

(d) Subject to article 63, paragraph 2, to be present at the trial, to conduct the defence in person or through legal assistance of the accused's choosing, to be informed, if the

accused does not have legal assistance, of this right and to have legal assistance assigned by the Court in any case where the interests of justice so require, and without payment if the accused lacks
sufficient means to pay for it;

(e) To examine, or have examined, the witnesses against him or her and to obtain the attendance and examination of witnesses on his or her behalf under the same conditions as witnesses against him or her. The accused shall also be entitled to raise defences and to present other evidence admissible under this Statute;

(f) To have, free of any cost, the assistance of a competent interpreter and such translations as are necessary to meet the requirements of fairness, if any of the proceedings of or documents presented to the Court are not in a language which the accused fully understands and speaks;

(g) Not to be compelled to testify or to confess guilt and to remain silent, without such silence being a consideration in the determination of guilt or innocence;

(h) To make an unsworn oral or written statement in his or her defence; and

(i) Not to have imposed on him or her any reversal of the burden of proof or any onus of rebuttal.

2. In addition to any other disclosure provided for in this Statute, the Prosecutor shall, as soon as practicable, disclose to the defence evidence in the Prosecutor's possession or control which he or she believes shows or tends to show the innocence of the accused, or to mitigate the guilt of the accused, or which may affect the credibility of prosecution evidence. In case of doubt as to the application of this paragraph, the Court shall decide.

Statute ICTY, art. 21. Rights of the accused. 1. All persons shall be equal before the International Tribunal.

2. In the determination of charges against him, the accused shall be entitled to a fair and public hearing, subject to article 22 of the Statute.

3. The accused shall be presumed innocent until proved guilty according to the provisions of the present Statute.

4. In the determination of any charge against the accused pursuant to the present Statute, the accused shall be entitled to the following minimum guarantees, in full equality:

(a) to be informed promptly and in detail in a language which he understands of the nature and cause of the charge against him;

(b) to have adequate time and facilities for the preparation of his defence and to communicate with counsel of his own choosing;

(c) to be tried without undue delay;

(d) to be tried in his presence, and to defend himself in person or through legal assistance of his own choosing; to be informed, if he does not have legal assistance, of this right; and to have legal assistance assigned to him, in any case where the interests of justice so require, and without payment by him in any such case if he does not have sufficient means to pay for it;

(e) to examine, or have examined, the witnesses against him and to obtain the attendance and examination of witnesses on his behalf under the same conditions as witnesses against him;

(f) to have the free assistance of an interpreter if he cannot understand or speak the language used in the International Tribunal;

(g) not to be compelled to testify against himself or to confess guilt.

Statute ICTR, art. 20. Rights of the Accused. 1. All persons shall be equal before the International Tribunal for Rwanda.

2. In the determination of charges against him or her, the accused shall be entitled to a fair and

public hearing, subject to Article 21 of the Statute.

3. The accused shall be presumed innocent until proven guilty according to the provisions of the present Statute.

4. In the determination of any charge against the accused pursuant to the present Statute, the accused shall be entitled to the following minimum guarantees, in full equality:

(a) To be informed promptly and in detail in a language which he or she understands of the nature and cause of the charge against him or her;

(b) To have adequate time and facilities for the preparation of his or her defence and to communicate with counsel of his or her own choosing;

(c) To be tried without undue delay;

(d) To be tried in his or her presence, and to defend himself or herself in person or through legal assistance of his or her own choosing; to be informed, if he or she does not have legal assistance, of this right; and to have legal assistance assigned to him or her, in any case where the interest of justice so require, and without payment by him or her in any such case if he or she does not have sufficient means to pay for it;

(e) To examine, or have examined, the witnesses against him or her and to obtain the attendance and examination of witnesses on his or her behalf under the same conditions as witnesses against him or her;

(f) To have the free assistance of an interpreter if he or she cannot understand or speak the language used in the International Tribunal for Rwanda;

(g) Not to be compelled to testify against himself or herself or to confess guilt.

Right to freedom of thought, conscience, religion and freedom of expression *(International Covenant on Civil and Political Rights. Adopted and opened for signature, ratification and accession by General Assembly resolution 2200A (XXI) of 16 December 1966. Part III, Art. 18, Art. 19, Art. 20 – Convention for the Protection of Human Rights and Fundamental Freedoms. Rome, 4.XI.1950. Art. 9. Freedom of thought, conscience and religion; Art. 10. Freedom of expression - American Convention on Human Rights "Pact of San Jose, Costa Rica", 22 November 1969. Art. 12. Freedom of Conscience and Religion; Art. 13. Freedom of Thought and Expression).*

International Covenant on Civil and Political Rights. Adopted and opened for signature, ratification and accession by General Assembly resolution 2200A (XXI) of 16 December 1966. Part III. Art. 18. 1. Everyone shall have the right to *freedom of thought, conscience and religion.* This right shall include freedom to have or to adopt a religion or belief of his choice, and freedom, either individually or in community with others and in public or private, to manifest his religion or belief in worship, observance, practice and teaching.

2. No one shall be subject to coercion which would impair his freedom to have or to adopt a religion or belief of his choice.

3. Freedom to manifest one's religion or beliefs may be subject only to such limitations as are prescribed by law and are necessary to protect public safety, order, health, or morals or the fundamental rights and freedoms of others.

4. The States Parties to the present Covenant undertake to have respect for the liberty of parents and, when applicable, legal guardians to ensure the religious and moral education of their children in conformity with their own convictions.

Art. 19. 1. Everyone shall have the right to hold opinions without interference.

2. Everyone shall have the right to *freedom of expression;* this right shall include freedom to seek, receive and impart information and ideas of all kinds, regardless of frontiers, either orally, in writing or in print, in the form of art, or through any other media of his choice.

3. The exercise of the rights provided for in paragraph 2 of this article carries with it special duties and responsibilities. It may therefore be subject to certain restrictions, but these shall only be such as are provided by law and are necessary:

(a) For respect of the rights or reputations of others;

(b) For the protection of national security or of public order (ordre public), or of public health or morals.

Art. 20. 1. Any propaganda for war shall be prohibited by law.

2. Any advocacy of national, racial or religious hatred that constitutes incitement to discrimination, hostility or violence shall be prohibited by law.

Convention for the Protection of Human Rights and Fundamental Freedoms. Rome, 4.XI.1950. Art. 9. Freedom of thought, conscience and religion. 1. Everyone has the right to freedom of thought, conscience and religion; this right includes freedom to change his religion or belief and freedom, either alone or in community with others and in public or private, to manifest his religion or belief, in worship, teaching, practice and observance.

2. Freedom to manifest one's religion or beliefs shall be subject only to such limitations as are prescribed by law and are necessary in a democratic society in the interests of public safety, for the protection of public order, health or morals, or for the protection of the rights and freedoms of others.

Art. 10. Freedom of expression. 1. Everyone has the right to freedom of expression. This right shall include freedom to hold opinions and to receive and impart information and ideas without interference by public authority and regardless of frontiers. This Article shall not prevent States from requiring the licensing of broadcasting, television or cinema enterprises.

2. The exercise of these freedoms, since it carries with it duties and responsibilities, may be subject to such formalities, conditions, restrictions or penalties as are prescribed by law and are necessary in a democratic society, in the interests of national security, territorial integrity or public safety, for the prevention of disorder or crime, for the protection of health or morals, for the protection of the reputation or rights of others, for preventing the disclosure of information received in confidence, or for maintaining the authority and impartiality of the judiciary.

American Convention on Human Rights *"Pact of San Jose, Costa Rica", 22 November 1969. Art. 12. Freedom of Conscience and Religion.* 1. Everyone has the right to freedom of conscience and of religion. This right includes freedom to maintain or to change one's religion or beliefs, and freedom to profess or disseminate one's religion or beliefs, either individually or together with others, in public or in private.

2. No one shall be subject to restrictions that might impair his freedom to maintain or to change his religion or beliefs.

3. Freedom to manifest one's religion and beliefs may be subject only to the limitations prescribed by law that are necessary to protect public safety, order, health, or morals, or the rights or freedoms of others.

4. Parents or guardians, as the case may be, have the right to provide for the religious and moral education of their children or wards that is in accord with their own convictions.

Art. 13. Freedom of Thought and Expression. 1. Everyone has the right to freedom of thought and expression. This right includes freedom to seek, receive, and impart information and ideas of all kinds, regardless of frontiers, either orally, in writing, in print, in the form of art, or through any other medium of one's choice.

2. The exercise of the right provided for in the foregoing paragraph shall not be subject to prior censorship but shall be subject to subsequent imposition of liability, which shall be expressly established by law to the extent necessary to ensure:

a. respect for the rights or reputations of others; or

b. the protection of national security, public order, or public health or morals.

3. The right of expression may not be restricted by indirect methods or means, such as the abuse of government or private controls over newsprint, radio broadcasting frequencies, or equipment used in the dissemination of information, or by any other means tending to impede the communication and circulation of ideas and opinions.

4. Notwithstanding the provisions of paragraph 2 above, public entertainments may be subject by law to prior censorship for the sole purpose of regulating access to them for the moral protection of childhood and adolescence.

5. Any propaganda for war and any advocacy of national, racial, or religious hatred that constitute incitements to lawless violence or to any other similar action against any person or group of persons on any grounds including those of race, color, religion, language, or national origin shall be considered as offenses punishable by law.

Right to life *(Universal Declaration of Human Rights, Paris, 10 December 1948. Art. 3; International Covenant on Civil and Political Rights. Adopted and opened for signature, ratification and accession by General Assembly resolution 2200A (XXI) of 16 December 1966. Art. 6; Convention for the Protection of Human Rights and Fundamental Freedoms. Rome, 4.XI.1950 (as amended by Protocols Nos. 11 and 14 with Protocols Nos. 1, 4, 6, 7, 12 and 13). Art. 2. Right to life; Charter of fundamental rights of the European Union (18.12.2000 EN Official Journal of the European Communities C 364/3). Art. 2. Right to life; American Convention on Human Rights "Pact of San Jose, Costa Rica", 22 November 1969. Art. 4. Right to life).*

Universal Declaration of Human Rights, Paris, 10 December 1948. *Art. 3.* Everyone has the right to life, liberty and security of person.

International Covenant on Civil and Political Rights. Adopted and opened for signature, ratification and accession by General Assembly resolution 2200A (XXI) of 16 December 1966. Art. 6. 1. Every human being has the inherent right to life. This right shall be protected by law. No one shall be arbitrarily deprived of his life.

2. In countries which have not abolished the death penalty, sentence of death may be imposed only for the most serious crimes in accordance with the law in force at the time of the commission of the crime and not contrary to the provisions of the present Covenant and to the Convention on the Prevention and Punishment of the Crime of Genocide. This penalty can only be carried out pursuant to a final judgement rendered by a competent court.

3. When deprivation of life constitutes the crime of genocide, it is understood that nothing in this article shall authorize any State Party to the present Covenant to derogate in any way from any obligation assumed under the provisions of the Convention on the Prevention and Punishment of the Crime of Genocide.

4. Anyone sentenced to death shall have the right to seek pardon or commutation of the sentence. Amnesty, pardon or commutation of the sentence of death may be granted in all cases.

5. Sentence of death shall not be imposed for crimes committed by persons below eighteen years of age and shall not be carried out on pregnant women.

6. Nothing in this article shall be invoked to delay or to prevent the abolition of capital punishment by any State Party to the present Covenant.

Convention for the Protection of Human Rights and Fundamental Freedoms. Rome, 4.XI.1950 (as amended by Protocols Nos. 11 and 14 with Protocols Nos. 1, 4, 6, 7, 12 and 13). Art. 2. Right to life. 1. Everyone's right to life shall be protected by law. No one shall be deprived of his life intentionally save in the execution of a sentence of a court following his conviction of a crime for which this penalty is provided by law.

2. Deprivation of life shall not be regarded as inflicted in contravention of this article when it results from the use of force which is no more than absolutely necessary:

a. in defence of any person from unlawful violence;

b. in order to effect a lawful arrest or to prevent the escape of a person lawfully detained;

c. in action lawfully taken for the purpose of quelling a riot or insurrection.

Charter of fundamental rights of the European Union (18.12.2000 EN Official Journal of the European Communities C 364/3). Art. 2. Right to life. 1. Everyone has the right to life.

2. No one shall be condemned to the death penalty, or executed.

American Convention on Human Rights *"Pact of San Jose, Costa Rica", 22 November 1969. Art. 4. Right to life.* 1. Every person has the right to have his life respected. This right shall be protected by law and, in general, from the moment of conception. No one shall be arbitrarily deprived of his life.

2. In countries that have not abolished the death penalty, it may be imposed only for the most serious crimes and pursuant to a final judgment rendered by a competent court and in accordance with a law establishing such punishment, enacted prior to

the commission of the crime. The application of such punishment shall not be extended to crimes to which it does not presently apply.

3. The death penalty shall not be reestablished in states that have abolished it.

4. In no case shall capital punishment be inflicted for political offenses or related common crimes.

5. Capital punishment shall not be imposed upon persons who, at the time the crime was committed, were under 18 years of age or over 70 years of age; nor shall it be applied to pregnant women.

6. Every person condemned to death shall have the right to apply for amnesty, pardon, or commutation of sentence, which may be granted in all cases. Capital punishment shall not be imposed while such a petition is pending decision by the competent authority.

Rights of the accused *(Rome Statute ICC, art. 67. Rights of the accused; Rights of the accused, Statute ICTY, art. 21; Rights of the Accused, Statute ICTR, art. 20).*
Rome Statute ICC, art. 67. 1. In the determination of any charge, the accused shall be entitled to a public hearing, having regard to the provisions of this Statute, to a fair hearing conducted impartially, and to the following minimum guarantees, in full equality:

(a) To be informed promptly and in detail of the nature, cause and content of the charge, in a language which the accused fully understands and speaks;

(b) To have adequate time and facilities for the preparation of the defence and to communicate freely with counsel of the accused's choosing in confidence;

(c) To be tried without undue delay;

(d) Subject to article 63, paragraph 2, to be present at the trial, to conduct the defence in person or through legal assistance of the accused's choosing, to be informed, if the accused does not have legal assistance, of this right and to have legal assistance assigned by the Court in any case where the interests of justice so require, and without payment if the accused lacks
sufficient means to pay for it;

(e) To examine, or have examined, the witnesses against him or her and to obtain the attendance and examination of witnesses on his or her behalf under the same conditions as witnesses against him or her. The accused shall also be entitled to raise defences and to present other evidence admissible under this Statute;

(f) To have, free of any cost, the assistance of a competent interpreter and such translations as are necessary to meet the requirements of fairness, if any of the proceedings of or documents presented to the Court are not in a language which the accused fully understands and speaks;

(g) Not to be compelled to testify or to confess guilt and to remain silent, without such silence being a consideration in the determination of guilt or innocence;

(h) To make an unsworn oral or written statement in his or her defence; and

(i) Not to have imposed on him or her any reversal of the burden of proof or any onus of rebuttal.

2. In addition to any other disclosure provided for in this Statute, the Prosecutor shall, as soon as practicable, disclose to the defence evidence in the Prosecutor's possession or control which he or she believes shows or tends to show the innocence of the accused, or to mitigate the guilt of the accused, or which may affect the

credibility of prosecution evidence. In case of doubt as to the application of this paragraph, the Court shall decide.

Rights of the accused (*Statute ICTY, art. 21*).
1. All persons shall be equal before the International Tribunal.
2. In the determination of charges against him, the accused shall be entitled to a fair and public hearing, subject to article 22 of the Statute.
3. The accused shall be presumed innocent until proved guilty according to the provisions of the present Statute.
4. In the determination of any charge against the accused pursuant to the present Statute, the accused shall be entitled to the following minimum guarantees, in full equality:
(a) to be informed promptly and in detail in a language which he understands of the nature and cause of the charge against him;
(b) to have adequate time and facilities for the preparation of his defence and to communicate with counsel of his own choosing;
(c) to be tried without undue delay;
(d) to be tried in his presence, and to defend himself in person or through legal assistance of his own choosing; to be informed, if he does not have legal assistance, of this right; and to have legal assistance assigned to him, in any case where the interests of justice so require, and without payment by him in any such case if he does not have sufficient means to pay for it;
(e) to examine, or have examined, the witnesses against him and to obtain the attendance and examination of witnesses on his behalf under the same conditions as witnesses against him;
(f) to have the free assistance of an interpreter if he cannot understand or speak the language used in the International Tribunal;
(g) not to be compelled to testify against himself or to confess guilt.

Rights of the Accused (*Statute ICTR, art. 20*).
1. All persons shall be equal before the International Tribunal for Rwanda.
2. In the determination of charges against him or her, the accused shall be entitled to a fair and
public hearing, subject to Article 21 of the Statute.
3. The accused shall be presumed innocent until proven guilty according to the provisions of the present Statute.
4. In the determination of any charge against the accused pursuant to the present Statute, the accused shall be entitled to the following minimum guarantees, in full equality:
(a) To be informed promptly and in detail in a language which he or she understands of the nature and cause of the charge against him or her;
(b) To have adequate time and facilities for the preparation of his or her defence and to communicate with counsel of his or her own choosing;
(c) To be tried without undue delay;
(d) To be tried in his or her presence, and to defend himself or herself in person or through legal assistance of his or her own choosing; to be informed, if he or she does

not have legal assistance, of this right; and to have legal assistance assigned to him or her, in any case where the interest of justice so require, and without payment by him or her in any such case if he or she does not have sufficient means to pay for it;

(e) To examine, or have examined, the witnesses against him or her and to obtain the attendance and examination of witnesses on his or her behalf under the same conditions as witnesses against him or her;

(f) To have the free assistance of an interpreter if he or she cannot understand or speak the language used in the International Tribunal for Rwanda;

(g) Not to be compelled to testify against himself or herself or to confess guilt.

"Rules of international law applicable in armed conflict" *(Protocol Additional to the Geneva Conventions of 12 August 1949, and relating to the Protection of Victims of International Armed Conflicts (Protocol I), 8 June 1977. Part I. General provisions. Art 2. Definitions). For the purposes of this Protocol (...)*
(b) "Rules of international law applicable in armed conflict" means the rules applicable in armed conflict set forth in international agreements to which the Parties to the conflict are Parties and the generally recognized principles and rules of international law which are applicable to armed conflict.

S

"Seafarer" *(International Convention on the protection of the rights of all migrant workers and members of their families. Adopted by General Assembly resolution 45/158 of 18 December 1990. Part. I., Scope and Definitions, Art. 2).* For the purposes of the present Convention: 2.(c) The term "seafarer", which includes a fisherman, refers to a migrant worker employed on board a vessel registered in a State of which he or she is not a national.

"Seasonal worker" (International Convention on the protection of the rights of all migrant workers and members of their families. Adopted by General Assembly resolution 45/158 of 18 December 1990. Part. I., Scope and Definitions, Art. 2). For the purposes of the present Convention: 2.(b) The term "seasonal worker" refers to a migrant worker whose work by its character is dependent on seasonal conditions and is performed only during part of the year.

Security Council (Charter of the United Nations, San Francisco, 26 June 1945, Chapter V. The Security Council. Composition, Art. 23; Functions and Powers, Art. 24, Art. 25; Art. 26; Voting, Art. 27(...)). Composition. Art. 23. 1. The Security Council shall consist of eleven Members of the United Nations. The Republic of China, France, the Union of Soviet Socialist Republics, the United Kingdom of Great Britain and Northern Ireland, and the United States of America shall be permanent members of the Security Council. The General Assembly shall elect six other Members of the United Nations to be non-permanent members of the Security Council, due regard being specially paid, in the first instance to the contribution of Members of the United Nations to the maintenance of international peace and security and to the other purposes of the Organization, and also to equitable geographical distribution.
2. The non-permanent members of the Security Council shall be elected for a term of two years. In the first election of the non-permanent members, however, three shall be chosen for a term of one year. A retiring member shall not be eligible for immediate re-election.
3. Each member of the Security Council shall have one representative.
Functions and Powers. Art. 24. 1. In order to ensure prompt and effective action by the United Nations, its Members confer on the Security Council primary responsibility for the maintenance of international peace and security, and agree that in carrying out its duties under this responsibility the Security Council acts on their behalf.

2. In discharging these duties the Security Council shall act in accordance with the Purposes
and Principles of the United Nations. The specific powers granted to the Security Council for the discharge of these duties are laid down in Chapters VI, VII, VIII, and XII.

3. The Security Council shall submit annual and, when necessary, special reports to the General Assembly for its consideration.

Art. 25. The Members of the United Nations agree to accept and carry out the decisions of the Security Council in accordance with the present Charter.

Art. 26. In order to promote the establishment and maintenance of international peace and security with the least diversion for armaments of the world's human and economic resources, the Security Council shall be responsible for formulating, with the assistance of the Military Staff Committee referred to in Article 47, plans to be submitted to the Members of the United Nations for the establishment of a system for the regulation of armaments.

Voting. Art. 27. 1. Each member of the Security Council shall have one vote.

2. Decisions of the Security Council on procedural matters shall be made by an affirmative
vote of seven members.

3. Decisions of the Security Council on all other matters shall be made by an affirmative vote
of seven members including the concurring votes of the permanent members; provided that, in decisions under Chapter VI, and under paragraph 3 of Article 52, a party to a dispute shall abstain from voting.

Self-determination of peoples (Charter of the United Nations, San Francisco, 26 June 1945. Chapter I. Purposes and principles, Art. 1; International Covenant on Civil and Political Rights. Adopted and opened for signature, ratification and accession by General Assembly resolution 2200A (XXI) of 16 December 1966. Part. I., Art. 1; *International Covenant on Economic, Social and Cultural Rights. New York*, 16 December 1966. Part. I. Art. 1).

Charter of the United Nations, San Francisco, 26 June 1945. Chapter I. Purposes and principles. Art. 1. The Purposes of the United Nations are: 1. To maintain international peace and security, and to that end: to take effective collective measures for the prevention and removal of threats to the peace, and for the suppression of acts of aggression or other breaches of the peace, and to bring about by peaceful means, and in conformity with the principles of justice and international law, adjustment or settlement of international disputes or situations which might lead to a breach of the peace;

2. To develop friendly relations among nations based on respect for the *principle of equal rights and self-determination of peoples*, and to take other appropriate measures to strengthen universal peace;

3. To achieve international cooperation in solving international problems of an economic, social, cultural, or humanitarian character, and in promoting and encouraging respect for human rights and for fundamental freedoms for all without distinction as to race, sex, language, or religion; and

4. To be a center for harmonizing the actions of nations in the attainment of these common ends.

International Covenant on Civil and Political Rights. Adopted and opened for signature, ratification and accession by General Assembly resolution 2200A (XXI) of 16 December 1966. Part. I., Art. 1. 1. All peoples have the right of self-determination. By virtue of that right they freely determine their political status and freely pursue their economic, social and cultural development.

2. All peoples may, for their own ends, freely dispose of their natural wealth and resources without prejudice to any obligations arising out of international economic co-operation, based upon the principle of mutual benefit, and international law. In no case may a people be deprived of its own means of subsistence.

3. The States Parties to the present Covenant, including those having responsibility for the administration of Non-Self-Governing and Trust Territories, shall promote the realization of the right of self-determination, and shall respect that right, in conformity with the provisions of the Charter of the United Nations.

International Covenant on Economic, Social and Cultural Rights*. New York,* 16 December 1966. Part. I. Art. 1. 1. All peoples have the right of self-determination. By virtue of that right they freely determine their political status and freely pursue their economic, social and cultural development.

2. All peoples may, for their own ends, freely dispose of their natural wealth and resources without prejudice to any obligations arising out of international economic co-operation, based upon the principle of mutual benefit, and international law. In no case may a people be deprived of its own means of subsistence.

3. The States Parties to the present Covenant, including those having responsibility for the administration of Non-Self-Governing and Trust Territories, shall promote the realization of the right of self-determination, and shall respect that right, in conformity with the provisions of the Charter of the United Nations.

"Self-employed worker" (International Convention on the protection of the rights of all migrant workers and members of their families. Adopted by General Assembly resolution 45/158 of 18 December 1990. Part. I., Scope and Definitions, Art. 2). For the purposes of the present Convention: 2.(h) The term "self-employed worker" refers to a migrant worker who is engaged in a remunerated activity otherwise than under a contract of employment and who earns his or her living through this activity normally working alone or together with members of his or her family, and to any other migrant worker recognized as self-employed by applicable legislation of the State of employment or bilateral or multilateral agreements.

Serious misconduct and serious breach of duty *(RPE – ICC, Chapter 2. Composition and administration of the Court, Section 4. Situations that may affect the functioning of the Court, Subsection 1. Removal from office and disciplinary measures, Rule 23. General principle, Rule 24. Definition of serious misconduct and serious breach of duty). Rule 23. General principle.* A judge, the Prosecutor, a Deputy Prosecutor, the Registrar and a Deputy Registrar shall be removed from

office or shall be subject to disciplinary measures in such cases and with such guarantees as are established in the Statute and the Rules.

Rule 24. Definition of serious misconduct and serious breach of duty. 1. For the purposes of article 46, paragraph 1 (a), 'serious misconduct' shall be constituted by conduct that:

(a) If it occurs in the course of official duties, is incompatible with official functions, and causes or is likely to cause serious harm to the proper administration of justice before the Court or the proper internal functioning of the Court, such as:

(i) Disclosing facts or information that he or she has acquired in the course of his or her duties or on a matter which is *sub judice*, where such disclosure is seriously prejudicial to the judicial proceedings or to any person;

(ii) Concealing information or circumstances of a nature sufficiently serious to have precluded him or her from holding office;

(iii) Abuse of judicial office in order to obtain unwarranted favourable treatment from any authorities, officials or professionals; or

(b) If it occurs outside the course of official duties, is of a grave nature that causes or is likely to cause serious harm to the standing of the Court.

2. For the purposes of article 46, paragraph 1 (a), a 'serious breach of duty' occurs where a person has been grossly negligent in the performance of his or her duties or has knowingly acted in contravention of those duties. This may include, *inter alia*, situations where the person:

(a) Fails to comply with the duty to request to be excused, knowing that there are grounds for doing so;

(b) Repeatedly causes unwarranted delay in the initiation, prosecution or trial of cases, or in the exercise of judicial powers.

"Shipwrecked" *(Protocol Additional to the Geneva Conventions of 12 August 1949, and relating to the Protection of Victims of International Armed Conflicts (Protocol I), 8 June 1977. Part. II. Wounded, sick and shipwrecked, Section I: General Protection. Art. 8. Terminology).* For the purposes of this Protocol: (...) b) "Shipwrecked" means persons, whether military or civilian, who are in peril at sea or in other waters as a result of misfortune affecting them or the vessel or aircraft carrying them and who refrain from any act of hostility. These persons, provided that they continue to refrain from any act of hostility, shall continue to be considered shipwrecked during their rescue until they acquire another status under the Conventions or this Protocol.

Social development. Copenhagen Declaration on Social Development *(United Nations. World Summit for Social Development. Copenhagen, Denmark, 6-12 March 1995. Annex I. Copenhagen Declaration on Social Development).* 1. For the first time in history, at the invitation of the United Nations, we gather as heads of State and Government to recognize the significance of social development and human well-being for all and to give to these goals the highest priority both now and into the twenty-first century.

2. We acknowledge that the people of the world have shown in different ways an urgent need to address profound social problems, especially poverty, unemployment

and social exclusion, that affect every country. It is our task to address both their underlying and structural causes and their distressing consequences in order to reduce uncertainty and insecurity in the life of
people.

3. We acknowledge that our societies must respond more effectively to the material and spiritual needs of individuals, their families and the communities in which they live throughout our diverse countries and regions. We must do so not only as a matter of urgency but also as a matter of sustained and unshakeable commitment through the years ahead.

4. We are convinced that democracy and transparent and accountable governance and administration in all sectors of society are indispensable foundations for the realization of social and people-centred sustainable development.

5. We share the conviction that social development and social justice are indispensable for the achievement and maintenance of peace and security within and among our nations. In turn, social development and social justice cannot be attained in the absence of peace and security or in the absence of respect for all human rights and fundamental freedoms. This essential interdependence was recognized 50 years ago in the Charter of the United Nations and has since grown ever stronger.

6. We are deeply convinced that economic development, social development and environmental protection are interdependent and mutually reinforcing components of sustainable development, which is the framework for our efforts to achieve a higher quality of life for all people. Equitable social development that recognizes empowering the poor to utilize environmental resources sustainably is a necessary foundation for sustainable development. We also recognize that broad-based and sustained economic growth in the context of sustainable development is necessary to sustain social development and social justice.

7. We recognize, therefore, that social development is central to the needs and aspirations of people throughout the world and to the responsibilities of Governments and all sectors of civil society. (...)

10. We make this solemn commitment on the eve of the fiftieth anniversary of the United Nations, with a determination to capture the unique possibilities offered by the end of the cold war to promote social development and social justice. We reaffirm and are guided by the principles of the Charter of the United Nations and by agreements reached at relevant international conferences, including the World Summit for Children, held at New York in 1990; 1/ the United Nations Conference on Environment and Development, held at Rio de Janeiro in 1992; 2/ the World Conference on Human Rights, held at Vienna in 1993; 3/ the Global Conference on the Sustainable Development of Small Island Developing States, held at Bridgetown, Barbados in 1994; 4/ and the International Conference on Population and Development, held at Cairo in 1994. 5/ (...)

20. The goals and objectives of social development require continuous efforts to reduce and eliminate major sources of social distress and instability for the family and for society. We pledge to place particular focus on and give priority attention to the fight against the world-wide conditions that pose severe threats to the health, safety, peace, security and well-being of our people. Among these conditions are chronic hunger; malnutrition; illicit drug problems; organized crime; corruption;

foreign occupation; armed conflicts; illicit arms trafficking, terrorism, intolerance and incitement to racial, ethnic, religious and other hatreds; xenophobia; and endemic, communicable and chronic diseases. To this end, coordination and cooperation at the national level and especially at the regional and international levels should be further strengthened. (...)

"Specified-employment worker" (International Convention on the protection of the rights of all migrant workers and members of their families. Adopted by General Assembly resolution 45/158 of 18 December 1990. Part. I., Scope and Definitions, Art. 2). For the purposes of the present Convention: 2.(g) The term "specified-employment worker" refers to a migrant worker: (i) Who has been sent by his or her employer for a restricted and defined period of time to a State of employment to undertake a specific assignment or duty; or

(ii) Who engages for a restricted and defined period of time in work that requires professional, commercial, technical or other highly specialized skill; or

(iii) Who, upon the request of his or her employer in the State of employment, engages for a restricted and defined period of time in work whose nature is transitory or brief;

and who is required to depart from the State of employment either at the expiration of his or her authorized period of stay, or earlier if he or she no longer undertakes that specific assignment or duty or engages in that work.

Spies *(Protocol Additional to the Geneva Conventions of 12 August 1949, and relating to the Protection of Victims of International Armed Conflicts (Protocol I), 8 June 1977. Part. III. Methods and Means of Warfare. Combatant and Prisoners-Of-War. Section II. Combatants and Prisoners of War. Art. 46. Spies).* 1. Notwithstanding any other provision of the Conventions or of this Protocol, any member of the armed forces of a Party to the conflict who falls into the power of an adverse Party while engaging in espionage shall not have the right to the status of prisoner of war and may be treated as a spy.

2. A member of the armed forces of a Party to the conflict who, on behalf of that Party and in territory controlled by an adverse Party, gathers or attempts to gather information shall not be considered as engaging in espionage if, while so acting, he is in the uniform of his armed forces.

3. A member of the armed forces of a Party to the conflict who is a resident of territory occupied by an adverse Party and who, on behalf of the Party on which he depends, gathers or attempts to gather information of military value within that territory shall not be considered as engaging in espionage unless he does so through an act of false pretences or deliberately in a clandestine manner. Moreover, such a resident shall not lose his right to the status of prisoner of war and may not be treated as a spy unless he is captured while engaging in espionage.

4. A member of the armed forces of a Party to the conflict who is not a resident of territory occupied by an adverse Party and who has engaged in espionage in that territory shall not lose his right to the status of prisoner of war and may not be treated as a spy unless he is captured before he has rejoined the armed forces to which he belongs.

"State of employment" *(International Convention on the protection of the rights of all migrant workers and members of their families. Adopted by General Assembly resolution 45/158 of 18 December 1990. Part. I., Scope and Definitions, Art. 6).* For the purposes of the present Convention: (b) The term "State of employment" means a State where the migrant worker is to be engaged, is engaged or has been engaged in a remunerated activity, as the case may be.

"State of origin" (International Convention on the protection of the rights of all migrant workers and members of their families. Adopted by General Assembly resolution 45/158 of 18 December 1990. Part. I., Scope and Definitions, Art. 6). For the purposes of the present Convention: (a) The term "State of origin" means the State of which the person concerned is a national.

"State of transit" *(International Convention on the protection of the rights of all migrant workers and members of their families. Adopted by General Assembly resolution 45/158 of 18 December 1990. Part. I., Scope and Definitions, Art. 6).* For the purposes of the present Convention: (c) The term "State of transit," means any State through which the person concerned passes on any journey to the State of employment or from the State of employment to the State of origin or the State of habitual residence.

"Substitute" *(Protocol Additional to the Geneva Conventions of 12 August 1949, and relating to the Protection of Victims of International Armed Conflicts (Protocol I), 8 June 1977. Part. I. General provisions. Art 2. Definitions; Art 5. Appointment of Protecting Powers and of their substitute; Art 1. General principles and scope of application; Art 4. Legal status of the Parties to the conflict). Art 2. Definitions.* For the purposes of this Protocol (…) (d) "Substitute" means an organization acting in place of a Protecting Power in accordance with Article 5.
Art 5. Appointment of Protecting Powers and of their substitute. 1. It is the duty of the Parties to a conflict from the beginning of that conflict to secure the supervision and implementation of the Conventions and of this Protocol by the application of the system of Protecting Powers, including inter alia the designation and acceptance of those Powers, in accordance with the following paragraphs. Protecting Powers shall have the duty of safeguarding the interests of the Parties to the conflict.
2. From the beginning of a situation referred to in Article 1, each Party to the conflict shall without delay designate a Protecting Power for the purpose of applying the Conventions and this Protocol and shall, likewise without delay and for the same purpose, permit the activities or a Protecting Power which has been accepted by it as such after designation by the adverse Party.
3. If a Protecting Power has not been designated or accepted from the beginning of a situation referred to in Article 1, the International Committee of the Red Cross, without prejudice to the right of any other impartial humanitarian organization to do likewise, shall offer its good offices to the Parties to the conflict with a view to the designation without delay of a Protecting Power to which the Parties to the conflict

consent. For that purpose it may inter alia ask each Party to provide it with a list of at least five States which that Party considers acceptable to act as Protecting Power on its behalf in relation to an adverse Party and ask each adverse Party to provide a list or at least five States which it would accept as the Protecting Power of the first Party; these lists shall be communicated to the Committee within two weeks after the receipt or the request; it shall compare them and seek the agreement of any proposed State named on both lists.

4. If, despite the foregoing, there is no Protecting Power, the Parties to the conflict shall accept without delay an offer which may be made by the International Committee of the Red Cross or by any other organization which offers all guarantees of impartiality and efficacy, after due consultations with the said Parties and taking into account the result of these consultations, to act as a substitute. The functioning of such a substitute is subject to the consent of the Parties to the conflict; every effort shall be made by the Parties to the conflict to facilitate the operations of the substitute in the performance of its tasks under the Conventions and this Protocol.

5. In accordance with Article 4, the designation and acceptance of Protecting Powers for the purpose of applying the Conventions and this Protocol shall not affect the legal status of the Parties to the conflict or of any territory, including occupied territory.

6. The maintenance of diplomatic relations between Parties to the conflict or the entrusting of the protection of a Party's interests and those of its nationals to a third State in accordance with the rules of international law relating to diplomatic relations is no obstacle to the designation of Protecting Powers for the purpose of applying the Conventions and this Protocol.

7. Any subsequent mention in this Protocol of a Protecting Power includes also a substitute. *Art 1. General principles and scope of application.* 1. The High Contracting Parties undertake to respect and to ensure respect for this Protocol in all circumstances.

2. In cases not covered by this Protocol or by other international agreements, civilians and combatants remain under the protection and authority of the principles of international law derived from established custom, from the principles of humanity and from dictates of public conscience.

3. This Protocol, which supplements the Geneva Conventions of 12 August 1949 for the protection of war victims, shall apply in the situations referred to in Article 2 common to those Conventions.

4. The situations referred to in the preceding paragraph include armed conflicts in which peoples are fighting against colonial domination and alien occupation and against racist regimes in the exercise of their right of self-determination, as enshrined in the Charter of the United Nations and the Declaration on Principles of International Law concerning Friendly Relations and Co-operation among States in accordance with the Charter of the United Nations.

Art 4. Legal status of the Parties to the conflict. The application of the Conventions and of this Protocol, as well as the conclusion of the agreements provided for therein, shall not affect the legal status of the Parties to the conflict. Neither the occupation of a territory nor the application of the Conventions and this Protocol shall affect the legal status of the territory in question.

"Surrender" *(Rome Statute ICC, art. 102. Use of terms, a); Rome Statute ICC, art. 89. Surrender of persons to the Court; Rome Statute ICC, art. 101. Rule of speciality; RPE – ICC, Rule 184. Arrangements for surrender; Rome Statute ICC, art. 91. Contents of request for arrest and surrender).*

Rome Statute ICC, art. 102. Use of terms. For the purposes of this Statute: (a) "surrender" means the delivering up of a person by a State to the Court, pursuant to this Statute. (...)

Rome Statute ICC, art. 89. **Surrender of persons to the Court.** 1. The Court may transmit a request for the arrest and surrender of a person, together with the material supporting the request outlined in article 91, to any State on the territory of which that person may be found and shall request the cooperation of that State in the arrest and surrender of such a person. States Parties shall, in accordance with the provisions of this Part and the procedure under their national law, comply with requests for arrest and surrender.

2. Where the person sought for surrender brings a challenge before a national court on the basis of the principle of *ne bis in idem* as provided in article 20, the requested State shall immediately consult with the Court to determine if there has been a relevant ruling on admissibility. If the case is admissible, the requested State shall proceed with the execution of the request. If an admissibility ruling is pending, the requested State may postpone the execution of the request for surrender of the person until the Court makes a determination on admissibility.

3. (a) A State Party shall authorize, in accordance with its national procedural law, transportation through its territory of a person being surrendered to the Court by another State, except where transit through that State would impede or delay the surrender.

(b) A request by the Court for transit shall be transmitted in accordance with article 87. The request for transit shall contain:

(i) A description of the person being transported;

(ii) A brief statement of the facts of the case and their legal characterization; and

(iii) The warrant for arrest and surrender;

(c) A person being transported shall be detained in custody during the period of transit;

(d) No authorization is required if the person is transported by air and no landing is scheduled on the territory of the transit State;

(e) If an unscheduled landing occurs on the territory of the transit State, that State may require a request for transit from the Court as provided for in subparagraph (b). The transit State shall detain the person being transported until the request for transit is received and the transit is effected, provided that detention for purposes of this subparagraph may not be extended beyond 96 hours from the unscheduled landing unless the request is received within that time.

4. If the person sought is being proceeded against or is serving a sentence in the requested State for a crime different from that for which surrender to the Court is sought, the requested State, after making its decision to grant the request, shall consult with the Court.

Rome Statute ICC, art. 101. **Rule of speciality.** 1. A person surrendered to the Court under this Statute shall not be proceeded against, punished or detained for any conduct committed prior to surrender, other than the conduct or course of conduct which forms the basis of the crimes for which that person has been surrendered.

2. The Court may request a waiver of the requirements of paragraph 1 from the State which surrendered the person to the Court and, if necessary, the Court shall provide additional information in accordance with article 91. States Parties shall have the authority to provide a waiver to the Court and should endeavour to do so.

RPE – ICC, Rule 184. Arrangements for surrender. 1. The requested State shall immediately inform the Registrar when the person sought by the Court is available for surrender.

2. The person shall be surrendered to the Court by the date and in the manner agreed upon between the authorities of the requested State and the Registrar.

3. If circumstances prevent the surrender of the person by the date agreed, the authorities of the requested State and the Registrar shall agree upon a new date and manner by which the person shall be surrendered.

4. The Registrar shall maintain contact with the authorities of the host State in relation to the arrangements for the surrender of the person to the Court.

Rome Statute ICC, art. 91. **Contents of request for arrest and surrender.** 1. A request for arrest and surrender shall be made in writing. In urgent cases, a request may be made by any medium capable of delivering a written record, provided that the request shall be confirmed through the channel provided for in article 87, paragraph 1 (a).

2. In the case of a request for the arrest and surrender of a person for whom a warrant of arrest has been issued by the Pre-Trial Chamber under article 58, the request shall contain or be supported by:

(a) Information describing the person sought, sufficient to identify the person, and information as to that person's probable location;

(b) A copy of the warrant of arrest; and

(c) Such documents, statements or information as may be necessary to meet the requirements for the surrender process in the requested State, except that those requirements should not be more burdensome than those applicable to requests for extradition pursuant to treaties or arrangements between the requested State and other States and should, if possible, be less burdensome, taking into account the distinct nature of the Court.

3. In the case of a request for the arrest and surrender of a person already convicted, the request shall contain or be supported by:

(a) A copy of any warrant of arrest for that person;

(b) A copy of the judgement of conviction;

(c) Information to demonstrate that the person sought is the one referred to in the judgement of conviction; and

(d) If the person sought has been sentenced, a copy of the sentence imposed and, in the case of a sentence for imprisonment, a statement of any time already served and the time remaining to be served.

4. Upon the request of the Court, a State Party shall consult with the Court, either generally or with respect to a specific matter, regarding any requirements under its national law that may apply under paragraph 2 (c). During the consultations, the State Party shall advise the Court of the specific requirements of its national law.

Sustainable Development. Johannesburg Declaration on Sustainable Development. United Nations. World Summit on Sustainable Development. Johannesburg, South Africa, 2-4 September 2002.

From our Origins to the Future

1. We, the representatives of the peoples of the world, assembled at the World Summit on Sustainable Development in Johannesburg, South Africa from 2-4 September 2002, reaffirm our commitment to sustainable development.

2. We commit ourselves to build a humane, equitable and caring global society cognizant of the need for human dignity for all.

3. At the beginning of this Summit, the children of the world spoke to us in a simple yet clear voice that the future belongs to them, and accordingly challenged all of us to ensure that through our actions they will inherit a world free of the indignity and indecency occasioned by poverty, environmental degradation and patterns of unsustainable development.

4. As part of our response to these children, who represent our collective future, all of us, coming from every corner of the world, informed by different life experiences, are united and moved by a deeply-felt sense that we urgently need to create a new and brighter world of hope.

5. Accordingly, we assume a collective responsibility to advance and strengthen the interdependent and mutually reinforcing pillars of sustainable development – economic development, social development and environmental protection – at local, national, regional and global levels.

6. From this Continent, the Cradle of Humanity we declare, through the Plan of Implementation and this Declaration, our responsibility to one another, to the greater community of life and to our children.

7. Recognizing that humankind is at a crossroad, we have united in a common resolve to make a determined effort to respond positively to the need to produce a practical and visible plan that should bring about poverty eradication and human development.

From Stockholm to Rio de Janeiro to Johannesburg

8. Thirty years ago, in Stockholm, we agreed on the urgent need to respond to the problem of environmental deterioration. Ten years ago, at the United Nations Conference on Environment and Development, held in Rio de Janeiro, we agreed that the protection of the environment, and social and economic development are fundamental to sustainable development, based on the Rio Principles. To achieve such development, we adopted the global programme, **Agenda 21**, and the Rio Declaration, to which we reaffirm our commitment. The Rio Summit was a significant milestone that set a new agenda for sustainable development.

9. Between Rio and Johannesburg the world's nations met in several major conferences under the guidance of the United Nations, including the Monterrey Conference on Finance for Development, as well as the Doha Ministerial Conference. These conferences defined for the world a comprehensive vision for the future of humanity.

10. At the Johannesburg Summit we achieved much in bringing together a rich tapestry of peoples and views in a constructive search for a common path, towards a

world that respects and implements the vision of sustainable development. Johannesburg also confirmed that significant progress has been made towards achieving a global consensus and partnership amongst all the people of our planet.

The Challenges we Face

11. We recognize that poverty eradication, changing consumption and production patterns, and protecting and managing the natural resource base for economic and social development are overarching objectives of, and essential requirements for sustainable development.

12. The deep fault line that divides human society between the rich and the poor and the ever-increasing gap between the developed and developing worlds pose a major threat to global prosperity, security and stability.

13. The global environment continues to suffer. Loss of biodiversity continues, fish stocks continue to be depleted, desertification claims more and more fertile land, the adverse effects of climate change are already evident, natural disasters are more frequent and more devastating and developing countries more vulnerable, and air, water and marine pollution continue to rob millions of a decent life.

14. Globalization has added a new dimension to these challenges. The rapid integration of markets, mobility of capital and significant increases in investment flows around the world have opened new challenges and opportunities for the pursuit of sustainable development. But the benefits and costs of globalization are unevenly distributed, with developing countries facing special difficulties in meeting this challenge.

15. We risk the entrenchment of these global disparities and unless we act in a manner that fundamentally changes their lives, the poor of the world may lose confidence in their representatives and the democratic systems to which we remain committed, seeing their representatives as nothing more than sounding brass or tinkling cymbals.

Our Commitment to Sustainable Development

16. We are determined to ensure that our rich diversity, which is our collective strength, will be used for constructive partnership for change and for the achievement of the common goal of sustainable development.

17. Recognizing the importance of building human solidarity, we urge the promotion of dialogue and cooperation among the world's civilizations and peoples, irrespective of race, disabilities, religion, language, culture and tradition.

18. We welcome the Johannesburg Summit focus on the indivisibility of human dignity and are resolved through decisions on targets, timetables and partnerships to speedily increase access to basic requirements such as clean water, sanitation, adequate shelter, energy, health care, food security and the protection of bio-diversity. At the same time, we will work together to assist one another to have access to financial resources, benefit from the opening of markets, ensure capacity building, use modern technology to bring about development, and make sure that there is technology transfer, human resource development, education and training to banish forever underdevelopment.

19. We reaffirm our pledge to place particular focus on, and give priority attention to, the fight against the worldwide conditions that pose severe threats to the sustainable development of our people. Among these conditions are: chronic hunger; malnutrition; foreign occupation; armed conflicts; illicit drug problems; organized

crime; corruption; natural disasters; illicit arms trafficking; trafficking in persons; terrorism; intolerance and incitement to racial, ethnic, religious and other hatreds; xenophobia; and endemic, communicable and chronic diseases, in particular HIV/AIDS, malaria and tuberculosis.

20. We are committed to ensure that women's empowerment and emancipation, and gender equality are integrated in all activities encompassed within **Agenda 21**, the Millennium Development Goals and the Johannesburg Plan of Implementation.

21. We recognize the reality that global society has the means and is endowed with the resources to address the challenges of poverty eradication and sustainable development confronting all humanity. Together we will take extra steps to ensure that these available resources are used to the benefit of humanity.

22. In this regard, to contribute to the achievement of our development goals and targets, we urge developed countries that have not done so to make concrete efforts towards the internationally agreed levels of Official Development Assistance.

23. We welcome and support the emergence of stronger regional groupings and alliances, such as the New Partnership for Africa's Development (NEPAD), to promote regional cooperation, improved international co-operation and promote sustainable development.

24. We shall continue to pay special attention to the developmental needs of Small Island Developing States and the Least Developed Countries.

25. We reaffirm the vital role of the indigenous peoples in sustainable development.

26. We recognize sustainable development requires a long-term perspective and broad-based participation in policy formulation, decision-making and implementation at all levels. As social partners we will continue to work for stable partnerships with all major groups respecting the independent, important roles of each of these.

27. We agree that in pursuit of their legitimate activities the private sector, both large and small companies, have a duty to contribute to the evolution of equitable and sustainable communities and societies.

28. We also agree to provide assistance to increase income generating employment opportunities, taking into account the International Labour Organization (ILO) Declaration of Fundamental Principles and Rights at Work.

29. We agree that there is a need for private sector corporations to enforce corporate accountability. This should take place within a transparent and stable regulatory environment.

30. We undertake to strengthen and improve governance at all levels, for the effective implementation of **Agenda 21**, the Millennium Development Goals and the Johannesburg Plan of Implementation.

Multilateralism is the Future

31. To achieve our goals of sustainable development, we need more effective, democratic and accountable international and multilateral institutions.

32. We reaffirm our commitment to the principles and purposes of the UN Charter and international law as well as the strengthening of multi-lateralism. We support the leadership role of the United Nations as the most universal and representative organization in the world, which is best placed to promote sustainable development.

33. We further commit ourselves to monitor progress at regular intervals towards the

achievement of our sustainable development goals and objectives.

Making it Happen!

34. We are in agreement that this must be an inclusive process, involving all the major groups and governments that participated in the historic Johannesburg Summit.

35. We commit ourselves to act together, united by a common determination to save our planet, promote human development and achieve universal prosperity and peace.

36. We commit ourselves to the Johannesburg Plan of Implementation and to expedite the achievement of the time-bound, socio-economic and environmental targets contained therein.

37. From the African continent, the Cradle of Humankind, we solemnly pledge to the peoples of the world, and the generations that will surely inherit this earth, that we are determined to ensure that our collective hope for sustainable development is realized. We express our deepest gratitude to the people and the Government of South Africa for their generous hospitality and excellent arrangements made for the World Summit on Sustainable Development.

T

The transfer, directly or indirectly, by the Occupying Power of parts of its own civilian population into the territory it occupies, or the deportation or transfer of all or parts of the population of the occupied territory within or outside this territory. *See: War crimes, Elements of Crimes.*

Torture *(International Covenant on Civil and Political Rights. Adopted and opened for signature, ratification and accession by General Assembly resolution 2200A (XXI) of 16 December 1966. Art. 7; Convention against Torture and Other Cruel, Inhuman or Degrading Treatment or Punishment. Adopted and opened for signature, ratification and accession by General Assembly resolution 39/46 of 10 December 1984. Art. 1; Convention for the Protection of Human Rights and Fundamental Freedoms. Rome, 4.XI.1950 (as amended by Protocols Nos. 11 and 14 with Protocols Nos. 1, 4, 6, 7, 12 and 13), Art. 3; See Crimes against humanity and War crimes).*

International Covenant on Civil and Political Rights. Adopted and opened for signature, ratification and accession by General Assembly resolution 2200A (XXI) of 16 December 1966. Art. 7. No one shall be subjected to torture or to cruel, inhuman or degrading treatment or punishment. In particular, no one shall be subjected without his free consent to medical or scientific experimentation.

Convention against Torture and Other Cruel, Inhuman or Degrading Treatment or Punishment. Adopted and opened for signature, ratification and accession by General Assembly resolution 39/46 of 10 December 1984. Art. 1. 1. For the purposes of this Convention, the term *"torture"* means any act by which severe pain or suffering, whether physical or mental, is intentionally inflicted on a person for such purposes as obtaining from him or a third person information or a confession, punishing him for an act he or a third person has committed or is suspected of having committed, or intimidating or coercing him or a third person, or for any reason based on discrimination of any kind, when such pain or suffering is inflicted by or at the instigation of or with the consent or acquiescence of a public official or other person acting in an official capacity. It does not include pain or suffering arising only from, inherent in or incidental to lawful sanctions.

2. This article is without prejudice to any international instrument or national legislation which does or may contain provisions of wider application.

Convention for the Protection of Human Rights and Fundamental Freedoms. *Rome, 4.XI.1950 (as amended by Protocols Nos. 11 and 14 with Protocols Nos. 1, 4,*

6, 7, 12 and 13), Art. 3. Prohibition of torture. No one shall be subjected to torture or to inhuman or degrading treatment or punishment.
See: Crimes against humanity, War crimes, Elements of Crimes.

"Trafficking in persons" (Protocol to Prevent, Suppress and Punish Trafficking in Persons Especially Women and Children, supplementing the United Nations Convention against Transnational Organized Crime. Adopted and opened for signature, ratification and accession by General Assembly resolution 55/25 of 15 November 2000. I. General provisions, Art. 3 Use of terms). For the purposes of this Protocol:
(a) "Trafficking in persons" shall mean the recruitment, transportation, transfer, harbouring or receipt of persons, by means of the threat or use of force or other forms of coercion, of abduction, of fraud, of deception, of the abuse of power or of a position of vulnerability or of the giving or receiving of payments or benefits to achieve the consent of a person having control over another person, for the purpose of exploitation. Exploitation shall include, at a minimum, the exploitation of the prostitution of others or other forms of sexual exploitation, forced labour or services, slavery or practices similar to slavery, servitude or the removal of organs;
(b) The consent of a victim of trafficking in persons to the intended exploitation set forth in subparagraph (a) of this article shall be irrelevant where any of the means set forth in subparagraph (a) have been used;
(c) The recruitment, transportation, transfer, harbouring or receipt of a child for the purpose of exploitation shall be considered "trafficking in persons" even if this does not involve any of the means set forth in subparagraph (a) of this article;
(d) "Child" shall mean any person under eighteen years of age.

U

United Nations Convention Against Transnational Organized Crime. New York, 15 November 2000. *(Art. 1 Statement of purpose; Art. 2 Use of terms; Art. 3 Scope of application).*

Art. 1 Statement of purpose. The purpose of this Convention is to promote cooperation to prevent and combat transnational organized crime more effectively.

Art. 2 Use of terms. For the purposes of this Convention:

(a) **"Organized criminal group"** shall mean a structured group of three or more persons, existing for a period of time and acting in concert with the aim of committing one or more serious crimes or offences established in accordance with this Convention, in order to obtain, directly or indirectly, a financial or other material benefit;

(b) **"Serious crime"** shall mean conduct constituting an offence punishable by a maximum deprivation of liberty of at least four years or a more serious penalty;

(c) **"Structured group"** shall mean a group that is not randomly formed for the immediate commission of an offence and that does not need to have formally defined roles for its members, continuity of its membership or a developed structure;

(d) **"Property"** shall mean assets of every kind, whether corporeal or incorporeal, movable or immovable, tangible or intangible, and legal documents or instruments evidencing title to, or interest in, such assets;

(e) **"Proceeds of crime"** shall mean any property derived from or obtained, directly or indirectly, through the commission of an offence;

(f) **"Freezing"** or **"seizure"** shall mean temporarily prohibiting the transfer, conversion, disposition or movement of property or temporarily assuming custody or control of property on the basis of an order issued by a court or other competent authority;

(g) **"Confiscation"**, which includes forfeiture where applicable, shall mean the permanent deprivation of property by order of a court or other competent authority;

(h) **"Predicate offence"** shall mean any offence as a result of which proceeds have been generated that may become the subject of an offence as defined in article 6 of this Convention;

(i) **"Controlled delivery"** shall mean the technique of allowing illicit or suspect consignments to pass out of, through or into the territory of one or more States, with the knowledge and under the supervision of their competent authorities, with a view to the investigation of an offence and the identification of persons involved in the commission of the offence;

(j) **"Regional economic integration organization"** shall mean an organization constituted by sovereign States of a given region, to which its member States have transferred competence in respect of matters governed by this Convention and which has been duly authorized, in accordance with its internal procedures, to sign, ratify, accept, approve or accede to it; references to **"States Parties"** under this Convention shall apply to such organizations within the limits of their competence.

Art. 3 Scope of application. 1. This Convention shall apply, except as otherwise stated herein,

to the prevention, investigation and prosecution of:

(a) The offences established in accordance with articles 5, 6, 8 and 23 of this Convention; and

(b) Serious crime as defined in article 2 of this Convention; where the offence is transnational in nature and involves an organized criminal group.

2. For the purpose of paragraph 1 of this article, an offence is transnational in nature if:

(a) It is committed in more than one State;

(b) It is committed in one State but a substantial part of its preparation, planning, direction or control takes place in another State;

(c) It is committed in one State but involves an organized criminal group that engages in criminal activities in more than one State; or

(d) It is committed in one State but has substantial effects in another State.

United Nations Convention to Combat Desertification in Countries Experiencing Serious Drought and/or Desertification, Particularly in Africa. Paris, 17 June 1994 *(Preamble. Part. I. Introduction. Art. 1. Use of terms: "desertification", "combating desertification", "drought", "mitigating the effects of drought", "land", "land degradation", "arid, semi-arid and dry sub-humid areas", "affected areas", "affected countries", "regional economic integration organization", "developed country Parties", Art. 2. Objective. Art. 3. Principles).*

Preamble. The Parties to this Convention,

Affirming that human beings in affected or threatened areas are at the centre of concerns to combat desertification and mitigate the effects of drought,

Reflecting the urgent concern of the international community, including States and international organizations, about the adverse impacts of desertification and drought,

Aware that arid, semi-arid and dry sub-humid areas together account for a significant proportion of the Earth's land area and are the habitat and source of livelihood for a large segment of its population,

Acknowledging that desertification and drought are problems of global dimension in that they affect all regions of the world and that joint action of the international community is needed to combat desertification and/or mitigate the effects of drought,

Noting the high concentration of developing countries, notably the least developed countries, among those experiencing serious drought and/or desertification, and the particularly tragic consequences of these phenomena in Africa,

Noting also that desertification is caused by complex interactions among physical, biological, political, social, cultural and economic factors,

Considering the impact of trade and relevant aspects of international economic relations on the ability of affected countries to combat desertification adequately,

Conscious that sustainable economic growth, social development and poverty eradication are priorities of affected developing countries, particularly in Africa, and are essential to meeting sustainability objectives,

Mindful that desertification and drought affect sustainable development through their interrelationships with important social problems such as poverty, poor health and nutrition, lack of food security, and those arising from migration, displacement of persons and demographic dynamics,

Appreciating the significance of the past efforts and experience of States and international organizations in combating desertification and mitigating the effects of drought, particularly in implementing the Plan of Action to Combat Desertification which was adopted at the United Nations Conference on Desertification in 1977,

Realizing that, despite efforts in the past, progress in combating desertification and mitigating the effects of drought has not met expectations and that a new and more effective approach is needed at all levels within the framework of sustainable development,

Recognizing the validity and relevance of decisions adopted at the United Nations Conference on Environment and Development, particularly of **Agenda 21** and its chapter 12, which provide a basis for combating desertification,

Reaffirming in this light the commitments of developed countries as contained in paragraph 13 of chapter 33 of **Agenda 21**,

Recalling General Assembly resolution 47/188, particularly the priority in it prescribed for Africa, and all other relevant United Nations resolutions, decisions and programmes on desertification and drought, as well as relevant declarations by African countries and those from other regions,

Reaffirming the Rio Declaration on Environment and Development which states, in its Principle 2, that States have, in accordance with the Charter of the United Nations and the principles of international law, the sovereign right to exploit their own resources pursuant to their own environmental and developmental policies, and the responsibility to ensure that activities within their jurisdiction or control do not cause damage to the environment of other States or of areas beyond the limits of national jurisdiction,

Recognizing that national Governments play a critical role in combating desertification and mitigating the effects of drought and that progress in that respect depends on local implementation of action programmes in affected areas,

Recognizing also the importance and necessity of international cooperation and partnership in combating desertification and mitigating the effects of drought,

Recognizing further the importance of the provision to affected developing countries, particularly in Africa, of effective means, inter alia substantial financial resources, including new and additional funding, and access to technology, without which it will be difficult for them to implement fully their commitments under this Convention,

Expressing concern over the impact of desertification and drought on affected countries in Central Asia and the Transcaucasus,

Stressing the important role played by women in regions affected by desertification and/or drought, particularly in rural areas of developing countries, and the importance of ensuring the full participation of both men and women at all levels in programmes to combat desertification and mitigate the effects of drought,

Emphasizing the special role of non-governmental organizations and other major groups in programmes to combat desertification and mitigate the effects of drought,

Bearing in mind the relationship between desertification and other environmental problems of global dimension facing the international and national communities,

Bearing also in mind the contribution that combating desertification can make to achieving the objectives of the United Nations Framework Convention on Climate Change, the Convention on Biological Diversity and other related environmental conventions,

Believing that strategies to combat desertification and mitigate the effects of drought will be most effective if they are based on sound systematic observation and rigorous scientific knowledge and if they are continuously re-evaluated,

Recognizing the urgent need to improve the effectiveness and coordination of international cooperation to facilitate the implementation of national plans and priorities,

Determined to take appropriate action in combating desertification and mitigating the effects of drought for the benefit of present and future generations,

Have agreed as follows:

Part. I. Introduction. Art. 1. Use of terms. For the purposes of this Convention:

(a) **"desertification"** means land degradation in arid, semi-arid and dry sub-humid areas resulting from various factors, including climatic variations and human activities;

(b) **"combating desertification"** includes activities which are part of the integrated development of land in arid, semi-arid and dry sub-humid areas for sustainable development which are aimed at:

(i) prevention and/or reduction of land degradation;

(ii) rehabilitation of partly degraded land; and

(iii) reclamation of desertified land;

(c) **"drought"** means the naturally occurring phenomenon that exists when precipitation has been significantly below normal recorded levels, causing serious hydrological imbalances that adversely affect land resource production systems;

(d) **"mitigating the effects of drought"** means activities related to the prediction of drought and intended to reduce the vulnerability of society and natural systems to drought as it relates to combating desertification;

(e) **"land"** means the terrestrial bio-productive system that comprises soil, vegetation, other biota, and the ecological and hydrological processes that operate within the system;

(f) **"land degradation"** means reduction or loss, in arid, semi-arid and dry sub-humid areas, of the biological or economic productivity and complexity of rainfed cropland, irrigated cropland, or range, pasture, forest and woodlands resulting from land uses or from a process or combination of processes, including processes arising from human activities and habitation patterns, such as:

(i) soil erosion caused by wind and/or water;

(ii) deterioration of the physical, chemical and biological or economic properties of soil; and

(iii) long-term loss of natural vegetation;

(g) **"arid, semi-arid and dry sub-humid areas"** means areas, other than polar and sub-polar regions, in which the ratio of annual precipitation to potential evapotranspiration falls within the range from 0.05 to 0.65;

(h) **"affected areas"** means arid, semi-arid and/or dry sub-humid areas affected or threatened by desertification;

(i) **"affected countries"** means countries whose lands include, in whole or in part, affected areas;

(j) **"regional economic integration organization"** means an organization constituted by sovereign States of a given region which has competence in respect of matters governed by this Convention and has been duly authorized, in accordance with its internal procedures, to sign, ratify, accept, approve or accede to this Convention;

(k) **"developed country Parties"** means developed country Parties and regional economic integration organizations constituted by developed countries.

Art. 2. Objective. 1. The objective of this Convention is to combat desertification and mitigate the effects of drought in countries experiencing serious drought and/or desertification, particularly in Africa, through effective action at all levels, supported by international cooperation and partnership arrangements, in the framework of an integrated approach which is consistent with Agenda 21, with a view to contributing to the achievement of sustainable development in affected areas.

2. Achieving this objective will involve long-term integrated strategies that focus simultaneously, in affected areas, on improved productivity of land, and the rehabilitation, conservation and sustainable management of land and water resources, leading to improved living conditions, in particular at the community level.

Art. 3. Principles. In order to achieve the objective of this Convention and to implement its provisions, the Parties shall be guided, inter alia, by the following:

(a) the Parties should ensure that decisions on the design and implementation of programmes to combat desertification and/or mitigate the effects of drought are taken with the participation of populations and local communities and that an enabling environment is created at higher levels to facilitate action at national and local levels;

(b) the Parties should, in a spirit of international solidarity and partnership, improve cooperation and coordination at subregional, regional and international levels, and better focus financial, human, organizational and technical resources where they are needed;

(c) the Parties should develop, in a spirit of partnership, cooperation among all levels of government, communities, non-governmental organizations and landholders to establish a better understanding of the nature and value of land and scarce water resources in affected areas and to work towards their sustainable use; and

(d) the Parties should take into full consideration the special needs and circumstances of affected developing country Parties, particularly the least developed among them. (...)

United Nations Framework Convention on Climate Change. New York, 9 may 1992 *(Preamble; Art. 1. Definitions: "Adverse effects of climate change", "Climate change", "Climate system", "Emissions", "Greenhouse gases",*

"Regional economic integration organization", "Reservoir", "Sink", "Source"; Art. 2. Objective).

Preamble. The Parties to this Convention,

Acknowledging that change in the Earth's climate and its adverse effects are a common concern of humankind,

Concerned that human activities have been substantially increasing the atmospheric concentrations of greenhouse gases, that these increases enhance the natural greenhouse effect, and that this will result on average in an additional warming of the Earth's surface and atmosphere and may adversely affect natural ecosystems and humankind,

Noting that the largest share of historical and current global emissions of greenhouse gases has originated in developed countries, that per capita emissions in developing countries are still relatively low and that the share of global emissions originating in developing countries will grow to meet their social and development needs,

Aware of the role and importance in terrestrial and marine ecosystems of sinks and reservoirs of greenhouse gases,

Noting that there are many uncertainties in predictions of climate change, particularly with regard to the timing, magnitude and regional patterns thereof,

Acknowledging that the global nature of climate change calls for the widest possible cooperation by all countries and their participation in an effective and appropriate international response, in accordance with their common but differentiated responsibilities and respective capabilities and their social and economic conditions,

Recalling the pertinent provisions of the Declaration of the United Nations Conference on the Human Environment, adopted at Stockholm on 16 June 1972,

Recalling also that States have, in accordance with the Charter of the United Nations and the principles of international law, the sovereign right to exploit their own resources pursuant to their own environmental and developmental policies, and the responsibility to ensure that activities within their jurisdiction or control do not cause damage to the environment of other States or of areas beyond the limits of national jurisdiction,

Reaffirming the principle of sovereignty of States in international cooperation to address climate change,

Recognizing that States should enact effective environmental legislation, that environmental standards, management objectives and priorities should reflect the environmental and developmental context to which they apply, and that standards applied by some countries may be inappropriate and of unwarranted economic and social cost to other countries, in particular developing countries,

Recalling the provisions of General Assembly resolution 44/228 of 22 December 1989 on the United Nations Conference on Environment and Development, and resolutions 43/53 of 6 December 1988, 44/207 of 22 December 1989, 45/212 of 21 December 1990 and 46/169 of 19 December 1991 on protection of global climate for present and future generations of mankind,

Recalling also the provisions of General Assembly resolution 44/206 of 22 December 1989 on the possible adverse effects of sea-level rise on islands and coastal areas, particularly low-lying coastal areas and the pertinent provisions of General Assembly resolution 44/172 of 19 December 1989 on the implementation of the Plan of Action to Combat Desertification,

Recalling further the Vienna Convention for the Protection of the Ozone Layer, 1985, and the Montreal Protocol on Substances that Deplete the Ozone Layer, 1987, as adjusted and amended on 29 June 1990,

Noting the Ministerial Declaration of the Second World Climate Conference adopted on 7 November 1990,

Conscious of the valuable analytical work being conducted by many States on climate change and of the important contributions of the World Meteorological Organization, the United Nations Environment Programme and other organs, organizations and bodies of the United Nations system, as well as other international and intergovernmental bodies, to the exchange of results of scientific research and the coordination of research,

Recognizing that steps required to understand and address climate change will be environmentally, socially and economically most effective if they are based on relevant scientific, technical and economic considerations and continually re-evaluated in the light of new findings in these areas,

Recognizing that various actions to address climate change can be justified economically in their own right and can also help in solving other environmental problems,

Recognizing also the need for developed countries to take immediate action in a flexible manner on the basis of clear priorities, as a first step towards comprehensive response strategies at the global, national and, where agreed, regional levels that take into account all greenhouse gases, with due consideration of their relative contributions to the enhancement of the greenhouse effect,

Recognizing further that low-lying and other small island countries, countries with low-lying coastal, arid and semi-arid areas or areas liable to floods, drought and desertification, and developing countries with fragile mountainous ecosystems are particularly vulnerable to the adverse effects of climate change,

Recognizing the special difficulties of those countries, especially developing countries, whose economies are particularly dependent on fossil fuel production, use and exportation, as a consequence of action taken on limiting greenhouse gas emissions,

Affirming that responses to climate change should be coordinated with social and economic development in an integrated manner with a view to avoiding adverse impacts on the latter, taking into full account the legitimate priority needs of developing countries for the achievement of sustained economic growth and the eradication of poverty,

Recognizing that all countries, especially developing countries, need access to resources required to achieve sustainable social and economic development and that, in order for developing countries to progress towards that goal, their energy consumption will need to grow taking into account the possibilities for achieving greater energy efficiency and for controlling greenhouse gas emissions in general, including through the application of new technologies on terms which make such an application economically and socially beneficial,

Determined to protect the climate system for present and future generations,

Have agreed as follows:

Art. 1. Definitions. For the purposes of this Convention:

1. "**Adverse effects of climate change**" means changes in the physical environment or biota resulting from climate change which have significant deleterious effects on the composition, resilience or productivity of natural and managed ecosystems or on the operation of socio-economic systems or on human health and welfare.

2. "**Climate change**" means a change of climate which is attributed directly or indirectly to human activity that alters the composition of the global atmosphere and which is in addition to natural climate variability observed over comparable time periods.

3. "**Climate system**" means the totality of the atmosphere, hydrosphere, biosphere and geosphere and their interactions.

4. "**Emissions**" means the release of greenhouse gases and/or their precursors into the atmosphere over a specified area and period of time.

5. "**Greenhouse gases**" means those gaseous constituents of the atmosphere, both natural and anthropogenic, that absorb and re-emit infrared radiation.

6. "**Regional economic integration organization**" means an organization constituted by sovereign States of a given region which has competence in respect of matters governed by this Convention or its protocols and has been duly authorized, in accordance with its internal procedures, to sign, ratify, accept, approve or accede to the instruments concerned.

7. "**Reservoir**" means a component or components of the climate system where a greenhouse gas or a precursor of a greenhouse gas is stored.

8. "**Sink**" means any process, activity or mechanism which removes a greenhouse gas, an aerosol or a precursor of a greenhouse gas from the atmosphere.

9. "**Source**" means any process or activity which releases a greenhouse gas, an aerosol or a precursor of a greenhouse gas into the atmosphere.

Art. 2. Objective. The ultimate objective of this Convention and any related legal instruments that the Conference of the Parties may adopt is to achieve, in accordance with the relevant provisions of the Convention, stabilization of greenhouse gas concentrations in the atmosphere at a level that would prevent dangerous anthropogenic interference with the climate system. Such a level should be achieved within a time frame sufficient to allow ecosystems to adapt naturally to climate change, to ensure that food production is not threatened and to enable economic development to proceed in a sustainable manner. (…)

United Nations Millennium Declaration.
Resolution adopted by the General Assembly [*without reference to a Main Committee (A/55/L.2)*] - 55/2. United Nations Millennium Declaration. 8th plenary meeting, 8 September 2000 *(I. Values and principles (Freedom, Equality, Solidarity, Tolerance, Respect for nature, Shared responsibility); II. Peace, security and disarmament; III. Development and poverty eradication; IV. Protecting our common environment; V. Human rights, democracy and good governance; VI. Protecting the vulnerable; VII. Meeting the special needs of Africa; VIII. Strengthening the United Nations)*

The General Assembly

Adopts the following Declaration:

United Nations Millennium Declaration

I. Values and principles

1. We, heads of State and Government, have gathered at United Nations Headquarters in New York from 6 to 8 September 2000, at the dawn of a new millennium, to reaffirm our faith in the Organization and its Charter as indispensable foundations of a more peaceful, prosperous and just world.

2. We recognize that, in addition to our separate responsibilities to our individual societies, we have a collective responsibility to uphold the principles of human dignity, equality and equity at the global level. As leaders we have a duty therefore to all the world's people, especially the most vulnerable and, in particular, the children of the world, to whom the future belongs.

3. We reaffirm our commitment to the purposes and principles of the Charter of the United Nations, which have proved timeless and universal. Indeed, their relevance and capacity to inspire have increased, as nations and peoples have become increasingly interconnected and interdependent.

4. We are determined to establish a just and lasting peace all over the world in accordance with the purposes and principles of the Charter. We rededicate ourselves to support all efforts to uphold the sovereign equality of all States, respect for their territorial integrity and political independence, resolution of disputes by peaceful means and in conformity with the principles of justice and international law, the right to self-determination of peoples which remain under colonial domination and foreign occupation, non-interference in the internal affairs of States, respect for human rights and fundamental freedoms, respect for the equal rights of all without distinction as to race, sex, language or religion and international cooperation in solving international problems of an economic, social, cultural or humanitarian character.

5. We believe that the central challenge we face today is to ensure that globalization becomes a positive force for all the world's people. For while globalization offers great opportunities, at present its benefits are very unevenly shared, while its costs are unevenly distributed. We recognize that developing countries and countries with economies in transition face special difficulties in responding to this central challenge. Thus, only through broad and sustained efforts to create a shared future, based upon our common humanity in all its diversity, can globalization be made fully inclusive and equitable. These efforts must include policies and measures, at the global level, which correspond to the needs of developing countries and economies in transition and are formulated and implemented with their effective participation.

6. We consider certain fundamental values to be essential to international relations in the twenty-first century. These include:

• **Freedom.** Men and women have the right to live their lives and raise their children in dignity, free from hunger and from the fear of violence, oppression or injustice. Democratic and participatory governance based on the will of the people best assures these rights.

•. **Equality.** No individual and no nation must be denied the opportunity to benefit from development. The equal rights and opportunities of women and men must be assured.

• **Solidarity.** Global challenges must be managed in a way that distributes the costs and burdens fairly in accordance with basic principles of equity and social justice. Those who suffer or who benefit least deserve help from those who benefit most.

• **Tolerance.** Human beings must respect one other, in all their diversity of belief, culture and language. Differences within and between societies should be neither feared nor repressed, but cherished as a precious asset of humanity. A culture of peace and dialogue among all civilizations should be actively promoted.

• **Respect for nature.** Prudence must be shown in the management of all living species and natural resources, in accordance with the precepts of sustainable development. Only in this way can the immeasurable riches provided to us by nature be preserved and passed on to our descendants. The current unsustainable patterns of production and consumption must be changed in the interest of our future welfare and that of our descendants.

• **Shared responsibility.** Responsibility for managing worldwide economic and social development, as well as threats to international peace and security, must be shared among the nations of the world and should be exercised multilaterally. As the most universal and most representative organization in the world, the United Nations must play the central role.

7. In order to translate these shared values into actions, we have identified key objectives to which we assign special significance.

II. Peace, security and disarmament

8. We will spare no effort to free our peoples from the scourge of war, whether within or between States, which has claimed more than 5 million lives in the past decade. We will also seek to eliminate the dangers posed by weapons of mass destruction.

9. We resolve therefore:

• To strengthen respect for the rule of law in international as in national affairs and, in particular, to ensure compliance by Member States with the decisions of the International Court of Justice, in compliance with the Charter of the United Nations, in cases to which they are parties.

• To make the United Nations more effective in maintaining peace and security by giving it the resources and tools it needs for conflict prevention, peaceful resolution of disputes, peacekeeping, post-conflict peace-building and reconstruction. In this context, we take note of the report of the Panel on United Nations Peace Operations and request the General Assembly to consider its recommendations expeditiously.

• To strengthen cooperation between the United Nations and regional organizations, in accordance with the provisions of Chapter VIII of the Charter.

• To ensure the implementation, by States Parties, of treaties in areas such as arms control and disarmament and of international humanitarian law and human rights law, and call upon all States to consider signing and ratifying the Rome Statute of the International Criminal Court.

• To take concerted action against international terrorism, and to accede as soon as possible to all the relevant international conventions.

• To redouble our efforts to implement our commitment to counter the world drug problem.

• To intensify our efforts to fight transnational crime in all its dimensions, including trafficking as well as smuggling in human beings and money laundering.

• To minimize the adverse effects of United Nations economic sanctions on innocent populations, to subject such sanctions regimes to regular reviews and to eliminate the adverse effects of sanctions on third parties.

• To strive for the elimination of weapons of mass destruction, particularly nuclear weapons, and to keep all options open for achieving this aim, including the possibility of convening an international conference to identify ways of eliminating nuclear dangers.

• To take concerted action to end illicit traffic in small arms and light weapons, especially by making arms transfers more transparent and supporting regional disarmament measures, taking account of all the recommendations of the forthcoming United Nations Conference on Illicit Trade in Small Arms and Light Weapons.

• To call on all States to consider acceding to the Convention on the Prohibition of the Use, Stockpiling, Production and Transfer of Anti-personnel Mines and on Their Destruction, as well as the amended mines protocol to the Convention on conventional weapons.

10. We urge Member States to observe the Olympic Truce, individually and collectively, now and in the future, and to support the International Olympic Committee in its efforts to promote peace and human understanding through sport and the Olympic Ideal.

III. Development and poverty eradication

11. We will spare no effort to free our fellow men, women and children from the abject and dehumanizing conditions of extreme poverty, to which more than a billion of them are currently subjected. We are committed to making the right to development a reality for everyone and to freeing the entire human race from want.

12. We resolve therefore to create an environment – at the national and global levels alike – which is conducive to development and to the elimination of poverty.

13. Success in meeting these objectives depends, *inter alia*, on good governance within each country. It also depends on good governance at the international level and on transparency in the financial, monetary and trading systems. We are committed to an open, equitable, rule-based, predictable and non-discriminatory multilateral trading and financial system.

14. We are concerned about the obstacles developing countries face in mobilizing the resources needed to finance their sustained development. We will therefore make every effort to ensure the success of the High-level International and Intergovernmental Event on Financing for Development, to be held in 2001.

15. We also undertake to address the special needs of the least developed countries. In this context, we welcome the Third United Nations Conference on the Least Developed Countries to be held in May 2001 and will endeavour to ensure its success. We call on the industrialized countries:

• To adopt, preferably by the time of that Conference, a policy of duty- and quota-free access for essentially all exports from the least developed countries;

• To implement the enhanced programme of debt relief for the heavily indebted poor countries without further delay and to agree to cancel all official bilateral debts of those countries in return for their making demonstrable commitments to poverty reduction; and

• To grant more generous development assistance, especially to countries that are genuinely making an effort to apply their resources to poverty reduction.

16. We are also determined to deal comprehensively and effectively with the debt problems of low- and middle-income developing countries, through various national and international measures designed to make their debt sustainable in the long term.

17. We also resolve to address the special needs of small island developing States, by implementing the Barbados Programme of Action and the outcome of the twenty-second special session of the General Assembly rapidly and in full. We urge the international community to ensure that, in the development of a vulnerability index, the special needs of small island developing States are taken into account.

18. We recognize the special needs and problems of the landlocked developing countries, and urge both bilateral and multilateral donors to increase financial and technical assistance to this group of countries to meet their special development needs and to help them overcome the impediments of geography by improving their transit transport systems.

19. We resolve further:

• To halve, by the year 2015, the proportion of the world's people whose income is less than one dollar a day and the proportion of people who suffer from hunger and, by the same date, to halve the proportion of people who are unable to reach or to afford safe drinking water.

• To ensure that, by the same date, children everywhere, boys and girls alike, will be able to complete a full course of primary schooling and that girls and boys will have equal access to all levels of education.

• By the same date, to have reduced maternal mortality by three quarters, and under-five child mortality by two thirds, of their current rates.

• To have, by then, halted, and begun to reverse, the spread of HIV/AIDS, the scourge of malaria and other major diseases that afflict humanity.

• To provide special assistance to children orphaned by HIV/AIDS.

• By 2020, to have achieved a significant improvement in the lives of at least 100 million slum dwellers as proposed in the "Cities Without Slums" initiative.

20. We also resolve:

• To promote gender equality and the empowerment of women as effective ways to combat poverty, hunger and disease and to stimulate development that is truly sustainable.

• To develop and implement strategies that give young people everywhere a real chance to find decent and productive work.

• To encourage the pharmaceutical industry to make essential drugs more widely available and affordable by all who need them in developing countries.

• To develop strong partnerships with the private sector and with civil society organizations in pursuit of development and poverty eradication.

• To ensure that the benefits of new technologies, especially information and communication technologies, in conformity with recommendations contained in the ECOSOC 2000 Ministerial Declaration, are available to all.

IV. Protecting our common environment

21. We must spare no effort to free all of humanity, and above all our children and grandchildren, from the threat of living on a planet irredeemably spoilt by human activities, and whose resources would no longer be sufficient for their needs.

22. We reaffirm our support for the principles of sustainable development, including those set out in Agenda 21, agreed upon at the United Nations Conference on Environment and Development.

23. We resolve therefore to adopt in all our environmental actions a new ethic of conservation and stewardship and, as first steps, we resolve:

• To make every effort to ensure the entry into force of the Kyoto Protocol, preferably by the tenth anniversary of the United Nations Conference on Environment and Development in 2002, and to embark on the required reduction in emissions of greenhouse gases.

• To intensify our collective efforts for the management, conservation and sustainable development of all types of forests.

• To press for the full implementation of the Convention on Biological Diversity and the Convention to Combat Desertification in those Countries Experiencing Serious Drought and/or Desertification, particularly in Africa.

• To stop the unsustainable exploitation of water resources by developing water management strategies at the regional, national and local levels, which promote both equitable access and adequate supplies.

• To intensify cooperation to reduce the number and effects of natural and man-made disasters.

• To ensure free access to information on the human genome sequence.

V. Human rights, democracy and good governance

24. We will spare no effort to promote democracy and strengthen the rule of law, as well as respect for all internationally recognized human rights and fundamental freedoms, including the right to development.

25. We resolve therefore:

• To respect fully and uphold the Universal Declaration of Human Rights.

• To strive for the full protection and promotion in all our countries of civil, political, economic, social and cultural rights for all.

• To strengthen the capacity of all our countries to implement the principles and practices of democracy and respect for human rights, including minority rights.

• To combat all forms of violence against women and to implement the Convention on the Elimination of All Forms of Discrimination against Women.

• To take measures to ensure respect for and protection of the human rights of migrants, migrant workers and their families, to eliminate the increasing acts of racism and xenophobia in many societies and to promote greater harmony and tolerance in all societies.

• To work collectively for more inclusive political processes, allowing genuine participation by all citizens in all our countries.

• To ensure the freedom of the media to perform their essential role and the right of the public to have access to information.

VI. Protecting the vulnerable

26. We will spare no effort to ensure that children and all civilian populations that suffer disproportionately the consequences of natural disasters, genocide, armed conflicts and other humanitarian emergencies are given every assistance and protection so that they can resume normal life as soon as possible.

We resolve therefore:

• To expand and strengthen the protection of civilians in complex emergencies, in conformity with international humanitarian law.

• To strengthen international cooperation, including burden sharing in, and the coordination of humanitarian assistance to, countries hosting refugees and to help all refugees and displaced persons to return voluntarily to their homes, in safety and dignity and to be smoothly reintegrated into their societies.

• To encourage the ratification and full implementation of the Convention on the Rights of the Child and its optional protocols on the involvement of children in armed conflict and on the sale of children, child prostitution and child pornography.

VII. Meeting the special needs of Africa

27. We will support the consolidation of democracy in Africa and assist Africans in their struggle for lasting peace, poverty eradication and sustainable development, thereby bringing Africa into the mainstream of the world economy.

28. We resolve therefore:

• To give full support to the political and institutional structures of emerging democracies in Africa.

• To encourage and sustain regional and subregional mechanisms for preventing conflict and promoting political stability, and to ensure a reliable flow of resources for peacekeeping operations on the continent.

• To take special measures to address the challenges of poverty eradication and sustainable development in Africa, including debt cancellation, improved market access, enhanced Official Development Assistance and increased flows of Foreign Direct Investment, as well as transfers of technology.

• To help Africa build up its capacity to tackle the spread of the HIV/AIDS pandemic and other infectious diseases.

VIII. Strengthening the United Nations

29. We will spare no effort to make the United Nations a more effective instrument for pursuing all of these priorities: the fight for development for all the peoples of the world, the fight against poverty, ignorance and disease; the fight against injustice; the fight against violence, terror and crime; and the fight against the degradation and destruction of our common home.

30. We resolve therefore:

• To reaffirm the central position of the General Assembly as the chief deliberative, policy-making and representative organ of the United Nations, and to enable it to play that role effectively.

• To intensify our efforts to achieve a comprehensive reform of the Security Council in all its aspects.

• To strengthen further the Economic and Social Council, building on its recent achievements, to help it fulfil the role ascribed to it in the Charter.

• To strengthen the International Court of Justice, in order to ensure justice and the rule of law in international affairs.

• To encourage regular consultations and coordination among the principal organs of the United Nations in pursuit of their functions.

• To ensure that the Organization is provided on a timely and predictable basis with the resources it needs to carry out its mandates.

• To urge the Secretariat to make the best use of those resources, in accordance with clear rules and procedures agreed by the General Assembly, in the interests of all

Member States, by adopting the best management practices and technologies available and by concentrating on those tasks that reflect the agreed priorities of Member States.

• To promote adherence to the Convention on the Safety of United Nations and Associated Personnel.

• To ensure greater policy coherence and better cooperation between the United Nations, its agencies, the Bretton Woods Institutions and the World Trade Organization, as well as other multilateral bodies, with a view to achieving a fully coordinated approach to the problems of peace and development.

• To strengthen further cooperation between the United Nations and national parliaments through their world organization, the Inter-Parliamentary Union, in various fields, including peace and security, economic and social development, international law and human rights and democracy and gender issues.

• To give greater opportunities to the private sector, non-governmental organizations and civil society, in general, to contribute to the realization of the Organization's goals and programmes.

31. We request the General Assembly to review on a regular basis the progress made in implementing the provisions of this Declaration, and ask the Secretary-General to issue periodic reports for consideration by the General Assembly and as a basis for further action.

32. We solemnly reaffirm, on this historic occasion, that the United Nations is the indispensable common house of the entire human family, through which we will seek to realize our universal aspirations for peace, cooperation and development. We therefore pledge our unstinting support for these common objectives and our determination to achieve them.

Keeping the promise: united to achieve the Millennium Development Goals.

United Nations A/65/L.1. New York, 22 September 2010. General Assembly, Sixty-fifth session, Agenda items 13 and 115: Integrated and coordinated implementation of and follow-up to the outcomes of the major United Nations conferences and summits in the economic, social and related fields. Follow-up to the outcome of the Millennium Summit. Draft resolution referred to the High-level Plenary Meeting of the General Assembly by the General Assembly at its sixty-fourth session. *Keeping the promise: united to achieve the Millennium Development Goals*

The General Assembly,

Adopts the following outcome document of the High-level Plenary Meeting of the sixty-fifth session of the General Assembly on the Millennium Development Goals:

Keeping the promise: united to achieve the Millennium Development Goals

1. We, Heads of State and Government, gathered at United Nations Headquarters in New York from 20 to 22 September 2010, welcome the progress made since we last met here in 2005 while expressing deep concern that it falls far short of what is needed. Recalling the development goals and commitments emanating from the Millennium Declaration (1 See resolution 55/2) and the 2005 World Summit Outcome,(2 See resolution 60/1) we reaffirm our resolve to work together for the promotion of the economic and social advancement of all peoples.

2. We reaffirm that we continue to be guided by the purposes and principles of the Charter of the United Nations, with full respect for international law and its principles.

3. We also reaffirm the importance of freedom, peace and security, respect for all human rights, including the right to development, the rule of law, gender equality and an overall commitment to just and democratic societies for development.

4. We underscore the continued relevance of the outcomes of all major United Nations conferences and summits in the economic, social and related fields and the commitments contained therein, including the Millennium Development Goals, which have raised awareness and continue to generate real and important development gains. Together these outcomes and commitments have played a vital role in shaping a broad development vision and constitute the overarching framework for the development activities of the United Nations. We strongly reiterate our determination to ensure the timely and full implementation of these outcomes and commitments.

5. We recognize that progress, including on poverty eradication, is being made despite setbacks, including setbacks caused by the financial and economic crisis. In this context, we recognize the deeply inspiring examples of progress made by countries in all regions of the world through cooperation, partnerships, actions and solidarity. We are deeply concerned, however, that the number of people living in extreme poverty and hunger surpasses 1 billion and that inequalities between and within countries remains a significant challenge. We are also deeply concerned about the alarming global levels of maternal and child mortality. We believe that eradication of poverty and hunger, as well as combating inequality at all levels, is essential to create a more prosperous and sustainable future for all.

6. We reiterate our deep concern at the multiple and interrelated crises, including the financial and economic crisis, volatile energy and food prices and ongoing concerns over food security, as well as the increasing challenges posed by climate change and the loss of biodiversity, which have increased vulnerabilities and inequalities and adversely affected development gains, in particular in developing countries. But this will not deter us in our efforts to make the Millennium Development Goals a reality for all.

7. We are determined to collectively advance and strengthen the global partnership for development, as the centrepiece of our cooperation, in the years ahead. The global partnership has been reaffirmed in the Millennium Declaration, the Monterrey Consensus of the International Conference on Financing for Development, (3 *Report of the International Conference on Financing for Development, Monterrey, Mexico, 18-22 March 2002* (United Nations publication, Sales No. E.02.II.A.7), chap. I, resolution 1, annex) the Plan of Implementation of the World Summit on Sustainable Development ("Johannesburg Plan of Implementation"), (4 *Report of the World Summit on Sustainable Development, Johannesburg, South Africa, 26 August- 4 September 2002* (United Nations publication, Sales No. E.03.II.A.1 and corrigendum), chap. I, resolution 1, annex) the 2005 World Summit Outcome and the Doha Declaration on Financing for Development: outcome document of the Follow-up International Conference on Financing for Development to Review the Implementation of the Monterrey Consensus. (5 See resolution 63/239).

8. We are committed to making every effort to achieve the Millennium Development Goals by 2015, including through actions, policies and strategies defined in the present Declaration in support of developing countries, in particular those countries that are lagging most behind and those goals that are most off track, thus improving the lives of the poorest people.

9. We are convinced that the Millennium Development Goals can be achieved, including in the poorest countries, with renewed commitment, effective implementation and intensified collective action by all Member States and other relevant stakeholders at both the domestic and international levels, using national development strategies and appropriate policies and approaches that have proved to be effective, with strengthened institutions at all levels, increased mobilization of resources for development, increased effectiveness of development cooperation and an enhanced global partnership for development.

10. We reaffirm that national ownership and leadership are indispensable in the development process. There is no one size fits all. We reiterate that each country has primary responsibility for its own economic and social development and that the role of national policies, domestic resources and development strategies cannot be overemphasized. At the same time, domestic
economies are now interwoven with the global economic system and, therefore, an effective use of trade and investment opportunities can help countries to fight poverty. Development efforts at the national level need to be supported by an enabling national and international environment that complements national actions and strategies.

11. We acknowledge that good governance and the rule of law at the national and international levels are essential for sustained, inclusive and equitable economic growth, sustainable development and the eradication of poverty and hunger.

12. We recognize that gender equality, the empowerment of women, women's full enjoyment of all human rights and the eradication of poverty are essential to economic and social development, including the achievement of all the Millennium Development Goals. We reaffirm the need for the full and effective implementation of the Beijing Declaration and Platform for Action. (6 *Report of the Fourth World Conference on Women, Beijing, 4-15 September 1995* (United Nations publication, Sales No. E.96.IV.13), chap. I, resolution 1, annexes I and II). Achieving gender equality and empowerment of women is both a key development goal and an important means for achieving all of the Millennium Development Goals. We welcome the establishment of the United Nations Entity for Gender Equality and the Empowerment of Women (UN Women), and pledge our full support for its operationalization.

13. We acknowledge that peace and security, development and human rights are the pillars of the United Nations system and the foundations for collective security and well-being. We recognize that development, peace and security and human rights are interlinked and mutually reinforcing. We reaffirm thatour common fundamental values, including freedom, equality, solidarity, tolerance, respect for all human rights, respect for nature and shared responsibility, are essential for achieving the Millennium Development Goals.

14. We are convinced that the United Nations, on the basis of its universal membership, legitimacy and unique mandate, plays a vital role in the promotion of international cooperation for development and in supporting the acceleration of the implementation of the internationally agreed development goals, including the Millennium Development Goals. We reaffirm the need for a strong United Nations to meet the challenges of the changing global
environment.

15. We recognize that all the Millennium Development Goals are interconnected and mutually reinforcing. We therefore underline the need to pursue these Goals through a holistic and comprehensive approach.

16. We acknowledge the diversity of the world and recognize that all cultures and civilizations contribute to the enrichment of humankind. We emphasize the importance of culture for development and its contribution to the achievement of the Millennium Development Goals.

17. We call on civil society, including non-governmental organizations, voluntary associations and foundations, the private sector and other relevant stakeholders at the local, national, regional and global levels, to enhance their role in national development efforts as well as their contribution to the achievement of the Millennium Development Goals by 2015, and commit as national Governments to the inclusion of these stakeholders.

18. We acknowledge the role of national parliaments in furthering the achievement of the Millennium Development Goals by 2015.

A mixed story: successes, uneven progress, challenges and opportunities

19. We recognize that developing countries have made significant efforts towards achieving the Millennium Development Goals and have had major successes in realizing some of the targets of the Millennium Development Goals. Successes have been made in combating extreme poverty, improving school enrolment and child health, reducing child deaths, expanding access to clean water, improving prevention of mother-to-child transmission of HIV, expanding access to HIV/AIDS prevention, treatment and care, and controlling malaria, tuberculosis and neglected tropical diseases.

20. We acknowledge that much more needs to be done in achieving the Millennium Development Goals as progress has been uneven among regions and between and within countries. Hunger and malnutrition rose again from 2007 through 2009, partially reversing prior gains. There has been slow progress in reaching full and productive employment and decent work for all, advancing gender equality and the empowerment of women, achieving environmental sustainability and providing basic sanitation, and new HIV infections still outpace the number of people starting treatment. In particular, we express grave concern over the slow progress being made on reducing maternal mortality and improving maternal and reproductive health. Progress on other Millennium Development Goals is fragile and must be sustained to avoid reversal.

21. We underline the central role of the global partnership for development and the importance of Goal 8 in achieving the Millennium Development Goals. We recognize that without substantial international support, several of the Goals are likely to be missed in many developing countries by 2015.

22. We are deeply concerned about the impact of the financial and economic crisis, the worst since the Great Depression. It has reversed development gains in many developing countries and threatens to seriously undermine the achievement of the Millennium Development Goals by 2015.

23. We take note of the lessons learned and successful policies and approaches in the implementation and achievement of the Millennium Development Goals and recognize that with increased political commitment these could be replicated and scaled up for accelerating progress, including by:

(a) Strengthening national ownership and leadership of development strategies;

(b) Adopting forward-looking, macroeconomic policies that promote sustainable development and lead to sustained, inclusive and equitable economic growth, increase productive employment opportunities and promote agricultural and industrial development;

(c) Promoting national food security strategies that strengthen support for smallholder farmers and contribute to poverty eradication;

(d) Adopting policies and measures oriented towards benefiting the poor and addressing social and economic inequalities;

(e) Supporting participatory, community-led strategies aligned with national development priorities and strategies;

(f) Promoting universal access to public and social services and providing social protection floors;

(g) Improving capacity to deliver quality services equitably;

(h) Implementing social policies and programmes, including appropriate conditional cash-transfer programmes, and investing in basic services for health, education, water and sanitation;

(i) Ensuring the full participation of all segments of society, including the poor and disadvantaged, in decision-making processes;

(j) Respecting, promoting and protecting all human rights, including the right to development;

(k) Increasing efforts to reduce inequality and eliminate social exclusion and discrimination;

(l) Enhancing opportunities for women and girls and advancing the economic, legal and political empowerment of women;

(m) Investing in the health of women and children to drastically reduce the number of women and children who die from preventable causes;

(n) Working towards transparent and accountable systems of governance at the national and international levels;

(o) Working towards greater transparency and accountability in international development cooperation, in both donor and developing countries, focusing on adequate and predictable financial resources as well as their improved quality and targeting;

(p) Promoting South-South and triangular cooperation, which complement North-South cooperation;

(q) Promoting effective public-private partnerships;

(r) Expanding access to financial services for the poor, especially poor women, including through adequately funded microfinance plans, programmes and initiatives supported by development partners;

(s) Strengthening statistical capacity to produce reliable disaggregated data for better programmes and policy evaluation and formulation.

24. We recognize that the scaling-up of the successful policies and approaches outlined above will need to be complemented by a strengthened global partnership for development, as set out in the action agenda below.

25. We take note of the first formal debate organized by the President of the General Assembly in which different views on the notion of **human security** were presented by Member States, as well as the ongoing efforts to define the notion of human security, and recognize the need to continue the discussion and to achieve an agreement on the definition of human security in the General Assembly.

26. We recognize that climate change poses serious risks and challenges to all countries, especially developing countries. We commit to addressing climate change in accordance with the principles and provisions of the United Nations Framework Convention on Climate Change, (7 United Nations, *Treaty Series*, vol. 1771, No. 30822) including the principle

of common but differentiated responsibilities and respective capabilities. We maintain the Framework Convention as the primary international, intergovernmental forum for negotiating the global response to climate change. Addressing climate change will be of key importance in safeguarding and advancing progress towards achieving the Millennium Development Goals.

27. We recognize that attention must be focused on the particular needs of developing countries and on the large and increasing economic and social inequalities. Disparities between developed and developing countries and inequalities between the rich and the poor, and between rural and urban populations, inter alia, remain persistent and significant and need to be addressed.

28. We also recognize that policies and actions must focus on the poor and those living in the most vulnerable situations, including persons with disabilities, so that they benefit from progress towards achieving the Millennium Development Goals. In this respect there is a particular need to provide more equitable access to economic opportunities and social services.

29. We recognize the urgency of paying attention to the many developing countries with specific needs, and the unique challenges they confront in achieving the Millennium Development Goals.

30. We acknowledge that the least developed countries face significant constraints and structural impediments in their development efforts. We express grave concern that the least developed countries are lagging behind in meeting internationally agreed development goals, including the Millennium Development Goals. In that context, we call for continued implementation of the Brussels Programme of Action for the Least Developed Countries for the Decade 2001-2010 (8 A/CONF.191/13, chap. II) and look forward to the Fourth United Nations Conference on the Least Developed Countries, to be held in Istanbul in 2011, which would further invigorate the international partnership to address the special needs of these countries.

31. We reiterate our recognition of the special needs of and challenges faced by the landlocked developing countries, caused by their lack of territorial access to the sea

aggravated by remoteness from world markets, and also the concern that the economic growth and social well-being of landlocked developing countries remain very vulnerable to external shocks. We stress the need to overcome these vulnerabilities and build resilience. We call for the full, timely and effective implementation of the Almaty Programme of Action: Addressing the Special Needs of Landlocked Developing Countries within a New Global Framework for Transit Transport Cooperation for Landlocked and Transit Developing Countries, (9 *Report of the International Ministerial Conference of Landlocked and Transit Developing Countries and Donor Countries and International Financial and Development Institutions on Transit Transport Cooperation, Almaty, Kazakhstan, 28 and 29 August 2003* (A/CONF.202/3), annex I) as presented in the Declaration of the highlevel meeting of the sixty-third session of the General Assembly on the midterm review of the Almaty Programme of Action. (10 See resolution 63/2).

32. We recognize the unique and particular vulnerabilities of small island developing States and reaffirm our commitment to take urgent and concrete action to address those vulnerabilities through the full and effective implementation of the Mauritius Strategy for the Further Implementation of the Programme of Action for the Sustainable Development of Small Island Developing States. (11 *See Report of the International Meeting to Review the Implementation of the Programme of Action for the Sustainable Development of Small Island Developing States, Port Louis, Mauritius, 10-14 January 2005* (United Nations publication, Sales No. E.05.II.A.4 and corrigendum), chap. I, resolution 1, annex II). We also recognize that the adverse effects of climate change and sea-level rise present significant risks to the sustainable development of small island developing States. We note the uneven progress of small island developing States in achieving the Millennium Development Goals and express concern that progress in some areas has been lagging. In this regard, we welcome the five-year high-level review of the Mauritius Strategy in September 2010 to assess progress made in addressing the vulnerabilities of small island developing States.

33. We recognize that more attention should be given to Africa, especially those countries most off track to achieve the Millennium Development Goals by 2015. Progress has been made in some African countries, but the situation in others remains a grave concern, not least because the continent is among the hardest hit by the financial and economic crisis. We note that aid to Africa has increased in recent years; however, it still lags behind the commitments that have been made. We therefore strongly call for the delivery of those commitments.

34. We recognize also the specific development challenges of middle-income countries. These countries face unique challenges in their efforts to achieve their national development goals, including the Millennium Development Goals. We also reiterate that their efforts in that regard should be based on national development plans that integrate the Millennium Development Goals and should be adequately supported by the international community, through various forms, taking into account the needs and the capacity to mobilize domestic resources of these countries.

35. We acknowledge that disaster risk reduction and increasing resilience to all types of natural hazard, including geological and hydro-meteorological hazards, in developing countries, in line with the Hyogo Framework for Action 2005-2015:

Building the Resilience of Nations and Communities to Disasters, (12 A/CONF.206/6 and Corr.1, chap. I, resolution 2) can have multiplier effects and accelerate achievement of the Millennium Development Goals. Reducing vulnerabilities to these hazards is therefore a high priority for developing countries. We recognize that small island developing States continue to grapple with natural disasters, some of which are of increased intensity, including as a result of the effects of climate change, impeding progress towards sustainable development.

The way forward: an action agenda for achieving the Millennium Development Goals by 2015

(...) Millennium Development Goal 1: Eradicate extreme poverty and hunger; Millennium Development Goal 2: Achieve universal primary education; Millennium Development Goal 3: Promoting gender equality and empowerment of women; Promoting global public health for all to achieve the Millennium Development Goals; Millennium Development Goal 4: Reduce child mortality; Millennium Development Goal 5: Improve maternal health; Millennium Development Goal 6: Combat HIV/AIDS, malaria and other diseases; Millennium Development Goal 7: Ensure environmental sustainability; Millennium Development Goal 8: Develop a Global Partnership for Development; Staying engaged to achieve the Millennium Development Goals.

Universal Declaration of Human Rights, Paris, 10 December 1948

(Preamble. Art. 1, Art. 2, Art. 3, Art. 4, Art. 5, Art. 6, Art. 7, Art. 8, Art. 9, Art. 10, Art. 11, Art. 12, Art. 13, Art. 14, Art. 15, Art. 16, Art. 17, Art. 18, Art. 19, Art. 20, Art. 21, Art. 22, Art. 23, Art. 24, Art. 25, Art. 26, Art. 27, Art. 28, Art. 29, Art. 30). Preamble.

Whereas recognition of the inherent dignity and of the equal and inalienable rights of all members of the human family is the foundation of freedom, justice and peace in the world,

Whereas disregard and contempt for human rights have resulted in barbarous acts which have outraged the conscience of mankind, and the advent of a world in which human beings shall enjoy freedom of speech and belief and freedom from fear and want has been proclaimed as the highest aspiration of the common people,

Whereas it is essential, if man is not to be compelled to have recourse, as a last resort, to rebellion against tyranny and oppression, that human rights should be protected by the rule of law,

Whereas it is essential to promote the development of friendly relations between nations,

Whereas the peoples of the United Nations have in the Charter reaffirmed their faith in fundamental human rights, in the dignity and worth of the human person and in the equal rights of men and women and have determined to promote social progress and better standards of life in larger freedom,

Whereas Member States have pledged themselves to achieve, in co-operation with the United Nations, the promotion of universal respect for and observance of human rights and fundamental freedoms,

Whereas a common understanding of these rights and freedoms is of the greatest importance for the full realization of this pledge,

Now, Therefore The General Assembly proclaims this Universal Declaration of Human Rights as a common standard of achievement for all peoples and all nations, to the end that every individual and every organ of society, keeping this Declaration constantly in mind, shall strive by teaching and education to promote respect for these rights and freedoms and by progressive measures, national and international, to secure their universal and effective recognition and observance, both among the peoples of Member States themselves and among the peoples of territories under their jurisdiction.

Art. 1. All human beings are born free and equal in dignity and rights. They are endowed with reason and conscience and should act towards one another in a spirit of brotherhood.

Art. 2. Everyone is entitled to all the rights and freedoms set forth in this Declaration, without distinction of any kind, such as race, colour, sex, language, religion, political or other opinion, national or social origin, property, birth or other status. Furthermore, no distinction shall be made on the basis of the political, jurisdictional or international status of the country or territory to which a person belongs, whether it be independent, trust, non-self-governing or under any other limitation of sovereignty.

Art. 3. Everyone has the right to life, liberty and security of person.

Art. 4. No one shall be held in slavery or servitude; slavery and the slave trade shall be prohibited in all their forms.

Art. 5. No one shall be subjected to torture or to cruel, inhuman or degrading treatment or punishment.

Art. 6. Everyone has the right to recognition everywhere as a person before the law.

Art. 7. All are equal before the law and are entitled without any discrimination to equal protection of the law. All are entitled to equal protection against any discrimination in violation of this Declaration and against any incitement to such discrimination.

Art. 8. Everyone has the right to an effective remedy by the competent national tribunals for acts violating the fundamental rights granted him by the constitution or by law.

Art. 9. No one shall be subjected to arbitrary arrest, detention or exile.

Art. 10. Everyone is entitled in full equality to a fair and public hearing by an independent and impartial tribunal, in the determination of his rights and obligations and of any criminal charge against him.

Art. 11. (1) Everyone charged with a penal offence has the right to be presumed innocent until proved guilty according to law in a public trial at which he has had all the guarantees necessary for his defence.

(2) No one shall be held guilty of any penal offence on account of any act or omission which did not constitute a penal offence, under national or international law, at the time when it was committed. Nor shall a heavier penalty be imposed than the one that was applicable at the time the penal offence was committed.

Art. 12. No one shall be subjected to arbitrary interference with his privacy, family, home or correspondence, nor to attacks upon his honour and reputation. Everyone has the right to the protection of the law against such interference or attacks.

Art. 13. (1) Everyone has the right to freedom of movement and residence within the borders of each state.

(2) Everyone has the right to leave any country, including his own, and to return to his country.

Art. 14. (1) Everyone has the right to seek and to enjoy in other countries asylum from persecution.

(2) This right may not be invoked in the case of prosecutions genuinely arising from non-political crimes or from acts contrary to the purposes and principles of the United Nations.

Art. 15. (1) Everyone has the right to a nationality.

(2) No one shall be arbitrarily deprived of his nationality nor denied the right to change his nationality.

Art. 16. (1) Men and women of full age, without any limitation due to race, nationality or religion, have the right to marry and to found a family. They are entitled to equal rights as to marriage, during marriage and at its dissolution.

(2) Marriage shall be entered into only with the free and full consent of the intending spouses.

(3) The family is the natural and fundamental group unit of society and is entitled to protection by society and the State.

Art. 17. (1) Everyone has the right to own property alone as well as in association with others.

(2) No one shall be arbitrarily deprived of his property.

Art. 18. Everyone has the right to freedom of thought, conscience and religion; this right includes freedom to change his religion or belief, and freedom, either alone or in community with others and in public or private, to manifest his religion or belief in teaching, practice, worship and observance.

Art. 19. Everyone has the right to freedom of opinion and expression; this right includes freedom to hold opinions without interference and to seek, receive and impart information and ideas through any media and regardless of frontiers.

Art. 20. (1) Everyone has the right to freedom of peaceful assembly and association.

(2) No one may be compelled to belong to an association.

Art. 21. (1) Everyone has the right to take part in the government of his country, directly or through freely chosen representatives.

(2) Everyone has the right of equal access to public service in his country.

(3) The will of the people shall be the basis of the authority of government; this will shall be expressed in periodic and genuine elections which shall be by universal and equal suffrage and shall be held by secret vote or by equivalent free voting procedures.

Art. 22. Everyone, as a member of society, has the right to social security and is entitled to realization, through national effort and international co-operation and in accordance with the organization and resources of each State, of the economic, social and cultural rights indispensable for his dignity and the free development of his personality.

Art. 23. (1) Everyone has the right to work, to free choice of employment, to just and favourable conditions of work and to protection against unemployment.

(2) Everyone, without any discrimination, has the right to equal pay for equal work.

(3) Everyone who works has the right to just and favourable remuneration ensuring for himself and his family an existence worthy of human dignity, and supplemented, if necessary, by other means of social protection.

(4) Everyone has the right to form and to join trade unions for the protection of his interests.

Art. 24. Everyone has the right to rest and leisure, including reasonable limitation of working hours and periodic holidays with pay.

Art. 25. (1) Everyone has the right to a standard of living adequate for the health and well-being of himself and of his family, including food, clothing, housing and medical care and necessary social services, and the right to security in the event of unemployment, sickness, disability, widowhood, old age or other lack of livelihood in circumstances beyond his control.

(2) Motherhood and childhood are entitled to special care and assistance. All children, whether born in or out of wedlock, shall enjoy the same social protection.

Art. 26. (1) Everyone has the right to education. Education shall be free, at least in the elementary and fundamental stages. Elementary education shall be compulsory. Technical and professional education shall be made generally available and higher education shall be equally accessible to all on the basis of merit.

(2) Education shall be directed to the full development of the human personality and to the strengthening of respect for human rights and fundamental freedoms. It shall promote understanding, tolerance and friendship among all nations, racial or religious groups, and shall further the activities of the United Nations for the maintenance of peace.

(3) Parents have a prior right to choose the kind of education that shall be given to their children.

Art. 27. (1) Everyone has the right freely to participate in the cultural life of the community, to enjoy the arts and to share in scientific advancement and its benefits.

(2) Everyone has the right to the protection of the moral and material interests resulting from any scientific, literary or artistic production of which he is the author.

Art. 28. Everyone is entitled to a social and international order in which the rights and freedoms set forth in this Declaration can be fully realized.

Art. 29. (1) Everyone has duties to the community in which alone the free and full development of his personality is possible.

(2) In the exercise of his rights and freedoms, everyone shall be subject only to such limitations as are determined by law solely for the purpose of securing due recognition and respect for the rights and freedoms of others and of meeting the just requirements of morality, public order and the general welfare in a democratic society.

(3) These rights and freedoms may in no case be exercised contrary to the purposes and principles of the United Nations.

Art. 30. Nothing in this Declaration may be interpreted as implying for any State, group or person any right to engage in any activity or to perform any act aimed at the destruction of any of the rights and freedoms set forth herein.

Use of force *(Charter of the United Nations, San Francisco, 26 June 1945, Chapter VII. Action with respect to threats to the peace, breaches of the peace, and* *acts of aggression. Art. 39, Art. 40, Art. 41, Art. 42, Art. 43, Art. 44, Art. 45, Art. 46, Art. 47, Art. 48, Art. 49, Art. 50, Art. 51).*

Art. 39. The Security Council shall determine the existence of any threat to the peace, breach of the peace, or act of aggression and shall make recommendations, or decide what measures shall be taken in accordance with Articles 41 and 42, to maintain or restore international peace and security.

Art. 40. In order to prevent an aggravation of the situation, the Security Council may, before making the recommendations or deciding upon the measures provided for in Article 39, call upon the parties concerned to comply with such provisional measures as it deems necessary or desirable. Such provisional measures shall be without prejudice to the rights, claims, or position of the parties concerned. The Security Council shall duly take account of failure to comply with such provisional measures.

Art. 41. The Security Council may decide what measures not involving the use of armed force are to be employed to give effect to its decisions, and it may call upon the Members of the United Nations to apply such measures. These may include complete or partial interruption of economic relations and of rail, sea, air, postal, telegraphic, radio, and other means of communication, and the severance of diplomatic relations.

Art. 42. Should the Security Council consider that measures provided for in Article 41 would be inadequate or have proved to be inadequate, it may take such action by air, sea, or land forces as may be necessary to maintain or restore international peace and security. Such action may include demonstrations, blockade, and other operations by air, sea, or land forces of Members of the United Nations.

Art. 43. 1. All Members of the United Nations, in order to contribute to the maintenance of international peace and security, undertake to make available to the Security Council, on its call and in accordance with a special agreement or agreements, armed forces, assistance, and facilities, including rights of passage, necessary for the purpose of maintaining international peace and security.

2. Such agreement or agreements shall govern the numbers and types of forces, their degree of
readiness and general location, and the nature of the facilities and assistance to be provided.

3. The agreement or agreements shall be negotiated as soon as possible on the initiative of the
Security Council. They shall be concluded between the Security Council and Members or between the Security Council and groups of Members and shall be subject to ratification by the signatory states in accordance with their respective constitutional processes.

Art. 44. When the Security Council has decided to use force it shall, before calling upon a Member not represented on it to provide armed forces in fulfillment of the obligations assumed under Article 43, invite that Member, if the Member so desires, to participate in the decisions of the Security Council concerning the employment of contingents of that Member's armed forces.

Art. 45. In order to enable the United Nations to take urgent military measures, Members shall hold immediately available national air-force contingents for combined international enforcement action. The strength and degree of readiness of these contingents and plans for their combined action shall be determined, within the limits laid down in the special agreement or agreements referred to in Article 43, by the Security Council with the assistance of the Military Staff Committee.

Art. 46. Plans for the application of armed force shall be made by the Security Council with the assistance of the Military Staff Committee.

Art. 47. 1. There shall be established a Military Staff Committee to advise and assist the Security Council on all questions relating to the Security Council's military requirements for the maintenance of international peace and security, the employment and command of forces placed at its disposal, the regulation of armaments, and possible disarmament.

2. The Military Staff Committee shall consist of the Chiefs of Staff of the permanent members

of the Security Council or their representatives. Any Member of the United Nations not permanently represented on the Committee shall be invited by the Committee to be associated with it when the efficient discharge of the Committee's responsibilities requires the participation of that Member in its work.

3. The Military Staff Committee shall be responsible under the Security Council for the strategic direction of any armed forces placed at the disposal of the Security Council. Questions relating to the command of such forces shall be worked out subsequently.

4. The Military Staff Committee, with the authorization of the Security Council and after consultation with appropriate regional agencies, may establish regional subcommittees.

Art. 48. 1. The action required to carry out the decisions of the Security Council for the maintenance of international peace and security shall be taken by all the Members of the United Nations or by some of them, as the Security Council may determine.

2. Such decisions shall be carried out by the Members of the United Nations directly and through their action in the appropriate international agencies of which they are members.

Art. 49. The Members of the United Nations shall join in affording mutual assistance in carrying out the measures decided upon by the Security Council.

Art. 50. If preventive or enforcement measures against any state are taken by the Security Council, any other state, whether a Member of the United Nations or not, which finds itself confronted with special economic problems arising from the carrying out of those measures shall have the right to consult the Security Council with regard to a solution of those problems.

Art. 51. Nothing in the present Charter shall impair the inherent right of individual or collective self-defense if an armed attack occurs against a Member of the United Nations, until the Security Council has taken the measures necessary to maintain international peace and security. Measures taken by Members in the exercise of this right of self-defense shall be immediately reported to the Security Council and shall not in any way affect the authority and responsibility of the Security Council under the present Charter to take at any time such action as it deems necessary in order to maintain or restore international peace and security.

V

Victims (RPE – ICC, Section 3. Victims and witnesses; Subsection 1. Definition and general principle relating to victims; Rule 85. Definition of victims; International Convention for the Protection of All Persons from Enforced Disappearance. 20 December 2006. Part. I., Art. 24).

RPE – ICC, Section 3. Victims and witnesses; Subsection 1. Definition and general principle relating to victims; Rule 85. Definition of victims. For the purposes of the Statute and the Rules of Procedure and Evidence:

(a) 'Victims' means natural persons who have suffered harm as a result of the commission of any crime within the jurisdiction of the Court;

(b) Victims may include organizations or institutions that have sustained direct harm to any of their property which is dedicated to religion, education, art or science or charitable purposes, and to their historic monuments, hospitals and other places and objects for humanitarian purposes.

International Convention for the Protection of All Persons from Enforced Disappearance. 20 December 2006. Part. I., Art. 24. 1. For the purposes of this Convention, "victim" means the disappeared person and any individual who has suffered harm as the direct result of an enforced disappearance.

2. Each victim has the right to know the truth regarding the circumstances of the enforced disappearance, the progress and results of the investigation and the fate of the disappeared person. Each State Party shall take appropriate measures in this regard.

3. Each State Party shall take all appropriate measures to search for, locate and release disappeared persons and, in the event of death, to locate, respect and return their remains.

4. Each State Party shall ensure in its legal system that the victims of enforced disappearance have the right to obtain reparation and prompt, fair and adequate compensation.

5. The right to obtain reparation referred to in paragraph 4 of this article covers material and moral damages and, where appropriate, other forms of reparation such as:

(*a*) Restitution;

(*b*) Rehabilitation;

(*c*) Satisfaction, including restoration of dignity and reputation;

(*d*) Guarantees of non-repetition.

6. Without prejudice to the obligation to continue the investigation until the fate of the disappeared person has been clarified, each State Party shall take the appropriate steps with regard to the legal situation of disappeared persons whose fate has not

been clarified and that of their relatives, in fields such as social welfare, financial matters, family law and property rights.

7. Each State Party shall guarantee the right to form and participate freely in organizations and associations concerned with attempting to establish the circumstances of enforced disappearances and the fate of disappeared persons, and to assist victims of enforced disappearance.

Violations of Article 3 Common to the Geneva Conventions and of Additional Protocol II (*Statute ICTR, art. 4*).

The International Tribunal for Rwanda shall have the power to prosecute persons committing or ordering to be committed serious violations of Article 3 common to the Geneva Conventions of 12 August 1949 for the Protection of War Victims, and of Additional Protocol II thereto of 8 June 1977. These violations shall include, but shall not be limited to:

(a) Violence to life, health and physical or mental well-being of persons, in particular murder as well as cruel treatment such as torture, mutilation or any form of corporal punishment;

(b) Collective punishments;

(c) Taking of hostages;

(d) Acts of terrorism;

(e) Outrages upon personal dignity, in particular humiliating and degrading treatment, rape, enforced prostitution and any form of indecent assault;

(f) Pillage;

(g) The passing of sentences and the carrying out of executions without previous judgement pronounced by a regularly constituted court, affording all the judicial guarantees which are recognized as indispensable by civilised peoples;

(h) Threats to commit any of the foregoing acts.

Violations of the laws or customs of war (*Statute ICTY, art. 3*).

The International Tribunal shall have the power to prosecute persons violating the laws or customs of war. Such violations shall include, but not be limited to:

(a) employment of poisonous weapons or other weapons calculated to cause unnecessary suffering;

(b) wanton destruction of cities, towns or villages, or devastation not justified by military necessity;

(c) attack, or bombardment, by whatever means, of undefended towns, villages, dwellings, or buildings;

(d) seizure of, destruction or wilful damage done to institutions dedicated to religion, charity and education, the arts and sciences, historic monuments and works of art and science;

(e) plunder of public or private property.

W

War crime of attacking civilian objects. *See: War crimes, Elements of Crimes.*

War crime of attacking civilians. *See: War crimes, Elements of Crimes.*

War crime of attacking objects or persons using the distinctive emblems of the Geneva Conventions. *See: War crimes, Elements of Crimes.*

War crime of attacking personnel or objects involved in a humanitarian assistance or peacekeeping mission. *See: War crimes, Elements of Crimes.*

War crime of attacking protected objects. *See: War crimes, Elements of Crimes.*

War crime of attacking undefended places. *See: War crimes, Elements of Crimes.*

War crime of biological experiments. *See: War crimes, Elements of Crimes.*

War crime of compelling participation in military operations. *See: War crimes, Elements of Crimes.*

War crime of compelling service in hostile forces. *See: War crimes, Elements of Crimes.*

War crime of cruel treatment. *See: War crimes, Elements of Crimes.*

War crime of denying a fair trial. *See: War crimes, Elements of Crimes.*

War crime of denying quarter. *See: War crimes, Elements of Crimes.*

War crime of depriving the nationals of the hostile power of rights or actions. *See: War crimes, Elements of Crimes.*

War crime of destroying or seizing the enemy's property. *See: War crimes, Elements of Crimes.*

War crime of destruction and appropriation of property. *See: War crimes, Elements of Crimes.*

War crime of displacing civilians. *See: War crimes, Elements of Crimes.*
War crime of employing poison or poisoned weapons. *See: War crimes, Elements of Crimes.*

War crime of employing prohibited bullets. *See: War crimes, Elements of Crimes.*

War crime of employing prohibited gases, liquids, materials or devices. *See: War crimes, Elements of Crimes.*

War crime of employing weapons, projectiles or materials or methods of warfare listed in the Annex to the Statute (ICC). *See: War crimes, Elements of Crimes.*

War crime of enforced prostitution. *See: War crimes, Elements of Crimes, Crimes against humanity.*

War crime of enforced sterilization. *See: War crimes, Elements of Crimes, Crimes against humanity.*

War crime of excessive incidental death, injury, or damage. *See: War crimes, Elements of Crimes.*

War crime of forced pregnancy. *See: War crimes, Elements of Crimes, Crimes against humanity.*

War crime of improper use of a flag, insignia or uniform of the hostile party. *See: War crimes, Elements of Crimes.*

War crime of improper use of a flag of truce. *See: War crimes, Elements of Crimes.*

War crime of improper use of the distinctive emblems of the Geneva Conventions. *See: War crimes, Elements of Crimes.*

War crime of improper use of a flag, insignia or uniform of the United Nations. *See: War crimes, Elements of Crimes.*

War crime of inhuman treatment. *See: War crimes, Elements of Crimes.*

War crime of killing or wounding a person hors de combat. *See: War crimes, Elements of Crimes.*

War crime of medical or scientific experiments. *See: War crimes, Elements of Crimes.*

War crime of murder. *See: War crimes, Elements of Crimes, Crimes against humanity.*

War crime of mutilation. *See: War crimes, Elements of Crimes.*

War crime of outrages upon personal dignity. *See: War crimes, Elements of Crimes.*

War crime of pillaging. *See: War crimes, Elements of Crimes.*

War crime of rape. *See: War crimes, Elements of Crimes, Crimes against humanity.*

War crime of sentencing or execution without due process. *See: War crimes, Elements of Crimes.*

War crime of sexual slavery. *See: War crimes, Elements of Crimes, Crimes against humanity.*

War crime of sexual violence. *See: War crimes, Elements of Crimes, Crimes against humanity.*

War crime of starvation as a method of warfare. *See: War crimes, Elements of Crimes.*

War crime of taking hostages. *See: War crimes, Elements of Crimes.*

War crime of torture. *See: Torture, War crimes, Elements of Crimes, Crimes against humanity.*

War crime of treacherously killing or wounding. *See: War crimes, Elements of Crimes.*

War crime of unlawful confinement. *See: War crimes, Elements of Crimes.*

War crime of unlawful deportation and transfer. *See: War crimes, Elements of Crimes.*

War crime of using, conscripting or enlisting children. *See: War crimes, Elements of Crimes.*

War crime of using protected persons as shields. *See: War crimes, Elements of Crimes.*

War crime of wilful killing. *See: War crimes, Elements of Crimes.*

War crime of wilfully causing great suffering. *See: War crimes, Elements of Crimes.*

War crimes *(London Agreement (8 August 1945), Charter of the International Military Tribunal. Art. 6. (b) - Rome Statute ICC, art. 8. War Crimes; Elements of Crimes, art. 8. War crimes: Introduction; Art. 8 (2) (a), Art. 8 (2) (a) (i) War crime of wilful killing. Elements; Art. 8 (2) (a) (ii)-1 War crime of torture. Elements; Art. 8 (2) (a) (ii)-2 War crime of inhuman treatment. Elements; Art. 8 (2) (a) (ii)-3 War crime of biological experiments. Elements; Art. 8 (2) (a) (iii) War crime of wilfully causing great suffering. Elements; Art. 8 (2) (a) (iv) War crime of destruction and appropriation of property. Elements; Art. 8 (2) (a) (v) War crime of compelling service in hostile forces. Elements; Art. 8 (2) (a) (vi) War crime of denying a fair trial. Elements; Art. 8 (2) (a) (vii)-1 War crime of unlawful deportation and transfer. Elements; Art. 8 (2) (a) (vii)-2 War crime of unlawful confinement. Elements; Art. 8 (2) (a) (viii) War crime of taking hostages. Elements; Art. 8 (2) (b), Art. 8 (2) (b) (i) War crime of attacking civilians. Elements; Art. 8 (2) (b) (ii) War crime of attacking civilian objects. Elements; Art. 8 (2) (b) (iii) War crime of attacking personnel or objects involved in a humanitarian assistance or peacekeeping mission. Elements; Art. 8 (2) (b) (iv) War crime of excessive incidental death, injury, or damage. Elements; Art. 8 (2) (b) (v) War crime of attacking undefended places. Elements; Art. 8 (2) (b) (vi) War crime of killing or wounding a person hors de combat. Elements; Art. 8 (2) (b) (vii)-1 War crime of improper use of a flag of truce. Elements; Art. 8 (2) (b) (vii)-2 War crime of improper use of a flag, insignia or uniform of the hostile party. Elements; Art. 8 (2) (b) (vii)-3 War crime of improper use of a flag, insignia or uniform of the United Nations. Elements; Art. 8 (2) (b) (vii)-4 War crime of improper use of the distinctive emblems of the Geneva Conventions. Elements; Art. 8 (2) (b) (viii) The transfer, directly or indirectly, by the Occupying Power of parts of* *its own civilian population into the territory it occupies, or the deportation or transfer of all or parts of the population of the occupied territory within or outside this territory. Elements; Art. 8 (2) (b) (ix) War crime of attacking protected objects. Elements; Art. 8 (2) (b) (x)-1 War crime of mutilation. Elements; Art. 8 (2) (b) (x)-1 War crime of mutilation. Elements; Art. 8 (2) (b) (x)-2 War crime of medical or scientific experiments. Elements; Art. 8 (2) (b) (xi) War crime of treacherously killing or wounding. Elements; Art. 8 (2) (b) (xii) War crime of denying quarter. Elements; Art. 8 (2) (b) (xiii) War crime of destroying or seizing the enemy's property. Elements; Art. 8 (2) (b) (xiv) War crime of depriving the nationals of the hostile power of rights or actions. Elements; Art. 8 (2) (b) (xv) War crime of compelling participation in military operations. Elements; Art. 8 (2) (b) (xvi) War crime of pillaging. Elements; Art. 8 (2) (b) (xvii) War crime of employing poison or poisoned weapons. Elements; Art. 8 (2) (b) (xviii) War crime of employing prohibited gases, liquids, materials or devices. Elements; Art. 8 (2) (b) (xix) War crime of employing prohibited bullets. Elements; Art. 8 (2) (b) (xx) War crime of employing weapons, projectiles or materials or methods of warfare listed in the Annex to the Statute. Elements; Art. 8 (2) (b) (xxi) War crime of outrages upon personal dignity. Elements; Art. 8 (2) (b) (xxii)-1 War crime of rape. Elements; Art. 8 (2) (b) (xxii)-2 War crime of sexual slavery. Elements; Art. 8 (2) (b) (xxii)-3 War crime of enforced prostitution. Elements; Art. 8 (2) (b) (xxii)-4 War crime of forced pregnancy. Elements; Art. 8 (2) (b) (xxii)-5 War crime of enforced sterilization. Elements; Art. 8 (2) (b) (xxii)-6 War crime of sexual violence. Elements; Art. 8 (2) (b) (xxiii) War crime of using protected persons as shields. Elements; Art. 8 (2) (b) (xxiv) War crime of attacking objects or persons using the distinctive emblems of the Geneva Conventions. Elements; Art. 8 (2) (b) (xxv) War crime of starvation as a method of warfare. Elements; Art. 8 (2) (b) (xxvi) War crime of using, conscripting or enlisting children. Elements; Art. 8 (2) (c), Art. 8 (2) (c) (i)-1 War crime of murder. Elements; Art. 8 (2) (c) (i)-2 War crime of mutilation. Elements; Art. 8 (2) (c) (i)-3 War crime of cruel treatment. Elements; Art. 8 (2) (c) (i)-4 War crime of torture. Elements; Art. 8 (2) (c) (ii) War crime of outrages upon personal dignity. Elements; Art. 8 (2) (c) (iii) War crime of taking hostages. Elements; Art. 8 (2) (c) (iv) War crime of sentencing or execution without due process. Elements; Art. 8 (2) (e), Art. 8 (2) (e) (i) War crime of attacking civilians. Elements; Art. 8 (2) (e) (ii) War crime of attacking objects or persons using the distinctive emblems of the Geneva Conventions. Elements; Art. 8 (2) (e) (iii) War crime of attacking personnel or objects involved in a humanitarian assistance or peacekeeping mission. Elements; Art. 8 (2) (e) (iv) War crime of attacking protected objects. Elements; Art. 8 (2) (e) (v) War crime of pillaging. Elements; Art. 8 (2) (e) (vi)-1 War crime of rape. Elements; Art. 8 (2) (e) (vi)-2 War crime of sexual slavery. Elements; Art. 8 (2) (e) (vi)-3 War crime of enforced prostitution. Elements; Art. 8 (2) (e) (vi)-4 War crime of forced pregnancy. Elements; Art. 8 (2) (e) (vi)-5 War crime of enforced sterilization. Elements; Art. 8 (2) (e) (vi)-6 War crime of sexual violence. Elements; Art. 8 (2) (e) (vii) War crime of using, conscripting and enlisting children. Elements; Art. 8 (2) (e) (viii) War crime of displacing civilians. Elements; Art. 8 (2) (e) (ix) War crime of treacherously killing or wounding. Elements; Art. 8 (2) (e) (x) War crime of denying quarter. Elements; Art. 8 (2) (e) (xi)-1 War crime of mutilation.*

Elements; Art. 8 (2) (e) (xi)-2 War crime of medical or scientific experiments. Elements).

London Agreement (8 August 1945), Charter of the International Military Tribunal. Art. 6. The Tribunal established by the Agreement referred to in Article 1 hereof for the trial and punishment of the major war criminals of the European Axis countries shall have the power to try and punish persons who, acting in the interests of the European Axis countries, whether as individuals or as members of organizations, committed any of the following crimes.

The following acts, or any of them, are crimes coming within the jurisdiction of the Tribunal for which there shall be individual responsibility: (...)

(b) *War Crimes:* namely, violations of the laws or customs of war. Such violations shall include, but not be limited to, murder, ill-treatment or deportation to slave labor or for any other purpose of civilian population of or in occupied territory, murder or ill-treatment of prisoners of war or persons on the seas, killing of hostages, plunder of public or private property, wanton destruction of cities, towns or villages, or devastation not justified by military necessity; (...)

Rome Statute ICC, art. 8. War crimes. 1. The Court shall have jurisdiction in respect of war crimes in particular when committed as part of a plan or policy or as part of a large-scale commission of such crimes.

2. For the purpose of this Statute, 'war crimes' means:

(a) Grave breaches of the Geneva Conventions of 12 August 1949, namely, any of the following acts against persons or property protected under the provisions of the relevant Geneva Convention:

(i) Wilful killing;

(ii) Torture or inhuman treatment, including biological experiments;

(iii) Wilfully causing great suffering, or serious injury to body or health;

(iv) Extensive destruction and appropriation of property, not justified by military necessity and carried out unlawfully and wantonly;

(v) Compelling a prisoner of war or other protected person to serve in the forces of a hostile Power;

(vi) Wilfully depriving a prisoner of war or other protected person of the rights of fair and regular trial;

(vii) Unlawful deportation or transfer or unlawful confinement;

(viii) Taking of hostages.

(b) Other serious violations of the laws and customs applicable in international armed conflict, within the established framework of international law, namely, any of the following acts:

(i) Intentionally directing attacks against the civilian population as such or against individual civilians not taking direct part in hostilities;

(ii) Intentionally directing attacks against civilian objects, that is, objects which are not military objectives;

(iii) Intentionally directing attacks against personnel, installations, material, units or vehicles involved in a humanitarian assistance or peacekeeping mission in accordance with the Charter of the United Nations, as long as they are entitled to the protection given to civilians or civilian objects under the international law of armed conflict;

(iv) Intentionally launching an attack in the knowledge that such attack will cause incidental loss of life or injury to civilians or damage to civilian objects or widespread, long-term and severe damage to the natural environment which would be clearly excessive in relation to the concrete and direct overall military advantage anticipated;

(v) Attacking or bombarding, by whatever means, towns, villages, dwellings or buildings which are undefended and which are not military objectives;

(vi) Killing or wounding a combatant who, having laid down his arms or having no longer means of defence, has surrendered at discretion;

(vii) Making improper use of a flag of truce, of the flag or of the military insignia and uniform of the enemy or of the United Nations, as well as of the distinctive emblems of the Geneva Conventions, resulting in death or serious personal injury;

(viii) The transfer, directly or indirectly, by the Occupying Power of parts of its own civilian population into the territory it occupies, or the deportation or transfer of all or parts of the population of the occupied territory within or outside this territory;

(ix) Intentionally directing attacks against buildings dedicated to religion, education, art, science or charitable purposes, historic monuments, hospitals and places where the sick and wounded are collected, provided they are not military objectives;

(x) Subjecting persons who are in the power of an adverse party to physical mutilation or to medical or scientific experiments of any kind which are neither justified by the medical, dental or hospital treatment of the person concerned nor carried out in his or her interest, and which cause death to or seriously endanger the health of such person or persons;

(xi) Killing or wounding treacherously individuals belonging to the hostile nation or army;

(xii) Declaring that no quarter will be given;

(xiii) Destroying or seizing the enemy's property unless such destruction or seizure be imperatively demanded by the necessities of war;

(xiv) Declaring abolished, suspended or inadmissible in a court of law the rights and actions of the nationals of the hostile party;

(xv) Compelling the nationals of the hostile party to take part in the operations of war directed against their own country, even if they were in the belligerent's service before the commencement of the war;

(xvi) Pillaging a town or place, even when taken by assault;

(xvii) Employing poison or poisoned weapons;

(xviii) Employing asphyxiating, poisonous or other gases, and all analogous liquids, materials or devices;

(xix) Employing bullets which expand or flatten easily in the human body, such as bullets with a hard envelope which does not entirely cover the core or is pierced with incisions;

(xx) Employing weapons, projectiles and material and methods of warfare which are of a nature to cause superfluous injury or unnecessary suffering or which are inherently indiscriminate in violation of the international law of armed conflict, provided that such weapons, projectiles and material and methods of warfare are the subject of a comprehensive prohibition and are included in an annex to this Statute, by an amendment in accordance with the relevant provisions set forth in articles 121 and 123;

(xxi) Committing outrages upon personal dignity, in particular humiliating and degrading treatment;

(xxii) Committing rape, sexual slavery, enforced prostitution, forced pregnancy, as defined in article 7, paragraph 2 (f), enforced sterilization, or any other form of sexual violence also constituting a grave breach of the Geneva Conventions;

(xxiii) Utilizing the presence of a civilian or other protected person to render certain points, areas or military forces immune from military operations;

(xxiv) Intentionally directing attacks against buildings, material, medical units and transport, and personnel using the distinctive emblems of the Geneva Conventions in conformity with international law;

(xxv) Intentionally using starvation of civilians as a method of warfare by depriving them of objects indispensable to their survival, including wilfully impeding relief supplies as provided for under the Geneva Conventions;

(xxvi) Conscripting or enlisting children under the age of fifteen years into the national armed forces or using them to participate actively in hostilities.

(c) In the case of an armed conflict not of an international character, serious violations of article 3 common to the four Geneva Conventions of 12 August 1949, namely, any of the following acts committed against persons taking no active part in the hostilities, including members of armed forces who have laid down their arms and those placed *hors de combat* by

sickness, wounds, detention or any other cause:

(i) Violence to life and person, in particular murder of all kinds, mutilation, cruel treatment and torture;

(ii) Committing outrages upon personal dignity, in particular humiliating and degrading treatment;

(iii) Taking of hostages;

(iv) The passing of sentences and the carrying out of executions without previous judgement pronounced by a regularly constituted court, affording all judicial guarantees which are generally recognized as indispensable.

(d) Paragraph 2 (c) applies to armed conflicts not of an international character and thus does not apply to situations of internal disturbances and tensions, such as riots, isolated and sporadic acts of violence or other acts of a similar nature.

(e) Other serious violations of the laws and customs applicable in armed conflicts not of an international character, within the established framework of international law, namely, any of the following acts:

(i) Intentionally directing attacks against the civilian population as such or against individual civilians not taking direct part in hostilities;

(ii) Intentionally directing attacks against buildings, material, medical units and transport, and personnel using the distinctive emblems of the Geneva Conventions in conformity with international law;

(iii) Intentionally directing attacks against personnel, installations, material, units or vehicles involved in a humanitarian assistance or peacekeeping mission in accordance with the Charter of the United Nations, as long as they are entitled to the protection given to civilians or civilian objects under the international law of armed conflict;

(iv) Intentionally directing attacks against buildings dedicated to religion, education, art, science or charitable purposes, historic monuments, hospitals and places where the sick and wounded are collected, provided they are not military objectives;

(v) Pillaging a town or place, even when taken by assault;

(vi) Committing rape, sexual slavery, enforced prostitution, forced pregnancy, as defined in article 7, paragraph 2 (f), enforced sterilization, and any other form of sexual violence also constituting a serious violation of article 3 common to the four Geneva Conventions;

(vii) Conscripting or enlisting children under the age of fifteen years into armed forces or groups or using them to participate actively in hostilities;

(viii) Ordering the displacement of the civilian population for reasons related to the conflict, unless the security of the civilians involved or imperative military reasons so demand;

(ix) Killing or wounding treacherously a combatant adversary;

(x) Declaring that no quarter will be given;

(xi) Subjecting persons who are in the power of another party to the conflict to physical mutilation or to medical or scientific experiments of any kind which are neither justified by the medical, dental or hospital treatment of the person concerned nor carried out in his or her interest, and which cause death to or seriously endanger the health of such person or persons;

(xii) Destroying or seizing the property of an adversary unless such destruction or seizure be imperatively demanded by the necessities of the conflict;

(f) Paragraph 2 (e) applies to armed conflicts not of an international character and thus does not apply to situations of internal disturbances and tensions, such as riots, isolated and sporadic acts of violence or other acts of a similar nature. It applies to armed conflicts that take place in the territory of a State when there is protracted armed conflict between governmental authorities and organized armed groups or between such groups.

3. Nothing in paragraph 2 (c) and (e) shall affect the responsibility of a Government to maintain or re-establish law and order in the State or to defend the unity and territorial integrity of the State, by all legitimate means.

Elements of Crimes, art. 8. War crimes. Introduction. The elements for war crimes under article 8, paragraph 2 (c) and (e), are subject to the limitations addressed in article 8, paragraph 2 (d) and (f), which are not elements of crimes.

The elements for war crimes under article 8, paragraph 2, of the Statute shall be interpreted within the established framework of the international law of armed conflict including, as appropriate, the international law of armed conflict applicable to armed conflict at sea.

With respect to the last two elements listed for each crime:

– There is no requirement for a legal evaluation by the perpetrator as to the existence of an armed conflict or its character as international or non-international;

– In that context there is no requirement for awareness by the perpetrator of the facts that established the character of the conflict as international or non-international;

– There is only a requirement for the awareness of the factual circumstances that established the existence of an armed conflict that is implicit in the terms 'took place in the context of and was associated with'.

Art. 8 (2) (a), Art. 8 (2) (a) (i) War crime of wilful killing. Elements. 1. The perpetrator killed one or more persons. (31).

2. Such person or persons were protected under one or more of the Geneva Conventions of 1949.

3. The perpetrator was aware of the factual circumstances that established that protected status. (32, 33).

4. The conduct took place in the context of and was associated with an international armed conflict. (34).

5. The perpetrator was aware of factual circumstances that established the existence of an armed conflict. *(31. The term 'killed' is interchangeable with the term 'caused death'. This footnote applies to all elements which use either of these concepts.*

32. This mental element recognizes the interplay between articles 30 and 32. This footnote also applies to the corresponding element in each crime under article 8 (2) (a), and to the element in other crimes in article 8 (2) concerning the awareness of factual circumstances that establish the status of persons or property protected under the relevant international law of armed conflict.

33. With respect to nationality, it is understood that the perpetrator needs only to know that the victim belonged to an adverse party to the conflict. This footnote also applies to the corresponding element in each crime under article 8 (2) (a).

34. The term 'international armed conflict' includes military occupation. This footnote also applies to the corresponding element in each crime under article 8 (2) (a)).

Art. 8 (2) (a) (ii)-1 War crime of torture. Elements (35). 1. The perpetrator inflicted severe physical or mental pain or suffering upon one or more persons.

2. The perpetrator inflicted the pain or suffering for such purposes as: obtaining information or a confession, punishment, intimidation or coercion or for any reason based on discrimination of any kind.

3. Such person or persons were protected under one or more of the Geneva Conventions of 1949.

4. The perpetrator was aware of the factual circumstances that established that protected status.

5. The conduct took place in the context of and was associated with an international armed conflict.

6. The perpetrator was aware of factual circumstances that established the existence of an armed conflict. *(35. As element 3 requires that all victims must be 'protected persons' under one or more of the Geneva Conventions of 1949, these elements do not include the custody or control requirement found in the elements of article 7 (1) (e)).*

Art. 8 (2) (a) (ii)-2 War crime of inhuman treatment. Elements. 1. The perpetrator inflicted severe physical or mental pain or suffering upon one or more persons.

2. Such person or persons were protected under one or more of the Geneva Conventions of 1949.

3. The perpetrator was aware of the factual circumstances that established that protected status.

4. The conduct took place in the context of and was associated with an international armed conflict.

5. The perpetrator was aware of factual circumstances that established the existence of an armed conflict.

Art. 8 (2) (a) (ii)-3 War crime of biological experiments. Elements. 1. The perpetrator subjected one or more persons to a particular biological experiment.

2. The experiment seriously endangered the physical or mental health or integrity of such person or persons.

3. The intent of the experiment was non-therapeutic and it was neither justified by medical reasons nor carried out in such person's or persons' interest.

4. Such person or persons were protected under one or more of the Geneva Conventions of 1949.

5. The perpetrator was aware of the factual circumstances that established that protected status.

6. The conduct took place in the context of and was associated with an international armed conflict.

7. The perpetrator was aware of factual circumstances that established the existence of an armed conflict.

Art. 8 (2) (a) (iii) War crime of wilfully causing great suffering. Elements. 1. The perpetrator caused great physical or mental pain or suffering to, or serious injury to body or health of, one or more persons.

2. Such person or persons were protected under one or more of the Geneva Conventions of 1949.

3. The perpetrator was aware of the factual circumstances that established that protected status.

4. The conduct took place in the context of and was associated with an international armed conflict.

5. The perpetrator was aware of factual circumstances that established the existence of an armed conflict.

Art. 8 (2) (a) (iv) War crime of destruction and appropriation of property. Elements.
1. The perpetrator destroyed or appropriated certain property.

2. The destruction or appropriation was not justified by military necessity.

3. The destruction or appropriation was extensive and carried out wantonly.

4. Such property was protected under one or more of the Geneva Conventions of 1949.

5. The perpetrator was aware of the factual circumstances that established that protected status.

6. The conduct took place in the context of and was associated with an international armed conflict.

7. The perpetrator was aware of factual circumstances that established the existence of an armed conflict.

Art. 8 (2) (a) (v) War crime of compelling service in hostile forces. Elements. 1. The perpetrator coerced one or more persons, by act or threat, to take part in military operations against that person's own country or forces or otherwise serve in the forces of a hostile power.

2. Such person or persons were protected under one or more of the Geneva Conventions of 1949.

3. The perpetrator was aware of the factual circumstances that established that protected status.

4. The conduct took place in the context of and was associated with an international armed conflict.

5. The perpetrator was aware of factual circumstances that established the existence of an armed conflict.

Art. 8 (2) (a) (vi) War crime of denying a fair trial. Elements. 1. The perpetrator deprived one or more persons of a fair and regular trial by denying judicial guarantees as defined, in particular, in the third and the fourth Geneva Conventions of 1949.

2. Such person or persons were protected under one or more of the Geneva Conventions of 1949.

3. The perpetrator was aware of the factual circumstances that established that protected status.

4. The conduct took place in the context of and was associated with an international armed conflict.

5. The perpetrator was aware of factual circumstances that established the existence of an armed conflict.

Art. 8 (2) (a) (vii)-1 War crime of unlawful deportation and transfer. Elements. 1. The perpetrator deported or transferred one or more persons to another State or to another location.

2. Such person or persons were protected under one or more of the Geneva Conventions of 1949.

3. The perpetrator was aware of the factual circumstances that established that protected status.

4. The conduct took place in the context of and was associated with an international armed conflict.

5. The perpetrator was aware of factual circumstances that established the existence of an armed conflict.

Art. 8 (2) (a) (vii)-2 War crime of unlawful confinement. Elements. 1. The perpetrator confined or continued to confine one or more persons to a certain location.

2. Such person or persons were protected under one or more of the Geneva Conventions of 1949.

3. The perpetrator was aware of the factual circumstances that established that protected status.

4. The conduct took place in the context of and was associated with an international armed conflict.

5. The perpetrator was aware of factual circumstances that established the existence of an armed conflict.

Art. 8 (2) (a) (viii) War crime of taking hostages. Elements. 1. The perpetrator seized, detained or otherwise held hostage one or more persons.

2. The perpetrator threatened to kill, injure or continue to detain such person or persons.

3. The perpetrator intended to compel a State, an international organization, a natural or legal person or a group of persons to act or refrain from acting as an explicit or implicit condition for the safety or the release of such person or persons.

4. Such person or persons were protected under one or more of the Geneva Conventions of 1949.

5. The perpetrator was aware of the factual circumstances that established that protected status.

6. The conduct took place in the context of and was associated with an international armed conflict.

7. The perpetrator was aware of factual circumstances that established the existence of an armed conflict.

Art. 8 (2) (b), Art. 8 (2) (b) (i) War crime of attacking civilians. Elements. 1. The perpetrator directed an attack.

2. The object of the attack was a civilian population as such or individual civilians not taking direct part in hostilities.

3. The perpetrator intended the civilian population as such or individual civilians not taking direct part in hostilities to be the object of the attack.

4. The conduct took place in the context of and was associated with an international armed conflict.

5. The perpetrator was aware of factual circumstances that established the existence of an armed conflict.

Art. 8 (2) (b) (ii) War crime of attacking civilian objects. Elements. 1. The perpetrator directed an attack.

2. The object of the attack was civilian objects, that is, objects which are not military objectives.

3. The perpetrator intended such civilian objects to be the object of the attack.

4. The conduct took place in the context of and was associated with an international armed conflict.

5. The perpetrator was aware of factual circumstances that established the existence of an armed conflict.

Art. 8 (2) (b) (iii) War crime of attacking personnel or objects involved in a humanitarian assistance or peacekeeping mission. *Elements.* 1. The perpetrator directed an attack.

2. The object of the attack was personnel, installations, material, units or vehicles involved in a humanitarian assistance or peacekeeping mission in accordance with the Charter of the United Nations.

3. The perpetrator intended such personnel, installations, material, units or vehicles so involved to be the object of the attack.

4. Such personnel, installations, material, units or vehicles were entitled to that protection given to civilians or civilian objects under the international law of armed conflict.

5. The perpetrator was aware of the factual circumstances that established that protection.

6. The conduct took place in the context of and was associated with an international armed conflict.

7. The perpetrator was aware of factual circumstances that established the existence of an armed conflict.

Art. 8 (2) (b) (iv) War crime of excessive incidental death, injury, or damage. Elements. 1. The perpetrator launched an attack.

2. The attack was such that it would cause incidental death or injury to civilians or damage to civilian objects or widespread, long-term and severe damage to the natural environment and that such death, injury or damage would be of such an extent as to

be clearly excessive in relation to the concrete and direct overall military advantage anticipated. (36).

3. The perpetrator knew that the attack would cause incidental death or injury to civilians or damage to civilian objects or widespread, long-term and severe damage to the natural environment and that such death, injury or damage would be of such an extent as to be clearly excessive in relation to the concrete and direct overall military advantage anticipated. (37).

4. The conduct took place in the context of and was associated with an international armed conflict.

5. The perpetrator was aware of factual circumstances that established the existence of an armed conflict. *(36. The expression 'concrete and direct overall military advantage' refers to a military advantage that is foreseeable by the perpetrator at the relevant time. Such advantage may or may not be temporally or geographically related to the object of the attack. The fact that this crime admits the possibility of lawful incidental injury and collateral damage does not in any way justify any violation of the law applicable in armed conflict. It does not address justifications for war or other rules related to jus ad bellum. It reflects the proportionality requirement inherent in determining the legality of any military activity undertaken in the context of an armed conflict.*

37. As opposed to the general rule set forth in paragraph 4 of the General Introduction, this knowledge element requires that the perpetrator make the value judgement as described therein. An evaluation of that value judgement must be based on the requisite information available to the perpetrator at the time).

Art. 8 (2) (b) (v) War crime of attacking undefended places *(38).* Elements. 1. The perpetrator attacked one or more towns, villages, dwellings or buildings.

2. Such towns, villages, dwellings or buildings were open for unresisted occupation.

3. Such towns, villages, dwellings or buildings did not constitute military objectives.

4. The conduct took place in the context of and was associated with an international armed conflict.

5. The perpetrator was aware of factual circumstances that established the existence of an armed conflict. *(38. The presence in the locality of persons specially protected under the Geneva Conventions of 1949 or of police forces retained for the sole purpose of maintaining law and order does not by itself render the locality a military objective).*

Art. 8 (2) (b) (vi) War crime of killing or wounding a person hors de combat. Elements.

1. The perpetrator killed or injured one or more persons.

2. Such person or persons were *hors de combat.*

3. The perpetrator was aware of the factual circumstances that established this status.

4. The conduct took place in the context of and was associated with an international armed conflict.

5. The perpetrator was aware of factual circumstances that established the existence of an armed conflict.

Art. 8 (2) (b) (vii)-1 War crime of improper use of a flag of truce. Elements. 1. The perpetrator used a flag of truce.

2. The perpetrator made such use in order to feign an intention to negotiate when there was no such intention on the part of the perpetrator.

3. The perpetrator knew or should have known of the prohibited nature of such use. (39).

4. The conduct resulted in death or serious personal injury.

5. The perpetrator knew that the conduct could result in death or serious personal injury.

6. The conduct took place in the context of and was associated with an international armed conflict.

7. The perpetrator was aware of factual circumstances that established the existence of an armed conflict. *(39. This mental element recognizes the interplay between article 30 and article 32. The term 'prohibited nature' denotes illegality).*

Art. 8 (2) (b) (vii)-2 War crime of improper use of a flag, insignia or uniform of the hostile party. Elements. 1. The perpetrator used a flag, insignia or uniform of the hostile party.

2. The perpetrator made such use in a manner prohibited under the international law of armed conflict while engaged in an attack.

3. The perpetrator knew or should have known of the prohibited nature of such use. (40).

5. The perpetrator knew that the conduct could result in death or serious personal injury.

6. The conduct took place in the context of and was associated with an international armed conflict.

7. The perpetrator was aware of factual circumstances that established the existence of an armed conflict. *(40. This mental element recognizes the interplay between article 30 and article 32. The term 'prohibited nature' denotes illegality).*

Art. 8 (2) (b) (vii)-3 War crime of improper use of a flag, insignia or uniform of the United Nations. Elements. 1. The perpetrator used a flag, insignia or uniform of the United Nations.

2. The perpetrator made such use in a manner prohibited under the international law of armed conflict.

3. The perpetrator knew of the prohibited nature of such use. (41).

4. The conduct resulted in death or serious personal injury.

5. The perpetrator knew that the conduct could result in death or serious personal injury.

6. The conduct took place in the context of and was associated with an international armed conflict.

7. The perpetrator was aware of factual circumstances that established the existence of an armed conflict. *(41. This mental element recognizes the interplay between article 30 and article 32. The 'should have known' test required in the other offences found in article 8 (2) (b) (vii) is not applicable here because of the variable and regulatory nature of the relevant prohibitions).*

Art. 8 (2) (b) (vii)-4 War crime of improper use of the distinctive emblems of the Geneva Conventions. Elements. 1. The perpetrator used the distinctive emblems of the Geneva Conventions.

2. The perpetrator made such use for combatant purposes (42) in a manner prohibited under the international law of armed conflict.

3. The perpetrator knew or should have known of the prohibited nature of such use. (43).

4. The conduct resulted in death or serious personal injury.

5. The perpetrator knew that the conduct could result in death or serious personal injury.

6. The conduct took place in the context of and was associated with an international armed conflict.

7. The perpetrator was aware of factual circumstances that established the existence of an armed conflict. *(42. 'Combatant purposes' in these circumstances means purposes directly related to hostilities and not including medical, religious or similar activities.*

43. This mental element recognizes the interplay between article 30 and article 32. The term 'prohibited nature' denotes illegality).

Art. 8 (2) (b) (viii) The transfer, directly or indirectly, by the Occupying Power of parts of its own civilian population into the territory it occupies, or the deportation or transfer of all or parts of the population of the occupied territory within or outside this territory. *Elements.* 1. The perpetrator:

(a) Transferred, (44) directly or indirectly, parts of its own population into the territory it occupies; or

(b) Deported or transferred all or parts of the population of the occupied territory within or outside this territory.

2. The conduct took place in the context of and was associated with an international armed conflict.

3. The perpetrator was aware of factual circumstances that established the existence of an armed conflict. *(44. The term 'transfer' needs to be interpreted in accordance with the relevant provisions of international humanitarian law).*

Art. 8 (2) (b) (ix) War crime of attacking protected objects (45). Elements. 1. The perpetrator directed an attack.

2. The object of the attack was one or more buildings dedicated to religion, education, art, science or charitable purposes, historic monuments, hospitals or places where the sick and wounded are collected, which were not military objectives.

3. The perpetrator intended such building or buildings dedicated to religion, education, art, science or charitable purposes, historic monuments, hospitals or places where the sick and wounded are collected, which were not military objectives, to be the object of the attack.

4. The conduct took place in the context of and was associated with an international armed conflict.

5. The perpetrator was aware of factual circumstances that established the existence of an armed conflict. *(45. The presence in the locality of persons specially protected under the Geneva Conventions of 1949 or of police forces retained for the sole purpose of maintaining law and order does not by itself render the locality a military objective).*

Art. 8 (2) (b) (x)-1 War crime of mutilation. Elements. 1. The perpetrator subjected one or more persons to mutilation, in particular by permanently disfiguring the person or persons, or by permanently disabling or removing an organ or appendage.

2. The conduct caused death or seriously endangered the physical or mental health of such person or persons.

3. The conduct was neither justified by the medical, dental or hospital treatment of the person or persons concerned nor carried out in such person's or persons' interest. (46).

4. Such person or persons were in the power of an adverse party.

5. The conduct took place in the context of and was associated with an international armed conflict.

6. The perpetrator was aware of factual circumstances that established the existence of an armed conflict.

(46. Consent is not a defence to this crime. The crime prohibits any medical procedure which is not indicated by the state of health of the person concerned and which is not consistent with generally accepted medical standards which would be applied under similar medical circumstances to persons who are nationals of the party conducting the procedure and who are in no way deprived of liberty. This footnote also applies to the same element for article 8 (2) (b) (x)-2).

Art. 8 (2) (b) (x)-2 War crime of medical or scientific experiments. Elements. 1. The perpetrator subjected one or more persons to a medical or scientific experiment.

2. The experiment caused death or seriously endangered the physical or mental health or integrity of such person or persons.

3. The conduct was neither justified by the medical, dental or hospital treatment of such person or persons concerned nor carried out in such person's or persons' interest.

4. Such person or persons were in the power of an adverse party.

5. The conduct took place in the context of and was associated with an international armed conflict.

6. The perpetrator was aware of factual circumstances that established the existence of an armed conflict.

Art. 8 (2) (b) (xi) War crime of treacherously killing or wounding. Elements. 1. The perpetrator invited the confidence or belief of one or more persons that they were entitled to, or were obliged to accord, protection under rules of international law applicable in armed conflict.

2. The perpetrator intended to betray that confidence or belief.

3. The perpetrator killed or injured such person or persons.

4. The perpetrator made use of that confidence or belief in killing or injuring such person or persons.

5. Such person or persons belonged to an adverse party.

6. The conduct took place in the context of and was associated with an international armed conflict.

7. The perpetrator was aware of factual circumstances that established the existence of an armed conflict.

Art. 8 (2) (b) (xii) War crime of denying quarter. Elements. 1. The perpetrator declared or ordered that there shall be no survivors.

2. Such declaration or order was given in order to threaten an adversary or to conduct hostilities on the basis that there shall be no survivors.

3. The perpetrator was in a position of effective command or control over the subordinate forces to which the declaration or order was directed.

4. The conduct took place in the context of and was associated with an international armed conflict.

5. The perpetrator was aware of factual circumstances that established the existence of an armed conflict.

Art. 8 (2) (b) (xiii) War crime of destroying or seizing the enemy's property. Elements. 1. The perpetrator destroyed or seized certain property.

2. Such property was property of a hostile party.

3. Such property was protected from that destruction or seizure under the international law of armed conflict.

4. The perpetrator was aware of the factual circumstances that established the status of the property.

5. The destruction or seizure was not justified by military necessity.

6. The conduct took place in the context of and was associated with an international armed conflict.

7. The perpetrator was aware of factual circumstances that established the existence of an armed conflict.

Art. 8 (2) (b) (xiv) War crime of depriving the nationals of the hostile power of rights or actions. Elements. 1. The perpetrator effected the abolition, suspension or termination of admissibility in a court of law of certain rights or actions.

2. The abolition, suspension or termination was directed at the nationals of a hostile party.

3. The perpetrator intended the abolition, suspension or termination to be directed at the nationals of a hostile party.

4. The conduct took place in the context of and was associated with an international armed conflict.

5. The perpetrator was aware of factual circumstances that established the existence of an armed conflict.

Art. 8 (2) (b) (xv) War crime of compelling participation in military operations. Elements. 1. The perpetrator coerced one or more persons by act or threat to take part in military operations against that person's own country or forces.

2. Such person or persons were nationals of a hostile party.

3. The conduct took place in the context of and was associated with an international armed conflict.

4. The perpetrator was aware of factual circumstances that established the existence of an armed conflict.

Art. 8 (2) (b) (xvi) War crime of pillaging. Elements. 1. The perpetrator appropriated certain property.

2. The perpetrator intended to deprive the owner of the property and to appropriate it for private or personal use. (47).

3. The appropriation was without the consent of the owner.

4. The conduct took place in the context of and was associated with an international armed conflict.

5. The perpetrator was aware of factual circumstances that established the existence of an armed conflict. *(47. As indicated by the use of the term 'private or personal use', appropriations justified by military necessity cannot constitute the crime of pillaging).*

Art. 8 (2) (b) (xvii) War crime of employing poison or poisoned weapons. *Elements.*
1. The perpetrator employed a substance or a weapon that releases a substance as a result of its employment.
2. The substance was such that it causes death or serious damage to health in the ordinary course of events, through its toxic properties.
3. The conduct took place in the context of and was associated with an international armed conflict.
4. The perpetrator was aware of factual circumstances that established the existence of an armed conflict.

Art. 8 (2) (b) (xviii) War crime of employing prohibited gases, liquids, materials or devices. Elements. 1. The perpetrator employed a gas or other analogous substance or device.
2. The gas, substance or device was such that it causes death or serious damage to health in the ordinary course of events, through its asphyxiating or toxic properties. (48).
3. The conduct took place in the context of and was associated with an international armed conflict.
4. The perpetrator was aware of factual circumstances that established the existence of an armed conflict. *(48. Nothing in this element shall be interpreted as limiting or prejudicing in any way existing or developing rules of international law with respect to the development, production, stockpiling and use of chemical weapons).*

Art. 8 (2) (b) (xix) War crime of employing prohibited bullets. *Elements.* 1. The perpetrator employed certain bullets.
2. The bullets were such that their use violates the international law of armed conflict because they expand or flatten easily in the human body.
3. The perpetrator was aware that the nature of the bullets was such that their employment would uselessly aggravate suffering or the wounding effect.
4. The conduct took place in the context of and was associated with an international armed conflict.
5. The perpetrator was aware of factual circumstances that established the existence of an armed conflict.

Art. 8 (2) (b) (xx) War crime of employing weapons, projectiles or materials or methods of warfare listed in the Annex to the Statute. *Elements.* [Elements will have to be drafted once weapons, projectiles or material or methods of warfare have been included in an annex to the Statute.]

Art. 8 (2) (b) (xxi) War crime of outrages upon personal dignity. Elements. 1. The perpetrator humiliated, degraded or otherwise violated the dignity of one or more persons. (49).
2. The severity of the humiliation, degradation or other violation was of such degree as to be generally recognized as an outrage upon personal dignity.
3. The conduct took place in the context of and was associated with an international armed conflict.
4. The perpetrator was aware of factual circumstances that established the existence of an armed conflict. *(49. For this crime, 'persons' can include dead persons. It is understood that the victim need not personally be aware of the existence of the humiliation or degradation or other violation. This element takes into account relevant aspects of the cultural background of the victim).*

Art. 8 (2) (b) (xxii)-1 War crime of rape. Elements. 1. The perpetrator invaded (50) the body of a person by conduct resulting in penetration, however slight, of any part of the body of the victim or of the perpetrator with a sexual organ, or of the anal or genital opening of the victim
with any object or any other part of the body.
2. The invasion was committed by force, or by threat of force or coercion, such as that caused by fear of violence, duress, detention, psychological oppression or abuse of power, against such person or another person, or by taking advantage of a coercive environment, or the invasion was committed against a person incapable of giving genuine consent. (51).
3. The conduct took place in the context of and was associated with an international armed conflict.
4. The perpetrator was aware of factual circumstances that established the existence of an armed conflict. *(50. The concept of 'invasion' is intended to be broad enough to be gender-neutral.*
51. It is understood that a person may be incapable of giving genuine consent if affected by natural, induced or age-related incapacity. This footnote also applies to the corresponding elements of article 8 (2) (b) (xxii)-3, 5 and 6).
Art. 8 (2) (b) (xxii)-2 War crime of sexual slavery *(52). Elements.* 1. The perpetrator exercised any or all of the powers attaching to the right of ownership over one or more persons, such as by purchasing, selling, lending or bartering such a person or persons, or by imposing on them a similar deprivation of liberty. (53).
2. The perpetrator caused such person or persons to engage in one or more acts of a sexual nature.
3. The conduct took place in the context of and was associated with an international armed conflict.
4. The perpetrator was aware of factual circumstances that established the existence of an armed conflict. *(52. Given the complex nature of this crime, it is recognized that its commission could involve more than one perpetrator as a part of a common criminal purpose.*
53. It is understood that such deprivation of liberty may, in some circumstances, include exacting forced labour or otherwise reducing a person to servile status as defined in the Supplementary Convention on the Abolition of Slavery, the Slave Trade, and Institutions and Practices Similar to Slavery of 1956. It is also understood that the conduct described in this element includes trafficking in persons, in particular women and children).
Art. 8 (2) (b) (xxii)-3 War crime of enforced prostitution. *Elements.* 1. The perpetrator caused one or more persons to engage in one or more acts of a sexual nature by force, or by threat of force or coercion, such as that caused by fear of violence, duress, detention, psychological oppression or abuse of power, against such person or persons or another person, or by taking advantage of a coercive environment or such person's or persons' incapacity to give genuine consent.
2. The perpetrator or another person obtained or expected to obtain pecuniary or other advantage in exchange for or in connection with the acts of a sexual nature.
3. The conduct took place in the context of and was associated with an international armed conflict.

4. The perpetrator was aware of factual circumstances that established the existence of an armed conflict.

Art. 8 (2) (b) (xxii)-4 War crime of forced pregnancy. Elements. 1. The perpetrator confined one or more women forcibly made pregnant, with the intent of affecting the ethnic composition of any population or carrying out other grave violations of international law.

2. The conduct took place in the context of and was associated with an international armed conflict.

3. The perpetrator was aware of factual circumstances that established the existence of an armed conflict.

Art. 8 (2) (b) (xxii)-5 War crime of enforced sterilization. Elements. 1. The perpetrator deprived one or more persons of biological reproductive capacity. (54).

2. The conduct was neither justified by the medical or hospital treatment of the person or persons concerned nor carried out with their genuine consent. (55).

3. The conduct took place in the context of and was associated with an international armed conflict.

4. The perpetrator was aware of factual circumstances that established the existence of an armed conflict. *(54. The deprivation is not intended to include birth-control measures which have a non-permanent effect in practice.*

55. It is understood that 'genuine consent' does not include consent obtained through deception).

Art. 8 (2) (b) (xxii)-6 War crime of sexual violence. *Elements.* 1. The perpetrator committed an act of a sexual nature against one or more persons or caused such person or persons to engage in an act of a sexual nature by force, or by threat of force or coercion, such as that caused by fear of violence, duress, detention, psychological oppression or abuse of power, against such person or persons or another person, or by taking advantage of a coercive environment or such person's or persons' incapacity to give genuine consent.

2. The conduct was of a gravity comparable to that of a grave breach of the Geneva Conventions.

3. The perpetrator was aware of the factual circumstances that established the gravity of the conduct.

4. The conduct took place in the context of and was associated with an international armed conflict.

5. The perpetrator was aware of factual circumstances that established the existence of an armed conflict.

Art. 8 (2) (b) (xxiii) War crime of using protected persons as shields. Elements. 1. The perpetrator moved or otherwise took advantage of the location of one or more civilians or other persons protected under the international law of armed conflict.

2. The perpetrator intended to shield a military objective from attack or shield, favour or impede military operations.

3. The conduct took place in the context of and was associated with an international armed conflict.

4. The perpetrator was aware of factual circumstances that established the existence of an armed conflict.

Art. 8 (2) (b) (xxiv) War crime of attacking objects or persons using the distinctive emblems of the Geneva Conventions. Elements. 1. The perpetrator attacked one or more persons, buildings, medical units or transports or other objects using, in conformity with international law, a distinctive emblem or other method of identification indicating protection under the Geneva Conventions.

2. The perpetrator intended such persons, buildings, units or transports or other objects so using such identification to be the object of the attack.

3. The conduct took place in the context of and was associated with an international armed conflict.

4. The perpetrator was aware of factual circumstances that established the existence of an armed conflict.

Art. 8 (2) (b) (xxv) War crime of starvation as a method of warfare. Elements. 1. The perpetrator deprived civilians of objects indispensable to their survival.

2. The perpetrator intended to starve civilians as a method of warfare.

3. The conduct took place in the context of and was associated with an international armed conflict.

4. The perpetrator was aware of factual circumstances that established the existence of an armed conflict.

Art. 8 (2) (b) (xxvi) War crime of using, conscripting or enlisting children. Elements. 1. The perpetrator conscripted or enlisted one or more persons into the national armed forces or used one or more persons to participate actively in hostilities.

2. Such person or persons were under the age of 15 years.

3. The perpetrator knew or should have known that such person or persons were under the age of 15 years.

4. The conduct took place in the context of and was associated with an international armed conflict.

5. The perpetrator was aware of factual circumstances that established the existence of an armed conflict.

Art. 8 (2) (c), Art. 8 (2) (c) (i)-1 War crime of murder. Elements. 1. The perpetrator killed one or more persons.

2. Such person or persons were either *hors de combat*, or were civilians, medical personnel, or religious personnel (56) taking no active part in the hostilities.

3. The perpetrator was aware of the factual circumstances that established this status.

4. The conduct took place in the context of and was associated with an armed conflict not of an international character.

5. The perpetrator was aware of factual circumstances that established the existence of an armed conflict. *(56. The term 'religious personnel' includes those non-confessional non-combatant military personnel carrying out a similar function).*

Art. 8 (2) (c) (i)-2 War crime of mutilation. Elements. 1. The perpetrator subjected one or more persons to mutilation, in particular by permanently disfiguring the person or persons, or by permanently disabling or removing an organ or appendage.

2. The conduct was neither justified by the medical, dental or hospital treatment of the person or persons concerned nor carried out in such person's or persons' interests.

3. Such person or persons were either *hors de combat*, or were civilians, medical personnel or religious personnel taking no active part in the hostilities.

4. The perpetrator was aware of the factual circumstances that established this status.

5. The conduct took place in the context of and was associated with an armed conflict not of an international character.

6. The perpetrator was aware of factual circumstances that established the existence of an armed conflict.

Art. 8 (2) (c) (i)-3 War crime of cruel treatment. Elements. 1. The perpetrator inflicted severe physical or mental pain or suffering upon one or more persons.

2. Such person or persons were either *hors de combat*, or were civilians, medical personnel, or religious personnel taking no active part in the hostilities.

3. The perpetrator was aware of the factual circumstances that established this status.

4. The conduct took place in the context of and was associated with an armed conflict not of an international character.

5. The perpetrator was aware of factual circumstances that established the existence of an armed conflict.

Art. 8 (2) (c) (i)-4 War crime of torture. Elements. 1. The perpetrator inflicted severe physical or mental pain or suffering upon one or more persons.

2. The perpetrator inflicted the pain or suffering for such purposes as: obtaining information or a confession, punishment, intimidation or coercion or for any reason based on discrimination of any kind.

3. Such person or persons were either *hors de combat*, or were civilians, medical personnel or religious personnel taking no active part in the hostilities.

4. The perpetrator was aware of the factual circumstances that established this status.

5. The conduct took place in the context of and was associated with an armed conflict not of an international character.

6. The perpetrator was aware of factual circumstances that established the existence of an armed conflict.

Art. 8 (2) (c) (ii) War crime of outrages upon personal dignity. Elements. 1. The perpetrator humiliated, degraded or otherwise violated the dignity of one or more persons. (57).

2. The severity of the humiliation, degradation or other violation was of such degree as to be generally recognized as an outrage upon personal dignity.

3. Such person or persons were either *hors de combat*, or were civilians, medical personnel or religious personnel taking no active part in the hostilities.

4. The perpetrator was aware of the factual circumstances that established this status.

5. The conduct took place in the context of and was associated with an armed conflict not of an international character.

6. The perpetrator was aware of factual circumstances that established the existence of an armed conflict. *(57. For this crime, 'persons' can include dead persons. It is understood that the victim need not personally be aware of the existence of the humiliation or degradation or other violation. This element takes into account relevant aspects of the cultural background of the victim).*

Art. 8 (2) (c) (iii) War crime of taking hostages. Elements. 1. The perpetrator seized, detained or otherwise held hostage one or more persons.

2. The perpetrator threatened to kill, injure or continue to detain such person or persons.

3. The perpetrator intended to compel a State, an international organization, a natural or legal person or a group of persons to act or refrain from acting as an explicit or implicit condition for the safety or the release of such person or persons.

4. Such person or persons were either *hors de combat*, or were civilians, medical personnel or religious personnel taking no active part in the hostilities.

5. The perpetrator was aware of the factual circumstances that established this status.

6. The conduct took place in the context of and was associated with an armed conflict not of an international character.

7. The perpetrator was aware of factual circumstances that established the existence of an armed conflict.

Art. 8 (2) (c) (iv) War crime of sentencing or execution without due process. Elements. 1. The perpetrator passed sentence or executed one or more persons. (58).

2. Such person or persons were either *hors de combat*, or were civilians, medical personnel or religious personnel taking no active part in the hostilities.

3. The perpetrator was aware of the factual circumstances that established this status.

4. There was no previous judgement pronounced by a court, or the court that rendered judgement was not 'regularly constituted', that is, it did not afford the essential guarantees of independence and impartiality, or the court that rendered judgement did not afford all other judicial guarantees generally recognized as indispensable under international law. (59).

5. The perpetrator was aware of the absence of a previous judgement or of the denial of relevant guarantees and the fact that they are essential or indispensable to a fair trial.

6. The conduct took place in the context of and was associated with an armed conflict not of an international character.

7. The perpetrator was aware of factual circumstances that established the existence of an armed conflict. *(58. The elements laid down in these documents do not address the different forms of individual criminal responsibility, as enunciated in articles 25 and 28 of the Statute.*

59. With respect to elements 4 and 5, the Court should consider whether, in the light of all relevant circumstances, the cumulative effect of factors with respect to guarantees deprived the person or persons of a fair trial).

Art. 8 (2) (e), Art. 8 (2) (e) (i) War crime of attacking civilians. *Elements.* 1. The perpetrator directed an attack.

2. The object of the attack was a civilian population as such or individual civilians not taking direct part in hostilities.

3. The perpetrator intended the civilian population as such or individual civilians not taking direct part in hostilities to be the object of the attack.

4. The conduct took place in the context of and was associated with an armed conflict not of an international character.

5. The perpetrator was aware of factual circumstances that established the existence of an armed conflict.

Art. 8 (2) (e) (ii) War crime of attacking objects or persons using the distinctive emblems of the Geneva Conventions. Elements. 1. The perpetrator attacked one or more persons, buildings, medical units or transports or other objects using, in conformity with international law, a distinctive emblem or other method of identification indicating protection under the Geneva Conventions.

2. The perpetrator intended such persons, buildings, units or transports or other objects so using such identification to be the object of the attack.

3. The conduct took place in the context of and was associated with an armed conflict not of an international character.

4. The perpetrator was aware of factual circumstances that established the existence of an armed conflict.

Art. 8 (2) (e) (iii) War crime of attacking personnel or objects involved in a humanitarian assistance or peacekeeping mission. Elements. 1. The perpetrator directed an attack.

2. The object of the attack was personnel, installations, material, units or vehicles involved in a humanitarian assistance or peacekeeping mission in accordance with the Charter of the United Nations.

3. The perpetrator intended such personnel, installations, material, units or vehicles so involved to be the object of the attack.

4. Such personnel, installations, material, units or vehicles were entitled to that protection given to civilians or civilian objects under the international law of armed conflict.

5. The perpetrator was aware of the factual circumstances that established that protection.

6. The conduct took place in the context of and was associated with an armed conflict not of an international character.

7. The perpetrator was aware of factual circumstances that established the existence of an armed conflict.

Art. 8 (2) (e) (iv) War crime of attacking protected objects (60). Elements. 1. The perpetrator directed an attack.

2. The object of the attack was one or more buildings dedicated to religion, education, art, science or charitable purposes, historic monuments, hospitals or places where the sick and wounded are collected, which were not military objectives.

3. The perpetrator intended such building or buildings dedicated to religion, education, art, science or charitable purposes, historic monuments, hospitals or places where the sick and wounded are collected, which were not military objectives, to be the object of the attack.

4. The conduct took place in the context of and was associated with an armed conflict not of an international character.

5. The perpetrator was aware of factual circumstances that established the existence of an armed conflict. *(60. The presence in the locality of persons specially protected under the Geneva Conventions of 1949 or of police forces retained for the sole purpose of maintaining law and order does not by itself render the locality a military objective).*

Art. 8 (2) (e) (v) War crime of pillaging. Elements. 1. The perpetrator appropriated certain property.

2. The perpetrator intended to deprive the owner of the property and to appropriate it for private or personal use. (61).

3. The appropriation was without the consent of the owner.

4. The conduct took place in the context of and was associated with an armed conflict not of an international character.

5. The perpetrator was aware of factual circumstances that established the existence of an armed conflict. *(61. As indicated by the use of the term 'private or personal*

use', appropriations justified by military necessity cannot constitute the crime of pillaging).

Art. 8 (2) (e) (vi)-1 War crime of rape. Elements. 1. The perpetrator invaded (62) the body of a person by conduct resulting in penetration, however slight, of any part of the body of the victim or of the perpetrator with a sexual organ, or of the anal or genital opening of the victim
with any object or any other part of the body.
2. The invasion was committed by force, or by threat of force or coercion, such as that caused by fear of violence, duress, detention, psychological oppression or abuse of power, against such person or another person, or by taking advantage of a coercive environment, or the invasion was committed against a person incapable of giving genuine consent. (63).
3. The conduct took place in the context of and was associated with an armed conflict not of an international character.
4. The perpetrator was aware of factual circumstances that established the existence of an armed conflict. *(62. The concept of 'invasion' is intended to be broad enough to be gender-neutral.*
63. It is understood that a person may be incapable of giving genuine consent if affected by natural, induced or age-related incapacity. This footnote also applies to the corresponding elements in article 8 (2) (e) (vi)-3, 5 and 6).

Art. 8 (2) (e) (vi)-2 War crime of sexual slavery (64). Elements. 1. The perpetrator exercised any or all of the powers attaching to the right of ownership over one or more persons, such as by purchasing, selling, lending or bartering such a person or persons, or by imposing on them a similar deprivation of liberty. (65).
2. The perpetrator caused such person or persons to engage in one or more acts of a sexual nature.
3. The conduct took place in the context of and was associated with an armed conflict not of an international character.
4. The perpetrator was aware of factual circumstances that established the existence of an armed conflict. *(64. Given the complex nature of this crime, it is recognized that its commission could involve more than one perpetrator as a part of a common criminal purpose.*
65. It is understood that such deprivation of liberty may, in some circumstances, include exacting forced labour or otherwise reducing a person to servile status as defined in the Supplementary Convention on the Abolition of Slavery, the Slave Trade, and Institutions and Practices Similar to Slavery of 1956. It is also understood that the conduct described in this element includes trafficking in persons, in particular women and children).

Art. 8 (2) (e) (vi)-3 War crime of enforced prostitution. Elements. 1. The perpetrator caused one or more persons to engage in one or more acts of a sexual nature by force, or by threat of force or coercion, such as that caused by fear of violence, duress, detention, psychological oppression or abuse of power, against such person or persons or another person, or by taking advantage of a coercive environment or such person's or persons' incapacity to give genuine consent.
2. The perpetrator or another person obtained or expected to obtain pecuniary or other advantage in exchange for or in connection with the acts of a sexual nature.

3. The conduct took place in the context of and was associated with an armed conflict not of an international character.

4. The perpetrator was aware of factual circumstances that established the existence of an armed conflict.

Art. 8 (2) (e) (vi)-4 War crime of forced pregnancy. Elements. 1. The perpetrator confined one or more women forcibly made pregnant, with the intent of affecting the ethnic composition of any population or carrying out other grave violations of international law.

2. The conduct took place in the context of and was associated with an armed conflict not of an international character.

3. The perpetrator was aware of factual circumstances that established the existence of an armed conflict.

Art. 8 (2) (e) (vi)-5 War crime of enforced sterilization. Elements. 1. The perpetrator deprived one or more persons of biological reproductive capacity. (66).

2. The conduct was neither justified by the medical or hospital treatment of the person or persons concerned nor carried out with their genuine consent. (67).

3. The conduct took place in the context of and was associated with an armed conflict not of an international character.

4. The perpetrator was aware of factual circumstances that established the existence of an armed conflict. *(66. The deprivation is not intended to include birth-control measures which have a non permanent effect in practice.*

67. It is understood that 'genuine consent' does not include consent obtained through deception).

Art. 8 (2) (e) (vi)-6 War crime of sexual violence. *Elements.* 1. The perpetrator committed an act of a sexual nature against one or more persons or caused such person or persons to engage in an act of a sexual nature by force, or by threat of force or coercion, such as that caused by fear of violence, duress, detention, psychological oppression or abuse of power, against such person or persons or another person, or by taking advantage of a coercive environment or such person's or persons' incapacity to give genuine consent.

2. The conduct was of a gravity comparable to that of a serious violation of article 3 common to the four Geneva Conventions.

3. The perpetrator was aware of the factual circumstances that established the gravity of the conduct.

4. The conduct took place in the context of and was associated with an armed conflict not of an international character.

5. The perpetrator was aware of factual circumstances that established the existence of an armed conflict.

Art. 8 (2) (e) (vii) War crime of using, conscripting and enlisting children. Elements.
1. The perpetrator conscripted or enlisted one or more persons into an armed force or group or used one or more persons to participate actively in hostilities.

2. Such person or persons were under the age of 15 years.

3. The perpetrator knew or should have known that such person or persons were under the age of 15 years.

4. The conduct took place in the context of and was associated with an armed conflict not of an international character.

5. The perpetrator was aware of factual circumstances that established the existence of an armed conflict.

Art. 8 (2) (e) (viii) War crime of displacing civilians. Elements. 1. The perpetrator ordered a displacement of a civilian population.

2. Such order was not justified by the security of the civilians involved or by military necessity.

3. The perpetrator was in a position to effect such displacement by giving such order.

4. The conduct took place in the context of and was associated with an armed conflict not of an international character.

5. The perpetrator was aware of factual circumstances that established the existence of an armed conflict.

Art. 8 (2) (e) (ix) War crime of treacherously killing or wounding. Elements. 1. The perpetrator invited the confidence or belief of one or more combatant adversaries that they were entitled to, or were obliged to accord, protection under rules of international law applicable in armed conflict.

2. The perpetrator intended to betray that confidence or belief.

3. The perpetrator killed or injured such person or persons.

4. The perpetrator made use of that confidence or belief in killing or injuring such person or persons.

5. Such person or persons belonged to an adverse party.

6. The conduct took place in the context of and was associated with an armed conflict not of an international character.

7. The perpetrator was aware of factual circumstances that established the existence of an armed conflict.

Art. 8 (2) (e) (x) War crime of denying quarter. Elements. 1. The perpetrator declared or ordered that there shall be no survivors.

2. Such declaration or order was given in order to threaten an adversary or to conduct hostilities on the basis that there shall be no survivors.

3. The perpetrator was in a position of effective command or control over the subordinate forces to which the declaration or order was directed.

4. The conduct took place in the context of and was associated with an armed conflict not of an international character.

5. The perpetrator was aware of factual circumstances that established the existence of an armed conflict.

Art. 8 (2) (e) (xi)-1 War crime of mutilation. Elements. 1. The perpetrator subjected one or more persons to mutilation, in particular by permanently disfiguring the person or persons, or by permanently disabling or removing an organ or appendage.

2. The conduct caused death or seriously endangered the physical or mental health of such person or persons.

3. The conduct was neither justified by the medical, dental or hospital treatment of the person or persons concerned nor carried out in such person's or persons' interest. (68).

4. Such person or persons were in the power of another party to the conflict.

5. The conduct took place in the context of and was associated with an armed conflict not of an international character.

6. The perpetrator was aware of factual circumstances that established the existence of an armed conflict. *(68. Consent is not a defence to this crime. The crime prohibits any medical procedure which is not indicated by the state of health of the person concerned and which is not consistent with generally accepted medical standards which would be applied under similar medical circumstances to persons who are nationals of the party conducting the procedure and who are in no way deprived of liberty. This footnote also applies to the similar element in article 8 (2) (e) (xi)-2).*

Art. 8 (2) (e) (xi)-2 War crime of medical or scientific experiments. Elements. 1. The perpetrator subjected one or more persons to a medical or scientific experiment.

2. The experiment caused the death or seriously endangered the physical or mental health or integrity of such person or persons.

3. The conduct was neither justified by the medical, dental or hospital treatment of such person or persons concerned nor carried out in such person's or persons' interest.

4. Such person or persons were in the power of another party to the conflict.

5. The conduct took place in the context of and was associated with an armed conflict not of an international character.

6. The perpetrator was aware of factual circumstances that established the existence of an armed conflict.

Art. 8 (2) (e) (xii) War crime of destroying or seizing the enemy's property. Elements. 1. The perpetrator destroyed or seized certain property.

2. Such property was property of an adversary.

3. Such property was protected from that destruction or seizure under the international law of armed conflict.

4. The perpetrator was aware of the factual circumstances that established the status of the property.

5. The destruction or seizure was not required by military necessity.

6. The conduct took place in the context of and was associated with an armed conflict not of an international character.

7. The perpetrator was aware of factual circumstances that established the existence of an armed conflict.

Warrant of arrest *(Rome Statute ICC, Part V. Investigation and prosecution. Art. 58. Issuance by the Pre-Trial Chamber of a warrant of arrest or a summons to appear - RPE – ICTY, Part 5. Pre-Trial Proceedings, Section 2. Orders & Warrants. Rule 54 General Rule; Rule 55 Execution of Arrest Warrants. See: Rule 54bis Orders Directed to States for the Production of Documents; Rule 56 Cooperation of States; Rule 57 Procedure after Arrest; Rule 58 National Extradition Provisions; Rule 59 Failure to Execute a Warrant or Transfer Order; Rule 59bis Transmission of Arrest Warrants; Rule 60 Advertisement of Indictment; Rule 61 Procedure in Case of Failure to Execute a Warrant - RPE – ICTR, Part 5. Pre-Trial proceedings, Section 2. Orders and Warrants. Rule 54 General Provision; Rule 55 Execution of Arrest Warrants; Rule 55bis Warrant of Arrest to All States. See: Rule 56 Cooperation of States; Rule 57 Procedure after Arrest; Rule 58 National Extradition Provisions; Rule 59 Failure to Execute a Warrant of Arrest or Transfer Order; Rule 60 Publication of Indictment; Rule 61 Procedure in Case of Failure to Execute a Warrant of Arrest; Rule 62 Initial Appearance of Accused and Plea; Rule 62bis Plea*

Agreement Procedure; Rule 63 Questioning of the Accused; Rule 64 Detention on Remand; Rule 65 Provisional Release; Rule 65bis Status Conferences).
Rome Statute ICC, **Part V. Investigation and prosecution. Art. 58. Issuance by the Pre-Trial Chamber of a warrant of arrest or a summons to appear.** 1. At any time after the initiation of an investigation, the Pre-Trial Chamber shall, on the application of the Prosecutor, issue a warrant of arrest of a person if, having examined the application and the evidence or other information submitted by the Prosecutor, it is satisfied that:
(a) There are reasonable grounds to believe that the person has committed a crime within the jurisdiction of the Court; and
(b) The arrest of the person appears necessary:
(i) To ensure the person's appearance at trial;
(ii) To ensure that the person does not obstruct or endanger the investigation or the court proceedings; or
(iii) Where applicable, to prevent the person from continuing with the commission of that crime or a related crime which is within the jurisdiction of the Court and which arises out of the same circumstances.
2. The application of the Prosecutor shall contain:
(a) The name of the person and any other relevant identifying information;
(b) A specific reference to the crimes within the jurisdiction of the Court which the person is alleged to have committed;
(c) A concise statement of the facts which are alleged to constitute those crimes;
(d) A summary of the evidence and any other information which establish reasonable grounds to believe that the person committed those crimes; and
(e) The reason why the Prosecutor believes that the arrest of the person is necessary.
3. The warrant of arrest shall contain:
(a) The name of the person and any other relevant identifying information;
(b) A specific reference to the crimes within the jurisdiction of the Court for which the person's arrest is sought; and
(c) A concise statement of the facts which are alleged to constitute those crimes.
4. The warrant of arrest shall remain in effect until otherwise ordered by the Court.
5. On the basis of the warrant of arrest, the Court may request the provisional arrest or the arrest and surrender of the person under Part 9.
6. The Prosecutor may request the Pre-Trial Chamber to amend the warrant of arrest by modifying or adding to the crimes specified therein. The Pre-Trial Chamber shall so amend the warrant if it is satisfied that there are reasonable grounds to believe that the person committed the modified or additional crimes.
7. As an alternative to seeking a warrant of arrest, the Prosecutor may submit an application requesting that the Pre-Trial Chamber issue a summons for the person to appear. If the Pre-Trial Chamber is satisfied that there are reasonable grounds to believe that the person committed the crime alleged and that a summons is sufficient to ensure the person's appearance, it shall issue the summons, with or without conditions restricting liberty (other than detention) if provided for by national law, for the person to appear. The summons shall contain:
(a) The name of the person and any other relevant identifying information;
(b) The specified date on which the person is to appear;

(c) A specific reference to the crimes within the jurisdiction of the Court which the person is alleged to have committed; and

(d) A concise statement of the facts which are alleged to constitute the crime.

The summons shall be served on the person.

RPE – ICTY, Part 5. Pre-Trial Proceedings, Section 2. Orders & Warrants. Rule 54 General Rule. At the request of either party or *proprio motu*, a Judge or a Trial Chamber may issue such orders, summonses, subpoenas, warrants and transfer orders as may be necessary for the purposes of an investigation or for the preparation or conduct of the trial. (...)

Rule 55 Execution of Arrest Warrants. (A) A warrant of arrest shall be signed by a permanent Judge. It shall include an order for the prompt transfer of the accused to the Tribunal upon the arrest of the accused.

(B) The original warrant shall be retained by the Registrar, who shall prepare certified copies bearing the seal of the Tribunal.

(C) Each certified copy shall be accompanied by a copy of the indictment certified in accordance with Rule 47 (G) and a statement of the rights of the accused set forth in Article 21 of the Statute, and in Rules 42 and 43 *mutatis mutandis*. If the accused does not understand either of the official languages of the Tribunal and if the language understood by the accused is known to the Registrar, each certified copy of the warrant of arrest shall also be accompanied by a translation of the statement of the rights of the accused in that language.

(D) Subject to any order of a Judge or Chamber, the Registrar may transmit a certified copy of a warrant of arrest to the person or authorities to which it is addressed, including the national authorities of a State in whose territory or under whose jurisdiction the accused resides, or was last known to be, or is believed by the Registrar to be likely to be found.

(E) The Registrar shall instruct the person or authorities to which a warrant is transmitted that at the time of arrest the indictment and the statement of the rights of the accused be read to the accused in a language that he or she understands and that the accused be cautioned in that language that the accused has the right to remain silent, and that any statement he or she makes shall be recorded and may be used in evidence.

(F) Notwithstanding paragraph (E), if at the time of arrest the accused is served with, or with a translation of, the indictment and the statement of rights of the accused in a language that the accused understands and is able to read, these need not be read to the accused at the time of arrest.

(G) When an arrest warrant issued by the Tribunal is executed by the authorities of a State, or an appropriate authority or international body, a member of the Office of the Prosecutor may be present as from the time of the arrest.

See: Rule 54bis Orders Directed to States for the Production of Documents; Rule 56 Cooperation of States; Rule 57 Procedure after Arrest; Rule 58 National Extradition Provisions; Rule 59 Failure to Execute a Warrant or Transfer Order; Rule 59 bis Transmission of Arrest Warrants; Rule 60 Advertisement of Indictment; Rule 61 Procedure in Case of Failure to Execute a Warrant.

RPE – ICTR, **Part 5. Pre-Trial proceedings, Section 2. Orders and Warrants.** *Rule 54 General Provision.* At the request of either party or *proprio motu*, a Judge or a Trial Chamber may issue such orders, summonses, subpoenas, warrants and transfer orders as may be necessary for the purposes of an investigation or for the preparation or conduct of the trial.

Rule 55 Execution of Arrest Warrants. (A) A warrant of arrest shall be signed by a Judge and shall bear the seal of the Tribunal. It shall be accompanied by a copy of the indictment, and a statement of the rights of the accused. These rights include those set forth in Article 20 of the Statute, and in Rules 42 and 43 *mutatis mutandis*, together with the right of the accused to remain silent, and to be cautioned that any statement he makes shall be recorded and may be used in evidence.

(B) The Registrar shall transmit to the national authorities of the State in whose territory or under whose jurisdiction or control the accused resides, or was last known to be, three sets of certified copies of:

(i) The warrant for arrest of the accused and an order for his surrender to the Tribunal;

(ii) The confirmed indictment;

(iii) A statement of the rights of the accused; and if necessary a translation thereof in a language understood by the accused.

(C) The Registrar shall instruct the said authorities to:

(i) Cause the arrest of the accused and his transfer to the Tribunal;

(ii) Serve a set of the aforementioned documents upon the accused;

(iii) Cause the documents to be read to the accused in a language understood by him and to caution him as to his rights in that language; and

(iv) Return one set of the documents together with proof of service, to the Tribunal.

(D) When an arrest warrant issued by the Tribunal is executed, a member of the Prosecutor's Office may be present as from the time of arrest.

Rule 55 bis Warrant of Arrest to All States. (A) Upon the request of the Prosecutor, and if satisfied that to do so would facilitate the arrest of an accused who may move from State to State, or whose whereabouts are unknown, a Judge may without having recourse to the procedures set out in Rule 61, and subject to sub-rule (B), address a warrant of arrest to all States.

(B) The Registrar shall transmit such a warrant to the national authorities of such States as may be indicated by the Prosecutor.

See: Rule 56 Cooperation of States; Rule 57 Procedure after Arrest; Rule 58 National Extradition Provisions; Rule 59 Failure to Execute a Warrant of Arrest or Transfer Order; Rule 60 Publication of Indictment; Rule 61 Procedure in Case of Failure to Execute a Warrant of Arrest; Rule 62 Initial Appearance of Accused and Plea; Rule 62bis Plea Agreement Procedure; Rule 63 Questioning of the Accused; Rule 64 Detention on Remand; Rule 65 Provisional Release; Rule 65bis Status Conferences.

"Worker on an offshore installation" *(International Convention on the protection of the rights of all migrant workers and members of their families. Adopted by General Assembly resolution 45/158 of 18 December 1990. Part. I., Scope and Definitions, Art. 2).* For the purposes of the present Convention: 2.(d) The term "worker on an offshore installation" refers to a migrant worker employed on an offshore installation that is under the jurisdiction of a State of which he or she is not a national.

Works and installations containing dangerous forces *(Protocol Additional to the Geneva Conventions of 12 August 1949, and relating to the Protection of Victims of International Armed Conflicts (Protocol I), 8 June 1977. Part. IV. Civilian Population. Section I. General Protection Against Effects of Hostilities. Chapter III. Civilian objects. Art. 56. Protection of works and installations containing dangerous forces).* 1. Works or installations containing dangerous forces, namely dams, dykes and nuclear electrical generating stations, shall not be made the object of attack, even where these objects are military objectives, if such attack may cause the release of dangerous forces and consequent severe losses among the civilian population. Other military objectives located at or in the vicinity of these works or installations shall not be made the object of attack if such attack may cause the release of dangerous forces from the works or installations and consequent severe losses among the civilian population. (…).

"Wounded" and "sick" *(Protocol Additional to the Geneva Conventions of 12 August 1949, and relating to the Protection of Victims of International Armed Conflicts (Protocol I), 8 June 1977. Part II. Wounded, sick and shipwrecked, Section I: General Protection. Art. 8. Terminology).* For the purposes of this Protocol: (…) a) "Wounded" and "sick" mean persons, whether military or civilian, who, because of trauma, disease or other physical or mental disorder or disability, are in need of medical assistance or care and who refrain from any act of hostility. These terms also cover maternity cases, new-born babies and other persons who may be in need of immediate medical assistance or care, such as the infirm or expectant mothers, and who refrain from any act of hostility.

LIST OF TERMS AND PHRASES

A

Admission of guilt - Guilty Plea (*Rome Statute ICC, Part 6. The trial (...),* *art. 64. Functions and powers of the Trial Chamber (...), paragraph 8. (a); Rome* *Statute ICC, art. 65. Proceedings on an admission of guilt; RPE – ICC, Rule 139.* *Decision on admission of guilt - RPE – ICTY, Rule 62. Initial Appearance of* *Accused; Rule 62bis. Guilty Pleas; Rule 62 ter. Plea Agreement Procedure - RPE –* *ICTR, Rule 62. Initial Appearance of Accused and Plea; Rule 62bis. Plea Agreement* *Procedure*).

African Charter on Human and Peoples' Rights. Adopted June 27, 1981, Kenya, Nairobi, entered into force October 21, 1986. *Preamble.*

African Court of Justice and Human Rights (*Protocol on the Statute of* *the African Court of Justice and Human Rights. Adopted by the 11th Ordinary* *Session of the Assembly of the Union, In Sharm El-Sheikh, Egypt, 01 July 2008.* *Preamble; Chapter 1. Merger of the African Court on Human and Peoples'Rights* *and the Court of Justice of the African Union. Art. 1. Replacement of the 1998 and* *2003 Protocols; Art. 2. Establishment of a single Court; Art. 3. Reference to the* *single Court in the Constitutive Act. (...) Annex – Statute of the African Court of* *Justice and Human Rights. (...) Art. 2. Functions of the Court; Art. 3. Composition;* *Art. 4. Qualifications of Judges (...); Art. 16. Sections of the Court; (...) Art. 25. Seat* *and Seal of the Court; (...) Chapter 3. Competence of the Court. Art. 28. Jurisdiction* *of the Court; Art. 29. Entities Eligible to Submit Cases to the Court; Art. 30. Other* *Entities Eligible to Submit Cases to the Court; Art. 31. Applicable Law; (...) Chapter* *5. Advisory opinion. Art. 53. Request for Advisory Opinion. (...)*).

Agenda 21 and sustainable development. United Nations. General Assembly. United Nations Conference on Environment and Development. Rio de Janeiro, 3-14 June 1992. *Chapter 1. Preamble (When the term "Governments" is* *used, it will be deemed to include the European Economic Community within its* *areas of competence. Throughout Agenda 21 the term "environmentally sound"* *means "environmentally safe and sound", in particular when applied to the terms* *"energy sources", "energy supplies", "energy systems" and "technology" or* *"technologies"*).

American Convention on Human Rights "Pact of San Jose, Costa Rica", 22 November 1969. *Preamble.*

Amicus curiae *(RPE – ICC, Rule 103. Amicus curiae and other forms of submission)*.

Arab Charter on Human Rights. Adopted by the Council of the League of Arab States, 22 May 2004, Tunis (Tunisia), entered into force March 15, 2008. *Preamble.*

Armed forces. Combatants *(Protocol Additional to the Geneva Conventions of 12 August 1949, and relating to the Protection of Victims of International Armed Conflicts (Protocol I), 8 June 1977. Part. III. Methods and Means of Warfare. Combatant and Prisoners-Of-War. Section II. Combatants and Prisoners of War. Art. 43. Armed forces)*.

Assembly of States Parties *(Rome Statute ICC. Part XI. Assembly of states parties, art. 112. Assembly of States Parties)*.

Attack directed against any civilian population. See: *Crimes against humanity.*

"Attacks" *(Protocol Additional to the Geneva Conventions of 12 August 1949, and relating to the Protection of Victims of International Armed Conflicts (Protocol I), 8 June 1977. Part. IV. Civilian Population. Section I. General Protection Against Effects of Hostilities. Chapter I. Basic rule and field of application. Art. 49. Definition of attacks and scope of application; Chapter IV. Precautionary measures. Art. 57. Precautions in attack; Art. 58. Precautions against the effects of attacks)*.

C

Chambers *(Rome Statute ICC, art. 39. Chambers; See RPE – ICC, Chapter 2. Composition and administration of the Court. Section I. General provisions relating to the composition and administration of the Court. Rules 4, 5, 6, 7, 8; Statute ICTY, art. 12. Composition of the Chambers; See RPE – ICTY, Part 3. Organization of the Tribunal. Section 1. The Judges; Section 4. The Chambers; Statute ICTR, art. 11. Composition of the Chambers; See RPE – ICTR, Part. 3. Organization of the Tribunal. Section 1. The Judges; Section 4. The Chambers)*.

Charter of fundamental rights of the European Union. C 364/1 - Official Journal of the European Communities, 18.12.2000. *Preamble.*

Charter of the United Nations, San Francisco, 26 June 1945 *(Preamble; Chapter I. Purposes and principles, Art. 1, Art. 2; Chapter II. Membership, Art. 3, Art. 4, Art. 5, Art. 6; Chapter III. Organs, Art. 7, Art. 8; Chapter XIV. The International Court of Justice, Art. 92).*

Child *(Convention on the rights of the child. Adopted and opened for signature, ratification and accession by General Assembly resolution 44/25 of 20 November 1989. Part. I., Art.1; Art. 2; Art. 3).*

"Civil defence", "Civil defence organizations", "Personnel" and "Matériel" of civil defence organizations *(Protocol Additional to the Geneva Conventions of 12 August 1949, and relating to the Protection of Victims of International Armed Conflicts (Protocol I), 8 June 1977. Part. IV. Civilian Population. Section I. General Protection Against Effects of Hostilities. Chapter VI. Civil defence. Art. 61. Definitions and scope).*

Civil defence in occupied territories *(Protocol Additional to the Geneva Conventions of 12 August 1949, and relating to the Protection of Victims of International Armed Conflicts (Protocol I), 8 June 1977. Part. IV. Civilian Population. Section I. General Protection Against Effects of Hostilities. Chapter VI. Civil defence. Art. 63. Civil defence in occupied territories).*

Civilian objects *(Protocol Additional to the Geneva Conventions of 12 August 1949, and relating to the Protection of Victims of International Armed Conflicts (Protocol I), 8 June 1977. Part. IV. Civilian Population. Section I. General Protection Against Effects of Hostilities. Chapter III. Civilian objects. Art. 52. General Protection of civilian objects).*

Civilians and civilian population *(Protocol Additional to the Geneva Conventions of 12 August 1949, and relating to the Protection of Victims of International Armed Conflicts (Protocol I), 8 June 1977. Part. IV. Civilian Population. Section I. General Protection Against Effects of Hostilities. Chapter II. Civilians and civilian population. Art. 50. Definition of civilians and civilian population).*

Combatants and prisoners of war *(Protocol Additional to the Geneva Conventions of 12 August 1949, and relating to the Protection of Victims of International Armed Conflicts (Protocol I), 8 June 1977. Part. III. Methods and Means of Warfare. Combatant and Prisoners-Of-War. Section II. Combatants and Prisoners of War. Art. 44. Combatants and prisoners of war).*

"Contact zone". Medical aircraft in contact or similar zones *(Protocol Additional to the Geneva Conventions of 12 August 1949, and relating to the Protection of Victims of International Armed Conflicts (Protocol I), 8 June 1977.*

Part. II. Wounded, sick and shipwrecked. Section II. Medical transportation. Art. 26. Medical aircraft in contact or similar zones).

Convention against torture and other cruel, inhuman or degrading treatment or punishment. Adopted and opened for signature, ratification and accession by General Assembly resolution 39/46 of 10 December 1984. *Preamble.*

Convention for the Protection of Human Rights and Fundamental Freedoms (as amended by Protocols Nos. 11 and 14 with Protocols Nos. 1, 4, 6, 7, 12 and 13). Rome, 4 November 1950. *Preamble.*

Convention on Biological Diversity. Rio de Janeiro, 5 June 1992 *(Authentic text. Preamble. Art. 1. Objectives. Art. 2. Use of Terms. "Biological diversity", "Biological resources", "Biotechnology", "Country of origin of genetic resources", "Country providing genetic resources", "Domesticated or cultivated species", "Ecosystem", "Ex-situ conservation", "Genetic material", "Genetic resources", "Habitat", "In-situ conditions", "In-situ conservation", "Protected area", "Regional economic integration organization", "Sustainable use", "Technology". Art. 3. Principle. Art. 4. Jurisdictional Scope. Art. 5. Cooperation).*

Convention on the elimination of all forms of discrimination against women. New York, 18 December 1979. *Preamble.*

Convention on the Prevention and Punishment of the Crime of Genocide.
Approved and proposed for signature and ratification or accession by General Assembly resolution 260 A (III) of 9 December 1948. *Preamble.*

Convention on the rights of the child. Adopted and opened for signature, ratification and accession by General Assembly resolution 44/25 of 20 November 1989. Preamble.

Convention relating to the Status of Refugees. Geneva, 28 July 1951. *Preamble.*

Copenhagen Accord. 18 December 2009. United Nations. Conference of the Parties. Fifteenth session. Copenhagen, 7.18 December 2009. Agenda item 9. High-level segment. Draft decision -/CP.15 (Climate change).

Crime against humanity of apartheid. *See: Crimes against humanity.*

Crime against humanity of deportation or forcible transfer of population. *See: Crimes against humanity.*

Crime against humanity of enforced disappearance of persons. *See: Crimes against humanity.*

Crime against humanity of enforced prostitution. *See: Crimes against humanity, War crimes, Elements of Crimes.*

Crime against humanity of enforced sterilization. *See: Crimes against humanity, War crimes, Elements of Crimes.*

Crime against humanity of enslavement. See: Crimes against humanity.

Crime against humanity of extermination. *See: Crimes against humanity.*

Crime against humanity of forced pregnancy. *See: Crimes against humanity, War crimes, Elements of Crimes.*

Crime against humanity of imprisonment or other severe deprivation of physical liberty. *See: Crimes against humanity.*

Crime against humanity of murder. *See: Crimes against humanity, War crimes, Elements of Crimes.*

Crime against humanity of other inhumane acts. *See: Crimes against humanity.*

Crime against humanity of persecution. *See: Crimes against humanity.*

Crime against humanity of rape. *See: Crimes against humanity, War crimes, Elements of Crimes.*

Crime against humanity of sexual slavery. *See: Crimes against humanity, War crimes, Elements of Crimes.*

Crime against humanity of sexual violence. *See: Crimes against humanity, War crimes, Elements of Crimes.*

Crime against humanity of torture. *See: Torture, Crimes against humanity, War crimes, Elements of Crimes.*

Crime of aggression *(Rome Statute ICC. Part II. Jurisdiction, admissibility and applicable law, art. 5. Crimes within the jurisdiction of the Court).*

Crime of apartheid. *See: Crimes against humanity.*

Crime of Genocide. *See: Genocide - Crime of Genocide.*

Crimes against humanity *(London Agreement (8 August 1945), Charter of the International Military Tribunal. Art. 6. (c) - Rome Statute ICC, art. 7 (Attack directed against any civilian population, Extermination, Enslavement, Deportation or forcible transfer of population, Torture, Forced pregnancy, Persecution, The crime of apartheid, Enforced disappearance of persons) - Rome Statute ICC, Elements of Crimes, art. 7. Crimes against humanity. Introduction; Art. 7 (1) (a). Crime against humanity of murder. Elements; Art. 7 (1) (b). Crime against humanity of extermination. Elements; Art. 7 (1) (c). Crime against humanity of enslavement. Elements; Art. 7 (1) (d). Crime against humanity of deportation or forcible transfer of population. Elements; Art. 7 (1) (e). Crime against humanity of imprisonment or other severe deprivation of physical liberty. Elements; Art. 7 (1) (f). Crime against humanity of torture. Elements; Art. 7 (1) (g)-1. Crime against humanity of rape. Elements; Art. 7 (1) (g)-2. Crime against humanity of sexual slavery. Elements; Art. 7 (1) (g)-3. Crime against humanity of enforced prostitution. Elements; Art. 7 (1) (g)-4. Crime against humanity of forced pregnancy. Elements; Art. 7 (1) (g)-5. Crime against humanity of enforced sterilization. Elements; Art. 7 (1) (g)-6. Crime against humanity of sexual violence. Elements; Art. 7 (1) (h). Crime against humanity of persecution. Elements; Art. 7 (1) (i). Crime against humanity of enforced disappearance of persons. Elements; Art. 7 (1) (j). Crime against humanity of apartheid. Elements; Art. 7 (1) (k). Crime against humanity of other inhumane acts. Elements - Statute ICTY, art. 5. Crimes against humanity; Statute ICTR, art. 3. Crimes against Humanity).*

Crimes against peace *(London Agreement (8 August 1945). Charter of the International Military Tribunal. Prosecution and punishment of major war criminals of European Axis. Agreement signed at London August 8, 1945, with charter of the International Military Tribunal. Entered into force August 8, 1945. Discrepancy in article 6 of charter rectified by protocol of October 6, 1945. Agreement by the government of the United States of America, the Provisional Government of the French Republic, the Government of the United Kingdom of Great Britain and Northern Ireland and the Government of the Union of Soviet Socialist Republics for the prosecution and punishment of the major war criminals of the European axis).*

D

Defence - Counsel for the defence *(RPE – ICC, Chapter 2. Composition and administration of the Court; Section 3. The Registry; Subsection 3. Counsel for the defence: Rule 20. Responsibilities of the Registrar relating to the rights of the defence: Rule 21. Assignment of legal assistance; Rule 22. Appointment and qualifications of Counsel for the defence - RPE – ICTY, Part 4. Investigations and rights of suspects; Section 2. Of Counsel. Rule 44. Appointment, Qualifications and Duties of Counsel; Rule 45. Assignment of Counsel; Rule 45bis. Detained Persons; Rule 45 ter. Assignment of Counsel in the Interests of Justice; Rule 46. Misconduct of Counsel - RPE – ICTR, Part 4. Investigations and rights of suspects; Section 2. Of Counsel. Rule 44. Appointment and Qualifications of Counsel; Rule 44bis. Duty Counsel; Rule 45. Assignment of Counsel; Rule 45bis. Detained Persons; Rule 45 ter. Availability of Counsel; Rule 45 quarter. Assignment of Counsel in the Interests of Justice; Rule 46. Misconduct of Counsel).*

Demilitarized zones *(Protocol Additional to the Geneva Conventions of 12 August 1949, and relating to the Protection of Victims of International Armed Conflicts (Protocol I), 8 June 1977. Part. IV. Civilian Population. Section I. General Protection Against Effects of Hostilities. Chapter V. Localities and zones under special protection. Art. 60. Demilitarized zones).*

Deportation or forcible transfer of population. *See: Crimes against humanity.*

Development. Right to Development. Declaration on the Right to Development *(Adopted by General Assembly resolution 41/128 of 4 December 1986).*

"Discrimination against women" *(Convention on the elimination of all forms of discrimination against women, New York, 18 December 1979. Part. I., Art. 2).*

"Distinctive emblem" *(Protocol Additional to the Geneva Conventions of 12 August 1949, and relating to the Protection of Victims of International Armed Conflicts (Protocol I), 8 June 1977. Part. II. Wounded, sick and shipwrecked, Section I: General Protection. Art. 8. Terminology).*

"Distinctive signal" *(Protocol Additional to the Geneva Conventions of 12 August 1949, and relating to the Protection of Victims of International Armed Conflicts (Protocol I), 8 June 1977. Part. II. Wounded, sick and shipwrecked, Section I: General Protection. Art. 8. Terminology).*

E

Elements of Crimes *(Rome Statute ICC, art. 9. Elements of Crimes; Elements of Crimes. General introduction).*

"Enforced disappearance" *(International Convention for the Protection of All Persons from Enforced Disappearance. 20 December 2006. Part. I., Art. 2).*

Enforced disappearance of persons. *See: Crimes against humanity.*

Enslavement. *See: Crimes against humanity.*

Environment and Development. Rio Declaration on Environment and Development. United Nations, General Assembly. Rio de Janeiro from 3 to 14 June 1992.

Escape *(Rome Statute ICC, Part X. Enforcement, art. 111. Escape; RPE – ICC, Section VI. Escape, Rule 225. Measures under article 111 in the event of escape).*

European Court of Human Rights *(Convention for the Protection of Human Rights and Fundamental Freedoms. Rome, 4.XI.1950. Section 2. European Court of Human Rights. Art. 19. Establishment of the Court; Art. 20. Number of judges; Art. 21. Criteria for office; (...) Art. 32. Jurisdiction of the Court; Art. 33. Inter-State cases; Art. 34. Individual applications; Art. 35. Admissibility criteria; Art. 36. Third party intervention - Rules of Court. Rule 19. Seat of the Court).*

Extermination. *See: Crimes against humanity.*

Extradition *(Rome Statute ICC, art. 102. Use of terms).*

F

Forced pregnancy. *See: Crimes against humanity, War crimes, Elements of Crimes.*

"Frontier worker" *(International Convention on the protection of the rights of all migrant workers and members of their families. Adopted by General Assembly resolution 45/158 of 18 December 1990. Part. I., Scope and Definitions, Art. 2).*

G

General protection *(Protocol Additional to the Geneva Conventions of 12 August 1949, and relating to the Protection of Victims of International Armed Conflicts (Protocol I), 8 June 1977. Part. IV. Civilian Population. Section I. General Protection Against Effects of Hostilities. Chapter VI. Civil defence. Art. 62. General protection; Art. 52. General Protection of civilian objects).*

General Protection of civilian objects *(Protocol Additional to the Geneva Conventions of 12 August 1949, and relating to the Protection of Victims of International Armed Conflicts (Protocol I), 8 June 1977. Part. IV. Civilian Population. Section I. General Protection Against Effects of Hostilities. Chapter III. Civilian objects. Art. 52. General Protection of civilian objects).*

General protection of medical duties *(Protocol Additional to the Geneva Conventions of 12 August 1949, and relating to the Protection of Victims of International Armed Conflicts (Protocol I), 8 June 1977. Part. II. Wounded, sick and shipwrecked. Section I. General Protection. Art. 16. General protection of medical duties).*

Geneva Conventions of 12 August 1949: "First Convention", "Second Convention", "Third Convention" and "Fourth Convention" *(Protocol Additional to the Geneva Conventions of 12 August 1949, and relating to the Protection of Victims of International Armed Conflicts (Protocol I), 8 June 1977. Part I. General provisions. Art 2. Definitions).* For the purposes of this Protocol (a) "First Convention", "Second Convention", "Third Convention" and

"Fourth Convention" mean, respectively, the Geneva Convention for the Amelioration of the Condition of the Wounded and Sick in Armed Forces in the Field of 12 August 1949; the Geneva Convention for the Amelioration of the Condition of Wounded, Sick and Ship-wrecked Members of Armed Forces at Sea of 12 August 1949; the Geneva Convention relative to the Treatment of Prisoners of War of 12 August 1949; the Geneva Convention relative to the Protection of Civilian Persons in Time of War of 12 August 1949; "the Conventions" means the four Geneva Conventions of 12 August 1949 for the protection of war victims.

(See: Protocol Additional to the Geneva Conventions of 12 August 1949, and relating to the Protection of Victims of International Armed Conflicts (Protocol I), 8 June 1977; Protocol Additional to the Geneva Conventions of 12 August 1949, and relating to the Protection of Victims of Non-International Armed Conflicts (Protocol II), 8 June 1977; Protocol additional to the Geneva Conventions of 12 August 1949, and relating to the adoption of an additional distinctive emblem (Protocol III), 8 December 2005).

Genocide by causing serious bodily or mental harm. *See: Genocide - Crime of Genocide.*

Genocide - Crime of Genocide *(Convention on the Prevention and Punishment of the Crime of Genocide, New York, 9 December 1948. Preamble. Art. 1; Art. 2; Art. 3: Art. 4; Art. 5; Art. 6; Art. 7; (...); Genocide (Rome Statute ICC, art. 6); Elements of Crimes. Art. 6. Genocide. Introduction; Art. 6 (a). Genocide by killing. Elements; Art. 6 (b). Genocide by causing serious bodily or mental harm. Elements; Art. 6 (c). Genocide by deliberately inflicting conditions of life calculated to bring about physical destruction. Elements; Art. 6 (d). Genocide by imposing measures intended to prevent births. Elements; Art. 6 (e). Genocide by forcibly transferring children. Elements; Genocide (Statute ICTY, art. 4); Genocide (Statute ICTR, art. 2)).*

Genocide by deliberately inflicting conditions of life calculated to bring about physical destruction. *See: Genocide - Crime of Genocide.*

Genocide by forcibly transferring children. *See: Genocide - Crime of Genocide.*

Genocide by imposing measures intended to prevent births. *See: Genocide - Crime of Genocide.*

Genocide by killing. *See: Genocide - Crime of Genocide.*

Grave breaches of the Geneva Conventions of 12 August 1949 and of the Additional Protocols *(Convention (I) for the Amelioration of the Condition of the Wounded and Sick in Armed Forces in the Field. Geneva, 12 August*

1949. Chapter IX. Repression of Abuses and Infractions. Art. 49; Art. 50. Convention (II) for the Amelioration of the Condition of Wounded, Sick and Shipwrecked Members of Armed Forces at Sea. Geneva, 12 August 1949. Chapter VIII. Repression of Abuses and Infractions. Art. 50; Art. 51. Convention (III) relative to the Treatment of Prisoners of War. Geneva, 12 August 1949. Part. VI. Execution of the Convention. Section I. General Provisions. Art. 129; Art. 130. Convention (IV) relative to the Protection of Civilian Persons in Time of War. Geneva, 12 August 1949. Part. IV. Execution of the Convention. Section I. General Provisions. Art. 146; Art. 147. Protocol Additional to the Geneva Conventions of 12 August 1949, and relating to the Protection of Victims of International Armed Conflicts (Protocol I), 8 June 1977. Part. II. Wounded, sick and shipwrecked. Section I. General Protection. Art. 11. Protection of persons. Part. V. Execution of the Conventions and of its Protocols. Section II. Repression of Breaches of the Conventions and of this Protocol. Art. 85. Repression of breaches of this Protocol).

H

Human Environment. Stockholm Declaration on the Human Environment. 16 June 1972. Declaration of the United Nations Conference on the Human Environment. Stockholm, 5-16 June 1972.

Human Rights. Vienna Declaration and Programme of Action (World Conference on Human Rights, 14-25 June 1993, Vienna, Austria. Vienna Declaration and Programme of Action, 25 June 1993. Preamble).

Human Settlements (United Nations Conference on Human Settlements (Habitat II), Istanbul, Turkey, 3-14 June 1996. Istanbul Declaration on Human Settlements).

I

Indictment *(Statute ICTY, art. 18. Investigation and preparation of indictment; art. 19. Review of the indictment; art. 20. Commencement and conduct of trial proceedings (See: RPE – ICTY, Part. 5. Pre-Trial proceedings, Section 1. Indictments: Rule 47 Submission of Indictment by the Prosecutor; Rule 48 Joinder of*

Accused; Rule 49 Joinder of Crimes; Rule 50 Amendment of Indictment; Rule 51 Withdrawal of Indictment; Rule 52 Public Character of Indictment; Rule 53 Non-disclosure; Rule 53 bis Service of Indictment) – Statute ICTR, art. 17. Investigation and Preparation of Indictment; art. 18. Review of the Indictment; art. 19. Commencement and conduct of trial proceedings (See: RPE – ICTR, Part 5. Pre-Trial Proceedings, Section 1. Indictments; Rule 47. Submission of Indictment by the Prosecutor ; Rule 48. Joinder of Accused; Rule 48 bis. Joinder of Trials; Rule 49. Joinder of Crimes; Rule 50. Amendment of Indictment; Rule 51. Withdrawal of Indictment; Rule 52. Public Character of Indictment; Rule 53. Non-Disclosure; Rule 53bis: Service of Indictment).

Indiscriminate attacks *(Protocol Additional to the Geneva Conventions of 12 August 1949, and relating to the Protection of Victims of International Armed Conflicts (Protocol I), 8 June 1977. Part. IV. Civilian Population. Section I. General Protection Against Effects of Hostilities. Chapter II. Civilians and civilian population. Art. 51. Protection of the civilian population).*

Inter-American Convention against terrorism *(AG/RES XXXII-0/02-Adopted at the second plenary session held on June 3, 2002). Preamble; Art. 1. Object and purposes (...)).*

Inter-American Court on Human Rights *(Statute of the Inter-American Court on Human Rights. O.A.S. Res. 448, October 1979, La Paz, Bolivia. Chapter 1. General provisions. Art. 1. Nature and Legal Organization; Art. 2. Jurisdiction; Art. 3. Seat; Chapter 2. Composition of the Court. Art. 4. Composition; Art. 5. Judicial Terms (...)).*

International Convention for the Protection of All Persons from Enforced Disappearance. 20 December 2006. Preamble.

International Convention on the Elimination of All Forms of Racial Discrimination *(Adopted and opened for signature and ratification by General Assembly resolution 2106 (XX) of 21 December 1965). Preamble.*

International Convention on the Protection of the Rights of All Migrant Workers and Members of their Families. Adopted by General Assembly resolution 45/158 of 18 December 1990. *Preamble.*

International Court of Justice – ICJ *(Charter of the United Nations, San Francisco, 26 June 1945, Chapter XIV. The International Court of Justice, Art. 92; Art. 93; Art. 94; Art. 95; Art. 96 – Statute ICJ, Art. 1; Chapter 1. Organization of the Court. Art. 2 (...); Chapter 2. Competence of the Court. Art. 34; Art. 35; Art. 36; Art. 37; Art. 38).*

International Covenant on Civil and Political Rights. Adopted and opened for signature, ratification and accession by General Assembly resolution 2200A (XXI) of 16 December 1966 *(Preamble. Part. I., Art. 1. Part. II., Art. 2; Art. 3; Art. 4. Part. III., Art. 6; Art. 7; Art. 8).*

International Covenant on Economic, Social and Cultural Rights. New York, 16 December 1966 *(Preamble. Part. I. Art. 1. Part. II. Art. 2; Art. 3; Art. 4; Art. 5. Part. III. Art. 6; Art. 7; Art. 8; Art. 9; Art. 10; Art. 11; Art. 12; Art. 13; Art. 14; Art. 15. Part. IV. Art. 16 (...); Art. 23; Art. 24; Art. 25 (...)).*

International Criminal Court – ICC. Text of the Rome Statute circulated as document A/CONF.183/9 of 17 July 1998 and corrected by process-verbaux of 10 November 1998, 12 July 1999, 30 November 1999, 8 May 2000, 17 January 2001 and 16 January 2002. The Statute entered into force on 1 July 2002 *(Preamble; Part I. Establishment of the Court. Art. 1. The Court; Art. 2. Relationship of the Court with the United Nations; Art. 3. Seat of the Court; Art. 4. Legal status and powers of the Court. Part II. Jurisdiction, admissibility and applicable law. Art. 5. Crimes within the jurisdiction of the Court; (...) Art. 11. Jurisdiction ratione temporis. (...) Art. 21. Applicable law. Part. III. General principles of Criminal Law. Art. 22. Nullum crimen sine lege; Art. 23. Nulla poena sine lege; Art. 24. Non-retroactivity ratione personae; Art. 25. Individual criminal responsibility; Art. 26. Exclusion of jurisdiction over persons under eighteen; Art. 27. Irrelevance of official capacity; Art. 28. Responsibility of commanders and other superiors; Art. 29. Non-applicability of statute of limitations. (...) Part. VII. Penalties. Art. 77. Applicable penalties).*

International Military Tribunal. London Agreement (8 August 1945). Charter of the International Military Tribunal. *Prosecution and punishment of major war criminals of European Axis. Agreement signed at London August 8, 1945, with charter of the International Military Tribunal. Entered into force August 8, 1945. Discrepancy in article 6 of charter rectified by protocol of October 6, 1945. Agreement by the government of the United States of America, the Provisional Government of the French Republic, the Government of the United Kingdom of Great Britain and Northern Ireland and the Government of the Union of Soviet Socialist Republics for the prosecution and punishment of the major war criminals of the European axis.*

"Itinerant worker" *(International Convention on the protection of the rights of all migrant workers and members of their families. Adopted by General Assembly resolution 45/158 of 18 December 1990. Part. I., Scope and Definitions, Art. 2).*

277

K

Kyoto Protocol to the United Nations Framework Convention on Climate Change. Kyoto, 11 December 1997 (*Preamble; Art. 1; Art. 3*).

M

"Medical aircraft" *(Protocol Additional to the Geneva Conventions of 12 August 1949, and relating to the Protection of Victims of International Armed Conflicts (Protocol I), 8 June 1977. Part. II. Wounded, sick and shipwrecked, Section I: General Protection. Art. 8. Terminology).*

"Medical personnel" *(Protocol Additional to the Geneva Conventions of 12 August 1949, and relating to the Protection of Victims of International Armed Conflicts (Protocol I), 8 June 1977. Part. II. Wounded, sick and shipwrecked, Section I: General Protection. Art. 8. Terminology).*

"Medical ships and craft" *(Protocol Additional to the Geneva Conventions of 12 August 1949, and relating to the Protection of Victims of International Armed Conflicts (Protocol I), 8 June 1977. Part. II. Wounded, sick and shipwrecked, Section I: General Protection. Art. 8. Terminology).*

"Medical transportation" *(Protocol Additional to the Geneva Conventions of 12 August 1949, and relating to the Protection of Victims of International Armed Conflicts (Protocol I), 8 June 1977. Part. II. Wounded, sick and shipwrecked, Section I: General Protection. Art. 8. Terminology).*

"Medical transports" *(Protocol Additional to the Geneva Conventions of 12 August 1949, and relating to the Protection of Victims of International Armed Conflicts (Protocol I), 8 June 1977. Part. II. Wounded, sick and shipwrecked, Section I: General Protection. Art. 8. Terminology).*

"Medical units" *(Protocol Additional to the Geneva Conventions of 12 August 1949, and relating to the Protection of Victims of International Armed Conflicts*

(Protocol I), 8 June 1977. Part. II. Wounded, sick and shipwrecked, Section I: General Protection. Art. 8. Terminology).

"Medical vehicles" *(Protocol Additional to the Geneva Conventions of 12 August 1949, and relating to the Protection of Victims of International Armed Conflicts (Protocol I), 8 June 1977. Part. II. Wounded, sick and shipwrecked, Section I: General Protection. Art. 8. Terminology).*

"Members of the family" *(International Convention on the protection of the rights of all migrant workers and members of their families. Adopted by General Assembly resolution 45/158 of 18 December 1990. Part. I., Scope and Definitions, Art. 4).*

Mercenaries *(Protocol Additional to the Geneva Conventions of 12 August 1949, and relating to the Protection of Victims of International Armed Conflicts (Protocol I), 8 June 1977. Part. III. Methods and Means of Warfare. Combatant and Prisoners-Of-War. Section II. Combatants and Prisoners of War. Art. 47. Mercenaries).*

"Migrant worker" *(International Convention on the protection of the rights of all migrant workers and members of their families. Adopted by General Assembly resolution 45/158 of 18 December 1990. Part. I., Scope and Definitions, Art. 2).*

Misconduct of a less serious nature *(Rome Statute ICC, Part 4. Composition and organization of the Court, art. 47. Disciplinary measures - RPE – ICC, Chapter 2. Composition and administration of the Court, Section 4. Situations that may affect the functioning of the Court, Subsection 1. Removal from office and disciplinary measures, Rule 23. General principle, Rule 25. Definition of misconduct of a less serious nature).*

N

NEPAD – New partnership for Africa's Development. Abuja, Nigeria, October 2001. Original document. (…) *I. Introduction.*

Non-defended localities *(Protocol Additional to the Geneva Conventions of 12 August 1949, and relating to the Protection of Victims of International Armed Conflicts (Protocol I), 8 June 1977. Part. IV. Civilian Population. Section I. General*

Protection Against Effects of Hostilities. Chapter V. Localities and zones under special protection. Art. 59. Non-defended localities).

O

Objects indispensable to the survival of the civilian population
(Protocol Additional to the Geneva Conventions of 12 August 1949, and relating to the Protection of Victims of International Armed Conflicts (Protocol I), 8 June 1977. Part. IV. Civilian Population. Section I. General Protection Against Effects of Hostilities. Chapter III. Civilian objects. Art. 54. Protection of objects indispensable to the survival of the civilian population).

P

Pacific settlement of disputes *(Charter of the United Nations, San Francisco, 26 June 1945, Chapter VI, Art. 33, Art. 34, Art. 35, Art. 36, Art. 37, Art. 38).*

Peace. An Agenda for Peace *(United Nations. General Assembly. Security Council. An Agenda for Peace. Preventive diplomacy, peacemaking and peace-keeping, post-conflict peace-building. Report of the Secretary-General pursuant to the statement adopted by the Summit Meeting of the Security Council on 31 January 1992. A/47/277 - S/24111, 17 June 1992. II. Definitions. III. Preventive diplomacy (...) Demilitarized zones; IV. Peacemaking (...) Use of military force).*

Perfidy and Ruses of war. Prohibition of Perfidy *(Protocol Additional to the Geneva Conventions of 12 August 1949, and relating to the Protection of Victims of International Armed Conflicts (Protocol I), 8 June 1977. Part III. Methods and Means of Warfare Combatant and Prisoners-Of-War. Section I. Methods and Means of Warfare. Art. 37. Prohibition of Perfidy).*

Persecution. *See: Crimes against humanity.*

Population and development. International Conference on Population and development, Cairo, 5-13 September 1994 *(Programme of Action. Chapter 1. Preamble; Chapter 2. Principles).*

Presumption of innocence *(Universal Declaration of Human Rights, Paris, 10 December 1948. Art. 11. (1); International Covenant on Civil and Political Rights. Adopted and opened for signature, ratification and accession by General Assembly resolution 2200A (XXI) of 16 December 1966. Art. 14. (2); Convention for the Protection of Human Rights and Fundamental Freedoms. Rome, 4.XI.1950 (as amended by Protocols Nos. 11 and 14 with Protocols Nos. 1, 4, 6, 7, 12 and 13). Art. 6. Right to a fair trial. (2); Rome Statute ICC. Part VI. The trial, art. 66. Presumption of innocence; ICTY - Rules Covering the Detention of Persons Awaiting Trial or Appeal Before the Tribunal or Otherwise Detained on the Authority of the Tribunal ("Rules of detention"). Basic principles, Rule 5; ICTR - Rules Covering the Detention of Persons Awaiting Trial or Appeal Before the Tribunal or Otherwise Detained on the Authority of the Tribunal ("Rules of detention"). Basic provisions, Rule 5).*

Prisoners of War *(Convention (III) relative to the Treatment of Prisoners of War. Geneva, 12 August 1949. Part. I. General Provisions. Art. 4 A) B) C); Art. 5. Part. II. General Protection of Prisoners of War. Art. 12; Art. 13; Art. 14; Art. 15; Art. 16. Part. III. Captivity. Section VI. Relations Between Prisoners of War and the Authorities. Chapter I. Complaints of Prisoners of War Respecting the Conditions of Captivity. Art. 78. Chapter II. Prisoner of War Representatives. Art. 79; Art. 80; Art. 81).*

Prisoners' representatives *(Convention (III) relative to the Treatment of Prisoners of War. Geneva, 12 August 1949. Part. III. Captivity. Section VI. Relations Between Prisoners of War and the Authorities. Chapter I. Complaints of Prisoners of War Respecting the Conditions of Captivity. Art. 78. Chapter II. Prisoner of War Representatives. Art. 79; Art. 80; Art. 81).*

"Project-tied worker" *(International Convention on the protection of the rights of all migrant workers and members of their families. Adopted by General Assembly resolution 45/158 of 18 December 1990. Part. I., Scope and Definitions, Art. 2).*

Prosecutor - The Office of the Prosecutor *(Rome Statute ICC, art. 42. The Office of the Prosecutor; See RPE – ICC, Chapter 2. Composition and administration of the Court. Section 2. The Office of the Prosecutor. Rules 9, 10, 11; Statute ICTY, art. 16. The Prosecutor; See RPE – ICTY, Part 3. Organization of the Tribunal. Section 6. The Prosecutor; Statute ICTR, art. 15. The Prosecutor; See RPE – ICTR, Part 3. Organization of the Tribunal. Section 6. The Prosecutor).*

Protection and care *(Protocol Additional to the Geneva Conventions of 12 August 1949, and relating to the Protection of Victims of International Armed Conflicts (Protocol I), 8 June 1977. Part. II. Wounded, sick and shipwrecked. Section I. General Protection. Art. 10. Protection and care).*

Protection of children *(Protocol Additional to the Geneva Conventions of 12 August 1949, and relating to the Protection of Victims of International Armed Conflicts (Protocol I), 8 June 1977. Part. IV. Civilian Population. Section III. Treatment of Persons in the Power of a Party to the Conflict. Chapter II. Measures in favour of women and children. Art. 77. Protection of children; Art. 78. Evacuation of children).*

Protection of civilian medical and religious personnel *(Protocol Additional to the Geneva Conventions of 12 August 1949, and relating to the Protection of Victims of International Armed Conflicts (Protocol I), 8 June 1977. Part. II. Wounded, sick and shipwrecked. Section I. General Protection. Art. 15. Protection of civilian medical and religious personnel).*

Protection of cultural objects and of places of worship *(Protocol Additional to the Geneva Conventions of 12 August 1949, and relating to the Protection of Victims of International Armed Conflicts (Protocol I), 8 June 1977. Part. IV. Civilian Population. Section I. General Protection Against Effects of Hostilities. Chapter III. Civilian objects. Art. 53. Protection of cultural objects and of places of worship).*

Protection of journalists. Measures or protection for journalists *(Protocol Additional to the Geneva Conventions of 12 August 1949, and relating to the Protection of Victims of International Armed Conflicts (Protocol I), 8 June 1977. Part. IV. Civilian Population. Section III. Treatment of Persons in the Power of a Party to the Conflict. Chapter III. Journalists. Art. 79. Measures or protection for journalists).*

Protection of medical units *(Protocol Additional to the Geneva Conventions of 12 August 1949, and relating to the Protection of Victims of International Armed Conflicts (Protocol I), 8 June 1977. Part. II. Wounded, sick and shipwrecked. Section I. General Protection. Art. 12. Protection of medical units).*

Protection of objects indispensable to the survival of the civilian population *(Protocol Additional to the Geneva Conventions of 12 August 1949, and relating to the Protection of Victims of International Armed Conflicts (Protocol I), 8 June 1977. Part. IV. Civilian Population. Section I. General Protection Against Effects of Hostilities. Chapter III. Civilian objects. Art. 54. Protection of objects indispensable to the survival of the civilian population).*

Protection of persons *(Protocol Additional to the Geneva Conventions of 12 August 1949, and relating to the Protection of Victims of International Armed Conflicts (Protocol I), 8 June 1977. Part. II. Wounded, sick and shipwrecked. Section I. General Protection. Art. 11. Protection of persons).*

Protection of persons who have taken part in hostilities *(Protocol Additional to the Geneva Conventions of 12 August 1949, and relating to the Protection of Victims of International Armed Conflicts (Protocol I), 8 June 1977. Part. III. Methods and Means of Warfare. Combatant and Prisoners-Of-War. Section II. Combatants and Prisoners of War. Art. 45. Protection of persons who have taken part in hostilities; Section III. Treatment of Persons in the Power of a Party to the Conflict. Chapter I. Field of application and protection of persons and objects. Art. 75. Fundamental guarantees).*

Protection of the civilian population *(Protocol Additional to the Geneva Conventions of 12 August 1949, and relating to the Protection of Victims of International Armed Conflicts (Protocol I), 8 June 1977. Part. IV. Civilian Population. Section I. General Protection Against Effects of Hostilities. Chapter II. Civilians and civilian population. Art. 51. Protection of the civilian population; Chapter IV. Precautionary measures. Art. 57. Precautions in attack; Art. 58. Precautions against the effects of attacks).*

Protection of the natural environment *(Protocol Additional to the Geneva Conventions of 12 August 1949, and relating to the Protection of Victims of International Armed Conflicts (Protocol I), 8 June 1977. Part. IV. Civilian Population. Section I. General Protection Against Effects of Hostilities. Chapter III. Civilian objects. Art. 55. Protection of the natural environment).*

Protection of the victims and witnesses *(Rome Statute ICC, art. 68. Protection of the victims and witnesses and their participation in the proceedings; RPE – ICC, Section 3. Victims and witnesses, Subsection 2. Protection of victims and witnesses - Statute ICTY, art. 22. Protection of victims and witnesses; RPE – ICTY, Rule 69. Protection of Victims and Witnesses - Statute ICTR, art. 21. Protection of Victims and Witnesses; RPE – ICTR, Rule 69. Protection of Victims and Witnesses).*

Protection of women *(Protocol Additional to the Geneva Conventions of 12 August 1949, and relating to the Protection of Victims of International Armed Conflicts (Protocol I), 8 June 1977. Part. IV. Civilian Population. Section III. Treatment of Persons in the Power of a Party to the Conflict. Chapter II. Measures in favour of women and children. Art. 76. Protection of women).*

Protection of works and installations containing dangerous forces *(Protocol Additional to the Geneva Conventions of 12 August 1949, and relating to the Protection of Victims of International Armed Conflicts (Protocol I), 8 June 1977.*

Part. IV. Civilian Population. Section I. General Protection Against Effects of Hostilities. Chapter III. Civilian objects. Art. 56. Protection of works and installations containing dangerous forces).

"Protecting Power" *(Protocol Additional to the Geneva Conventions of 12 August 1949, and relating to the Protection of Victims of International Armed Conflicts (Protocol I), 8 June 1977. Part I. General provisions. Art 2. Definitions).*

Protocol to Prevent, Suppress and Punish Trafficking in Persons Especially Women and Children, supplementing the United Nations Convention against Transnational Organized Crime. Adopted and opened for signature, ratification and accession by General Assembly resolution 55/25 of 15 November 2000. *Preamble.*

Q

Qualified persons *(Protocol Additional to the Geneva Conventions of 12 August 1949, and relating to the Protection of Victims of International Armed Conflicts (Protocol I), 8 June 1977. Part I. General provisions. Art 6. Qualified persons).*

R

"Racial discrimination" *(International Convention on the Elimination of All Forms of Racial Discrimination (Adopted and opened for signature and ratification by General Assembly resolution 2106 (XX) of 21 December 1965. Part. I., Art. 1).*

"Refugee" *(Convention relating to the Status of Refugees. Geneva, 28 July 1951.Chapter I. General provisions, Art. 1. Definition of the term "refugee").*

Registry *(Rome Statute ICC, art. 43. The Registry; See RPE – ICC, Chapter 2. Composition and administration of the Court. Section 3. The Registry. Subsection 1. General provisions relating to the Registry. Rules 12, 13, 14, 15; Subsection 3. Counsel for the defence. Rules 20, 21, 22; Statute ICTY, art. 17. The Registry; See RPE – ICTY, Part 3. Organization of the Tribunal. Section 5. The Registry; Statute*

ICTR, art. 16. The Registry; See RPE – ICTR, Part 3. Organization of the Tribunal. Section 5. The Registrar).

"Religious personnel" *(Protocol Additional to the Geneva Conventions of 12 August 1949, and relating to the Protection of Victims of International Armed Conflicts (Protocol I), 8 June 1977. Part. II. Wounded, sick and shipwrecked, Section I: General Protection. Art. 8. Terminology).*

Right to a fair trial *(International Covenant on Civil and Political Rights. Adopted and opened for signature, ratification and accession by General Assembly resolution 2200A (XXI) of 16 December 1966. Art. 14; Convention for the Protection of Human Rights and Fundamental Freedoms. Rome, 4.XI.1950 (as amended by Protocols Nos. 11 and 14 with Protocols Nos. 1, 4, 6, 7, 12 and 13). Art. 6. Right to a fair trial; Rome Statute ICC, art. 67. Rights of the accused; Statute ICTY, art. 21. Rights of the accused; Statute ICTR, art. 20. Rights of the Accused).*

Right to freedom of thought, conscience, religion and freedom of expression *(International Covenant on Civil and Political Rights. Adopted and opened for signature, ratification and accession by General Assembly resolution 2200A (XXI) of 16 December 1966. Part III, Art. 18, Art. 19, Art. 20 – Convention for the Protection of Human Rights and Fundamental Freedoms. Rome, 4.XI.1950. Art. 9. Freedom of thought, conscience and religion; Art. 10. Freedom of expression - American Convention on Human Rights "Pact of San Jose, Costa Rica", 22 November 1969. Art. 12. Freedom of Conscience and Religion; Art. 13. Freedom of Thought and Expression).*

Right to life *(Universal Declaration of Human Rights, Paris, 10 December 1948. Art. 3; International Covenant on Civil and Political Rights. Adopted and opened for signature, ratification and accession by General Assembly resolution 2200A (XXI) of 16 December 1966. Art. 6; Convention for the Protection of Human Rights and Fundamental Freedoms. Rome, 4.XI.1950 (as amended by Protocols Nos. 11 and 14 with Protocols Nos. 1, 4, 6, 7, 12 and 13). Art. 2. Right to life; Charter of fundamental rights of the European Union (18.12.2000 EN Official Journal of the European Communities C 364/3). Art. 2. Right to life; American Convention on Human Rights "Pact of San Jose, Costa Rica", 22 November 1969. Art. 4. Right to life).*

Rights of the accused *(Rome Statute ICC, art. 67. Rights of the accused; Rights of the accused, Statute ICTY, art. 21; Rights of the Accused, Statute ICTR, art. 20).*

"Rules of international law applicable in armed conflict" *(Protocol Additional to the Geneva Conventions of 12 August 1949, and relating to the Protection of Victims of International Armed Conflicts (Protocol I), 8 June 1977. Part I. General provisions. Art 2. Definitions).*

S

"Seafarer" *(International Convention on the protection of the rights of all migrant workers and members of their families. Adopted by General Assembly resolution 45/158 of 18 December 1990. Part. I., Scope and Definitions, Art. 2).*

"Seasonal worker" *(International Convention on the protection of the rights of all migrant workers and members of their families. Adopted by General Assembly resolution 45/158 of 18 December 1990. Part. I., Scope and Definitions, Art. 2).*

Security Council *(Charter of the United Nations, San Francisco, 26 June 1945, Chapter V. The Security Council. Composition, Art. 23; Functions and Powers, Art. 24, Art. 25; Art. 26; Voting, Art. 27(...)).*

Self-determination of peoples *(Charter of the United Nations, San Francisco, 26 June 1945. Chapter I. Purposes and principles, Art. 1; International Covenant on Civil and Political Rights. Adopted and opened for signature, ratification and accession by General Assembly resolution 2200A (XXI) of 16 December 1966. Part. I., Art. 1; International Covenant on Economic, Social and Cultural Rights. New York, 16 December 1966. Part. I. Art. 1).*

"Self-employed worker" *(International Convention on the protection of the rights of all migrant workers and members of their families. Adopted by General Assembly resolution 45/158 of 18 December 1990. Part. I., Scope and Definitions, Art. 2).*

Serious misconduct and serious breach of duty *(RPE – ICC, Chapter 2. Composition and administration of the Court, Section 4. Situations that may affect the functioning of the Court, Subsection 1. Removal from office and disciplinary measures, Rule 23. General principle, Rule 24. Definition of serious misconduct and serious breach of duty).*

"Shipwrecked" *(Protocol Additional to the Geneva Conventions of 12 August 1949, and relating to the Protection of Victims of International Armed Conflicts (Protocol I), 8 June 1977. Part. II. Wounded, sick and shipwrecked, Section I: General Protection. Art. 8. Terminology).*

Social development. Copenhagen Declaration on Social Development *(United Nations. World Summit for Social Development. Copenhagen, Denmark, 6-12 March 1995. Annex I. Copenhagen Declaration on Social Development).*

"Specified-employment worker" *(International Convention on the protection of the rights of all migrant workers and members of their families. Adopted by General Assembly resolution 45/158 of 18 December 1990. Part. I., Scope and Definitions, Art. 2).*

Spies *(Protocol Additional to the Geneva Conventions of 12 August 1949, and relating to the Protection of Victims of International Armed Conflicts (Protocol I), 8 June 1977. Part. III. Methods and Means of Warfare. Combatant and Prisoners-Of-War. Section II. Combatants and Prisoners of War. Art. 46. Spies).*

"State of employment" *(International Convention on the protection of the rights of all migrant workers and members of their families. Adopted by General Assembly resolution 45/158 of 18 December 1990. Part. I., Scope and Definitions, Art. 6).*

"State of origin" *(International Convention on the protection of the rights of all migrant workers and members of their families. Adopted by General Assembly resolution 45/158 of 18 December 1990. Part. I., Scope and Definitions, Art. 6).*

"State of transit" *(International Convention on the protection of the rights of all migrant workers and members of their families. Adopted by General Assembly resolution 45/158 of 18 December 1990. Part. I., Scope and Definitions, Art. 6).*

"Substitute" *(Protocol Additional to the Geneva Conventions of 12 August 1949, and relating to the Protection of Victims of International Armed Conflicts (Protocol I), 8 June 1977. Part. I. General provisions. Art 2. Definitions; Art 5. Appointment of Protecting Powers and of their substitute; Art 1. General principles and scope of application; Art 4. Legal status of the Parties to the conflict).*

"Surrender" *(Rome Statute ICC, art. 102. Use of terms, a); Rome Statute ICC, art. 89. Surrender of persons to the Court; Rome Statute ICC, art. 101. Rule of speciality; RPE – ICC, Rule 184. Arrangements for surrender; Rome Statute ICC, art. 91. Contents of request for arrest and surrender).*

Sustainable Development. Johannesburg Declaration on Sustainable Development. *United Nations. World Summit on Sustainable Development. Johannesburg, South Africa, 2-4 September 2002.*

T

The transfer, directly or indirectly, by the Occupying Power of parts of its own civilian population into the territory it occupies, or the deportation or transfer of all or parts of the population of the occupied territory within or outside this territory. *See: War crimes, Elements of Crimes.*

Torture *(International Covenant on Civil and Political Rights. Adopted and opened for signature, ratification and accession by General Assembly resolution 2200A (XXI) of 16 December 1966. Art. 7; Convention against Torture and Other Cruel, Inhuman or Degrading Treatment or Punishment. Adopted and opened for signature, ratification and accession by General Assembly resolution 39/46 of 10 December 1984. Art. 1; Convention for the Protection of Human Rights and Fundamental Freedoms. Rome, 4.XI.1950 (as amended by Protocols Nos. 11 and 14 with Protocols Nos. 1, 4, 6, 7, 12 and 13), Art. 3; See Crimes against humanity and War crimes).*

"Trafficking in persons" *(Protocol to Prevent, Suppress and Punish Trafficking in Persons Especially Women and Children, supplementing the United Nations Convention against Transnational Organized Crime. Adopted and opened for signature, ratification and accession by General Assembly resolution 55/25 of 15 November 2000. I. General provisions, Art. 3 Use of terms).*

U

United Nations Convention Against Transnational Organized Crime. New York, 15 November 2000. *(Art. 1 Statement of purpose; Art. 2 Use of terms; Art. 3 Scope of application).*

United Nations Convention to Combat Desertification in Countries Experiencing Serious Drought and/or Desertification, Particularly in Africa. Paris, 17 June 1994 *(Preamble. Part. I. Introduction. Art. 1. Use of terms: "desertification", "combating desertification", "drought", "mitigating the* *effects of drought", "land", "land degradation", "arid, semi-arid and dry sub-humid areas", "affected areas", "affected countries", "regional economic integration organization", "developed country Parties", Art. 2. Objective. Art. 3. Principles).*

United Nations Framework Convention on Climate Change. New York, 9 may 1992 *(Preamble; Art. 1. Definitions: "Adverse effects of climate change", "Climate change", "Climate system", "Emissions", "Greenhouse gases", "Regional economic integration organization", "Reservoir", "Sink", "Source"; Art. 2. Objective).*

United Nations Millennium Declaration. Resolution adopted by the General Assembly *[without reference to a Main Committee (A/55/L.2)]* - 55/2. United Nations Millennium Declaration. 8th plenary meeting, 8 September 2000 *(I. Values and principles (Freedom, Equality, Solidarity, Tolerance, Respect for nature, Shared responsibility); II. Peace, security and disarmament; III. Development and poverty eradication; IV. Protecting our common environment; V. Human rights, democracy and good governance; VI. Protecting the vulnerable; VII. Meeting the special needs of Africa; VIII. Strengthening the United Nations).*

Universal Declaration of Human Rights, Paris, 10 December 1948 *(Preamble. Art. 1, Art. 2, Art. 3, Art. 4, Art. 5, Art. 6, Art. 7, Art. 8, Art. 9, Art. 10, Art. 11, Art. 12, Art. 13, Art. 14, Art. 15, Art. 16, Art. 17, Art. 18, Art. 19, Art. 20, Art. 21, Art. 22, Art. 23, Art. 24, Art. 25, Art. 26, Art. 27, Art. 28, Art. 29, Art. 30).*

Use of force *(Charter of the United Nations, San Francisco, 26 June 1945, Chapter VII. Action with respect to threats to the peace, breaches of the peace, and acts of aggression. Art. 39, Art. 40, Art. 41, Art. 42, Art. 43, Art. 44, Art. 45, Art. 46, Art. 47, Art. 48, Art. 49, Art. 50, Art. 51).*

V

Victims (RPE – ICC, Section 3. Victims and witnesses; Subsection 1. Definition and general principle relating to victims; Rule 85. Definition of victims; International Convention for the Protection of All Persons from Enforced Disappearance. 20 December 2006. Part. I., Art. 24).

Violations of Article 3 Common to the Geneva Conventions and of Additional Protocol II (Statute ICTR, art. 4).

Violations of the laws or customs of war *(Statute ICTY, art. 3).*

W

War crime of attacking civilian objects. *See: War crimes, Elements of Crimes.*

War crime of attacking civilians. *See: War crimes, Elements of Crimes.*

War crime of attacking objects or persons using the distinctive emblems of the Geneva Conventions. *See: War crimes, Elements of Crimes.*

War crime of attacking personnel or objects involved in a humanitarian assistance or peacekeeping mission. *See: War crimes, Elements of Crimes.*

War crime of attacking protected objects. *See: War crimes, Elements of Crimes.*

War crime of attacking undefended places. *See: War crimes, Elements of Crimes.*

War crime of biological experiments. *See: War crimes, Elements of Crimes.*

War crime of compelling participation in military operations. *See: War crimes, Elements of Crimes.*

War crime of compelling service in hostile forces. *See: War crimes, Elements of Crimes.*

War crime of cruel treatment. *See: War crimes, Elements of Crimes.*

War crime of denying a fair trial. *See: War crimes, Elements of Crimes.*

War crime of denying quarter. *See: War crimes, Elements of Crimes.*

War crime of depriving the nationals of the hostile power of rights or actions. *See: War crimes, Elements of Crimes.*

War crime of destroying or seizing the enemy's property. *See: War crimes, Elements of Crimes.*

War crime of destruction and appropriation of property. *See: War crimes, Elements of Crimes.*

War crime of displacing civilians. *See: War crimes, Elements of Crimes.*

War crime of employing poison or poisoned weapons. *See: War crimes, Elements of Crimes.*

War crime of employing prohibited bullets. *See: War crimes, Elements of Crimes.*

War crime of employing prohibited gases, liquids, materials or devices. *See: War crimes, Elements of Crimes.*

War crime of employing weapons, projectiles or materials or methods of warfare listed in the Annex to the Statute (ICC). *See: War crimes, Elements of Crimes.*

War crime of enforced prostitution. *See: War crimes, Elements of Crimes, Crimes against humanity.*

War crime of enforced sterilization. *See: War crimes, Elements of Crimes, Crimes against humanity.*

War crime of excessive incidental death, injury, or damage. *See: War crimes, Elements of Crimes.*

War crime of forced pregnancy. *See: War crimes, Elements of Crimes, Crimes against humanity.*

War crime of improper use of a flag, insignia or uniform of the hostile party. *See: War crimes, Elements of Crimes.*

War crime of improper use of a flag of truce. *See: War crimes, Elements of Crimes.*

291

War crime of improper use of the distinctive emblems of the Geneva Conventions. *See: War crimes, Elements of Crimes.*

War crime of improper use of a flag, insignia or uniform of the United Nations. *See: War crimes, Elements of Crimes.*

War crime of inhuman treatment. *See: War crimes, Elements of Crimes.*

War crime of killing or wounding a person hors de combat. *See: War crimes, Elements of Crimes.*

War crime of medical or scientific experiments. *See: War crimes, Elements of Crimes.*

War crime of murder. *See: War crimes, Elements of Crimes, Crimes against humanity.*

War crime of mutilation. *See: War crimes, Elements of Crimes.*

War crime of outrages upon personal dignity. *See: War crimes, Elements of Crimes.*

War crime of pillaging. *See: War crimes, Elements of Crimes.*

War crime of rape. *See: War crimes, Elements of Crimes, Crimes against humanity.*

War crime of sentencing or execution without due process. *See: War crimes, Elements of Crimes.*

War crime of sexual slavery. *See: War crimes, Elements of Crimes, Crimes against humanity.*

War crime of sexual violence. *See: War crimes, Elements of Crimes, Crimes against humanity.*

War crime of starvation as a method of warfare. *See: War crimes, Elements of Crimes.*

War crime of taking hostages. *See: War crimes, Elements of Crimes.*

War crime of torture. *See: Torture, War crimes, Elements of Crimes, Crimes against humanity.*

War crime of treacherously killing or wounding. *See: War crimes, Elements of Crimes.*

War crime of unlawful confinement. *See: War crimes, Elements of Crimes.*

War crime of unlawful deportation and transfer. *See: War crimes, Elements of Crimes.*

War crime of using, conscripting or enlisting children. *See: War crimes, Elements of Crimes.*

War crime of using protected persons as shields. *See: War crimes, Elements of Crimes.*

War crime of willful killing. *See: War crimes, Elements of Crimes.*

War crime of willfully causing great suffering. *See: War crimes, Elements of Crimes.*

War crimes *(London Agreement (8 August 1945), Charter of the International Military Tribunal. Art. 6. (b) - Rome Statute ICC, art. 8. War Crimes; Elements of Crimes, art. 8. War crimes: Introduction; Art. 8 (2) (a), Art. 8 (2) (a) (i) War crime of wilful killing. Elements; Art. 8 (2) (a) (ii)-1 War crime of torture. Elements; Art. 8 (2) (a) (ii)-2 War crime of inhuman treatment. Elements; Art. 8 (2) (a) (ii)-3 War crime of biological experiments. Elements; Art. 8 (2) (a) (iii) War crime of wilfully causing great suffering. Elements; Art. 8 (2) (a) (iv) War crime of destruction and appropriation of property. Elements; Art. 8 (2) (a) (v) War crime of compelling service in hostile forces. Elements; Art. 8 (2) (a) (vi) War crime of denying a fair trial. Elements; Art. 8 (2) (a) (vii)-1 War crime of unlawful deportation and transfer. Elements; Art. 8 (2) (a) (vii)-2 War crime of unlawful confinement. Elements; Art. 8 (2) (a) (viii) War crime of taking hostages. Elements; Art. 8 (2) (b), Art. 8 (2) (b) (i) War crime of attacking civilians. Elements; Art. 8 (2) (b) (ii) War crime of attacking civilian objects. Elements; Art. 8 (2) (b) (iii) War crime of attacking personnel or objects involved in a humanitarian assistance or peacekeeping mission. Elements; Art. 8 (2) (b) (iv) War crime of excessive incidental death, injury, or damage. Elements; Art. 8 (2) (b) (v) War crime of attacking undefended places. Elements; Art. 8 (2) (b) (vi) War crime of killing or wounding a person hors de combat. Elements; Art. 8 (2) (b) (vii)-1 War crime of improper use of a flag of truce. Elements; Art. 8 (2) (b) (vii)-2 War crime of improper use of a flag, insignia or uniform of the hostile party. Elements; Art. 8 (2) (b) (vii)-3 War crime of improper use of a flag, insignia or uniform of the United Nations. Elements; Art. 8 (2) (b) (vii)-4 War crime of* *improper use of the distinctive emblems of the Geneva Conventions. Elements; Art. 8 (2) (b) (viii) The transfer, directly or indirectly, by the Occupying Power of parts of its own civilian population into the territory it occupies, or the deportation or transfer of all or parts of the population of the occupied territory within or outside this territory. Elements; Art. 8 (2) (b) (ix) War crime of attacking protected objects. Elements; Art. 8 (2) (b) (x)-1 War crime of mutilation. Elements; Art. 8 (2) (b) (x)-1 War crime of mutilation. Elements; Art. 8 (2) (b) (x)-2 War crime of medical or scientific experiments. Elements; Art. 8 (2) (b) (xi) War crime of treacherously killing or wounding. Elements; Art. 8 (2) (b) (xii) War crime of denying quarter. Elements; Art. 8 (2) (b) (xiii) War crime of destroying or seizing the enemy's property. Elements; Art. 8 (2) (b) (xiv) War crime of depriving the nationals of the hostile power of rights or actions. Elements; Art. 8 (2) (b) (xv) War crime of compelling participation in military operations. Elements; Art. 8 (2) (b) (xvi) War crime of pillaging. Elements; Art. 8 (2) (b) (xvii) War crime of employing poison or poisoned weapons. Elements; Art. 8 (2) (b) (xviii) War crime of employing prohibited gases, liquids, materials or devices. Elements; Art. 8 (2) (b) (xix) War crime of employing prohibited bullets. Elements; Art. 8 (2) (b) (xx) War crime of employing weapons, projectiles or materials or methods of warfare listed in the Annex to the Statute. Elements; Art. 8 (2) (b) (xxi) War crime of outrages upon personal dignity. Elements; Art. 8 (2) (b) (xxii)-1 War crime of rape. Elements; Art. 8 (2) (b) (xxii)-2 War crime of sexual slavery. Elements; Art. 8 (2) (b) (xxii)-3 War crime of enforced prostitution. Elements; Art. 8 (2) (b) (xxii)-4 War crime of forced pregnancy. Elements; Art. 8 (2) (b) (xxii)-5 War crime of enforced sterilization. Elements; Art. 8 (2) (b) (xxii)-6 War crime of sexual violence. Elements; Art. 8 (2) (b) (xxiii) War crime of using protected persons as shields. Elements; Art. 8 (2) (b) (xxiv) War crime of attacking objects or persons using the distinctive emblems of the Geneva Conventions. Elements; Art. 8 (2) (b) (xxv) War crime of starvation as a method of warfare. Elements; Art. 8 (2) (b) (xxvi) War crime of using, conscripting or enlisting children. Elements; Art. 8 (2) (c), Art. 8 (2) (c) (i)-1 War crime of murder. Elements; Art. 8 (2) (c) (i)-2 War crime of mutilation. Elements; Art. 8 (2) (c) (i)-3 War crime of cruel treatment. Elements; Art. 8 (2) (c) (i)-4 War crime of torture. Elements; Art. 8 (2) (c) (ii) War crime of outrages upon personal dignity. Elements; Art. 8 (2) (c) (iii) War crime of taking hostages. Elements; Art. 8 (2) (c) (iv) War crime of sentencing or execution without due process. Elements; Art. 8 (2) (e), Art. 8 (2) (e) (i) War crime of attacking civilians. Elements; Art. 8 (2) (e) (ii) War crime of attacking objects or persons using the distinctive emblems of the Geneva Conventions. Elements; Art. 8 (2) (e) (iii) War crime of attacking personnel or objects involved in a humanitarian assistance or peacekeeping mission. Elements; Art. 8 (2) (e) (iv) War crime of attacking protected objects. Elements; Art. 8 (2) (e) (v) War crime of pillaging. Elements; Art. 8 (2) (e) (vi)-1 War crime of rape. Elements; Art. 8 (2) (e) (vi)-2 War crime of sexual slavery. Elements; Art. 8 (2) (e) (vi)-3 War crime of enforced prostitution. Elements; Art. 8 (2) (e) (vi)-4 War crime of forced pregnancy. Elements; Art. 8 (2) (e) (vi)-5 War crime of enforced sterilization. Elements; Art. 8 (2) (e) (vi)-6 War crime of sexual violence. Elements; Art. 8 (2) (e) (vii) War crime of using, conscripting and enlisting children. Elements; Art. 8 (2) (e) (viii) War crime of displacing civilians. Elements; Art. 8 (2) (e) (ix)*

War crime of treacherously killing or wounding. Elements; Art. 8 (2) (e) (x) War crime of denying quarter. Elements; Art. 8 (2) (e) (xi)-1 War crime of mutilation. Elements; Art. 8 (2) (e) (xi)-2 War crime of medical or scientific experiments. Elements).

Warrant of arrest *(Rome Statute ICC, Part V. Investigation and prosecution. Art. 58. Issuance by the Pre-Trial Chamber of a warrant of arrest or a summons to appear - RPE – ICTY, Part 5. Pre-Trial Proceedings, Section 2. Orders & Warrants. Rule 54 General Rule; Rule 55 Execution of Arrest Warrants. See: Rule 54bis Orders Directed to States for the Production of Documents; Rule 56 Cooperation of States; Rule 57 Procedure after Arrest; Rule 58 National Extradition Provisions; Rule 59 Failure to Execute a Warrant or Transfer Order; Rule 59bis Transmission of Arrest Warrants; Rule 60 Advertisement of Indictment; Rule 61 Procedure in Case of Failure to Execute a Warrant - RPE – ICTR, Part 5. Pre-Trial proceedings, Section 2. Orders and Warrants. Rule 54 General Provision; Rule 55 Execution of Arrest Warrants; Rule 55bis Warrant of Arrest to All States. See: Rule 56 Cooperation of States; Rule 57 Procedure after Arrest; Rule 58 National Extradition Provisions; Rule 59 Failure to Execute a Warrant of Arrest or Transfer Order; Rule 60 Publication of Indictment; Rule 61 Procedure in Case of Failure to Execute a Warrant of Arrest; Rule 62 Initial Appearance of Accused and Plea; Rule 62bis Plea Agreement Procedure; Rule 63 Questioning of the Accused; Rule 64 Detention on Remand; Rule 65 Provisional Release; Rule 65bis Status Conferences).*

"Worker on an offshore installation" *(International Convention on the protection of the rights of all migrant workers and members of their families. Adopted by General Assembly resolution 45/158 of 18 December 1990. Part. I., Scope and Definitions, Art. 2).*

Works and installations containing dangerous forces *(Protocol Additional to the Geneva Conventions of 12 August 1949, and relating to the Protection of Victims of International Armed Conflicts (Protocol I), 8 June 1977. Part. IV. Civilian Population. Section I. General Protection Against Effects of Hostilities. Chapter III. Civilian objects. Art. 56. Protection of works and installations containing dangerous forces).*

"Wounded" and "sick" *(Protocol Additional to the Geneva Conventions of 12 August 1949, and relating to the Protection of Victims of International Armed Conflicts (Protocol I), 8 June 1977. Part II. Wounded, sick and shipwrecked, Section I: General Protection. Art. 8. Terminology).*

REFERENCE TEXTS

A

African Charter on Human and Peoples' Rights. Adopted June 27, 1981, Kenya, Nairobi, entered into force October 21, 1986.

Agenda 21 and sustainable development. United Nations. General Assembly. United Nations Conference on Environment and Development. Rio de Janeiro, 3-14 June 1992.

Agenda for Peace. United Nations. General Assembly. Security Council. An Agenda for Peace. Preventive diplomacy, peacemaking and peace-keeping, post-conflict peace-building. Report of the Secretary-General pursuant to the statement adopted by the Summit Meeting of the Security Council on 31 January 1992. A/47/277 - S/24111, 17 June 1992.

American Convention on Human Rights "Pact of San Jose, Costa Rica", 22 November 1969.

Arab Charter on Human Rights. Adopted by the Council of the League of Arab States, 22 May 2004, Tunis (Tunisia), entered into force March 15, 2008.

C

Charter of fundamental rights of the European Union. C 364/1 - Official Journal of the European Communities, 18.12.2000.

Charter of the United Nations, San Francisco, 26 June 1945.

Convention against torture and other cruel, inhuman or degrading treatment or punishment. Adopted and opened for signature, ratification and accession by General Assembly resolution 39/46 of 10 December 1984.

Convention for the Protection of Human Rights and Fundamental Freedoms (*as amended by Protocols Nos. 11 and 14 with Protocols Nos. 1, 4, 6, 7, 12 and 13*). Rome, 4 November 1950.

Convention on Biological Diversity. Rio de Janeiro, 5 June 1992.

Convention on the elimination of all forms of discrimination against women. New York, 18 December 1979.

Convention on the Prevention and Punishment of the Crime of Genocide. Approved and proposed for signature and ratification or accession by General Assembly resolution 260 A (III) of 9 December 1948. New York.

Convention on the rights of the child. Adopted and opened for signature, ratification and accession by General Assembly resolution 44/25 of 20 November 1989.

Convention relating to the Status of Refugees. Geneva, 28 July 1951.

Copenhagen Accord. 18 December 2009. United Nations. Conference of the Parties. Fifteenth session. Copenhagen, 7.18 December 2009. Agenda item 9. High-level segment. Draft decision -/CP.15 (Climate change).

Copenhagen Declaration on Social Development. United Nations. World Summit for Social Development. Copenhagen, Denmark, 6-12 March 1995. Annex I. Copenhagen Declaration on Social Development.

D

Declaration on the Right to Development. Adopted by General Assembly resolution 41/128 of 4 December 1986.

E

Elements of Crimes. Rome Statute of the International Criminal Court.

G

Geneva Conventions of 12 August 1949: "First Convention", "Second Convention", "Third Convention" and "Fourth Convention" (*Protocol Additional to the Geneva Conventions of 12 August 1949, and relating to the Protection of Victims of International Armed Conflicts (Protocol I), 8 June 1977. Part I. General provisions. Art 2. Definitions*). For the purposes of this Protocol (a) "First Convention", "Second Convention", "Third Convention" and "Fourth Convention" mean, respectively, the Geneva Convention for the Amelioration of the Condition of the Wounded and Sick in Armed Forces in the Field of 12 August 1949; the Geneva Convention for the Amelioration of the Condition of Wounded, Sick and Ship-wrecked Members of Armed Forces at Sea of 12 August 1949; the Geneva Convention relative to the Treatment of Prisoners of War of 12 August 1949; the Geneva Convention relative to the Protection of Civilian Persons in Time of War of 12 August 1949; "the Conventions" means the four Geneva Conventions of 12 August 1949 for the protection of war victims.
(*See: Protocol Additional to the Geneva Conventions of 12 August 1949, and relating to the Protection of Victims of International Armed Conflicts (Protocol I), 8 June 1977; Protocol Additional to the Geneva Conventions of 12 August 1949, and relating to the Protection of Victims of Non-International Armed Conflicts (Protocol II), 8 June 1977; Protocol additional to the Geneva Conventions of 12 August 1949, and relating to the adoption of an additional distinctive emblem (Protocol III), 8 December 2005*).

I

Inter-American Convention against terrorism. AG/RES XXXII-0/02-
Adopted at the second plenary session held on June 3, 2002.

International Conference on Population and development, Cairo, 5-13
September 1994. Programme of Action.

International Convention for the Protection of All Persons from
Enforced Disappearance. 20 December 2006.

International Convention on the Elimination of All Forms of Racial
Discrimination. Adopted and opened for signature and ratification by General
Assembly resolution 2106 (XX) of 21 December 1965.

International Convention on the protection of the rights of all migrant
workers and members of their families. Adopted by General Assembly
resolution 45/158 of 18 December 1990.

International Covenant on Civil and Political Rights. Adopted and opened
for signature, ratification and accession by General Assembly resolution 2200A
(XXI) of 16 December 1966.

International Covenant on Economic, Social and Cultural Rights. New
York, 16 December 1966.

Istanbul Declaration on Human Settlements. United Nations Conference on
Human Settlements (Habitat II), Istanbul, Turkey, 3-14 June 1996.

J

Johannesburg Declaration on Sustainable Development. United Nations. World Summit on Sustainable Development. Johannesburg, South Africa, 2-4 September 2002.

K

Kyoto Protocol to the United Nations Framework Convention on Climate Change. Kyoto, 11 December 1997.

L

London Agreement (8 August 1945). Charter of the International Military Tribunal. Prosecution and punishment of major war criminals of European Axis. Agreement signed at London August 8, 1945, with charter of the International Military Tribunal. Entered into force August 8, 1945. Discrepancy in article 6 of charter rectified by protocol of October 6, 1945. Agreement by the government of the United States of America, the Provisional Government of the French Republic, the Government of the United Kingdom of Great Britain and Northern Ireland and the Government of the Union of Soviet Socialist Republics for the prosecution and punishment of the major war criminals of the European axis.

N

NEPAD – New partnership for Africa's Development. Abuja, Nigeria, October 2001. Original document.

P

Protocol additional to the Geneva Conventions of 12 August 1949, and relating to the adoption of an additional distinctive emblem (Protocol III), 8 December 2005.

Protocol Additional to the Geneva Conventions of 12 August 1949, and relating to the Protection of Victims of International Armed Conflicts (Protocol I), 8 June 1977.

Protocol Additional to the Geneva Conventions of 12 August 1949, and relating to the Protection of Victims of Non-International Armed Conflicts (Protocol II), 8 June 1977.

Protocol on the Statute of the African Court of Justice and Human Rights. Adopted by the 11th Ordinary Session of the Assembly of the Union, In Sharm El-Sheikh, Egypt, 01 July 2008.

Protocol to Prevent, Suppress and Punish Trafficking in Persons Especially Women and Children, supplementing the United Nations Convention against Transnational Organized Crime. Adopted and opened for signature, ratification and accession by General Assembly resolution 55/25 of 15 November 2000.

R

Rio Declaration on Environment and Development. United Nations, General Assembly. Rio de Janeiro from 3 to 14 June 1992.

Rome Statute of the International Criminal Court.

Rules of Procedure and Evidence of the International Criminal Court.

Rules of Procedure and Evidence of the International Criminal for the former Yugoslavia.

Rules of Procedure and Evidence of the International Criminal Tribunal for Rwanda.

S

Statute of the African Court of Justice and Human Rights. Protocol on the Statute of the African Court of Justice and Human Rights. Adopted by the 11th Ordinary Session of the Assembly of the Union, In Sharm El-Sheikh, Egypt, 01 July 2008.

Statute of the European Court of Human Rights.

Statute of the Inter-American Court on Human Rights. O.A.S. Res. 448, October 1979, La Paz, Bolivia.

Statute of the International Court of Justice.

Statute of the International Criminal Tribunal for the former Yugoslavia.

Statute of the International Criminal Tribunal for Rwanda.

Stockholm Declaration on the Human Environment. 16 June 1972. Declaration of the United Nations Conference on the Human Environment. Stockholm, 5-16 June 1972.

U

United Nations Convention Against Transnational Organized Crime. New York, 15 November 2000.

United Nations Convention to Combat Desertification in Countries Experiencing Serious Drought and/or Desertification, Particularly in Africa. Paris, 17 June 1994.

United Nations Framework Convention on Climate Change. New York, 9 may 1992.

United Nations Millennium Declaration. Resolution adopted by the General Assembly [*without reference to a Main Committee (A/55/L.2)*] - 55/2. United Nations Millennium Declaration. 8th plenary meeting, 8 September 2000.

Universal Declaration of Human Rights. Paris, 10 December 1948.

V

Vienna Declaration and Programme of Action, 25 June 1993. World Conference on Human Rights, 14-25 June 1993, Vienna, Austria.

Editions Innovations and Information

In English

- Serejski, Eric. The Jesuits Driven Away from Masonry and Their Dagger Shattered by Freemasons. Translation from *Les Jésuites chassés de la Maçonnerie et leur poignard brisé par les Maçons* (1788) par Nicholas de Bonneville. 2011.
- Serejski, Eric. *The Chinese Kama Sutra. Sexuality and Sexual Dysfunctions in Ancient China.* Translation from Chinese. 2007
- Serejski, Eric. *Shan Hai Jing. Volume 1 - The Classics of Mountains.* Translation from Chinese. 2010.

In French

- Serejski, Eric. *Le Kama Sutra chinois. Sexualité et dysfonctions sexuelles.* 2007.
- Serejski, Ivar. *Au pays des joies et des drames. Notre vie au Burundi.* 2012.

www.ingramcontent.com/pod-product-compliance
Lightning Source LLC
Chambersburg PA
CBHW021030210326
41598CB00016B/974